THE JUDICIARY IN CANADA:

THE THIRD BRANCH OF GOVERNMENT

SERIES LIST
McGraw-Hill Ryerson Series in Canadian Politics
General Editor—Paul W. Fox

POLITICS: Canada, Fifth Edition
Paul W. Fox
CANADIAN FOREIGN POLICY
D.C. Thomson and R.F. Swanson
THE CONSTITUTIONAL PROCESS IN CANADA, Second Edition
R.I. Cheffins and R.N. Tucker
POLITICAL PARTIES AND IDEOLOGIES IN CANADA,
Second Edition
W. Christian and C. Campbell
PRESSURE GROUP BEHAVIOUR IN CANADIAN POLITICS
A. Paul Pross
POLITICAL PARTIES IN CANADA
C. Winn and J.C. McMenemy
GOVERNMENT IN CANADA
T.A. Hockin
LOCAL GOVERNMENT IN CANADA, Second Edition
C.R. Tindal and S. Nobes Tindal
PUBLIC POLICY AND PROVINCIAL POLITICS
M. Chandler and W. Chandler
POLITICAL CHOICE IN CANADA (Abridged Edition)
Harold D. Clarke, Jane Jenson, Lawrence LeDuc, Jon H. Pammett
CANADIAN FOREIGN POLICY: Contemporary Issues and Themes
Michael Tucker
POLITICS AND THE MEDIA IN CANADA
Arthur Siegel
CANADA IN QUESTION: Federalism in the Eighties, Third Edition
D.V. Smiley
THE L-SHAPED PARTY: The Liberty Party of Canada 1958-1980
Joseph Wearing
WOMEN AND POLITICS IN CANADA
Janine Brodie
THE REVISED CANADIAN CONSTITUTION: Politics as Law
R. Cheffins and P. Johnson
SOUTHERN EXPOSURE: Canadian Perspectives on the U.S.
David Flaherty and William McKercher
FEDERAL CONDITION IN CANADA
D.V. Smiley
POLITICS: Canada, Sixth Edition
Paul W. Fox

THE JUDICIARY IN CANADA: The Third Branch of Government
Peter Russell

Forthcoming

POLITICAL PARTIES AND IDEOLOGIES IN CANADA,
Third Edition
W. Christian and C. Campbell
GOVERNMENT IN CANADA, Second Edition
T.A. Hockin
CANADIAN PARLIAMENTARY SYSTEM
Paul G. Thomas
CANADIAN FOREIGN POLICY, Second Edition
Michael J. Tucker

THE JUDICIARY IN CANADA:
THE THIRD BRANCH OF GOVERNMENT

Peter H. Russell
Department of Political Science
University of Toronto

McGraw-Hill Ryerson Limited

Toronto   Montreal   New York   Auckland   Bogotá   Cairo
Hamburg   Lisbon   London   Madrid   Mexico   Milan   New Delhi
Panama   Paris   San Juan   São Paulo   Singapore   Sydney   Tokyo

THE JUDICIARY IN CANADA:
THE THIRD BRANCH OF GOVERNMENT

ISBN 0-07-548843-4

1 2 3 4 5 6 7 8 9 0 W 6 5 4 3 2 1 0 9 8 7

Printed and bound in Canada

Care has been taken to trace ownership of copyright material contained in this text. The publishers will gladly take any information that will enable them to rectify any reference or credit in subsequent editions.

Canadian Cataloguing in Publication Data

Russell, Peter H.
    The judiciary in Canada

(McGraw-Hill Ryerson series in Canadian politics)
Bibliography: p.
Includes index.
ISBN 0-07-548843-4

1. Judicial power—Canada.   2. Courts—Canada.
3. Judges—Canada.   I. Title.   II. Series.

JL183.R87 1987   347.71   C87-094719-2

73167

For my mother, Jean Russell

CONTENTS

TABLES AND FIGURES

FOREWORD

It is with great pleasure that I welcome *The Judiciary in Canada: The Third Branch of Government* into the McGraw-Hill Ryerson Series in Canadian Politics.

When I learned a number of years ago of Professor Peter Russell's developing academic interest in the role of the judiciary in the Canadian political system, I encouraged him to think about writing a book on the subject for inclusion in this Series. It seemed to me that there was a great need for such a book. Canadian students—and, for that matter, the Canadian public—were not sufficiently aware of the significant part that the judiciary played in the everyday process of Canadian government. It was also clear that they knew very little about the organization and operation of our courts and probably even less about the judges and officials who served in them.

Though there may have been some legal textbooks which dealt with certain aspects of the subject and there certainly were some political science texts which devoted a routine chapter or two to the judiciary, there was, to my knowledge, no single monograph which described the structure and functioning of the courts and examined them as a branch of government in a manner similar to the way in which the legislature or executive had been studied. In short, political scientists had neglected the judiciary, or at any rate they had not given it as much attention as they had paid to the other major institutions of government.

This omission is all the more surprising in view of the fact that several of the leading political scientists of that day were themselves trained in the law and might have been expected therefore to put more emphasis upon the judiciary. But their lack of attention is probably to be explained by the prevailing attitude of the time. The traditional view was that the judiciary was not really part of the political process. It existed as one of the classic organs of government which, like all Gaul, was divided into three parts—the executive, legislature, and judiciary—but the judiciary did not share in the nitty-gritty, mundane machinations of government. The courts were above and beyond the hurly-burly of politics and the sweaty and sometimes seamy side of the daily round. They were detached—remote, objective, pure, arcane, and rather unreal.

It is from this rather archaic view of the judiciary that Professor Russell has rescued us. He has brought us down to earth and provided us with a very practical guide book to our courts as part of the political system. He approaches the subject as a political scientist, examining the way in which the Canadian judiciary functions as well as describing the actual structure and organization of the courts. He more than fulfils his stated purpose for the book which is "to examine the extent and nature of judicial power in the Canadian political system."

It is not too much to say that Professor Russell, by his research, his teaching, and now by his book, has opened up a new branch of study in Canadian political science—the examination of the judiciary as part of the actual *process* of government in Canada. In doing so he has added immeasurably to the knowledge and perception of not only political scientists but members of the legal and judicial professions as well as the general public. Students also can be grateful to him for broadening their horizons while informing their minds. Finally, scholars will appreciate the fact that Professor Russell's achievements as a political scientist working in the field of law demonstrate the value of interdisciplinary research.

Ontario Council on University Affairs,   Paul W. Fox
Toronto, Ontario,   General Editor
July 1987.

PREFACE

This book had its origins in a course on the judiciary I have taught for a good many years to political science students at the University of Toronto. The aim of this course has been to give those who are studying politics and government an opportunity to think about where the judiciary fits in. My central theoretical interest has been to probe the peculiar nature of judicial power. What is the proper role of the judiciary in the liberal democratic state? What is distinctive and interesting about Canada's judicial system?

As my students and I explored these questions we were frustrated by the absence of a text describing and giving a political science analysis of the Canadian judicial system. Thus when I was approached by Professor Paul Fox, the general editor of the McGraw-Hill Ryerson Series in Canadian Politics, I was delighted to accept his invitation to write a book for that series on the Canadian judicial system.

When I first began, as a political scientist, to teach and write about the judiciary, there was little awareness on the part of the general public that the judiciary was a branch of Canadian government; and there was little willingness on the part of lawyers or judges to acknowledge that there was anything political about the judiciary. Over the period I have been working on this project I sense that both our political and legal cultures have changed—somewhat. The Charter of Rights and Freedoms has no doubt been a catalyst for this change. Today non-academic friends outside the legal profession are not totally mystified when I refer to the judiciary as our third branch of government; nor do all lawyers and judges become physically ill on hearing that political scientists might take an interest in "their" branch of government. I hope that this book will be of some interest to Canadian citizens, including professional lawyers and judges, who are concerned about the nature, organization, and growth of judicial power in Canada.

I began to work on this book in 1976-77 when I spent a year of sabbatical leave at the Osgoode Hall Law School, York University. At Osgoode I enjoyed the company of a stimulating group of colleagues and the support of that institution's fine library. During that year, with the help of a Canada Council grant and the good offices of Professor Allen Linden, who was then the executive director of the Canadian Institute for the Administration of Justice, I was able to travel across Canada visiting the courts in every province. In each province I interviewed judges, lawyers, and members of justice ministries. I am most grateful for the time these individuals spent with me and for their thoughtful responses to my many questions.

This book should have been written immediately following that sabbatical leave. However, I soon became distracted by a Royal Commission on Certain

Activities of the Royal Canadian Mounted Police, and then by the constitutional politics that produced the Constitution Act, 1982. I did not get back to work on the book until 1983. This at least had the benefit of enabling me to take into account the Charter of Rights and its implications for the Canadian judiciary. The latter stages of the research and writing were supported by grants from the Social Science and Humanities Research Council of Canada and the University of Toronto's Connaught Fund.

All along I planned to conclude the book with a Part Five on court administration. It is only very recently that the modern administrative sciences have begun to be applied to the courts. The Canadian judicial system is just now entering an era when efforts are being made not simply to administer courts but to manage them. The information base and administrative skills needed for intelligent management are being assembled in a number of jurisdictions. This development raises important questions about the goals of court management, in particular the balance to be struck between economy and adjudicative fairness in achieving expeditious justice. It also raises important political questions about the appropriate role for an independent judiciary on the one hand, and officials responsible to politically accountable ministers on the other, in the direction of burgeoning court bureaucracies. These questions were to be taken up in Part Five; alas, my ambition outstripped my time, my space and, most important, my knowledge.

I particularly regret not being able to make use of the excellent research on court administration done for me by Barbara Holman. Her work on delays in the courts, on public expenditures on courts, and on the reporting relationship of court administrators to executive and judicial authorities would have contributed greatly to what I might have written on the public administration of courts. I am confident that Ms. Holman's valuable work will be used in other publications. I am also consoled by the fact that there is already some outstanding published scholarship on court administration in Canada. I refer, in particular, to *Judicial Administration in Canada* by Perry S. Millar and Carl Baar, *Maîtres Chez Eux* by Justice Jules Deschênes in collaboration with Professor Baar, and the volume entitled *Expeditious Justice*, published by the Canadian Institute for the Adminstration of Justice, which contains the seminal article by Dr. Shimon Shetreet. The political scientist who wishes to explore the administrative dimensions of the third branch of government is already well served by these works.

My students have been my main collaborators in my enterprise. Their questions about courts and judges have shaped my agenda. Their answers have been a source of constant refreshment. They may be surprised to find some of their ideas popping up in the pages that follow.

In the early stages of my work I received much appreciated research assistance from Laura Bradbury and Michael Watson, who were then studying at Osgoode Hall Law School, and later from Murray Adams and Barbara Holman, students at the University of Toronto's faculty of law. For many years the faculty of law has been my second home at the University of Toronto. It has served as my senate—a chamber of sober second thoughts. The other institutional support outside my own department for which I am most grateful is the Centre of Criminology at the University of Toronto. The assistance I have received there over the past two years has been indispensable in completing this book.

Carl Baar, Martin Friedland, Peter Hogg and Hudson Janisch were kind enough to read various chapters of the manuscript, and the Honourable John D. Arnup the entire manuscript. I have benefited greatly from their comments and hasten to add erroneous or questionable passages that survive are entirely my own responsibility. Last but not least I would like to express my thanks to Sandra McAuslan and Sylvia Brown in my own department and Wendy Burgess, Marie Pierce, Monica Sandor, and Gail Landau in the Centre of Criminology for their skill and hard work in transforming my incorrigibly illegible handwriting into a neatly typed manuscript. It was reassuring to learn how essential the human element still is in the age of the word processor.

Peter H. Russell
University of Toronto
December 1986

PART ONE

THE JUDICIARY AS A
BRANCH OF GOVERNMENT

CHAPTER 1
THE NATURE OF JUDICIAL POWER

Canadians are not conditioned to think of courts as part of the political system. Judicial institutions are not regarded as an important item in the agenda of political science. The role of the judiciary is perceived as being essentially technical and non-political: it is there to apply the laws made by the political branches of government. Indeed, the most important normative expectations of judges and courts would seem to be a thorough-going impartiality requiring total independence of the political process.

And yet this book and others like it are devoted to studying the judiciary as an integral part of a country's political system.[1] Such undertakings are built on the firm conviction that judges exercise political power and that courts are part of the machinery of government. In virtually all societies persons holding judicial office have the function of ensuring compliance with prevailing norms and of strengthening allegiance to the regime. In some political systems (including the Canadian) judges not only maintain order, they may also promote change in public policies and assist individuals and groups who are challenging the activities of other branches of government. The purpose of this book is to examine the extent and nature of judicial power in the Canadian political system; it will identify the areas of public life in which judicial power is most influential, the ways in which that power is organized and administered, and the social interests and political values it serves.

The addition of a Charter of Rights and Freedoms to Canada's Constitution in 1982 will make Canadians much more conscious of judicial power. Whatever Canadian judges do with the Charter—whether they use it as a basis for overriding policies of federal and provincial governments, or whether they respond in a much more conservative fashion and give the "political branches" the benefit of the doubt when their activities are subjected to Charter challenges—in either case, their decisions are bound to be politically contentious. The reality of judicial choice will be more clearly exposed. The idea that judging is a technical, non-political function will be less easily maintained. Much more attention will be given to the appointment of judges, especially those at the commanding heights of the judicial structure.

There can be no doubt that the Charter deals the Canadian judiciary into a wider range of political issues and in that sense increases judicial power in Canada; it is a mistake, nonetheless, to regard this involvement as a revolutionary development. Canadian judges all along have been exercising a considerable influence on policy—by making decisions on the common law, by interpreting statutes, and by umpiring the federal division of powers in Canada's written constitution, as well as by such non-adjudicative activities as the sentencing in criminal courts and mediation in family courts. An intriguing feature of the exercise of judicial power in Canada is how well it has been masked and hidden from political scrutiny. It may be, as I have suggested elsewhere, that the quiet nature of this traditional exercise of judicial power has been a major source of its strength.[2] What the new Charter threatens to do is unmask that power. The effect this may have on judicial power is an important question for contemporary political scientists.

Given the perception of the judicial process that prevails in our political culture, such an unmasking is likely to be a somewhat scandalous activity. In fact, some members of the judiciary who in professional circles acknowledge the policy-making role of judges, believe that news of this judicial realism should not reach the ears of the public. In their view, public confidence in the impartiality of the judiciary requires that the perception of the judicial function as technical and non-political be maintained as a kind of Platonic "noble lie."[3] Even if this myth of courts and judges as political neuters could survive indefinitely (which is extremely doubtful), it is surely not part of the task of scholars and teachers of political science to be co-conspirators in this project of public hoodwinking.

But those who engage in the political analysis of the judicial branch of government do have a responsibility to give serious attention to the normative dimensions of the judicial process. Notions of judicial impartiality and independence should not be cynically dismissed as rhetorical façades behind which judges are free to exercise raw political power on behalf of themselves or their "political masters," or against their political or economic opponents. It is one thing to acknowledge the power of judges in shaping public policy through the interpretation and case-by-case application of the constitution, statutes, and common law. That does not commit us to condoning a phone call from a cabinet minister pressuring a judge to handle a case in a manner favourable to the minister's constituent, or to accepting a system of criminal justice that has a built-in tendency to punish non-Caucasian youths more harshly than others who may have committed similar offences. An adequate political science analysis of the judicial process must be built on a political theory which recognizes that the ideals of judicial impartiality and independence are not pieces of folklore cleverly manufactured by a governing class; rather, they represent normative concerns arising from the fundamental needs of a just and effective political order. The most profound challenge to the branch of political science that studies the judiciary is to consider how the judiciary's capacity to meet fundamental normative requirements can be reconciled with the inescapably political nature of so much of its activities.

We can begin to deal with this challenge by coming to grips with the essential function of all judicial bodies: adjudication. For inherent in the adjudicative function is the tension between the requirements of political neutrality and independence on the one hand, and the reality of political power on the other.

The Adjudicative Function

The political power of the judiciary differs from the power exercised by the executive and legislative branches of government in that whatever power judges exercise accrues to them because of their adjudicative responsibilities—that is, their responsibility for providing authoritative settlements in disputes about the law. The performance of this adjudicative dispute-settling function is the raison d'être of courts of law presided over by judges.

In placing adjudication as a form of dispute settlement at the centre of the judicial function, it is necessary to distinguish adjudication from other methods of dispute settlement that exist within a society. Adjudication should be distinguished from other forms of conflict resolution in terms of both the method it employs and the type of dispute to which it applies.

First, in terms of method, adjudication involves the engagement of the judge as a third party to settle a dispute which the participants in the dispute are unable or unwilling to settle on their own. Thus it is to be distinguished from more normal and certainly more economical methods of settling interpersonal and intergroup conflict: the abandonment of the dispute by one or all of the parties or a negotiated settlement worked out by the parties themselves.

Adjudication by judges is not the only kind of third party dispute-settlement process. It must be further distinguished from two other forms of third party or "triadic" approaches to conflict resolution: mediation and arbitration.[4] Mediation differs from adjudication in two vital respects. First, the mediator does not seek to determine which of the disputants is right and which is wrong, but by going back and forth between the parties, attempts to arrive at a solution which both will accept. Secondly, the mediator is not supposed to impose a settlement on the parties. The success of this method depends entirely on helping the parties work out their own solution. In arbitration, unlike mediation, the arbitrator is usually empowered to impose a settlement on the disputants. But this occurs only after the parties have chosen the arbitrator and have agreed to be bound by his or her decision.

It is this element of consent, of voluntariness, which is the key difference between both mediation and arbitration as methods of dispute settlement and adjudication by judges. It is precisely the coercive element in judicial decision-making—the judge's ties to the coercive powers of the state—that imbues adjudication with a political character lacking in the other two forms of third-party dispute settlement. The judge is a state-appointed, public office holder. The judge's power to determine a dispute does not depend entirely on the consent of the disputants. It is true that a dispute will not be brought before a judge until one of the parties takes the initiative and asserts before a court a legal claim that the other party denies. But once the court is seized of the case and the judge recognizes the claim as one that comes within his or her jurisdiction, the judge's intervention in the dispute no longer depends on the consent of the parties. Nor is it the judge's primary function as an adjudicator to work out a solution to the dispute which both parties find agreeable. His or her basic responsibility is to determine which of the disputants is legally right. Unlike the outcome of negotiated or mediated settlements, or even of arbitrated settlements, the outcome of adjudication is much less likely to be a compromise acceptable to both sides than a winner-take-all solution in favour of the party whom the judge decides has legal right on its side.

This last point brings us to the second distinctive dimension of adjudication as a method of dispute settlement: the type of dispute to which it applies. Adjudication by judges applies only to disputes about the law. A great many of the conflict situations which occur in a society do not involve claims to legal rights. For instance, in Canada disputes between spouses over the spending of the family income, competition between business rivals for larger shares of a market, disagreement between students and professors over the curriculum, arguments between critics over the merits of a movie, or conflicts between political organizations about the proper content of public policy normally do not involve disputes about legal rights and powers and would therefore not be accepted for adjudication by courts. But the situation changes when a legal element is introduced. If the spouses are arguing about the distribution of the family's assets in the process of dissolving their marriage; if a business firm alleges that its rival has infringed its copyright; if a student claims to have been academically penalized without a fair hearing; if a film distributor contests a charge by the police that a film is obscene; if a political group claims that legislation supported by its opponents is unconstitutional—in all these cases where the parties do not effect a reconciliation of their differences on their own, the dispute may well be brought before the courts for adjudication. It is the function of the judge to provide an authoritative resolution of the legal point at issue.

Often it is disputed matters of fact that are at issue in judicial decision-making. Courts of appeal, especially the highest court of appeal in a nation, will be preoccupied with complex issues concerning the proper interpretation and development of the law. But the disputes that come before trial courts (which as courts of first instance carry out by far the bulk of adjudication) more typically take the form of factual questions: Who did what to whom? Whose version of events is to be believed? These disputes about facts are decided by judges in courts, however, only because they are relevant to a disputed legal claim. No court will hear the kind of factual dispute I so often have with my wife as to whether the wind is blowing from the west or the northwest or with my son as to whether the runner is safe or out at first base. But courts will determine whether the evidence adduced about a person's behaviour meets the legal standard of tortious negligence or criminal liability. These disputes go beyond the private to the public realm, for what is at issue is whether or how the law, as society's system of binding rules, is to be applied. Here again we see the inherently political dimension of adjudication—its connection to the law, its application of the norms of the political community which are backed by the coercive powers of the state.

It should be noted that adjudication by judges may by no means settle all aspects of a dispute. The decisions of courts are authoritative only on those issues in a dispute which are directly relevant to the legal claim being asserted. But most conflicts, including many that come before the courts, have dimensions that extend well beyond the legal points at issue. To use Lon Fuller's phrase, social conflicts are frequently, if not most often, "polycentric."[5] For instance, in the conflict that gives rise to a criminal case involving an inter-spousal assault, there will be much more at stake than whether the evidence submitted to the court constitutes grounds for finding the accused guilty. Yet it is that narrow issue on which the judge and jury will focus. While the court's decision will be authoritative on that point, it will not settle the conflict between the warring spouses.

The limitations of judicial decision-making as a method of resolving disputes raise important policy questions about the proper scope and application of adjudication by courts. Excessive reliance on formal adjudication may erode a community's capacity for handling disputes more informally and in a way that deals more directly and effectively with the sources of conflict. Recognition of this possibility is at the root of contemporary law reform proposals, which aim to divert from the courts disputes involving criminal offences between individuals who have family, neighbourhood, or workplace relationships.[6] On the other hand there are many situations in which judicial resolution of the legal dimension of a dispute may be a helpful step in resolving a larger conflict. The Supreme Court of Canada's decisions in the late 1970s limiting provincial powers over natural resources did not settle the basic political conflict over the proper distribution of resource power within the Canadian federation. But even though the Court's decisions were far from acceptable to a number of provinces, it is arguable that, by clarifying the rights of the federal and provincial governments under the existing constitution, the decisions paved the way for negotiating an amendment to the constitution which represents a more satisfactory balancing of national and provincial interests.[7]

The desirability of adjudication does not depend solely on the likelihood that it will produce amicable solutions to social conflict. A dispute may involve a legal claim of great importance both to one of the parties and to society—for example, a wife's right to protection from physical assault by her husband— which sometimes can be effectively asserted only by submitting or threatening to submit the dispute to the courts. In such a situation, diversion from formal adjudication could entail the denial of an important legal right.

Even on legal matters, while the decisions of courts may be authoritative on paper, their effect on the rights people actually enjoy may be much more limited and, in the long run, far from definitive in determining the content of the law. The effectiveness of judicial decisions in shaping not only the law in books but the law in practice depends on compliance with court decisions. Compliance, however mandatory it may be in a legal sense, is not an automatic consequence of court decisions. Although courts can order that those who fail to comply with their rulings be punished for contempt of court, judges do not have under their direct command the executive instruments of law enforcement. The judiciary's very lack of its own coercive forces is the basis for its description as the "least dangerous branch."[8]

Where the decisions of courts are reasonably in line with the prevailing constellation of social forces, compliance with judicial decisions will be the norm. Such is probably the situation in Canada. But even here compliance is far from 100 per cent. Non-compliance with court decisions ranges all the way from failure to enforce the maintenance payments courts have awarded to deserted wives[9] to the ineffectiveness of court decisions in upholding the constitutional language rights of Manitoba francophones. In the latter instance, there was virtually no compliance with lower court decisions in the 1890s that Manitoba's "Charter of the English Language" was unconstitutional. Many years later, in 1979, when Canada's highest court reached a similar decision and found that Manitoba's laws must be enacted in both French and English,[10] problems of compliance immediately arose. The process of producing French translations of the province's statutes and regulations which had accumulated over ninety years could not be accomplished overnight. After the failure of politicians to work out a constitutional amendment that would have provided a breathing period in which the province could get its laws translated, the Supreme Court itself had to handle the compliance issue. In 1985 it virtually amended the Constitution by ruling that Manitoba's English-only laws would be constitutionally valid during a translation period, which it set as three years for the consolidated statutes and regulations, and five years for other laws.[11] It is a measure of the growth in judicial power in Canada that there seemed to be more public support for having the Supreme Court rather than the politicians regulate the compliance process.

The conditions affecting compliance with court decisions indicate the way in which judicial power interacts with other components of the political system. Judicial decisions are often powerful factors in shaping conduct and influencing the outcome of political contests. A favourable political decision can be an important resource to an individual, an interest group, or a government. But even in Canada, where the rule of law and respect for courts are well ingrained in our political culture, there are very real limits to the extent that judges can counter powerful political interests. In the words of J.W. Peltason, "Most of the time the judicial rulings will 'stick', although without significant support they will not stick for long."[12] Those who have championed a constitutional charter of rights as a means of "guaranteeing" the rights of minorities against the will of the majority ignore this fundamental fact about political reality. In the long run, no judiciary can be effective in upholding interests or rights which are opposed by the dominant forces and sentiment in a society.

The limits on judicial power in shaping the content of law are even more obvious. While the reality of judicial law-making in the process of adjudication is no longer seriously questioned and will be an important part of the analysis presented in this book, there can be no question about the political limits on judicial legislation. In countries such as Canada, whose legal systems derive largely from the English common law tradition, judge-made common law has been one of the primary sources of law. But these countries have also followed the British in accepting the principle of parliamentary or legislative supremacy, at least to the extent of acknowledging the power of the legislature (within the limits imposed on it by the written constitution) to enact legislation altering the rules of common law developed by the courts. Again, the judiciary's interpretation of legislation in the case-by-case process of adjudication often has a major bearing on the policies effected through legislation. But if there is considerable political opposition to the policy resulting from judicial interpretation of legislation and that opposition can be effectively mobilized in the legislature (and that is often a big if!), the legislature may override the policies read into the legislation by the judiciary. A good example is judicial interpretation of Canada's anti-monopoly legislation. The judges' approach has made it nearly impossible to convict corporations for monopolistic practices. Federal ministers of consumer and corporate affairs have experienced great difficulty politically in overcoming the effects of judicial decision-making on competition policy.

Where the written constitution comes into play as a third source of law, it is sometimes suggested that here judicial determination of the meaning of the Constitution must be legally authoritative and final. Certainly when a written constitutional text is associated with the process of judicial review, as it is in Canada, and the judiciary settles disputes about the constitutional limits on the other branches of government, judicial decisions provide authoritative determinations of constitutional rights and powers which normally cannot be overridden by ordinary legislation.[13] Even here, however, judicial decisions are not final. At the very least, judicial interpretation of a constitution can be altered by constitutional amendment. Even though formal amendment is usually a difficult political process, it is occasionally used to reverse the judiciary's constitutional interpretations, especially when they are strongly opposed by major forces in the political system. The reversals by constitutional amendment of the U.S. Supreme Court's ruling against the constitutional validity of income tax and of the Canadian Supreme Court's ruling against the validity of federal unemployment insurance legislation are clear examples.

But consideration of limits to the finality of judicial decisions on the meaning of the constitution must not be confined to the relatively rare instances of reversal by constitutional amendment. Much more pervasive is the political pressure which can be applied through a variety of processes to bring about changes in the constitutional policies of the judiciary. Such pressure can be quite blatant, as with the threats of President Roosevelt to pack the U.S. Supreme Court following its veto of his New Deal legislation, or the demands of some of Canada's provincial premiers to restructure the Supreme Court of Canada as a way of countering what they perceived to be that court's centralist bias in interpreting the division of powers in the Canadian constitution. Or it may be exercised much more subtly—for example, through the influence of a court's intellectual critics on the education of lawyers who eventually take their place on the bench and alter established judicial doctrines.

It must be recognized that the relationship between courts and the other branches of government cannot be understood adequately in terms of formal constitutional precepts. The legal formalist makes the mistake of thinking that these relationships are governed by concepts such as legislative supremacy or judicially enforced constitutional supremacy. But in the real world of politics no one is supreme and no institution ever has the last word. Political history, of which judicial events form a part, is a continuous process with ever fluctuating power relationships. The relationships among political institutions, including those between the judiciary and other centres of power in the political system, are much too free-flowing and complex to be grasped by simple constitutional formulas. Still, the political scientist must recognize that judicial enforcement of the constitution against the other branches of government as a practice of constitutional government may attract and retain a powerful body of political support. The United States is a clear example of a state in which judicial enforcement of constitutional norms has strong political support within the polity. By way of contrast, in India political support for judicial review is not nearly so strong, with the result that it is easier for elected politicians to resist. What is essential from the perspective of political science in coming to terms with judicial power is to avoid the shortcomings of legal formalism while at the same time giving sufficient weight to the political power of legal phenomena.

The Non-Adjudicative Functions of the Judiciary

Adjudication may be at the centre of the judicial function, but it is certainly not the only function of the judiciary or the only one of political significance. On the contrary, judges and courts are frequently engaged in activities which cannot be classified as adjudicative. Indeed, if you were to walk into a court house anywhere in Canada, you might have difficulty finding a judge doing what has been defined as adjudication. In a criminal court you are more likely to find judges concerned with processing requests for adjournments, or considering the sentence appropriate for an accused person who has pleaded guilty, than you are to find them in the process of hearing arguments about disputed points of law or fact. In a civil court you will often find judges acting not as adjudicators determining legal rights but as mediators trying to guide the parties to a compromise solution which will make formal adjudication of their dispute unnecessary. Family court judges may well be found assisting families and social agencies to find some better means of keeping a young person out of trouble, and small claims court judges involved in counselling individuals on the management of their debts.

The variety of activities above and beyond adjudication as we have strictly defined it will be examined in Part Four, where we will analyse the business of the principal types of Canadian courts. As these chapters show, the differences between types of courts as social and political institutions are so great that it can be quite misleading to label them all as "courts." And yet it is the core of adjudication at the heart of their work that in each case must be the institution's raison d'être and the reason for appointing, almost always, professional lawyers as their key decision makers. It is only because courts and judges are first perceived as having an adjudicative function that they are put in a position which enables them to take on non-adjudicative activities.

The combination of adjudicative and non-adjudicative activities in judicial institutions generates important policy questions. The performance of a non-adjudicative function by a court or judges—for example, working out a negotiated settlement in a civil dispute, or involvement in plea bargaining in a criminal case—may compromise their capacity to adjudicate legal claims at issue in disputes. Formal adjudication may in fact become so peripheral to the day-to-day activities of a court that the question must be asked whether decision makers with knowledge and skills different from those of legal professionals should be appointed to the court, or whether some of the court's functions should be diverted to non-judicial institutions. Organizational structures and administrative approaches designed to meet the requirements of an institution engaged primarily in formal adjudication may be ill suited for an institution which has come to devote most of its resources and energies to non-adjudicative activities.[14]

Consideration of the non-adjudicative functions of the judiciary should not be confined to activities that might be observed if one were to visit the courtroom or judge's chambers. Judges in Canada, as in many other societies, exercise important political functions off the bench and outside the court house in contexts which involve them with other actors and institutions in the political system. Two such functions are of particular interest to Canadian political scientists: the administrative role of judges, and their appointment to royal commissions and commissions of inquiry.

Until quite recently the phrase "the administration of justice" had nothing to do with the art or science of public administration. Judicial institutions were administered more by osmosis than by intelligent direction. In the latter half of the twentieth century, in Canada and in most of the other western democracies, burgeoning caseloads, coupled with public demands for greater efficiency in the provision of court services, have led to the introduction of much more intensive and systematic machinery for controlling the flow of court business. In varying degrees judges have become involved in managing this expanding machinery of judicial administration. In particular, chief justices and senior judges in multi-judge urban trial courts and in courts of appeal are increasingly called upon to act as administrators and managers.

In this process Canadian judges have not simply been the passive recipients of enlarged administrative responsibilities. Recently some of them have begun a vigorous campaign to increase the judiciary's control over court administration. In 1981 a report entitled *Maîtres Chez Eux*, prepared by the chief justice of Quebec's Superior Court, Jules Deschênes, and sponsored by organizations whose membership includes both federally and provincially appointed judges, proposed a series of reforms aimed at transferring from the executive branch to the judiciary control over virtually all aspects of court administration except collective bargaining with court staff.[15] In the final stage of the Deschênes plan, judges would negotiate court budgets directly with legislative committees. Ironically, while the rationale for these proposals is the better protection of judicial independence, the struggle to obtain this power and its exercise once obtained will inevitably involve judges more openly in political activity. The issue of who should control the new and expanding bureaucracies of court administration raises questions about the judiciary's role in government that up to now have received little political attention in Canada.

While the Canadian judiciary is still contesting its role in the direction and control of court bureaucracies, collectively it has already assumed more substantial powers with regard to the personnel management of judges themselves. The 1970s witnessed the introduction of judicial councils at both the federal and provincial levels in Canada. These bodies, composed entirely of judges in the case of the Canadian Judicial Council and partly of judges in the case of the provincial and territorial judicial councils, are concerned, for the most part, with the discipline, continuing education, and the selection of judges.[16] The activities of these new agencies of judicial governance will be examined in Part Three. Here I wish only to draw attention to the way in which these councils add a further dimension to judicial power. The investigation of Justice Thomas Berger's intervention in Canada's constitutional debate and the ensuing reprimand administered by the Canadian Judicial Council provide a vivid illustration of the political controversy which may be associated with the exercise of judicial council powers.[17] This episode brings into focus important constitutional questions about the collective power of the judiciary over its individual members and the relationship between this power and the concept of judicial independence.

In Canada, as in Britain and other Commonwealth countries, judges are frequently appointed by the executive branch of government to serve on commissions to inquire into and make recommendations on matters of public concern and political controversy.[18] When serious charges have been made about the misconduct of ministers or officials, or when there is need to review a field of public policy, governments in parliamentary systems have often favoured appointing a royal commission rather than permitting the matter to be investigated by a legislative committee. There are two obvious reasons for appointing judges to royal commissions. First, from a technical point of view, they are experienced in conducting proceedings in which contending views are given a fair hearing. But the second reason is essentially political: the judge has an aura of impartiality which lends credibility to the inquiry. Such credibility may be an important political asset to the government; in circumstances where the establishment of a commission has removed a contentious issue from parliamentary debate and scrutiny by its political opponents, it is essential for the government to be able to maintain that the commission is not a means of serving its own partisan interests.

The use of judges on royal commissions is a fragile instrument of government. The subjects investigated by commissions—whether they be major policy issues such as federal-provincial relations or medicare, or the improprieties of cabinet ministers, or allegations of illegal activities by the national police and security service[19]—are usually topics of great political interest and partisan debate. The participation of judges in these commissions is bound to contribute to the politicization of the judiciary and will likely diminish the aura of impartiality—which is one of the reasons for appointing judges to royal commissions in the first place. If this resulted merely in fewer royal commissions or fewer judicial royal commissioners, there would be no serious loss; there are other means of conducting public inquiries into government misconduct and public policy. The more serious danger is to the judicial branch of government itself and its capacity for effectively performing its essential function of adjudication. As we shall argue below in discussing the normative requirements of adjudication, to be effective as adjudicators judges need to be perceived as politically impartial at least in the sense of not favouring members of the government (or for that matter members of any other political body) in cases in which they are directly involved.

The Influence of Adjudication on Law and Policy

The process of adjudication influences and shapes the public policies that are given effect through laws. For this reason the adjudicative work of judges itself is of political significance.

This is a paradoxical and deeply problematic feature of adjudication. For in theory judges are supposed to be settling disputes according to pre-existing law, to be upholding rights and enforcing duties that exist under the law. But the fact remains that judges also shape and develop the law in the very process of settling disputes about it. The key to this most intriguing feature of adjudication is the inescapable generality of law. No body of rules could ever be comprehensive and detailed enough to anticipate explicitly the circumstances of the specific disputes which may arise under a legal system.[20] A rule of common law can be enunciated stipulating the "consideration" necessary for a binding contract, "murder" can be defined in the Criminal Code, the constitution may contain lists spelling out the powers of the two levels of government, but difficult questions requiring adjudication will still arise as to whether the circumstances of this particular business transaction constitutes consideration, or whether the facts of this particular homicide constitute murder, or whether a particular law is primarily concerned with "property and civil rights" (a provincial responsibility) or with the "peace, order and good government of Canada" (a federal responsibility). In settling disputes of this kind, the judiciary puts flesh on the bare skeleton of the law and in the process shapes the substance of the law.

The generality of legal rules is not the only reason for judicial law-making. Many disputes that come before the courts involve a number of legal arguments based on different and competing legal rules and principles. A good example is the famous case of *Roncarelli* v. *Duplessis*, in which the restauranteur Roncarelli challenged the action of the premier and attorney general of Quebec, Maurice Duplessis, in ordering the province's liquor commissioner to cancel Roncarelli's liquor licence because Roncarelli had been supporting the Jehovah's Witnesses.[21] Here there were two rules of law which seemed to go against Roncarelli: the statute which granted the liquor commissioner his powers did not specifically limit the grounds upon which he could cancel a licence; and Roncarelli had failed to initiate his action within the time period required by Quebec's Code of Civil Procedure. But there was another principle of public law involved in the case to which, in the end, a majority of the Supreme Court of Canada gave precedence—namely, that statutory powers are not to be used by the executive for purposes for which it is unreasonable to believe they were intended by the legislature. Often, in more mundane cases, clearly applicable legal rules will stand in the way of doing justice in the circumstances of a particular situation.[22] One of the judge's (and jury's) most important tasks is to establish priorities among competing legal rules and principles.

The process whereby judges in settling disputes about the law play a part in shaping the substance of law has two dimensions. First, not unlike administrators or bureaucrats, judges affect how legal rights are enjoyed in practice through the cumulative weight of their day-to-day, case-by-case decision-making. It is in this way that trial courts have their major impact on public policy. Bail reform policy, for instance, will be influenced as much by the ways in which judges assess the trustworthiness and danger to society of accused persons as by new provisions of the Criminal Code.[23]

Over the last century in Canada, and indeed in most other countries, the growth of the non-judicial administrative arm of government has far exceeded that of the judiciary. As a result, the proportion of policy formation subject to judicial influence has declined. This is true even when we take into account the extent to which judges in common law countries have insisted on maintaining their power to review the legality of administrative actions and the expanded basis of constitutional review in many of the democracies. In the domain of criminal law, for example, police forces in Canada (which have grown faster than the judiciary), whose members usually make the crucial decisions as to which offences to investigate and prosecute, probably have a considerably greater influence on the way in which criminal law affects our society than do judges.[24] Still, Canada's trial courts will have a significant impact in those areas where adjudication still looms large: on the rights of parents and children involved in family break-ups, for example, and on the rights of debtors and creditors in declining economic circumstances.

The second dimension of judicial policy-making through adjudication which takes a more formal law-making mode is the process whereby the decisions of courts themselves become rules of law. Those who have studied Canada's constitutional history will have encountered this kind of judicial law-making in studying the Judicial Committee of the Privy Council's and the Supreme Court of Canada's interpretations of Canada's Constitution.[25] These decisions become part of the law of the Canadian constitution—many observers would say a more important part than the actual text of the Constitution. The real meaning of the general phrases in the constitutional text—terms like "peace, order and good government" and "property and civil rights," which play such an important role in the federal division of powers—depends entirely on judicial interpretation. Judicial law-making of this kind also goes on in the development of the common law and the interpretation of ordinary statutes. It is especially evident in common law countries such as Canada, where the reported decisions of appeal courts are recognized as legal precedents binding on courts of lower jurisdiction. But such judicial law-making is far from unknown even in those civil law countries where judicial decisions are not formally accorded such a status.[26]

In recent years the spread of judicial review based on written constitutions has increased the political significance of judicial law-making. In theory at least, judicial interpretations of constitutional provisions have more political importance because they are not so easily reversed by other components of the political system. Certainly the political prominence of judicial policy-making has increased in countries such as Ireland, Italy, Japan, and West Germany which have adopted constitutions containing fundamental rights and have accepted courts as the mechanism for settling disputes about such rights.[27] Similarly, the visibility of judicial policy-making will now increase in Canada as a result of adopting a constitutional charter of rights and freedoms.

Providing an adequate account of judicial law-making has become a central preoccupation in the study of judicial decision-making. This is particularly so in democratic cultures where the mandate of appointed judges to make law is not recognized by the prevailing ideology. In addition to this democratic concern, legal scholars have found it difficult to square the reality of judicial law-making with the theoretical notion that judges in deciding cases are not applying their own subjective will but a pre-existing and objective law.

Three kinds of reaction are evident. Some judges have reacted to this debate by denying the reality of judicial legislation. They would have us believe that in applying the law to new and unforeseeable circumstances and in sorting out conflicts within the corpus of legal rules and principles, judges do not make the law but "declare" it.[28] Increasingly, however, this reaction has been recognized as a rhetorical device for masking the power of the judiciary.

A more frequent response has been to acknowledge the reality of judicial law-making but to insist that it is extremely limited, both in the sense that it is interstitial (i.e., within limits established by clear rules of law) and that it does not occur in most of the cases that judges are called upon to decide.[29] But this response is hardly satisfactory either. Judicial law-making may be interstitial, but so is law-making by the other branches of government. Normally legislators and policy makers do not have the luxury of working in a vacuum unencumbered by either the weight of the existing legal system or obvious political constraints. The decisions of Canadian judges as to what limits on freedom of speech are "reasonable" and "demonstrably justifiable in a free and democratic society" are hardly more interstitial than most decisions of Canada's formal legislators. The obvious policy-making implications of judicial decisions on the meaning of concepts in a new constitutional charter of rights may not be present in most court cases; still, if the processes of pre-trial dispute settlement are working reasonably well so that adjudication is reserved for legal disputes involving well-supported claims on each side, then even in mundane cases adjudication is likely to require more than the mechanical application of obviously relevant rules of law. Finally, even if it were empirically true that most of the time the law relevant to the disputes before judges was perfectly clear, the apparent creativity or subjectivity of judges in the residue of cases—some of which are likely to involve matters of great importance to a country's constitution and legal system—remains to be explained.

The need to cope with the problem of subjectivity in judicial decision-making has given rise to a third kind of response in modern jurisprudence. This attempts to identify and prescribe a methodology which can bring to judicial decision-making (even in those hard cases where the requirements of the law are far from clear) an objectivity consonant both with the requirements of the judicial role in a democracy and with the inherent nature of adjudication itself. A common theme in these approaches is to insist that in deciding disputes about the proper meaning of legal rules and sorting out conflicts and priorities within a legal system, judges must search for the principles underlying rules of law.[30] In deciding which competing position on the proper application of the law is correct, the judge should be guided not by the political or social result he or she personally favours but by consideration of society's reasons for having laws in regard to the matters at issue. So, in a sense, this third response to the problem of judicial law-making comes back to the first in that those who espouse it would deny that judges, by going beyond the letter of legal rules to consider the social and political values at the base of legal institutions, are going "outside the law." By seeking to interpret the law in terms of its broader purposes and hierarchy of underlying principles, the judge may "discover" the law in all its fullness.[31]

Some political scientists (and legal scholars) in their study of judicial decision-making have tried to avoid this whole debate by treating judges as political actors whose decisions reflect simply their personal values and interests.[32] For such radical realists, judicial decision-making should be studied solely from the point of view of "who gets what, when, and how." From this perspective the distinctive aspects of judicial institutions and the judicial process—the concern for the independence and impartiality of the judge, the procedural requirement of giving each side a fair hearing, and the provision of reasons explaining a decision in terms of legal rules and principles—are presumably nothing more than a cunning camouflage behind which judges are free to indulge their own political fancies. The position taken in this book is not that of the radical realist. The normative requirements of judicial decision-making in a liberal democracy will be taken seriously as posing a fundamental challenge to the proper exercise and organization of the judicial power in Canada. Although political science students of the judicial process should not expect to find a single, comprehensive formula for comprehending the role of judges in deciding difficult and politically significant law cases, they should become fully aware of the problematic nature of adjudication and of the risks involved in contracting or expanding the judicial role.

Alternative Structures for Adjudication

Adjudication is a function which must be performed in virtually all countries. Only in an extremely small and socially homogeneous society could the rules or customs governing acceptable social behaviour be so clear and spontaneously observed that the need for mechanisms to settle disputes about their meaning and proper application might never arise. But while rule adjudication is a universal function of government, the structures through which this function is performed vary greatly. Not only are there important variations in judicial institutions but, even more fundamentally, there are variations in the extent to which adjudication is carried out by specialized judicial structures separate and distinct from other institutions of government.

In Canada in the late twentieth century we tend to think that a system of courts staffed by professional lawyer-judges specializing in the adjudication of legal disputes and independent of the other branches of government is a sine qua non of an acceptable system of government. But this expectation is far from universal, nor has it always prevailed in our own society. Indeed, Martin Shapiro, surveying the performance of the adjudicative function through history and on a global basis, finds that a stress on the institutional separation of courts from the remainder of the political system is "the most deviant case." "The universal pattern," he states, "is that judging runs as an integral part of the mainstream of political authority."[33]

We do not have to go far back in Canadian history to find a time when the judiciary was joined much more closely to the other branches of government than would be acceptable today. Throughout most of the colonial period until well on into the nineteenth century, the highest court of appeal in the British North American colonies was the governor and his Executive Council, and judges participated in both the executive and legislative institutions of government.[34] By Confederation, adjudication of most civil disputes by professional judges in courts was well established. But in the field of criminal justice, where chiefly the working class was involved, the performance of adjudication by persons with executive responsibilities, notably municipal officials and police officers, continued long after Confederation. Well into this century, the Canadian Senate functioned as a divorce court for Quebec and the provincial cabinet did the same for Prince Edward Island.[35] Indeed, the family courts of Nova Scotia are still formally treated as a part of the Social Services Ministry rather than as part of a separate judicial branch of government.

The fusion of judicial and executive powers reflects the fact that adjudication can contribute to the consolidation and maintenance of a political regime. This social control function tends to be paramount when the judicial power is joined closely to the executive arm of government. This is evident in the history of the English Royal Courts of Justice. Originally the judges of these courts were members of the King's Council. The extension of the jurisdiction of these royal judges over local courts was a crucial step in centralizing political power under the English monarch.[36] Similarly, in Canada the establishment of a court system after the British conquest of New France contributed to the consolidation of the new British North American regime, just as the Hudson's Bay Company's establishment of the court of the Recorder of Rupert's Land and later the extension of police courts across the prairies were means of maintaining order on the frontier and affirming European domination over the native peoples.[37] The coercive, social control aspect of adjudication is apt to be most apparent in imperial contexts, where the judiciary has the function of applying an alien law to an indigenous population.

The extent to which the judicial function comes to be performed in institutions separate from the other branches of government depends in part on how much knowledge of the law becomes the monopoly of a special profession. Certainly the emergence of the common law in England as an enormously complex body of judge-made, legal rules, totally impenetrable to all but those schooled and trained by the professional lawyers' guild, had much to do with the development of the large degree of independence of the English courts from both the monarchy and Parliament. Legal specialization can be an important factor in promoting a degree of institutional differentiation for the judiciary, even in communist countries where there is no ideological basis for an independent judiciary.[38]

Some political scientists have suggested that the performance of rule adjudication by distinct judicial structures is a function of the specialization characteristic of institutional developments in modern political systems.[39] But this point of view tends to overlook the ideological or normative grounds for the performance of adjudication by institutions beyond the direct control of other parts of the political system. Modernization, with its accompanying emphasis on sophisticated skills and the division of labour, may go a long way in accounting for the development of specialized judicial institutions (i.e., courts) in virtually all contemporary political systems. But the relationship between these courts and other parts of the political system and, in this sense, the independence of the judiciary, depend much more on ideological factors which have not been a universal feature of political modernization.   The key ideological factor is the emergence of a strong element of liberalism in the prevailing norms of the political culture. This liberal perspective attaches a high value to insulating judicial institutions from direct interference by other branches of government as a means of enhancing liberty, and accounts for the relatively high degree of institutional independence acquired by the courts of Canada and of other liberal democracies.

The independence of judicial institutions from other parts of the political system in reality, of course, is never complete. The political system of which the judiciary is a component part is a set of interdependent institutions and processes. Still, differences in the degree of independence accorded judicial institutions in different polities may amount to differences of kind.[40] Judicial independence, though a relative concept in an empirical sense, is a much more potent and politically salient ideal in the practice of government in liberal societies which attach a positive value to the fracturing of governmental power and the protection of individual rights. In studying the Canadian judiciary, close attention must be paid to the way in which these liberal concerns are reflected in Canada's judicial arrangements.

Even where a judiciary functions through courts separate and distinct from the other branches of government, a considerable amount of adjudication may be done through institutions other than the courts. This is indeed the case in Canada and other modern political systems experiencing the same general expansion of governmental activities. Both the provincial and federal governments have established a vast array of administrative tribunals outside the regular courts to settle disputes arising under particular statutes or in particular areas of public policy. Calling to mind just a few of these bodies—workers' compensation boards, assessment appeal boards, labour relations boards, the Immigration Appeal Board, the Tariff Board—gives some idea of the scale of this development.[41] In Canada today, in purely quantitative terms, more adjudication is probably carried out by these non-curial institutions than by judges in courts. While no data are available on the number of decision makers serving on these administrative tribunals, it is likely that the number far exceeds Canada's 1750 judges.[42]

An examination of adjudication by these non-curial, adjudicative bodies is beyond the scope of this book, which will focus on adjudication by judges in courts. Still, consideration must be given to the growth of these agencies as alternatives to the formal judiciary and to issues that arise concerning the proper relationship of these tribunals to the courts. The reasons for assigning adjudicative tasks to these non-courts generally reflect the institutional limitation of courts: the need for decision makers with specialized knowledge and experience not possessed by the generalist lawyers who become judges; the demand for less expensive and complex procedures than are usually associated with the judicial process; and a more direct and open consideration of the policy implications of decisions. But these very advantages may become controversial in terms of the normative requirements of adjudication. Previous experience in a policy field may bring with it a strong policy bias or close associations with government agencies or private organizations frequently involved in proceedings before the tribunal; expeditious procedures may fail to afford litigants a fair and full hearing in determining their rights; and a concern for policy rather than consistency with previous decisions may produce results that seem unpredictable and capricious.

The growth of administrative tribunals as adjudicative agencies raises the fundamental question of the extent to which these tribunals' determinations of legal issues should be subject to review by the ordinary courts. In Canada and other countries in the English common law tradition there is a strong tendency, especially within the legal profession, to look upon the judiciary as the branch of government which on matters of legal rights and wrongs provides a single fountain of justice. This point of view resists attempts to eliminate or reduce the review of the decisions of administrative tribunals by the regular courts. It would look with great disfavour on an institution such as the French Conseil d'État, which is entirely apart from the formal courts and has complete and final responsibility for adjudicating most of the legal disputes that arise between the citizen and administrative agencies, as well as those that arise between and within branches of the administration.[43] One of the underlying concerns in the political science study of the judiciary must be the validity of regarding the judiciary as the single fountain of justice on disputed matters of law.

Normative Dimensions of Adjudication

A basic normative requirement inheres in the very concept of adjudication. Since adjudication is a form of *third*-party conflict resolution, the adjudicator-judge must appear to be genuinely a third party and not an ally or active supporter of one of the disputing parties. A process of adjudication which involves judges making decisions on the basis of their assessment of the competing submissions of the parties would be an open farce and difficult to sustain as a public institution if the judges were openly aligned with particular disputants.

The possibility of submitting disputes about one's rights to impartial judges is one of the primary benefits to be realized in civil society. For John Locke, the availability of common and impartial judges to settle disputes about rights was, indeed, the most fundamental reason for man to quit the state of nature and live under civil government:

> I easily grant that civil government is the proper remedy for the inconveniences of the state of nature, which must certainly be great where men may be judges in their own case.[44]

And later in the same *Treatise*, he wrote that

> wherever any two men are who have no standing rule and common judge to appeal to on earth for the determination of controversies of right betwixt them, they are still in a state of nature.[45]

Locke also recognized that this adjudicative need would not be satisfied if the judges had no independence from those with political authority in civil society:

> I desire to know what kind of government that is, and how much better it is than

the state of nature, where one man commanding a multitude has the liberty to be judge in his own case, and may do to all his subjects whatever he pleases, without the least liberty to any one to question or control those who exercise his pleasure.[46]

Thus, if government is to be based on the rational consent of human beings, adjudication by impartial and independent judges must be regarded as an inherent requirement of political society.

Although judicial independence and impartiality are normative requirements of adjudication, it must be recognized that such qualities can never be realized in an absolute sense in the judicial arrangements of any society, no matter how liberal that society may be. The ineluctable connection between judges and the system of official state authority of which they are a part must qualify both their independence and their impartiality. These ties to the power structure of the political community can be reduced and minimized but never entirely eliminated. John Locke implicitly recognized this fundamental paradox of judicial power when he placed the judiciary within the executive branch of government, despite his insistence that judges be independent of others with political authority.

Independence, as has already been noted, is a relative relationship. Even in a liberal democratic state which places great value on judicial independence, judges are connected to the power structure of the state in a number of important ways. Once appointed, judges may be secured against removal for decisions which displease politicians or officials, but their appointment in the first place will depend either on election or selection by other members of the governing elite. Also, as we have seen, the enforcement of judicial decisions and, in this sense, their effectiveness, depend on the support of other branches of government. Further, the maintenance of judicial institutions, no matter how successful judges may be in gaining control over the internal administration of courts, will always require resources that can only be secured through the cooperation of the other branches of government.

The law itself is the basis of the other primary link between the judiciary and the authority structure of the state. There will necessarily be considerable scope for discretion and law development by judges in deciding disputes about the proper application of laws to the circumstances of particular cases. Nevertheless, the broad contours and structure of a society's legal system will be built upon a general scheme and hierarchy of values. The legal systems of western liberal democracies continue, for example, to attach great value to protecting individuals in the enjoyment of their personal property, a value essential to maintaining capitalist economic relations; in the same way, the legal systems of communist states emphasize the importance of promoting social behaviour which conforms with an ideological conception of communist society. Laws and legal systems are not politically neutral and judges who adjudicate disputes about rights under a particular system of laws cannot be indifferent to the value orientation contained in the laws of their society. Indeed, in part, it is their function to provide leadership in articulating the social purposes underlying the law.

These ties between the judiciary and the authority structure of the state mean that there will always be some tension between judicial independence and impartiality as normative requirements of adjudication and the realities of judicial power. But it would be a serious mistake to assume that, because judicial independence and impartiality cannot be realized in an absolute sense, they should be dismissed as meaningless ideals devoid of significance in the real world of politics. Wherever there is a serious effort to have judges function as third party adjudicators in disputes involving legal rights, as a basic minimum, judges must at least appear to be free from direct interference in deciding individual cases and without close personal ties to either of the parties. And there must be some measure of reality behind this appearance if belief in this minimum element of integrity in the judicial process is to be sustained. Moving out from this rock bottom minimum of judicial independence and impartiality, the degree and character of the judiciary's political subordination and partiality can vary greatly in different political systems. Generally, the more liberal a political system—the more value it places on individual liberty and political and social pluralism—the stricter will be the boundaries between the judiciary and other centres of power, the greater the range and diversity of values that find expression in law, and the greater the opportunity of successfully asserting legal claims against political authorities through the courts.

Even in a relatively illiberal state such as the Soviet Union, where an independent judiciary is not stressed to the extent of regarding the courts as a major check on the governing party, there is still recognition of the minimum measure of judicial independence and impartiality. An official press explanation of the position of the judiciary under the 1977 constitution explains that

> The party organs oversee the selection, placement and ideological education of juridical cadres. But, at the same time, any kind of interference in the administration of justice in specific cases is absolutely ruled out.[47]

Without official recognition of at least this amount of independence for those deciding disputes about legal rights, the population would be unlikely to seriously believe the law embodied a significant corpus of rights and obligations. Thus, where political revolutions have temporarily uprooted judicial institutions possessing a minimum of independence and impartiality, the post-revolutionary need to stabilize the regime has invariably led to the revival of a legal order as the basis for more orderly social and economic relations. With this revival of law comes the restoration of a judicial system which can meet, in a minimal sense, the normative requirements of adjudication.[48]

Of course, there will be breaches of even this minimum notion of independence. Despite the Soviet Union's formal recognition of judicial independence in deciding individual cases, there is ample evidence of situations in which party and government officials pressure judges to decide particular cases in a certain way. There is also evidence, as we shall see in the next chapter, of attempts at such interference in Canada. However, when such interference is exposed in this country it becomes the centre of a major political scandal, sometimes leading to the resignation of the interfering politician; whereas in the Soviet Union such interference is not publicized, nor does it lead to open political criticism of the government. While this points to a significant difference in the degree of independence actually enjoyed by the judiciary in the two societies, nevertheless the Soviet regime's very suppression of information about interference with the judiciary shows that it recognizes how indispensable is the public's belief in at least a minimum degree of judicial independence.

To understand the political importance of the judiciary in different societies, it is essential to observe the very great differences that can exist in the extent to which judges are bound and subordinate to other centres of power in the political system. In Canada judicial independence, while by no means an absolute, is well toward the maximum end of the spectrum. But even here there are important limits. Because the selection of judges is controlled by the political heads of the executive branch of government, the general outlook and political orientation of the judges, to the extent that it is known, will not be drastically out of line with the political outlook of the groups of politicians who dominate both the executive and the legislature. Further, because judges are recruited from the ranks of relatively successful legal practitioners, they will tend to share the social and economic interests of the upper middle class. Still, given the diversity of political beliefs within both political parties and the legal profession, as well as some dispersal of appointing authority among federal and provincial governments, these factors need not produce monolithic selection criteria. Although Canadian judges after their appointment are basically secure from interference by the politicians who appointed them, the politicians' control of promotion within the judicial hierarchy may be a disincentive for some judges to become too well known for bringing down decisions contrary to the interests of the government of the day.[49]

Any limitation on judicial independence or impartiality arising from this factor in the Canadian system looms much larger in the judicial systems of continental Europe. There, most judges never engage in private legal practice but join the judiciary immediately after the completion of their professional education; for the rest of their careers they are on a promotional ladder controlled by politicians or fellow judges.[50] Even closer are the ties to the party hierarchy in a one-party state such as the Soviet Union, where the judges are drawn from and remain members of the legal cadres of the Communist Party. Both before and after their "election," these communist judges are subject to party direction as to the policy interests they are expected to promote through their decision-making.[51]

The independence of the judiciary has more political significance in those countries whose governmental systems are so constituted that the judicial process can serve as a means of challenging the policies and actions of those who for the moment control the main levers of political power. This is pre-eminently the case where, as in Canada, a formal written constitution imposes limitations on the political branches of government, and the judiciary through the process of judicial review is authoritative in interpreting those constitutional limits. Under a federal constitution such as Canada's, judicial review enables one level of government to challenge the other in the courts. It also provides opportunities for private interest groups to defeat policies initiated at each level of government. Adjudication of disputes concerning constitutional guarantees of individual and corporate rights can also become, as Canadians are rapidly finding out, an important rallying point for political interests to overcome defeats they have suffered in the administrative or legislative process. There are often significant changes in the complexion of the political groups that may, in a liberal state, use judicial review as a means of challenging their political opponents. In the late nineteenth and early twentieth century the process of judicial review was used in the United States mainly by conservative economic interests as a base for challenging the collectivist policies of elected governments; but later in the twentieth century it has been resorted to as much, if not more, by radicals and liberals on the left of the political spectrum as a means of resisting policies pursued by politicians elected with right-wing support.[52]

This function of the judicial process in providing opposition political groups with a vehicle through which they can challenge and sometimes thwart the government is not confined to judicial review under a written constitution. In England earlier in this century, social and economic interests opposed to the expansion of government regulation and the welfare state used judicial review of the legality of administrative action, often with considerable success, to check the advance of this policy development.[53] In many of the western liberal democracies, radical opposition movements whose members have been charged with criminal offences have effectively exploited the publicity which a free press gives to a political trial to rally public sympathy for their cause and to challenge the legitimacy not just of the government but of the whole political regime.[54] The trial of Louis Riel is an outstanding Canadian example.

Again, it is the fracturing of effective political power in a liberal, relatively pluralistic, political system that is the key to this dimension of judicial power. There is no room for the judiciary to provide an arena for this kind of political contest in a state where organized opposition to the ruling government is not tolerated. In such states the trial of political dissidents is far more likely to be stage-managed as a device for strengthening loyalty to the regime. The normative value of this difference between the role of the judiciary in liberal and non-liberal states depends on the significance one attaches to the political pluralism of the liberal democratic state. To those of a Marxist or neo-Marxist persuasion who reduce all significant political struggle to antagonistic class interests it could be of value only as a means of challenging "bourgeois" government. But to liberals who are distrustful of an excessive concentration of power in the hands of any group of politicians or bureaucrats, the political pluralism fostered by a judiciary enjoying a high degree of independence is fundamental to maintaining political liberty.

The normative dimensions of adjudication point not only to certain structural features of the judiciary but also generate a concern for certain procedural features of judicial decision-making.[55] As a third party deciding a dispute about legal rights, the judge should not render his decision without first allowing each of the parties to put forward its side of the case. If there is no opportunity for one or the other side to make its submissions and counter those of its adversary, or if the judge's decision is based on considerations extraneous to the arguments of the parties, the adjudicative process will appear to be less a process for impartially and objectively settling disputes about legal rights than a device for imposing the will of the judge and the political forces with which he seems to be aligned.

In a very basic sense all judicial systems that purport to adjudicate disputes are adversarial in that both sides have some opportunity to present their side of the case to the court. There are, however, remarkable variations in the lengths to which judicial systems go in recognizing the rights of litigants and in making their submissions the primary materials from which the judicial decision is fashioned. In countries whose judicial processes are based on the common law tradition, we find the adversarial system in its purest form. The procedures of this tradition evolved in conjunction with a system of trial by jury in which disputed issues of fact must be established in open court before a panel of lay persons who are responsible for the final verdict.[56] Even though jury trials for both civil and criminal cases, in Canada as in England, have come to be the exception rather than the rule, court procedures still emphasize the role of the judge as that of a referee ensuring that the evidence and legal arguments submitted to the court by the adversaries are relevant to the legal points at issue and fair to both sides. In this process it is the adversaries or their professional representatives and not the judges who have the primary responsibility for bringing to light the facts and advancing the legal considerations on which the judicial decision is to be based. The principal difference between this system and the so-called inquisitorial systems of continental Europe and other countries in the civil law tradition is that in the latter the judge is far less dependent on the adversaries for assembling the legal and factual materials on which the court bases its decision.[57]

Insofar as the adversary system practised in most Canadian courts puts a premium on the rights and responsibilities of the litigants in the process of judicial decision-making, it reflects a strong commitment to individualism. Such a system tends to assume that the individuals (or their professional representatives) whose rights are at stake should be in the best position to ascertain the strongest arguments with which to support their respective claims. At the philosophical core of such a system is the perception that a person is the bearer and prudent preserver of individual rights. An emphasis on the rights of the individual is evident in numerous other procedural features of our judicial system, notably the presumption of innocence and the requirement of proof beyond a reasonable doubt in criminal trials.

While these features of the adversary system followed in our courts are attractive from the point of view of liberal individualism, they may produce results which are questionable from an egalitarian perspective if the resources of effective advocacy are maldistributed. This certainly was the case for many years in our own country when the adversary system was dominated by professional lawyers whose services were not equally available to all segments of society. In recent years the extension of publicly funded legal aid to the economically disadvantaged has gone some way toward overcoming this injustice. But litigation is never likely to be a socially or economically neutral process. One of the political scientist's interests in the study of the judicial process is to identify the interests or groups that have easier access to, or a greater propensity to use, litigation and the judicial process as a means of defending their rights and advancing their interests.[58]

The normative requirement of adjudication by judges which is perhaps its most essential political feature is the provision of reasons to justify the judicial decision. It is not that the decisions of other branches of government necessarily are lacking in rationality, but that the judicial decision is apt to find its strongest basis of public support in its capacity to persuade those whose rights and interests it affects that it is the correct decision—indeed, the legally required decision. In this sense the reasons which judges give for their decisions, although such reasons may be quite different from the psychological processes through which they actually reach their conclusions,[59] are, in our society, the prime basis of the judicial decision's moral authority. In earlier epochs judges and political rulers could base their legitimacy on religious or mystical beliefs, or simply on the threat of superior coercive power. In a modern democratic culture the decisions of institutions nominally controlled by elected politicians can rest their authority on a democratic mandate. But for appointed judges functioning in such a society, unable to claim a democratic mandate for their decisions, it is the rationality of the judicial decision—its being demonstably based not on arbitrary exercise of judicial will but on a correct application of the law—that provides its strongest claim to legitimacy.

But here again we confront the paradoxical yet unavoidable element of choice or discretion in judicial decision-making. For it is precisely the uncertainties in the law—its vagueness, its ambiguities, its internal conflicts—that require judges to develop and shape the law in the very process of adjudicating disputes about it. Yet the judge must persuade us that his or her decision is based not on an arbitrary exercise of will but on the most reasonable application of our law. This is no easy task, especially in a society which tends to be increasingly sceptical about the possibility of objective rationality in human affairs.

Because of this central, inescapable challenge to the legitimacy of the judicial process, we should be concerned about the conservation of judicial energy. The capacity of a judiciary to maintain public confidence in the rationality of its decision-making may be over-taxed if it is called upon to resolve too many disputes which are deeply divisive in our society and on which the law may give great scope for, indeed may even require, a great deal of judicial law-making.

It was this concern for the conservation of judicial energy that prompted critics of a constitutional charter of rights and freedoms in Canada to warn that such a charter would accelerate the politicization of the judiciary. The Charter of Rights and Freedoms has the potential of significantly expanding the policy-making power of Canadian judges. But, ironically, the increase in this power of Canadian judges could bring with it some erosion of their political authority. Canadians will now have an opportunity to test the validity of this concern.

Notes to Chapter 1

1. Leading examples of political science studies of the judiciaries of other countries are: Fred. L. Morrison, *Courts and the Political Process in England* (Beverley Hills: Sage, 1973) and Walter F. Murphy and Herman C. Pritchett, eds., *Courts, Judges and Politics*, 4th ed. (New York: Random House, 1986). For comparative political science studies of the judiciary, see Theodore L. Becker, *Comparative Judicial Politics* (Chicago: Rand McNally, 1970) and Martin Shapiro, *Courts: A Comparative and Political Analysis* (Chicago: University of Chicago Press, 1981).
2. See Peter H. Russell, "Judicial Power in Canada's Political Culture," in M.L. Friedland, ed., *Courts and Trials: A Multi-disciplinary Approach* (Toronto: University of Toronto Press, 1975).
3. For an analysis of English judges who take this position, see P. S. Atiyah, "Judges and Policy," *Israeli Law Review* (1980), pp. 346-71.
4. For a discussion of different forms of dispute settlement, see Vilhelm Aubert, "Law as a Way of Resolving Conflicts," in Laura Nader, ed., *Law in Culture and Society* (Chicago: Aldine, 1969), pp. 282-303, and Torstein Eckhoff, "The Mediator and the Judge," in Vilhelm Aubert, ed., *Sociology of Law* (Harmsworth: Penguin Books, 1969).
5. Lon L. Fuller, "Adjudication and the Rule of Law," in L. Friedman and S. Macaulay, eds., *Law and the Behavioral Sciences* (Indianapolis: Bobbs-Merrill, 1977), pp. 736-45.
6. See, for instance, Law Reform Commission of Canada, *Studies on Diversion* (Ottawa: Information Canada, 1975).
7. The decisions were rendered in *Canadian Industrial Gas & Oil Ltd.* v. *Government of Saskatchewan* [1978] 2 SCR 545, and *Central Canada Potash Co. Ltd. and A.G. Canada* v. *Government of Saskatchewan* [1979] 1 SCR 42. The constitutional amendment is Part VI of the Constitution Act, 1982.
8. This idea is developed by Alexander Hamilton in B.F. Wright, ed., *The Federalist* (Cambridge, Mass.: Harvard University Press, 1961), Paper No. 78. See Alexander M. Bickel, *The Least Dangerous Branch* (Indianapolis: Bobbs-Merrill, 1962).
9. See Ellen Baar and Dorothy Moore, "Ineffective Enforcement: The Growth of Child Support Arrears," *Windsor Yearbook of Access to Justice* (1980), pp. 94-120.
10. *A. G. Manitoba* v. *Forest* [1979] 2 SCR 1032.
11. *Re Manitoba Language Rights* [1985] 1 SCR 721; *Order: Manitoba Language Rights* [1985] 2 SCR 347.

12. "Judicial Process," *International Encyclopaedia of the Social Sciences* 8 (New York: Crowell Collier and Macmillan, 1968), p. 291.

13. Under s 33 of the Canadian Charter of Rights Freedoms, a legislature could, for five years at a time, override a judicial decision applying the fundamental freedoms, legal, or equality rights in the Charter.

14. For an examination of these issues, see Perry S. Millar and Carl Baar, *Judicial Administration in Canada* (Montreal and Toronto: McGill/Queen's University Press with the Institute of Public Administration of Canada, 1981), esp. ch. 14.

15. Jules Deschênes in collaboration with Carl Baar, *Maîtres Chez Eux* (Ottawa: Canadian Judicial Council, 1981.)

16. For a survey of the features of judicial councils in Canada, see ibid., pp. 173-76.

17. Canadian Judicial Council, *Re: Mr. Justice Thomas Berger*, report submitted to the Hon. Jean Chrétien, minister of justice (Ottawa: Canadian Judicial Council, 31 May 1982).

18. See John Courtney, "Judges as Royal Commissioners," *Dalhousie Review* (1964-65), pp. 413-17. For a discussion of judges as royal commissioners in England, see Morrison, *Courts and the Political Process*, pp. 183-88.

19. In Canada judges have participated in royal commissions on all of these subjects.

20. A classic enunciation of this point can be found in H.L.A. Hart, *The Concept of Law* (Oxford: Clarendon Press, 1961), ch. 7.

21. *Roncarelli* v. *Duplessis* [1959] SCR 121.

22. For a good discussion of this aspect of judicial discretion, see Patrick Devlin, *The Judge* (London: Oxford University Press, 1979), ch. 4.

23. For an empirical account of the judge's role in shaping bail policy, see M.L. Friedland, *Detention Before Trial* (Toronto: University of Toronto Press, 1965).

24. See, for example, Richard V. Ericson, *Making Crime* (Toronto: Butterworths, 1981).

25. References to Canada's Constitution with a capital C are to "The Constitution of Canada" as defined in section 52(2) of the Constitution Act, 1982. This is the formal part of the constitution and includes the original Constitution, the British North America Act, 1867, which has been renamed The Constitution Act, 1867, all of the amendments to the original constitution and the Constitution Act of 1982. Besides this formal Constitution, the Canadian constitutional system includes some ordinary statutes, customs and conventions, and judicial decisions interpreting the Constitution. Where this broader constitutional system is being referred to, "constitution" will be written in the lower case.

26. See, for example, John Henry Merryman, *The Civil Law Tradition* (Stanford: Stanford University Press, 1969), esp. ch. 7.

27. For a survey of these developments, see Walter F. Murphy and Joseph Tanenhaus, *Comparative Constitutional Law* (New York: St. Martin's Press, 1977).

28. Blackstone is regarded as a leading exponent of this school. For a discussion, see Atiyah, "Judges and Policy," pp. 346-47.

29. The chief justice of the Supreme Court of Canada, Brian Dickson, emphasizes the interstitial nature of judicial law-making in his "Comment on the Judge as Law Maker," in A.M. Linden, ed., *The Canadian Judiciary* (Toronto: Osgoode Hall Law School, 1976), pp. 80-84. The infrequency of judicial law-making was claimed by Benjamin N. Cardozo, *The Nature of the Judicial Process* (New Haven: Yale University Press, 1921).

30. A leading Canadian exponent of this approach is Paul Weiler. See his *In The Last Resort: A Critical Study of The Supreme Court of Canada* (Toronto: Carswell/ Methuen, 1974), ch. 2. A leading American scholar in this tradition is Ronald Dworkin, *Taking Rights Seriously* (Cambridge, Mass.: Harvard University Press, 1977). See esp. ch. 4.
31. For an impressive articulation of this approach, see Graham Hughes, "Rules, Policy and Decision Making," *Yale Law Journal* (1968), p. 411.
32. This, I take it, is the underlying assumption of many behaviouralists who study the judicial process. See, for example, Glendon Schubert, *Human Jurisprudence: Public Law as Political Science* (Honolulu: University Press of Hawaii, 1975).
33. Shapiro, *Courts*, p. 20.
34. For a description of British North American judicial institutions during this colonial period, see W.R. Lederman, "The Independence of the Judiciary," *Canadian Bar Review* (1956), pp. 1145-58.
35. The former is described in R.A. MacKay, *The Unreformed Senate of Canada* (London: Oxford University Press, 1926), and the latter in Frank MacKinnon, *The Government of Prince Edward Island* (Toronto: University of Toronto Press, 1951).
36. For a description of this process, see John P. Dawson, *The Oracles of the Law* (Ann Arbor, Mich.: University of Michigan Law School, 1968), ch. 1.
37. See Hilda Neatby, *The Administration of Justice Under the Quebec Act* (Minneapolis: University of Minnesota Press, 1937, and Dale and Lee Gibson, *Substantial Justice: Law and Lawyers in Manitoba 1670-1970* (Winnipeg: Peguis, 1972).
38. See Robert Sharlet, "The Communist Party and the Administration of Justice in the USSR," in Donald Barry et al., *Soviet Law after Stalin* (Germantown, Maryland: Sijthoff and Noordhoff, 1979).
39. See, for example, Gabriel A. Almond and James S. Coleman, eds., *The Politics of the Developing Areas* (Princeton: Princeton University Press, 1960), Introduction.
40. This point is forcefully made in Samuel Shuman, "Philosophy and the Concept of Judicial Independence," *Wayne Law Review* (1962), pp. 363-75.
41. For a perceptive analysis of these bodies and their relationship to the courts, see John Willis, "The Administrator as Judge: The Citizens' Right to an Impartial Tribunal," in J.E. Hodgetts and D.C. Corbett, *Canadian Public Administration* (Toronto: Macmillan of Canada, 1960), pp. 514-23.
42. See table 3.2, p. 52.
43. For a discussion of the Conseil d'État, see Henry J. Abraham, *The Judicial Process*, 4th ed. (New York: Oxford University Press, 1980), pp. 281-86.
44. From John Locke, *The Second Treatise on Government*, edited by Thomas P. Peardon. New York: Macmillan Publishing Company, 1952, 1985, p. 9. Reprinted by permission of the publisher.
45. Ibid., p. 51.
46. Ibid., pp. 9-10.
47. Sharlet, *"The Communist Party,"*, p. 324.
48. For an analysis of the establishment of judicial systems in the communist world, see John N. Hazard, *Communists and their Law* (Chicago: University of Chicago Press, 1969).
49. For a discussion of this threat to judicial independence, see Shimon Shetreet,

Judges on Trial (Amsterdam: North Holland Publishing Co., 1976), pp. 78-84.

50. Abraham, *The Judicial Process*, pp. 97-99.

51. Sharlet, *"The Communist Party."*

52. For a discussion of the increasing reliance of the U.S. left on litigation as a political strategy, see Jon Gottschall, "Nixon's Judicial Appointments and the Emergence of the New Right," paper delivered at the annual meeting of the Law and Society Association, Toronto, 6 June 1982.

53. For an analysis of the role of English courts in the early years of the welfare state, see Brian Abel-Smith and Robert Stevens, *Lawyers and the Courts* (London: Heinemann, 1967), ch. 5. For an account of the efforts of lawyers and judges in nineteenth-century England to defeat adjudicative pluralism, see H.W. Arthurs, *"Without the Law": Administrative Justic and Legal Pluralism in Nineteenth-Century England* (Toronto: University of Toronto Press, 1985).

54. See Otto Kirchheimer, *Political Justice: The Use of Legal Procedure for Political Ends* (Princeton: Princeton University Press, 1961). For a discussion of political trials in Canada, see Kenneth McNaught, "Political Trials and the Canadian Political Tradition," in Friedland, ed., *Courts and Trials*.

55. This theme is carefully explored in Torstein Eckhoff, "Impartiality, Separation of Powers and Judicial Independence," *Scandinavian Studies in Law* (1965), pp. 9-52.

56. For a discussion of the roots of the adversary system,see Devlin, *The Judge*, ch. 3.

57. For an analysis of the differences between the two systems, see Neil Brooks, "The Judge and the Adversary System," in Linden, *Canadian Judiciary*, pp. 89-133.

58. For an analysis of this dimension of litigation, see Marc Galanter, "Why the 'Haves' Come Out Ahead: Speculations on the Limits of Legal Change," *Law and Society Review* (1975), pp. 95-160.

59. For an analysis of the differing logics of law, see Joseph Horowitz, *Law and Logic* (Vienna: Springer-Verlag, 1972).

CHAPTER 2

THE ENVIRONMENT OF CANADA'S JUDICIAL SYSTEM

While adjudication has certain universal features in all organized political communities, there are extremely important variations in the power of this branch of government and in the structures and procedures through which it is wielded. These broad variations stem from certain general characteristics of social and political systems. In the discussion that follows three kinds of societal influences are identified as being of central importance: the general level of social and economic development, the dominant currents of political philosophy or ideology, and the society's legal culture and traditions. In this chapter we will draw together the salient features of each of these dimensions of Canadian society as they impinge on Canada's judicial system. Taken together, these features of the social and political context in which the Canadian judiciary operates form what might be referred to as its "environment."[1] These environmental factors provide the social forces that shape and support the judicial power. They also generate potent pressures for change in the functioning of the judicial system.

Social and Economic Development

As an industrialized and urbanized society, Canada has experienced, to a relatively high degree, what the political sociologists refer to as "modernization." This modernization has been accompanied by increased complexity in Canadian law and increased professionalization of Canada's legal institutions. For the judicial system this has meant, among other things, an increased insistence on the possession of professional legal credentials by those adjudicating disputes about the law. Thus in Canada we have witnessed nearly a complete repudiation of the lay person as judge and a tendency to regard juries as technically too incompetent to be reliable fact-finders. Growing professionalism has also been felt, although in a much more delayed fashion, in the administration of Canadian courts, where there is increasing recognition of the merit of applying specialized administrative skills and the techniques of the computer age to managing court case flows.

But the effects of the modernization of Canadian society on its judicial system have been more pervasive and profound than a tendency to specialization. As industrialization and urbanization weaken traditional social bonds of family and community, basic social attitudes and relations are altered. We become a society of strangers relying increasingly, each of us, on formal positive law to define our rights and obligations; as a consequence, we turn increasingly to formal adjudication to settle our differences.[2] This transformation of social relations from those based on custom and informal sources of authority to a system depending much more on legally defined rights and duties tends to expand the role of adjudicative agencies. This can be seen in fields as far apart as family law and federalism: as squabbling spouses and governments turn to positive law as a guide to good conduct, they resort increasingly to courts to adjudicate conflict. Another facet of the social alienation accompanying modernity is increased reliance on enforcement of the criminal law rather than more informal communal sanctions as a means of maintaining social order. This, too, places increased burdens on Canadian courts, not so much to adjudicate disputes (few criminal charges produce not guilty pleas and formal court adjudication) but to provide a judicial presence in the processing of those selected by the police for criminal prosecution.

Socio-economic development does not affect the business of courts in industrialized societies in a uniform way. The impact is considerably influenced by the litigiousness of a people—that is to say, their general propensity to settle disputes by pressing claims to formal adjudication rather than negotiating settlements more informally. A litigious tendency may be present in a society quite independently of its level of modernization.[3] Among modern industrialized countries, England, New Zealand, and the United States have much higher civil case loads per capita than Italy, Japan, or Spain.[4] The preference of the Japanese for mediation and conciliation over adjudication is reflected in the small size of their legal profession: 1 lawyer for each 10 000 of population compared with a ratio of 1 to 400 in the United States.[5] No systematic research has been done on the litigiousness of Canadians, but the fact that on a per capita basis the Canadian judiciary and legal profession are roughly comparable in size to their American counterparts suggests that Canada is one of the more litigious of the industrialized and urbanized countries, perhaps only slightly less so than the United States. Canadian patterns may have been brought closer to American ones by the rapid expansion of the legal profession and legal aid programs over the past decade or so.[6] These developments, while not necessarily altering the general disposition of Canadians to litigate, have made the option of taking disputes to court more available to people of limited means.

Increases in the number and complexity of laws, in the number of lawyers, and even in the litigiousness of the population, do not necessarily lead to a mushrooming of court business and expansion of the courts. Much depends on the relative attractiveness of judicial institutions as dispute-settling mechanisms and the availability of alternatives.[7] The evidence in Canada suggests that very little of the increased need for adjudicative services generated by social change and industrial development has been taken care of by the general jursidiction trial courts (i.e., the superior, district, and county courts of the provinces), which at the time of Confederation were regarded as the most important of Canada's judicial institutions.[8] These provincial courts, staffed by federally appointed judges—the original linchpins of Canada's judicial system—have scarcely expanded at all. Whereas the number of judges serving at this level was 2.52 per 100 000 of population in 1867, by 1975 the ratio had actually declined to 2.23 per 100 000.[9] Some of this increased demand for adjudication, especially in the field of criminal justice, has been met by the provincially appointed judges in the so-called lower courts of the provinces, and a little, on the civil side, by the major federally established trial court, the Federal Court of Canada.[10] But probably a great deal more has been taken care of outside the formal court system through private arbitration and administrative tribunals. Improvements in the administration of courts may begin to reverse this trend by reducing some of the delay and inconvenience which in the past drove business away from the courts. Another factor working in the same direction is the Canadian version of what in the United States is referred to as the "public law explosion."[11] On the one hand, the expanded use of the criminal sanction by the state; on the other hand, the expanded range of statutory and even constitutional rights that can be claimed by the individual or corporation against the state generate disputes which in our society must finally be settled by the courts.

Political Beliefs and Ideology

Here we encounter the second environmental influence on the judicial system: political beliefs and ideology. An increase in the degree of independence enjoyed by Canadian courts and their added capacity to serve as vehicles for challenging government has been closely related to a strengthening of support for liberalism in Canada's political culture. This growth in respect for liberal values—for the rights of individuals and the value of preventing excessive and illegal exercises of governmental authority—has not, to be sure, developed to the point of extinguishing strong conservative tendencies in Canada's political culture. Canada was founded by counter-revolutionaries suspicious of the excesses of American democracy.[12] The continued popularity of the national police force, the RCMP (despite the exposure of its infringements of the legal rights of Canadians and its intolerance of political dissent), as well as popular support for the invocation of the War Measures Act in the 1970 October crisis, point to the survival of this conservative strain. But liberal critics of these recent manifestations of Canadians' respect for authority and fear of disorder often fail to mark the liberalization of political attitudes that has been occurring in Canada.[13] Manifestations of moral outrage and the favourable treatment it receives in the popular media are, in themselves, an indication of this change.

   A growing egalitarianism in Canadian society has fostered the extension of liberal values to all classes in society. This tendency has had important consequences for the functioning of the courts. Legal aid (the provision of publicly funded legal counsel to indigent persons) is, as we have noted, a leading example of this trend. Another is reform of the criminal justice system which has taken place over the last century.[14] The reduction of close ties between the criminal courts and the police, bail reform, and an up-grading of the qualifications of the judges who preside over the country's busiest criminal courts are part of this movement. These reforms are relatively modest; none goes as far as critics of the system might wish. But the direction of change is clearly liberal.

A further illustration of this liberalization of attitudes and its effect on the judicial system is the change which has taken place in the appeal system in criminal cases. Up until 1892 there was no right of appeal in criminal cases. When a right of appeal was included in the Criminal Code, it was typical of the mixture of values in Canadian society that not only was the accused given a right to appeal his conviction but the crown was also given a right to appeal the accused's acquittal, even if the verdict was rendered by a jury. The review of trial court decisions in criminal cases has become an increasingly important function of Canada's courts of appeal. We can get some idea of how much Canadian attitudes have changed by noting that in 1975 when the crown successfully appealed a jury's acquittal of Dr. Morgentaler, a Montreal physician who ran an abortion clinic, there was a sufficient public outcry to bring about an amendment of the Criminal Code removing the power of appeal courts to substitute a guilty verdict for an acquittal in a case heard by judge and jury.[15]

An egalitarian extension of legal rights has also affected the work of courts in non-criminal areas. New legal rights have been established for classes of persons whose bargaining position was relatively weak: for example, wives in relation to husbands, children in relation to parents, employees in relation to employers, students and professors in relation to university officials. The establishment of these rights means that disputes which might have been settled informally are now often litigated and go to court. Dispute settlement through informal negotiation becomes less acceptable when social and economic "underdogs" believe their interests will be better protected by claiming rights in court rather than counting on the benevolence of those in positions of power.

A similar reduction of trust in those exercising political authority has made Canadians more interested in the liberal notion of building checks and balances into their system of government. Canadians may continue to believe that the purpose of government is as much to provide for peace, order and good government as it is to protect the rights and liberties of the individual, but they have become increasingly apprehensive about the problems of controlling the governmental leviathan. Several generations of experience under big government have generated scepticism about the inherent good sense and self-restraint of those who govern. The nineteenth-century achievement of responsible government has proved to be no panacea for ensuring that government is accountable to the people. The decline of the legislature's significance in law-making and in its capacity for monitoring government operations has been evident for many years.[16] Cabinet government concentrates enormous power in the hands of a very few politicians and officials. There may be some dim recognition that the vitality of the division of powers and competition between federal and provincial governments in Canada by dispersing power enhances political liberty. Still, both provincial and federal governments are recognized as centres of power against whose arbitrary and unlawful activities citizens need further institutional protection.

Increasingly this liberal impulse looks to the judiciary for such protection. Where there is fear that government will abuse newly acquired powers, the judiciary is brought in to guard against this danger. A good example is the inclusion of a requirement for judicial warrants in the legislation that legalized electronic eavesdropping by the police.[17] More recently, in the debate over a federal Access to Information Act, distrust of the government forced the inclusion of a provision giving the courts, in most instances, the final word in deciding whether government refusals to provide information fall within statutory criteria.[18]

This tendency in the Canadian political system to rely on the judicial process as a means of preventing abuse of power and protecting rights may now be at a turning point. Canada's new constitutional Charter of Rights and Freedoms significantly expands expectations about the judiciary's capacity and inclination to check government. The apparent popularity of increasing the power of judges at the expense of the power of politicians and officials demonstrates the extent to which Canadians, at this point in their history, regard their judges as less tied to the interests of government; they are seen in a fundamental sense as being less political and more trustworthy than those holding executive and legislative positions. But, again, it is important to point out that this perception of the judiciary as the politically neutered branch of government may well be undermined by the political nature of the judiciary's responsibilities under the new Charter.

Canada's Legal Culture

The third and most direct of the environmental influences on the judicial system is a country's legal culture. The basic character of Canada's legal system, and hence of its judicial system, might be expected to reflect the legal cultures of the two European peoples, the English and the French, who founded Canada. But this expectation is not borne out by the facts. So dominant has the English common law system been that it is misleading to think of Canada's legal culture as fundamentally dualistic. This is especially true of its judicial system, which has been even more thoroughly anglicized than the substantive law. As far as the legal culture of Canada's original inhabitants is concerned, it was totally ignored and for all practical purposes obliterated by the European settlers.[19] Thus, in legal terms, Canada today belongs essentially to the common law world although, as with all the common law countries, there are some distinctive wrinkles stemming from the country's particular circumstances.

There is a strong element of legal dualism in Quebec's history. Soon after the British conquest of New France, through the Quebec Act of 1774, the laws of the French Canadians were made the basis of the colony's civil law, while its criminal law was to be British. Despite this original dualism, French civil law was subjected to powerful common law influences. The principal vehicle for this process of anglicization was the judicial system. British governors selected the judges and for the most part they chose persons whose legal knowledge, if it existed at all, was based on English experience.[20] Most importantly, the appeal process was dominated by English Canadians and British judges. Consequently the judicial method in both civil and criminal law became the common law method, with its emphasis on judicial precedent. These common law techniques were so firmly embedded by the time a Civil Code was adopted in Quebec that English-style judicial precedents rather than French civilian doctrine became the dominant force in interpreting the code. The anglicization of Quebec's civil law system is a testament to the quiet way in which power can flow through a judicial system, especially one with a powerful appeals hierarchy.

An essential part of the Confederation settlement in 1867 was that Quebec, as the province in which the French Canadians could maintain a majority, would be able to preserve the distinctive language, religion, and laws of the French-Canadian people. Section 92(13) of the British North America Act gave all the provinces jurisdiction over ''property and civil rights''—a concept that embraces most of the subjects included in Quebec's Civil Code and Code of Procedure.[21] Thus Quebec has retained legislative jurisdiction over those matters which are central to the French civil law tradition. On particular points of substantive law and civil procedure Quebec civil law differs from the laws of the common law provinces, although under the impact of secularization and modern commerce these differences have narrowed and may not be more significant than differences that exist in some areas of statutory law among the common law provinces. Since Confederation the highest court of appeal, whose opinions interpreting Quebec's civil law bind Quebec judges, has been, first, an imperial court, the Judicial Committee of the Privy Council, and then the Supreme Court of Canada. Although Quebec judges have always been in a minority position on the latter court,[22] more often than not they have been the dominant influence on the panels hearing civil law cases from Quebec.

For our purposes here the most important point is that the judicial institutions of Quebec, despite any residue of French civil law and procedure that survives, bear the essential features of English common law courts. A lawyer from English-speaking Canada, or for that matter from virtually any other part of the English-speaking world, who wished to practise in Quebec, would not have to adapt to an alien judicial system. It is only in very recent years that Quebec court reformers have begun to look to continental French institutions for inspiration—for instance, to the idea of a career judiciary based on a special legal education for judges.[23] So far, this application of Quebec nationalism to judicial institutions has not borne fruit in any concrete changes.

Some of the features of the common law tradition that have important consequences for the role of the judiciary in Canada (for example, the use of juries and the adversary system) have already been mentioned and will be referred to later in the text. In this introductory discussion of judicial power there are two features of common law systems that deserve special emphasis: the central importance of the judges, and the power of the legal profession.

In any legal system based on the common law tradition, the judge has a preeminent position as compared with other legal functionaries. Common law is indeed judge-made law. Judge-made common law is not, of course, the only source of law. On many subjects of contemporary legislative interest, common law rules are dwarfed in importance by statutes enacted by the legislature, by delegated legislation or regulations enacted by the executive, and in Canada by the written Constitution. Long ago common law judges accepted their subordination to Parliament as a sovereign law maker, and in Canada they must accept the Constitution of Canada as the highest source of law.[24] Even so, judicial decisions applying and interpreting regulations, statutes, and the Constitution, as we have already stressed, can have a tremendous influence on the policies that are actually effected and the rights that are actually established through these other sources of law. It is true that the difference between the legislative role of the judge in the common law system as compared with the civil law system has been exaggerated. Modern scholarship on civil law systems has revealed the important role that judicial interpretation and judicial opinions play in applying civil law codes, despite the civil law system's theoretical denial of their importance. Nevertheless, the fact remains that it is the common law system that openly accepts the judicial opinion with all its potential for law development as an integral part of the system.

The pre-eminence of the judge in the common law system extends beyond the judge's law-making role. It is also manifest in the social and political status of the judge. In continental Europe the legal scholar has as high, if not a higher, status than the judge.[25] This is certainly not the case in Canada. The lustre of the judicial position in Canada is reflected in the practice, already commented upon, of assigning judges major extra-judicial responsibilities, notably on royal commissions and commissions of inquiry, on matters of great public interest. A symbolic indication of the high status of the judicial office in Canada is that the chief justice of the country's highest court, the Supreme Court of Canada, in the absence or incapacity of the governor general, represents the head of state.[26] Whether or not there is validity in the generalization that Canadian judges are self-restrained or uncreative in the exercise of their judicial powers, the high status accorded them in the Canadian legal and political systems continues to be a significant political resource for the Canadian judiciary.

The prestige and power of judges in the common law system is closely related to the strength of the legal profession. It might even be said that the pre-eminent position of the bench within common law legal systems largely derives from the pre-eminent position of the bar within common law societies. Going back to the roots of the common law judicial system in England, it was the ability of a small guild of private legal practitioners centred in the Inns of Court in London—first the sergeants, then the barristers—to monopolize appointments to the Royal Courts of Justice that was decisive in ensuring that the common law judiciary would not develop in the continental fashion as a career branch of government service.[27] Instead, judicial positions in the higher courts would be awarded to persons who had distinguished themselves in private legal practice. The bench in Canada, even at its lowest levels, is recruited almost exclusively from the bar. Thus, in studying the forces that shape the Canadian judiciary it is essential to take into account the nature of the Canadian legal profession. Access to that profession, its education system, and the characteristics of private practice will have a great deal to do with determining what kinds of men and women become judges in Canada.

In Canada the bar is considerably less elitist than in England. Instead of the English division between a small group of barristers who plead cases in court and a great mass of solicitors advising clients and transacting legal business out of court, or France's four or five separate legal professions (advocates, avoues, notaries, and judges), Canada has a fused and unified legal profession.[28] There are specializations within this profession, but all Canadian lawyers belong to a single profession. Further, the Canadian bar is not concentrated in a single metropolitan centre but is dispersed across the country; there are centres of professional activity in every Canadian province. Thus the professional pool from which Canadian judges are recruited is much larger and more diverse than the tiny côterie of London-based barristers from which English judges are drawn. As a social interest group, geographical dispersal is more than compensated for by professional unity. The Canadian bar's ability to assert itself as a unified profession has few parallels in other countries.

Some lawyers might object to the suggestion that they belong to a private interest group. Formally, as members of the bar, they are "officers of the court," and in that sense belong to a public institution. Nevertheless, the profession has emphasized the need to maintain its independence of government. It has insisted, successfully, on its own self-government, on controlling the standards of professional education and, in most provinces, on keeping private legal practitioners, rather than salaried lawyers, as the mainstay of publicly funded legal aid programs. The rationale for this commitment to the profession's independence has been fundamentally ideological: recognition of the value in a liberal state under the rule of law of ensuring that individuals and groups have access to legal counsel not controlled by the government.

If the press can be referred to as the fourth estate, the legal profession as a private organization providing an essential public service might be thought of as a fifth estate in Canada. The power of this fifth estate is exercised through its professional activities and advocacy, and also through the participation of so many of its members at the highest levels of the political branches of government. The private practice of law provides exceptional opportunities for those who wish to take their chances in electoral competition. No other profession or occupational group has been so well represented in legislatures and cabinets at both the federal and provincial levels.[29] Among other things, the political prominence of the profession means that the views of professional lawyers are paramount in shaping policies with regard to judicial institutions and judicial reform. No major changes in the structure or functioning of Canada's courts can take place without the approval of leaders of the bar.

It would be a mistake, however, to think of the bar as an unchanging mon-

olithic force. The winds of change which affect all other important social institutions are beginning to bring about significant changes in the size and shape of
Canada's legal profession. The last decade has seen a major transformation. The
ranks of the profession have expanded so that on a per capita basis it approximates
the size of the American profession. The dominant position of males and the
charter ethnic groups has declined.[30] Most significantly, the political diversity
of the profession would appear to have increased with the formation of radical
breakaway organizations outside of the professional establishment. In the long
run, all of this is likely to have profoundly important effects on the social and
political orientation of the Canadian judiciary.

Summary and Conclusion to Part One

In this introductory section of the book we have attempted to place the study of the judiciary within the general context of political science. While judges and courts are properly regarded as "political" in the sense that they are part of the process whereby a society is governed, political scientists are urged not to assume that they are simply "political." It would be a mistake to move from a legalistic formalism according to which the judiciary is regarded as entirely apolitical, impartially administering the law, to a realism that regards the judiciary as an undifferentiated component of the political process.

An appreciation of the distinctive role of courts in the political process must be grounded in an understanding of the essential judicial function: adjudication. Adjudication is the function of settling disputes about legal rights and duties. It is a political activity insofar as it is authoritative and backed by the power of the state. But the power exercised through the process of adjudication is an unusual kind of power in that it is subject to exceptional constraints and normative expectations. Judges are constrained to respect the laws governing the disputes which they adjudicate. Yet their decision-making contributes—and often in a very substantial way—to the development of the law. Adjudicators settling disputes as third parties are expected to decide disputes fairly and without partiality to either of the disputing parties. Thus they should be independent and not controlled by private parties or the government. But as social scientists we are sceptical of the possibility of complete or absolute independence and impartiality. This scepticism may be well founded, but it does not justify dismissing the ideals of independence and impartiality as irrelevant to a   proper understanding of the judicial process. The challenge to political scientists is to ascertain the degree to which these ideals can and must be realized if a society's judicial system is to perform its essential adjudicative function.

Although adjudication has been identified as the essential function of judicial institutions, we have pointed out that there is not a perfect, one-to-one relationship between the function of adjudication and the structures called courts. Judges and courts perform other functions in the polity besides adjudication, and institutions other than courts carry out some of the adjudicative function. Certainly this is true in Canada, where judges have important administrative responsibilities within the judicial system and as royal commissioners advise government on policy matters. In addition, there is the important contribution judicial decisions make to the law-making process in Canada. On the other hand, to an ever-increasing extent both federal and provincial policy makers in Canada have decided, for a variety of reasons, to give adjudicative responsibilities to non-curial institutions. Quantitatively, the work of these administrative tribunals probably accounts for more adjudication in Canada today than is done by judges in courts.

The nature of the power exercised by courts in any given society is largely determined by three "environmental" factors: the level of development, the prevailing political ideology, and the society's legal culture. The relatively high level of industrialization and urbanization in Canada has been associated with an increased reliance on law and formal adjudication to define one's rights and duties. Modernization has also been accompanied by an increasing emphasis on individualism and a distrust of government. This evolution of the prevailing political ideology in a more liberal direction has fostered a tendency in Canada to turn to the courts as a means of checking government. The adoption of a constitutional Charter of Rights may signal a high watermark in this tendency, as the court's interpretation of the Charter increases public awareness of the political nature of adjudication. In Canada common law approaches and traditions have dominated the country's judicial system despite the strong normative commitment of elites to biculturalism. The common law system gives extraordinary power to lawyers representing the adversaries in producing the materials on which courts base their decisions. It also recruits its judges from the ranks of experienced members of the legal profession. No other legal culture gives its judges the prestige and power of the lawyer-judges of the common law system. At the same time no other corporate interest or profession is as well represented as the legal profession in the other branches of Canadian government.

Taking all of these factors into consideration, it is safe to say that, despite considerable competition from administrative tribunals staffed by non-judges and often non-lawyers, Canadian judges and courts are relatively powerful. If one put the judiciaries of all the nations of the world on a continuum from least powerful to most powerful, the Canadian judiciary would be well toward the most powerful end of the spectrum. Canadian courts and judges in the past may not have exercised as much power as their American counterparts, but they have certainly been considerably more powerful than the judiciaries in most non-industrialized societies, in civil law countries, or in any of the one-party, totalitarian polities. Indeed, the façade of powerlessness which up to now has hidden the power of Canadian courts from public purview may have given them as much opportunity to block if not to promote change as American courts possess. Under Canada's new Charter of Rights, which is much more comprehensive than the American Bill of Rights, the judicial branch of government in Canada may become more powerful than its counterpart in the United States.

In the next part we shall move from this discussion of the general features of the Canadian judicial system to an examination of the constitutional framework within which Canadian judges and courts operate. The constitutional rules and principles we will look at have a large bearing on how Canada's judges and courts are related both to the country's federal system of government and to the other branches of government at the federal and provincial levels.

Notes to Chapter 2

1. The "environment" of the courts is discussed here in the same way that Van Loon and Whittington discuss the "environment" of the Canadian political system. See R.J. Van Loon and Michael S. Whittington, *The Canadian Political System:*

Environment, Structure and Process, 3rd ed. (Toronto: McGraw-Hill Ryerson, 1981).

2. A classic sociological analysis of this transformation is Ferdinand Tonnies, *Community and Association* (Gemeinschaft und Gesellschaft), translated and supplemented by Charles P. Loomis (London, 1965).

3. For an account of a highly litigious non-industrialized society, see Lloyd A. Fallers, *Law Without Precedent: Legal Ideas in Action in the Courts of Colonial Basoga* (Chicago: University of Chicago Press, 1969).

4. Marc Galanter, "Reading the Landscape of Disputes: What We Know and Don't Know (And Think We Know) Abour Our Allegedly Contentious and Litigious Society," *UCLA Law Review* 4 (1983), table 3 (p. 52), shows a civil case load per capita for Ontario which is slightly higher than that of the United States.

5. Frank Gibney, *Mirage By Design: The Real Reasons Behind Japan's Economic Success* (New York: Times Books, 1982), ch. 7.

6. Even though the Canadian legal profession has roughly doubled in size over the past decade, there may still be fewer lawyers per capita in Canada than in the United States. In Ontario in 1980 the ratio of lawyers to the general population was estimated to be 1:599 as opposed to 1:410 in the United States. See Bruce Felthusen, "Are There Too Many Lawyers?" *The Law Society of Upper Canada Gazette* (1982) p. 278.

7. For an interesting exploration of this question, see H.W. Arthurs, "Alternatives to the Formal Justice System: Reminiscing about the Future," in Canadian Institute for the Administration of Justice, *Cost of Justice* (Toronto: Carswell, 1980), pp. 1-21.

8. For an analysis of the difficulties of Canadian courts in handling increased case loads, see Jules Deschênes, *The Sword and the Scales* (Toronto: Butterworths, 1979), ch. 6.

9. See below, table 3.1, p.52.

10. The original federal trial court, the Exchequer Court of Canada, founded in 1875, was replaced by the Federal Court of Canada in 1970.

11. See, for example, Harry W. Jones, ed., *The Courts, the Public and the Law Explosion* (Englewood Cliffs, N.J: Prentice-Hall, 1965).

12. For a lucid account of the political philosophy of Canada's Founding Fathers, see Donald Creighton, *The Road to Confederation* (Toronto: Macmillan of Canada, 1965), ch. 5.

13. See, for example, Edgar Z. Freidenberg, *Deference to Authority: The Case of Canada* (White Plains, NY: M.E. Sharpe, 1980).

14. For a discussion of a number of these reforms, see M.L. Friedland, "Pressure Groups and the Development of the Criminal Law," in P.R. Glazebrook, ed., *Reshaping the Criminal Law: Essays in Honour of Glanville Williams* (London: Stevens and Sons, 1978).

15. Statutes of Canada 1974-75-76, c. 93, s. 75.

16. See W.A.W. Neilson and J.C. MacPherson, eds., *The Legislative Process in Canada: The Need for Reform* (Toronto: Institute for Research on Public Policy, 1978).

17. Statutes of Canada 1973-74, c. 50, s. 2.

18. 29-30-31 Elizabeth II, c. 111. The one exception is cabinet documents.

19. See Robert Vachon, "The Incomplete Justice of the 'Civilized'," in *Native People*

and Justice in Canada (Ottawa: National Legal Aid Research Centre, 1982), pp. 177-79.

20. See Louis Baudouin, "Méthode d'interprétation judiciaire du Code civil du Québec," *Revue du Barreau* (1950), pp. 397-419.
21. Quebec was exempted from s. 94 which empowers the federal Parliament, with the permission of the provinces, to make provision for the uniformity of their laws relating to property and civil rights.
22. See Peter H. Russell, *The Supreme Court of Canada as a Bilingual and Bicultural Institution* (Ottawa: Queen's Printer, 1969), and David J. Wheat, "Disposition of Civil Law Appeals by the Supreme Court of Canada," *Supreme Court Review* (1980), p. 454.
23. See Jean de Montigny and Pierre Robert, *Analyse Comparative des Législations et des Perspectives de Réforme* (Montréal: Université de Montréal Centre international de Criminologie Comparée, 1973).
24. S.52 of the Constitution Act, 1982, states that "The Constitution of Canada is the supreme law of Canada, and any law that is inconsistent with the provisions of the Constitution is, to the extent of the inconsistency, of no force or effect."
25. See Martin Shapiro, *Courts: A Comparative and Political Analysis* (Chicago: University of Chicago Press, 1981), ch. 3.
26. When acting in this capacity he is to be known as "Our Administrator." See Peter W. Hogg, *Constitutional Law of Canada* (Toronto: Carswell, 1977), p. 143.
27. See John P. Dawson, *The Oracles of the Law* (Ann Arbor, Mich.: University of Michigan Law School, 1968).
28. See Gerald L. Gall, *The Canadian Legal System* (Toronto: Carswell, 1977), pp. 114-17. Notaries function as a separate branch of the profession in Quebec.
29. Van Loon and Whittington, *Canadian Political System*, ch. 14.
30. For a brief analysis of changes in access to legal education, see *Law and Learning* (Ottawa: Social Sciences and Humanities Research Council of Canada, 1982), pp. 20-23.

PART TWO
THE CONSTITUTIONAL FRAMEWORK

CHAPTER 3
THE JUDICIARY'S RELATIONSHIP TO THE FEDERAL SYSTEM

The provisions of Canada's formal Constitution concerning the judiciary are rather scant. The former chief justice of Quebec's Superior Court, Jules Deschênes, comparing these provisions with sections of the American and French constitutions establishing the judiciary as one of the three branches of government, remarked that "it is astounding that the Fathers of Confederation and, after them, the Parliament of Westminster proved so lacking in eloquence on the subject of the judicial power."[1]

Actually it is not surprising that the authors of Canada's Constitution had so little to say about the judicial power. Unlike the revolutionary constitutions of the United States and France, the Canadian Constitution did not purport to be a comprehensive plan for a new and ideal system of government. The British North Americans, including their francophone members, did not see any need to spell out the features of the main institutions of government. The principal objective of the confederation project was to combine the legacy of British institutions with a federal system of government. Thus the judicial branch did not have to be created in 1867: its main components already existed. Superior courts of civil and criminal jurisdiciton had been functioning in the founding colonies for many years prior to Confederation and there was a general court of appeal, the Judicial Committee of the Privy Council, in the imperial capital. The continuity of judicial institutions is manifest in section 129, which provides that "all Courts of Civil and Criminal Jurisdiction . . . shall continue in Ontario, Quebec, Nova Scotia, and New Brunswick respectively as if the Union had not been made."[2]

A few details concerning the judiciary are set out in Part VII—of the Constitution Act, 1867, entitled "Judicature." The six sections comprising Part VII are set out below:

VII.—JUDICATURE.

96. The Governor General shall appoint the Judges of the Superior, District, and County Courts in each Province, except those of the Courts of Probate in Nova Scotia and New Brunswick.

97. Until the laws relative to Property and Civil Rights in Ontario, Nova Scotia, and New Brunswick, and the Procedure of the Courts in those Provinces, are made uniform, the Judges of the Courts of those Provinces appointed by the Governor General shall be selected from the respective Bars of those Provinces.

98.   The Judges of the Courts of Quebec shall be selected from the Bar of that Province.

99.   (1) Subject to subsection two of this section, the Judges of the Superior Courts shall hold office during good behaviour, but shall be removable by the Governor General on Address of the Senate and House of Commons. (2) A Judge of a Superior Court, whether appointed before or after the coming into force of this section, shall cease to hold office upon attaining the age of seventy-five years, or upon the coming into force of this section if at that time he has already attained that age. [Added in 1960.]

100.   The Salaries, Allowances, and Pensions of the Judges of the Superior, District, and County Courts (except the Courts of Probate in Nova Scotia and New Brunswick), and of the Admiralty Courts in Cases where the Judges thereof are for the Time being paid by Salary, shall be fixed and provided by the Parliament of Canada.

101.   The Parliament of Canada may, notwithstanding anything in this Act, from Time to Time provide for the Constitution, Maintenance, and Organization of a General Court of Appeal for Canada, and for the Establishment of any additional Courts for the better Administration of the Laws of Canada.

Five of these sections, it should be noted, deal with the superior, district and county courts of the provinces. Section 101 is the only section that deals with what might be referred to as federal courts. That section does not recognize the existence of such courts (for they did not exist in 1867), nor does it establish these courts. It simply gives the federal Parliament the power to create "federal courts" at the trial and appeal level in the future. Clearly, in the minds of the Fathers of Confederation, the essential judicial institutions of the new nation were not the federal courts, which might or might not be established under section 101, but the provincial courts or "section 96 courts" as they have come to be known, staffed by federally appointed judges for whom the Constitution specified the qualifications, tenure, and method of remuneration.

Although the judges of the section 96 courts are appointed and paid by the central government, they are provincial courts in the sense that their establishment and maintenance are provincial responsibilities. Under section 92(14), "The Administration of Justice in the Province, including the Constitution, Maintenance, and Organization of Provincial Courts, both of Civil and of Criminal Jurisdiction" is assigned exclusively to the legistatures of the provinces. But section 96 courts, with federally appointed judges, are not the only courts which come under section 92(14). The provinces may also establish courts staffed by provincially appointed judges. Just how far the provinces can go in developing courts presided over by provincial rather than federal appointees is an enduring issue of Canadian constitutional law and will be discussed in some detail below. Here, the important point to bear in mind is that the term "provincial courts" in the Canadian context is ambiguous, in that it may refer to all of the courts established and maintained by the provinces including those whose judges are federally appointed, or it may refer only to those courts whose judges are provincially appointed. When the term Provincial Courts is used in this text it refers only to the latter.

The Integrated Nature of Canada's Judicial System

In no federation is there a division of judicial power exactly paralleling the division of legislative and executive power.[3] Even in a federal country such as the United States, with a highly developed dual court system, the adjudication of disputes arising under federal law is by no means confined to federal courts; indeed, the jurisdiction of courts established by the states extends to wide areas of federal law. There is a good reason for this. The disputes which generate the business of courts do not come neatly packaged in the categories of national or local law. Frequently the laws at issue in a court case include laws subject to the jurisdiction of the central legislature as well as laws under the jurisdiction of the constituent units of the federation. Rarely do litigants perceive their disputes as being "federal" or "provincial." A federation that insisted on a perfect match between the division of judicial power and the division of legislative and executive power would be afflicted with an enormously inconvenient system of adjudication. Thus in all federations there is some pull in the direction of a unified system of courts.

But there is also a pull in the opposite direction. Courts are a source of power. The way courts "administer" law can have a significant bearing on the meaning and impact of laws—even if it is only a matter of the vigour and efficiency with which they process disputes arising under the laws. A level of government without a judicial branch would seem incomplete. While federations have generally relied on locally established courts of general jurisdiction to play a primary role as courts of first instance, they have all recognized the need for a national court of appeal to provide some measure of uniformity, at least in the interpretation of federal laws and the constitution. Some have also developed federal trial courts specializing in the adjudication of issues of national significance. Just how far countries have gone or should go in this direction is an interesting question of comparative federalism.

Comparatively speaking, the Canadian judicial system ranks as one of the most integrated, or least federalized. The judicial provisions of the Canadian Constitution lean strongly in the direction of the judicial system of a unitary state. Unlike the American Constitution, which refers to the "judicial Power of the United States" and vests that jurisdiction in the Supreme Court of the United States and such federal courts as Congress may establish, and the Australian Constitution, which similarily vests "the judicial power of the Commonwealth' in the High Court of Australia and such federal courts as the national Parliament creates," the Canadian Constitution does not refer to a federal judicial power. The only judicial arrangements specifically provided for in the Constitution are the very essence of an integrated federal-provincial system: federally appointed judges of provincial superior and intermediate courts. No other federation has this element of judicial integration.

There are other ingredients of integration. Section 101 gives the federal Parliament the power to establish a national court of appeal, a court of appeal which is not limited to federal law and constitutional law, but is referred to as a "General Court of Appeal." Here the Canadian Constitution should be contrasted not only with the American, which restricts the judicial power vested in the national Supreme Court to cases involving the constitution and a specific list of federal matters, but also with those of European federations such as Switzerland and West Germany, whose constitutions establish federal courts of appeal to ensure uniformity in the application of federal laws and the constitution but not to serve as final courts of appeal in the interpretation of local laws. Under the Canadian Constitution a national supreme court can function, and indeed has done so, as the ultimate arbiter of both federal and provincial law. This surely reflects the strong British influence. In 1867 the Judicial Committee of the Privy Council was functioning as a general court of appeal for the whole empire and continued as Canada's final court of appeal until 1949. There was no room in the English judicial model for a national supreme court whose jurisdiction did not extend to all areas of law.[4]

A further mark of integration is that while the federal Parliament has exclusive jurisdiction in the area of criminal law, the provincial legislatures are empowered to establish courts of criminal jurisdiction. Here the Constitution contemplates provincially established courts administering federal law. Indeed, far from requiring that a minimum core of federal jurisdiction be excerised by federally established courts, the presumption under the Canadian Constitution is that "if federal law calls for the excercise of adjudication, but is silent as to the forum, the appropriate forum will be the provincial courts."[5] Thus, it would have been possible for Canada to have a complete judicial system for the administration of federal and provincial laws without the federal Parliament ever exercising its jurisdiction under section 101 to establish courts "for the better Administration of the Laws of Canada."

Integration is also evident with respect to court procedure. Although the provinces establish and maintain courts of criminal jurisdiction, the federal Parliament has exclusive jurisdiction to make laws governing procedure in criminal courts. Civil procedure is essentially a provincial responsibility, although the federal Parliament may prescribe the procedure to be followed by provincial courts in administering a particular federal law. These and the other provisions discussed above suggest that the underlying theme of the judicial sections of the Canadian Constitution is best characterized in terms of integration rather than unity. A unitary judicial system connotes a system in which one government, the national government, is responsible for maintaining the judicial system. That is clearly the situation in a unitary state such as Great Britain. But, while the Canadian Constitution points to a single hierarchy of courts responsible for settling disputes under both provincial and federal law, it does not assign responsibility for this system exclusively (or even primarily) to one level of government. Both the federal and provincial governments are given important responsibilities in relation to the judicial system. In this respect the unitary British model was adapted in the Canadian Constitution to the requirements of a federal state.

In emphasizing the integrated nature of Canada's judicial system it is important to bear in mind that there is often a considerable difference between the intent of the original constitutional provisions and the development of the institutions governed by those provisions. In the case at hand, there has been a tendency, more accentuated in recent years, to move away from the integrated model to a more bifurcated system of dual courts. This process has witnessed the expansion of courts entirely provincial in nature, established and staffed by the provinces, as well as courts which are entirely federal, established and staffed by the central government.

The expansion of Provincial Courts has been a more continuous process. Soon after Confederation the provinces, and the municipalities under their jurisdiction, began developing local courts for hearing minor civil and criminal cases. Provincial legislation assigning jurisdiction to courts with provincially and municipally appointed judges was frequently challenged, on the grounds that it encroached on the constitutionally entrenched jurisdiction of section 96 courts. Although a number of these challenges were successful, a substantial provincially appointed judiciary survived. Today the number of provincially appointed judges considerably exceeds the number of federally appointed judges, including those appointed to both section 96 and section 101 courts. As table 3.1 indicates, the number of federally appointed judges serving on section 96 courts in the provinces has scarcely kept pace with the increase in population. The real growth sector of the Canadian judicial system has been the Provincial Courts presided over by provincially appointed judges—courts and judges not expressly provided for in the country's original constitution (although sections 92(14) and 129 contemplate such courts).

Table 3.2 shows how the Canadian judiciary is distributed over the three basic types of courts in the Canadian constitutional system. In the middle are the section 96 judges: the federally appointed judges who serve on courts established and maintained by the provinces and territories. In the left hand column are the judges who serve on courts established under section 101 of the Constitution. We have labelled these "purely federal" because the judges are federally appointed and the courts are established and maintained by the central government. On the right side are the judges of the "purely provincial" courts: judges appointed by provincial governments serving on courts established and maintained by those governments. This table clearly indicates how the section 96 courts, the original linchpins of an integrated judicial system, have been outflanked by institutions subject to the unilateral jurisdiction of one or other level of government.

TABLE 3.1   SECTION 96 JUDGES,* CONFEDERATION TO 1982

YEAR	NUMBER	PER 100 000 OF POPULATION
1867	85	2.52
1886	158	3.56
1906	188	3.16
1927	277	2.85
1952	295	2.05
1975	508	2.23
1982	663	2.73

* Includes all federally appointed judges serving on provincial courts. Excludes territorial courts.

Source: Figures for all years to 1982 are based on judgeships provided for in federal and provincial statutes. The 1982 figures are based on *Manpower, Resources and Costs of Courts and Criminal Prosecutions in Canada 1980-82* (Ottawa: Canadian Centre for Judicial Statistics, 1983). Reproduced with permission of the Minister of Supply and Services Canada.

The most spectacular development of the provincial judiciary has occurred on the criminal side, where courts presided over by provincially appointed judges have become responsible for hearing virtually all minor cases as well as over

TABLE 3.2   CANADIAN COURTS AND JUDGES, 1982

PURE FEDERAL COURTS		SECTION 96	COURTS	PURE PROVINCIAL COURTS
Supreme Court	9	Alta.	62	102
Federal Court	25	B.C.	89	114
Tax Court	10	Man.	31	33
		N.B.	21	25
		Nfld.	18	32
		N.S.	26	36
		Ont.	209	326
		P.E.I.	7	3
		Que.	154	287
		Sask.	38	50
		N.W.T.	1	2
		Yukon	1	3
Total No. of Judges: 44			657	1013

Source: As Table 3.1 Reproduced with permission of the Minister of Supply and Services Canada.

90 per cent of the cases involving more serious indictable offences.[6] This development, it should be emphasized, occurred not as the result of aggressive province-building but because the federal Parliament continually expanded the criminal jurisdiction of provincially appointed magistrates and judges. In the twentieth century the work of purely provincial courts has also grown significantly in the area of family law. In part this reflects the expansion of provincial activities in the field of social welfare. But it also results from the federal government's decision to use provincially staffed courts for juvenile criminal justice. Most recently some provinces have begun to expand the civil jurisdiction of their provincial judiciary to suits involving sums of money beyond the traditional small claims jurisdictions of local judges.[7] This development is the clearest manifestation of the politics of province-building in the expansion of provincial judiciaries.

In itself the expansion of courts staffed by provincially appointed judges would not constitute a major departure from an integrated judicial system. It might only mean that the federal government increasingly relies on judges appointed and paid by the provinces to administer justice under federal laws. Whether or not there is significant movement in the direction of a dual court system depends on the extent to which the federal government elects to exercise the power it has under section 101 to establish a system of federal trial courts for cases involving federal laws. Shortly after Confederation, when Sir John A. Macdonald turned his mind to establishing a Supreme Court of Canada, he considered giving it an extensive trial jurisdiction in a wide range of federal matters in addition to its general appellate jurisdiction.[8] If Macdonald had proceeded with these plans he would have committed Canada to the development of an American-style dual court system. However, he soon backed away from these plans, partly as the result of pressure from judges of superior courts in the provinces. It was not until 1875, when the Exchequer Court of Canada was established along with the Supreme Court of Canada, that any use was made of Parliament's power under section 101 to establish federal trial courts. The Exchequer Court had a very limited jurisdiction, comprised mostly of cases involving federal revenue and the specialized field of law relating to patents and copyright. It did not have a full-time judge of its own until 1887[9] and by 1970 its bench numbered only eight.

In 1971 the Exchequer Court was replaced by the Federal Court of Canada. Although the Federal Court has a significant new jurisdiction, notably in federal administrative law, by American standards it does not amount to a substantial system of federal courts. Even allowing for the fact that Canada's population is one-tenth that of the United States, its twenty-five judges scarcely compare with over six hundred judges of the US district courts and circuit courts of appeal.[10] Nonetheless, some have seen the federal government's decision to expand the jurisdiction of "its own courts" at the expense of the integrated section 96 courts as the thin edge of the wedge and a decisive (and for many, unfortunate) move toward the federalization of Canada's judicial structure.

A further move in this direction was taken in 1983 when Parliament established the Tax Court of Canada.[11] In fact, this was not so much the establishment of a new federal court as the judicialization of an administrative tribunal. The 1983 legislation converted the federal Tax Review Board into a judicial body. Among other things, the legislation required that new appointees to the Tax Court have the same qualifications and terms of office as judges of the Federal Court.[12]

Section 96 under Attack

Canada is one of those federations which has become much more federal as it has aged. Increasing devotion to the requirements of a rather purist version of federalism has put the future of section 96 as an enduring feature of Canada's constitution in jeopardy; for, from the perspective of "classical federalism," K.C. Wheare's verdict on section 96 is surely correct. By giving the central government the power of appointing the judges of the higher provincial courts, it treats the provinces as a subordinate level of government and "contradicts the federal principle" according to which the general and regional governments should be "co-ordinate and independent."[13] Although the Fathers of Confederation did not have a clear commitment to this conception of federalism, gradually it has taken hold among the country's political elites.

The Fathers of Confederation did not have a coherent theory of federalism.[14] The leading politicians from the English-speaking section of central Canada who dominated the political coalition that achieved Confederation believed in the British unitary system of government, not federalism. A federal division of legislative powers was something they had to concede to secure the support of French-Canadian and Maritime politicians for the unification of British North America. But to protect Canada from what they regarded as the centrifugal perils of American-style federalism, Macdonald and his colleagues were able to insert a number of elements of central control into the constitutional scheme. These components of the Canadian Constitution are imperial rather than federal in nature in that they put the federal government in a relationship to the provinces similar to that which pertained between the imperial government in London and colonial governments. The federal executive's power to disallow provincial legislation, to appoint the lieutenant-governors of the provinces and instruct them to reserve provincial bills, and the federal legislature's power to bring any "work or undertaking" within a province under federal jurisdiction by declaring it "to be for the general Advantage of Canada"—these are clear examples of the imperial elements. In the judicial realm, section 96 is another example, as is the federal Parliament's plenary power in section 101 over what was potentially the Supreme Court of the federation.

The process whereby the prevailing constitutional ethic in Canada came to be something very close to Wheare's conception of classical federalism is one of the central themes of Canadian history. The judiciary itself played an important role in this process. The Judicial Committee of the Privy Council, which until

1949 was Canada's final court of appeal, based its interpretation of the division of powers in the BNA Act on a conception of federalism much closer to Wheare's than to the more centralist ideas of John A. Macdonald and company. Important as this judicial contribution was, it could not have had the impact it did unless it reinforced powerful social, economic and political forces at work in the country. Whatever the cause, there can be no doubt about the result. As Canada moved through the twentieth century, the instruments of direct federal control over the provinces—reservation, disallowance, and the declaratory power—became virtually unusable. This was not because the courts had declared these imperial powers to be unconstitutional but because federal politicians came to regard their use as politically unwise.[15]

This change in prevailing conceptions of federalism did not begin to catch up with section 96 until the 1970s. Earlier, as far as the judicial branch of government was concerned, it was the Supreme Court that had been the main target of federalist concerns. In 1956 Quebec's Royal Commission on Constitutional Problems contended that federal government control over appointments to the Supreme Court, the court that was now the final umpire of constitutional disputes, was incompatible with federalism.[16] In the 1960s there was some academic concern about section 96,[17] but it was not on the politician's agenda during the era of constitutional reform that culminated in the abortive Victoria Charter of 1971. However, in 1976 Jérôme Choquette, minister of justice in Robert Bourassa's Liberal administration in Quebec, issued a ringing denunciation of section 96 and called for a revision of that section of the Constitution.[18] In 1978 Ontario's Advisory Committee on Confederation recommended that provincial governments be given control over the appointment of judges to all provincial courts.[19] By 1980, when the federal and provincial ministers made their last effort to agree on a complete package of provincially and federally initiated reforms, nine of the ten provinces were calling for the elimination of section 96 and the acquisition by the provinces of the power to appoint the judges of all provincial courts.[20]

Judicial Interpretation of Section 96

Changing conceptions of federalism have not been the only factor in undermining support for section 96. Judicial interpretation of this section has severely limited the flexibility of the provinces to exercise their responsibility for the administration of justice in the provinces. The tortuous path which judicial construction of section 96 has followed is a classic example of the opportunities for judicial policy-making created by constitutional guarantees of court jurisdiction.[21]

It may seem odd that this section of the Constitution should have provided a basis for judicial review of legislation. Section 96 empowers the governor general to appoint the judges of superior, district and county courts in each province. It appears to deal only with the executive power of appointment, not the legislative power to create courts and alter their jurisdiction. But logically, the purpose of section 96—federal control of appointments to the higher provincial courts—could be completely defeated if the provinces were not limited in the changes they can make to their court structures. By transferring jurisdiction traditionally exercised by section 96 courts to new tribunals staffed by provincially appointed personnel, section 96 could be rendered an empty shell.

This is not the only rationale for judicial review of legislation affecting section 96 courts. The only elements of judicial independence explicitly provided for in Canada's original Constitution relate to the judges of section 96 courts. Section 99 guarantees the tenure of "Judges of the Superior Courts" on the terms secured for the judges of England's superior courts by the Act of Settlement in 1701. Section 100 guarantees a modicum of financial independence for all section 96 judges by providing that their salaries are to be fixed and provided for by Parliament. Other Canadian judges have their tenure of office and other aspects of independence secured by statute. But the judges of the superior courts are the only judges whose tenure of office is the subject of an explicit constitutional guarantee. Again the principle behind these sections of the Constitution could be defeated if there were no limit on the extent to which legislatures could bestow jurisdiction on courts whose judges' independence was not constitutionally protected. Logically, this rationale for judicial review should apply equally to federal and provincial legislation. However, as we shall see, until very recently it has been treated exclusively as a restraint on provincial legislatures.

For some years after Confederation the federal government claimed that the power to appoint judges of any kind was based on an undivided crown prerogative vested exclusively in the Dominion crown. Thus federal authorities questioned whether the provinces could cloak any provincial appointees with judicial powers. The premier of Ontario, Oliver Mowat, attacked this federal claim at the political level and was backed up by the courts. A series of judicial decisions upheld provincial legislation which had established courts staffed by provincially appointed judges and empowered them to decide cases involving minor criminal matters and small civil claims.[22] The coup de grâce for this assertion of a federal monopoly of the power to appoint judges came in 1892 when the Judicial Committee of the Privy Council rendered its important decision in the *Maritime Bank* case.[23] Here the English law lords held that Canadian federalism entailed a dual sovereignty such that the prerogative powers of the crown were divided along federal-provincial lines. After this decision there was no question about the basic power of the provincial executive to appoint judges. There were still, however, plenty of challenges to legislation conferring responsibilities on provincially appointed judicial officials on the grounds that they were being given jurisdiction constitutionally reserved for section 96 judges.

The occasions for challenging legislation in this area increased as the provinces reorganized their judicial structures and innovated in public administration in order to cope with increases in both the volume and complexity of legislation. The toughest judicial scrutiny focused on novel administrative schemes that assigned adjudicative responsibilities to non-judges. The courts were more tolerant of additions to the jurisdiction of the traditional provincial lower courts. In the latter case, it must be remembered, the most significant change was the steady expansion of the criminal jurisdiction of provincial magistrates; and this resulted from federal not provincial legislation. Provincial legislation establishing administrative boards and tribunals was another matter. Frequently private interests endeavoured to resist these new forms of regulation by invoking section 96 arguments in the courts. In the early decades of the century most of the challenged provincial schemes survived.

But beneath this litigation lurked a broader separation-of-powers doctrine that potentially could bar the assignment of any judicial function to administrative bodies. This tendency came to a head in the 1930s in several decisions of the Judicial Committee of the Privy Council. In *Martineau and Sons* v. *Montreal* the Privy Council upheld the Quebec Public Service Commission's jurisdiction to assess compensation for expropriation, but Lord Blanesburgh's opinion took a broad view of the underlying purpose of section 96. He viewed it as "at the root of the means adopted by the framers of the [BNA Act] to secure the impartiality and the independence of the Provincial judiciary." Blanesburgh suggested that this part of the Canadian Constitution, like certain sections of the Australian Constitution, called for the separation of judicial and administrative functions.[24] A few years later, in *Toronto* v. *York*[25] the Privy Council went further and overruled Ontario legislation empowering the Ontario Municipal Board to rule on variations in local water rates, on the grounds that this was a judicial function which could not be given to what was primarily an administration body. Lord Atkin based the decision on sections 96, 99, and 100 which he referred to as the "three principal pillars in the temple of justice."[26] His opinion enunciated a separation-of-powers doctrine which, if it had stood up over time, would have constituted a formidable constitutional barrier to administrative agencies exercising any functions deemed to be inherently judicial.

This broad separation-of-powers approach did not stand for long. The process of deflation was initiated by the Supreme Court in the *Adoption Reference* of 1938[27] in which the Court affirmed provincial power to confer on provincially appointed justices of the peace or magistrates jurisdiction over a wide range of matters relating to adoption, neglected children, illegitimate children and deserted wives. Chief Justice Duff, who wrote the Court's opinion, put aside the broad judicial function test of *Toronto* v. *York* in favour of a narrower historical approach: provinces could establish courts presided over by provincially appointed judges and give these courts a considerable jurisdiction in fields of adjudication which were unheard of at the time of Confederation, providing such jurisdiction "broadly conforms" to that "generally exercisable by courts of summary jurisdiction rather than the jurisdiction exercised by courts within the purview of s. 96."

After World War Two, a Judicial Committee less hostile to the collectivist age endorsed Duff's more restrained and pragmatic approach to section 96. In *John East Iron Works*,[28] the Privy Council, in one of its last important decisions on the Canadian Constitution, rejected a challenge to Saskatchewan's Labour Relations Board. Although some of that board's powers were clearly adjudicative and resembled responsibilities traditionally carried out by superior, district, and county court judges (e.g., the settlement of disputes concerning contracts of employment), Lord Simonds insisted that these functions were not to be treated in isolation; they should be seen as integral elements of a complex policy instrument in a field of activity not subject to regulation at the time of Confederation. The constitutional test, he said, was whether for performing adjudicative functions in a particular context it was "desirable that the Judges should have the same qualifications as those which distinguish the Judges of Superior or other Courts." In the case at hand, he felt that this was not desirable and that therefore Saskatchewan's legislation did not violate section 96. This case makes it clear that in deciding section 96 cases the judiciary is second-guessing the legislature as to the institutional arrangements appropriate for new fields of public administration. In these cases judges must determine not only whether any function of a regulatory body resembles a power historically exercised by section 96 courts; they must further determine whether "its setting in the institutional arrangement in which it appears"[29] transforms the nature of the judicial function by making it an integral element of a regulatory activity (for instance, maintaining a system of collective bargaining) which is inappropriate for superior courts to perform.

The Supreme Court of Canada after taking over as Canada's final court of appeal in 1949 continued to follow a relatively restrained approach to the enforcement of section 96. Up until the late 1970s the only serious damage inflicted on provincial administrative machinery by section 96 jurisprudence came in 1955 in *Toronto* v. *Olympia Edward Recreation Club*,[30] when the Supreme Court affirmed a holding of Ontario's Court of Appeal that the province's Municipal Board could not determine disputes concerning the liability of property owners to municipal assessment. But this stripping of an adjudicative function from an integrated regulatory system appeared increasingly anomalous, especially after the arrival of Bora Laskin on the Court. Laskin had been a leading academic advocate of a more pragmatic, policy-oriented approach to section 96, and as chief justice, it was he who enunciated the "institutional setting" test in the 1977 *Tomko* case.[31] During this period, the Court also showed its tolerance of the expansion of the civil jurisdiction of provincially appointed magistrates and lower court judges. In 1965 the Supreme Court upheld Quebec legislation expanding the civil jurisdiction of the Quebec magistrate's courts from $200 to $500.[32] The only serious reversal for the provinces in this area was the Supreme Court's 1972 decision in the *Seminary of Chicoutimi* case[33] ruling that Quebec could not transfer from its Superior Court to its Provincial Court the power to hear cases contesting the legality of municipal by-laws.

The late 1970s witnessed a reversal in the pattern of section 96 litigation and its results. The volume of section 96 cases rose sharply: between 1976 and 1982 the Supreme Court was called upon to decide eleven cases involving section 96.

During this period no other constitutional issue generated as many cases. In several of these cases the provinces suffered reversals of important policy initiatives. These defeats strengthened provincial demands for a constitutional amendment aimed at dismantling section 96.

In a 1981 reference case the Supreme Court held that Ontario legislation endowing the Residential Tenancy Commission with power to settle landlord-tenant disputes and issue eviction orders was unconstitutional. This decision indicates the constitutional philosophy underlying this tougher approach to section 96. Justice Brian Dickson, who wrote the Court's opinion, acknowledged that in interpreting the Constitution the judiciary should "attempt to determine and give effect to the broad objectives and purposes of the constitution viewed as a 'living tree,' . . ." The Court viewed section 96 as "one of the important compromises of the Fathers of Confederation"—a centralizing element designed to offset what were viewed as the centrifugal tendencies of the division of legislative powers.[34] Thus provincial competence to endow a provincial tribunal with judicial power must be limited, otherwise "what was conceived as a strong constitutional base for national unity, through a unitary judicial system, would be gravely undermined."[35] Dickson carefully examined the institutional setting in which the Residential Tenancy Commission exercised responsibilities traditionally carried out by section 96 courts and concluded that far from being a peripheral or ancillary element, these judicial powers were central to the commission's work as a body performing primarily an adjudicative role in relation to disputes about the legal rights of landlords and tenants.

Two Quebec appeals decided during this period display another facet of the contemporary Supreme Court's concern for retaining a substantial residue of judicial power in superior courts. In *A.G. Québec* v. *Farrah*[36] the Court overturned Quebec legislation giving a provincially appointed transport tribunal final appellate jurisdiction on questions of law determined by the provincial Transport Commission. Three years later Quebec experienced another setback in the *Crevier* case[37] when the Superior Court, on section 96 grounds, found *ultra vires* legislation establishing a professions tribunal. This tribunal, consisting of six Provincial Court judges, had been made the final court of appeal on all issues of law and jurisdiction appealed from discipline committees established for the various professional groups in the province. These decisions made it clear that so far as provincial legislation was concerned, no constitutional amendment was needed to preserve the traditional power of superior courts to review the decisions of administrative tribunals on matters of law and jurisdiction.[38]

The case which represented perhaps the most significant loss for a number of provinces was the *B.C. Family Relations Act Reference* of 1982.[39] For many years all of the provinces have been interested in having one court exercise a comprehensive jurisdiction over all aspects of family law. For some provinces the most attractive way of achieving this goal was to unify family law jurisdiction in the provincial family court—a court in which adjudication could be closely related to various counselling and welfare services and whose judges are selected

by the provincial government. But here they ran up against section 96 which seemed to bar transferring to lower provincial courts the traditional superior court jurisdiction over contested divorces. Nonetheless, as the grounds for divorce were relaxed and family litigation focused increasingly on collateral questions arising out of a divorce, it appeared that considerable progress might be made if jurisdiction to settle most of these collateral matters could be transferred to provincial family courts. In the *B.C. Family Relations Act* case, the Supreme Court ruled that the adjudication of issues concerning the guardianship and custody of children could be transferred to provincial family courts, but responsibility for deciding issues concerning occupancy of and access to the family home must remain (along with other questions concerning the division of family property) under the jurisdiction of superior courts. This decision meant that without a constitutional amendment, unification of family law jurisdiction could be accomplished only by virtually closing down the provincial family courts and transferring all jurisdiction to courts staffed by the federally appointed judiciary— a move which a number of provinces, at this stage in the evolution of their family court systems, are unwilling to contemplate.

The Supreme Court's guardianship of the traditional jurisdiction of superior courts has proved to be an obstacle not only to a unified family court but also to a unified criminal court. Here, too, a number of provinces have become interested in the possibility of unifying criminal jurisdiction in a single court presided over by provincially appointed judges. Although there is no evidence of the federal government's willingness to co-operate in this type of reform, the province of New Brunswick in the *McEvoy* case[40] was able to extract a decision from the Supreme Court on the hypothetical possibility that the federal Parliament would co-operate with New Brunswick to give a court staffed by provincially appointed judges jurisdiction to try *all* indictable offences. The Supreme Court's decision in *McEvoy* is remarkable, for it holds that section 96 limits the federal Parliament as well as the provincial legislatures: "Parliament can no more give away federal constitutional powers than a province can usurp them." The Court held that it was beyond the federal Parliament's power to confer a comprehensive criminal jurisdiction on provincially appointed judges even if that jurisdiction was exercised concurrently with superior courts. The solicitude expressed in this case for preserving superior court jurisdiction appears to be based not on the federal control aspect of section 96 but on the constitutional guarantee of superior court independence. This rationale of the Court's decision in *McEvoy* will be discussed further in the next chapter, where we focus on judicial independence. Here it is important to note that this limitation of Parliament's power to assign adjudicative responsibilities to Provincial Courts is not easily squared with Parliament's assignment over the years of a vast jurisdiction in criminal matters to provincially appointed magistrates and judges.

Costs and Benefits of Section 96

The more activist approach of the Supreme Court to section 96 reinvigorated the provinces' attack on that section. Amendments to overcome what were regarded as the worst consequences of judicial interpretation of section 96 were on the agenda of the constitutional conference held in March 1983.[41] One of the proposed amendments would remove any constitutional limits on the power of provinces to assign judicial functions to administrative bodies but would preserve the right of superior courts to review the decisions of such tribunals on questions of jurisdiction.[42] The other amendment was designed to facilitate a unified family court at the provincial level by empowering the provinces to assign jurisdiction over all family matters to provincially appointed judges. The 1983 conference, preoccupied as it was with aboriginal rights, did not get around to dealing with these proposals. There would appear to be little opposition, even from the federal government, to amendments designed to dismantle section 96 and increase the judicial establishment under total provincial control. Before Canadians succumb to this pressure, however, they would be wise to review the costs and benefits of section 96 and consider the alternatives to it.

We have already seen some of the costs. Section 96 is out of keeping not only with the textbook definition of federalism but with the conception of federalism accepted by most Canadians today. The original rationale of section 96— that provincial governments could not be trusted to make good judicial appointments—is no longer acceptable.[43] In addition, there are the restrictions which section 96 has imposed on public administration and judicial reform in the provinces. A case like the *Residential Tenancy Commission* reference indicates how section 96 may deprive provincial residents of the advantage of an accessible and low-cost forum tailor-made for dealing with landlord-tenant disputes. The *Family Relations Act* reference and the *McEvoy* case demonstrate that section 96 prevents a solution to the fragmentation of family and criminal jurisdictions within the Canadian judicial system unless the provinces are willing to acquiesce in concentrating all jurisdiction in judges appointed unilaterally by the federal government.

Section 96 has also adversely affected the administration and management of court systems. The division of responsibility for the development of provincial court systems has been a recipe for 'divide and abdicate' so far as a system of responsible court management is concerned. Under these sections, one level of government, the federal, is responsible for appointing and paying the judges of courts which the other level of government, the provincial is responsible for maintaining. Sir Wilfrid Laurier once referred to this system of divided responsibility as a "strong defect" and on another occasion a "failure" in the Canadian Constitution.[44] The Constitution was silent on whether the federal government was bound to accede to provincial requests for additional judges for their superior, county, or district courts. Neither level of government kept track of the case load of section 96 courts, so there was no objective or rational basis for assessing the manpower needs of these courts. While the bifurcation of responsibility resulting from the constitutional framework has by no means been the only factor retarding the development of effective techniques of court administration in Canada, it has certainly made a coherent attack on these problems more difficult to sustain.[45]

A further disadvantage of section 96 has been its tendency to promote a two-class system of Canadian trial courts. Judges appointed by the provinces can serve only on "inferior" courts. So long as the adjudicative responsibilities of the provincially appointed judiciary were confined to very minor cases this implication of section 96 may have been tolerable. But, as we have pointed out, the jurisdiction of the purely Provincial Courts (the courts presided over by provincially appointed judges) has expanded well beyond minor matters. In criminal cases provincial judges can give sentences of up to life imprisonment; and they have had the entire responsibility for juvenile criminal justice. In family law, their jurisdiction, although badly fragmented, is nonetheless of great social significance. Their civil jurisdiction, as we have seen, in several provinces has been extended to suits involving significant amounts of money. Much has been done in recent years to improve the status of provincially appointed judges and the quality of the services provided by their courts. These improvements will be described in subsequent chapters. Still, section 96 perpetuates an invidious class distinction between the two groups of Canadian judges in Canada. This distinction has more than symbolic significance. Among other things it adversely affects recruitment to the "inferior courts" and impedes the integration of adjudicative services.

Manifest as the negative features of section 96 are, they should not blind us to this section's positive consequences. On the plus side of the ledger, it is a key to the integrated judicial system established in the British North America Act. Whether or not integration was the prime motive behind section 96, it was unquestionably its prime benefit.[46] For a federation such as Canada's, in which regional jealousies and provincial loyalties have continued to be particularly strong, this contribution to the development of a national community has been an important benefit. Section 96 has fostered mobility by removing the threat of parochial justice. A manifestation of this is the fact that the concept of "diversity suits"—suits between citizens of different provinces—which originally constituted one of the main reasons for establishing an extensive network of federal trial courts in the United States and for including a special federal jurisdiction in the Australian Constitution has not been a major issue in Canada.[47] The willingness of federal authorities (at least until recently) to rely primarily on provincial courts to administer federal laws may in no small measure be a consequence of the fact that the federal government appoints the judges of the senior provincial courts. Thus section 96 has been a factor in saving Canadian consumers of justice the inconvenience of a dual court system.

The foundation section 96 provided for a truly national judicial system should be kept in mind in considering the various proposals to reform this part of the

Canadian Constitution. Thus far the push for reform has come entirely from provincial political elites, and nearly all the proposals favour moving in the direction of expanding the jurisdiction of the purely provincial judiciary. While proposals of this kind may overcome many of the disadvantages of section 96, they may also undermine the integration and unity which section 96 has contributed to the Canadian judicial system. It is not far-fetched to anticipate that moves in this direction will accelerate the federalization of the Canadian court structure. As the provinces, free from the constraints of section 96, expand the jurisdiction of "their own" judges, the federal government may well be tempted to expand the jurisdiction of "its judges," judges of the federal courts established under section 101. The main losers in such a competition in judicial empire-building will be Canadian litigants and their lawyers, who will be required to find their way through an increasingly confusing jurisdictional jungle. Just how inconvenient this might become can be better seen when the complexities resulting from judicial review of federal court jurisdiction are examined in the next section.

The challenge in this area of constitutional reform is to find a way of overcoming the negative features of section 96 while retaining its integrative benefits. This is not the place to bring forward detailed recommendations; nevertheless, it seems reasonable to suggest that the key might be to change the system of appointing judges so that both levels of government participate in selecting the judges of the provincial superior courts. In Part Three we will discuss proposals for reforming the method of appointing judges, including the use of federal-provincial nominating commissions.[48] Whether or not this modification of ministerial control over judicial recruitment is accepted, there seems to be no alternative to some system of joint federal-provincial participation if the integration resulting from section 96 is to be maintained in a manner that is acceptable to both federal and provincial political leaders.[49]

The Application and Interpretation of Section 101

Section 101 of the Constitution Act, 1867, it will be recalled, gives the federal Parliament power to establish courts and, in this sense, deals with what might be termed "federal courts." This section has two branches. First, it permits Parliament to establish a General Court of Appeal for Canada. It is by virtue of this branch that Parliament established the Supreme Court of Canada in 1875. The second branch empowers Parliament to establish "any additional Courts for the better Administration of the Laws of Canada." Under this branch Parliament can establish courts for the adjudication of disputes arising under federal laws. Parliament has used its power under this branch to establish the Exchequer Court, its successor, the Federal Court of Canada, and the Tax Court of Canada.

The political will and judgment of federal politicians have been the principal factors in determining the extent to which the powers granted under section 101 have been used. But judicial interpretation has also played an important role in determining the scope of these powers. The interesting feature of judicial interpretation is the unevenness in its treatment of the two aspects of section 101. While the courts have given the widest possible interpretation of the General Court of Appeal aspect, they have given the narrowest possible construction of the "additional Courts" dimension. This pattern of judicial interpretation has had the effect of strengthening the integrative tendencies of section 101 while diminishing its capacity to serve as the basis for a dual court system.

It was not until eight years after Confederation that Parliament exercised its power to establish the Supreme Court of Canada. This was not an urgent matter because the Judicial Committee of the Privy Council continued to provide this service for Canada. Granted, the Judicial Committee was not a terribly convenient court of appeal for Canadian litigants; still, it was manned by leading members of the British judiciary who were much revered by politicans and lawyers in both English and French Canada. Indeed, the most contentious issue in the founding of the Supreme Court was the charge made by the Conservative opposition that its establishment would deprive Canadians of their appeal to "the foot of the throne."[50] In the end, despite a clause inserted in the Supreme Court Act by the more nationalist Liberals making the Supreme Court's judgment final in all but special "prerogative" appeals to the Privy Council, the Supreme Court remained a thoroughly intermediate court of appeal until 1949. Not only were its own decisions appealable to the Judicial Committee, but it could be bypassed altogether by taking appeals directly to London from the highest courts in the provinces.

When the Supreme Court was established in 1875 its jurisdiction was based on both branches of section 101. While its primary function was to serve as a court of appeal, its individual judges, sitting alone, could function as the Exchequer Court with original jurisdiction in cases involving federal revenue laws and suits in which the federal crown was a party. Twelve years later this original jurisdiction was transferred to a separate Exchequer Court. Thus, throughout most of its history, Canada's Supreme Court (unlike the highest courts of the United States and Australia) has functioned essentially as a court of appeal.[51]

From the beginning the Supreme Court's appellate jurisdiction has been general, covering disputes arising under provincial laws as well as disputes involving federal laws and the Constitution. In 1875 the Supreme Court's power to review the decisions of provincial courts in provincial law matters was attacked mainly by French-Canadian MPs from Quebec. Their criticism focused on the policy of "submitting the laws relating to property, to civil rights and civil procedure in the Province of Quebec . . . to judges, who, for the most part are strangers to their language, their manners, their usages."[52] The Supreme Court Act of 1875 made just two slight concessions to this point of view: there would be no right of appeal from Quebec courts unless the matter in dispute was $2000 or more, and two of the Supreme Court's six judges would have to come from the bar or bench of Quebec. The attack on the Supreme Court's jurisdiction in provincial law matters continued for the next thirty years.[53] It inspired proposals for amendments to the Supreme Court Act which would either terminate appeals in cases concerned solely with provincial laws, or require that civil law appeals from Quebec be heard by a special Supreme Court panel with a majority of Quebec judges. But all of these efforts came to naught. During this period the constitutional power of a province to restrict or terminate appeals to the Supreme Court in provincial law matters was also tested in the courts. The leading case was provoked by Ontario, where the legal profession's scepticism about the quality of the Court had aroused considerable hostility. In the *Crown Grain* case the Judicial Committee ruled decisively against the provinces.[54] Pointing to the language of section 101, which prefaces Parliament's power to establish a General Court of Appeal with the words "notwithstanding anything in this Act," their Lordships held that, if there was a conflict between federal and provincial legislation concerning appeals to the Supreme Court, federal law was paramount.

The decisive and final test of the federal Parliament's power to control the Supreme Court's appellate jurisdiction in all areas of law came when federal legislation terminating Privy Council appeals and making the Supreme Court Canada's exclusive ultimate court of appeal was referred to the courts. The only serious constitutional question raised by this legislation concerned federalism, not imperialism. The imperial question in effect had been resolved in 1931 when the Statute of Westminster made it possible for a Canadian law to override any conflicting imperial law. But the question that remained was whether, within Canada, Parliament's power to regulate appeals was broad enough to deny the provinces the power to make the highest court of appeal in the province the final court of appeal with respect to provincial laws or to carry on with Privy Council appeals in these matters. Given the Judicial Committee's earlier decision in the *Crown Grain* case, it was not surprising that in 1947 it upheld federal jurisdiction over appeals in provincial law matters.[55] What is more interesting is the broad language used by Lord Jowitt in justifying a federal hegemony over the appeal system in Canada. He emphasized that in the Canadian federation "the judicial and legislative spheres are not coterminous." He did not rest his decision solely on the notwithstanding clause at the beginning of section 101, but advanced the thesis that for Canada to function as a sovereign independent state it must have a single ultimate court of appeal for all legal issues. "It is," he said, "in fact, a prime element in the self-government of the Dominion, that it should be able to secure through its own courts of justice that the law should be one and the same for all its citizens."[56] It is remarkable that the British law lords who had protected with such tender loving care the division of legislative power in Canada were so convinced of the need for a unified judicial system.

There can be no question that the breadth of the Supreme Court's (and the Judicial Committee's) appellate jurisdiction has had a unifying influence on Canadian law. From its foundation in 1875 until well into the modern period, cases involving provincial laws were the predominant element in its case load. In this respect the Canadian Supreme Court has been in marked contrast to the American Supreme Court and the national supreme courts of the West German and Swiss federations. It is important to bear in mind here that "provincial law" includes a good deal of judge-made common law as well as provincial statutes. In the early years when, outside of Quebec, so many legal relationships concerning property and civil rights were regulated by common law rather than by legislation, resolving differences among provincial courts on disputed points of common law was perhaps the Supreme Court's most important function. The uniformity in the law relating to property and civil rights obtainable through this judicial avenue certainly proved to be far more significant than the opportunity created by section 94 of the Constitution for obtaining uniformity through legislative co-operation between the common law provinces and the federal Parliament.[57]

Since 1949 when the Supreme Court became Canada's highest court of appeal in fact as well as in name, cases focusing on questions of provincial law have been diminishing as a component of the Court's workload. Gradually the Supreme Court has been moving in the direction of its American counterpart, concentrating more and more of its attention on cases involving federal laws and the constitution. Among other things, this shift results from a steady expansion of the federal statute book and of litigation in areas of federal law. Criminal law, which in Canada is under federal legislative jurisdiction, has been the largest single source of federal law appeals.[58] An intensification of federal-provincial conflict has meant that the Supreme Court, particularly since the mid-1970s, has been increasingly called upon to adjudicate constitutional disputes. The addition of a Charter of Rights and Freedoms to the Canadian Constitution in 1982 has significantly increased the Court's constitutional work. The Court's capacity to concentrate on federal and constitutional law was significantly increased by a 1974 amendment to the Supreme Court Act that removed the right of appeal in cases involving $10 000 or more and made access to the Court in civil cases dependent on leave being granted by the Supreme Court or by the court being appealed from. Leave is only to be granted when cases raise issues of "public importance."[59] While this criterion does not preclude issues of provincial law, leave will rarely be granted where a case is confined to an issue of concern to a single province. Thus, without any formal constitutional change, provincial courts of appeal in Canada increasingly assume the role of their counterparts in the United States as final courts of appeal on questions of provincial law.

This transformation of the Supreme Court's docket has occurred during a period when political opposition to its provincial law role appears to have virtually disappeared. In the 1950s there was a revival of Quebec's protests against the Supreme Court's jurisdiction over Quebec civil law. In the 1960s and early 1970s a constitutional amendment which would give provinces the option of eliminating provincial law appeals to the Supreme Court received some support outside of Quebec.[60] The 1972 report of the Joint Parliamentary Committee on the Constitution contained such a proposal.[61] But the Supreme Court proposals brought forward during the period of constitutional agitation following the Quebec Referendum took a very different approach. Quebeckers who wished their province to remain in Confederation were anxious that Quebec civil law remain an integral part of the Supreme Court's work. The constitutional proposals of both the Quebec Liberal party and the federal Task Force on Canadian Unity called for a retention of the Supreme Court's jurisdiction in civil law appeals from Quebec.[62] Even the idea of a special panel of Quebec Supreme Court justices to hear such appeals was discarded. Ironically, the integrative nature of the Supreme Court's jurisdiction in provincial law matters was gaining a wide appreciation at the very time this dimension of the Court's work was receding in importance.[63] In the future, the main integrative or centralizing influence of the Supreme Court is likely to be felt, as it is in the United States, through the Court's application of the norms contained in the new constitutional Charter of Rights to the activities of provincial governments.

Constitutional proposals concerning the Supreme Court were not one of the elements in the settlement which was negotiated by the federal prime minister and nine provincial premiers in November 1981 and which was eventually incorporated in the Constitution Act, 1982. Nonetheless that act, by referring to the Supreme Court in its constitutional amendment formula, created some confusion concerning the constitutional status of the Court. Section 41(d) refers to "the composition of the Supreme Court of Canada" as one of the parts of the Constitution which cannot be amended without the unanimous agreement of the federal Parliament and all of the provincial legislatures. In Section 42(d) "the Supreme Court of Canada" (except for its composition) is included in the list of matters which are subject to the normal amendment rule (agreement of the federal Parliament and two-thirds of the provinces representing 50 per cent of the population) but which cannot be opted out of by dissenting provinces. The question arises: To what provisions of the existing Constitution do these amending rules apply? Remember that the Supreme Court of Canada is not specifically provided for in the formal Constitution. There is still only section 101 of the BNA Act (now the Constitution Act, 1867) permitting Parliament to establish a General Court of Appeal for Canada. All of the rules governing the Court's jurisdiction, the qualifications, method of appointment, and tenure of its judges are contained in the Supreme Court Act which is an ordinary act of the federal Parliament. Except for the requirement in the Supreme Court Act that three of the Court's nine judges must come from Quebec, the practice of ensuring regional representation in its composition is a matter of custom or convention. So, do the references to the Court and its composition in the amending formula apply to these statutory and customary rules, or do they only apply to some clause that may eventually be put in the formal Constitution establishing the Court and regulating its composition?

Constitutional experts do not agree on this question. Peter Hogg, for example, believes that section 41(d) and 42(d) do not apply to the Supreme Court Act. In his view these sections apply only to some future constitutional amendment entrenching the Supreme Court in the Constitution.[64] But Ronald Cheffins, while acknowledging that the Supreme Court Act is not in the list of items which, according to section 52(2) of the Constitution Act, 1982, are included in "the

Constitution of Canada,'' argues that this list is not exhaustive. In Cheffins's view, the Supreme Court Act is part of the Constitution of Canada which section 52 establishes as the "supreme law of Canada."[65] If Cheffins is right, then the Constitution Act, 1982 not only entrenched the Supreme Court in the Constitution but the entire Supreme Court Act, including sections setting down rather fine points of court procedure. It is difficult to imagine that this was the intention of those who drafted and agreed to the Constitution Act, 1982. A more plausible explanation of the references to the Supreme Court in the amending formula is the desire to design a comprehensive formula that would cover any possible additions that might be made to the Constitution in the future. Still, the situation is far from clear, and the uncertainty surrounding the rather off-hand references to the Supreme Court in the "new Constitution" provide an added incentive for attending to proposals to entrench certain features of the Supreme Court in Canada's formal Constitution.

Turning now to the second branch of section 101, we find a rather different pattern of development. As we have seen, until quite recently the federal government showed little inclination to make use of the power it has under this section to establish a system of federal courts. For the most part, Ottawa relied on provincial courts to adjudicate disputes arising under federal laws. The major exception was the Exchequer Court, whose limited jurisdiction and modest growth was described earlier. The Federal Court of Canada which, replaced the Exchequer Court in 1971, represented a substantial expansion of the responsibilities of federal courts especially with respect to judicial review of the federal bureaucracy. The work of this new court will be examined in chapter 13. What must be analysed here in terms of the constitutional framework of Canada's judicial system is the way the Supreme Court of Canada has dealt with a series of challenges to the Federal Court's jurisdiction. The Supreme Court's decision-making in this area has put the narrowest possible construction on the second branch of section 101. The practical inconvenience to litigants resulting from these decisions has created a strong disincentive to any further moves by federal politicians in the direction of a dual court system. Here we may have a case of judicial activism fostering political restraint!

In interpreting section 101, it was very early established that the phrase "for the better Administration of the Laws of Canada" refers not to all laws in force in Canada but only to "federal laws." But just how narrow the concept of "federal laws" might be did not become clear until 1977 when the Supreme Court decided two cases concerning the new Federal Court. Both of these cases, *McNamara Construction* and *Quebec North Shore*, involved suits in which the federal government or one of its agencies was a party.[66] The Federal Court, like the Exchequer Court, had exclusive jurisdiction to hear civil suits against the federal crown and a concurrent jurisdiction with provincial superior courts to hear suits brought by the federal crown as a plaintiff. It was the latter part of the Federal Court's jurisdiction—the provision which gives the federal government the option of suing in the Federal Court or a provincial court—that the

Supreme Court found unconstitutional. In reaching this conclusion the Court overruled one of its previous decisions which had upheld this aspect of the Exchequer Court's jurisdiction.[67] Chief Justice Laskin, who wrote the Court's opinion in both of the 1977 cases, held that the "judicial jurisdiction contemplated by s.101 is not co-extensive with federal legislative jurisdiction."[68] The phrase "laws of Canada" in section 101 did not permit Parliament to extend the jurisdiction of federal courts to all matters in relation to which Parliament was competent to legislate, but only to those matters which were actually regulated by federal laws. Since there was federal legislation governing suits *against* the federal crown, the Federal Court could hear breach of contract suits brought against the federal government, but there was no operative federal law governing the opposite situation in which the federal crown was the plaintiff. Although the Supreme Court did not deny that the federal Parliament could pass legislation governing such suits, Parliament had not done so and consequently the applicable law was the common law and Quebec civil law. Thus the Court concluded that the Constitution did not permit the Federal Court's jurisdiction to apply to these cases.[69]

These decisions had a deleterious effect on civil litigation involving the federal government. Very often in such litigation (for instance, suits involving large construction contracts), there are claims and counter claims and claims against third parties. As a result of these rulings, disputes of this kind where the federal government is both a plaintiff and a defendant cannot now be tried in a single court. The federal crown can only be sued in the Federal Court, but it cannot, in situations such as those involved in the *McNamara Construction* and *Quebec North Shore* cases, bring its suit in the Federal Court.

The Supreme Court's strictness in enforcing constitutional limits on Federal Court jurisdiction was further demonstrated two years later in the *Fuller Construction* case.[70] Here the Court rejected the doctrines of ancillary and pendent jurisdiction which had been developed by the United States Supreme Court. These doctrines make it possible for courts exercising a constitutionally limited federal jurisdiction to deal with issues of state law if these are closely associated with the main action concerning federal law. As a result, federal trial courts in Canada have constitutionally less capacity than their American counterparts to adjudicate disputes involving elements of both federal and provincial law. As two commentators on the *Fuller* case have suggested, "It is as if the Supreme Court had declared that 'the better administration of the laws of Canada' requires that parliament *not* exercise its jurisdiction under section 101."[71]

In addition to the fragmentation of court proceedings resulting from the judicial interpretation of section 101, a number of tortuous jurisdictional complexities have arisen in applying the terms of the Federal Court Act, especially the division of jurisdiction between its trial and appellate divisions. This accumulation of jurisdictional difficulties has done nothing to alleviate the hostile scepticism that greeted the arrival of this new federal tribunal on the Canadian judicial scene. These problems may prompt Canadians to question whether the Constitution should continue with a clause that invites federal politicians to develop a separate tier of federal courts. It is doubtful that Canadian citizens, however wedded they may be to a federal division of legislative power, wish to see that division duplicated in the judicial branch of government. They have reason to hope that any attempt to reform the judicature sections of the Canadian Constitution will take its inspiration from Sir Zelman Cowan who, in reviewing the difficulties Australia has experienced with federal jurisdiction, suggested that

> it should not be beyond the wit of man to refashion the Judicature Chapter of the Constitution and the legislation enacted thereunder so as to provide for the orderly administration of justice within the framework of a single integrated court system— free of the Gothic complexities of the law of federal jurisdiction.[72]

Having examined how the constitution regulates the relationship between the judicial branch of government and the two levels of government in the Canadian federation, we will turn in the next chapter to the relationship between the judiciary and the so-called political branches of government at both the federal and provincial level.

Notes to Chapter 3

1. Jules Deschênes in collaboration with Carl Baar, *Maîtres Chez Eux* (Ottawa: Canadian Judicial Council, 1981), p. 13.
2. Constitution Act, 1867, s. 129.
3. For the classical federations (Australia, Canada, Switzerland, United States and West Germany), see Robert R. Bowie and Carl J. Frederich, *Studies in Federalism* (Boston: Little, Brown, 1954), pp. 106-72. W.J. Wagner, *The Federal States and Their Judiciary* (Gravenhage: Mouton, 1959), covers the Latin American federations as well as the classical federations. The judiciaries of new Commonwealth federations are discussed in R.L. Watts, *New Federations: Experiments in the Commonwealth* (Oxford: Clarendon Press, 1966).
4. The influence of the English model is similarly reflected in Australia's Constitution. Although in most other respects the judicial provisions of the Australian Constitution are modelled on the American Constitution, s. 73 extends the jurisdiction of Australia's High Court to matters of state law.
5. Peter W. Hogg, *Constitutional Law of Canada* 2nd ed. (Toronto: Carswell, 1985), p. 135.
6. Darrell Roberts, "The Structure and Jurisdiction of the Courts and Classification of Offences," paper prepared for the Law Reform Commission of Canada, 1973. On the basis of 1968 data, Roberts found that provincially appointed judges hear 93% of all indictable cases.
7. Quebec has led the way. Quebec's Provincial Court can now hear civil actions involving up to $15 000. SQ 1984, c. 83, s. 3.
8. Public Archives of Canada (PAC) Macdonald Papers, 159, Bill no. 80.
9. From 1875 to 1887 the Exchequer Court was constituted by judges of the Supreme Court of Canada sitting alone.
10. See table 13.1 below for data on the growth of the Federal Court of Canada. The figure for the number of judges serving in the US Federal Court system is based

on data in Henry J. Abraham, *The Judicial Process*, 4th ed. (New York: Oxford University Press, 1980).

11. House of Commons, *Debates*, 28 June 1983, pp. 26891-94. The legislation was assented to on 29 June 1983 (29-30-31-32 Elizabeth II, c. 158).
12. Another "court" established by Parliament under s. 101 is the Court Martial Appeal Court of Canada. This court does not have its own judges but uses judges from superior courts of criminal jurisdiction.
13. K.C. Wheare, *Federal Government*, 3rd ed. (London: Oxford University Press, 1953), pp. 11 and 71.
14. For an account of conceptions of federalism at the time of Confederation, see P.B. Waite, *The Life and Time of Confederation, 1864-1867* (Toronto: University of Toronto Press, 1962), ch. 8.
15. For an account of these powers, see Hogg, *Constitutional Law*, pp. 141-43, 329-32.
16. *Report of Quebec Royal Commission of Inquiry on Constitutional Problems* (Tremblay Report) (Quebec, 1956), 2, part IV, chs. 1 and 4.
17. See, for example, Gerard Trudel, "La Pouvoir Judiciaire au Canada," *Revue du Barreau* (1965), p. 193, and Peter H. Russell, "Constitutional Reform of the Canadian Judiciary," *Alberta Law Review* (1969), p. 103.
18. Jérôme Choquette, *Justice Today* (Quebec: Gouvernement de Québec, 1975), pp. 11-30.
19. *First Report of the Advisory Committee on Confederation* (Toronto, 1978), p. 12.
20. *Report to Cabinet on Constitutional Discussions, Summer 1980 and the Outlook for the First Ministers Conference and Beyond* ("Kirby Memorandum"), p. 26.
21. For a critical evaluation of this jurisprudence, see John Willis, "Section 96 of the British North American Act," *Canadian Bar Review* (1940), p. 517; Morris C. Shumiatcher, "Section 96 of the British North America Act Re-examined," ibid. (1949), p. 131; William Lederman, "The Independence of the Judiciary," ibid., (1956), pp. 1166-74.
22. For instance, Quebec fire marshalls' courts in *R. v. Coote* (1873) 4 AC 599, provincial appointment of justices of the peace in *R. v. Bush* 15 OR 398, and the small debts jurisdiction of justices of the peace in *In re Small Debts Act* 5 BCR 246.
23. *Liquidators of the Maritime Bank of Canada v. Receiver General of New Brunswick* (1892) AC 437.
24. [1932] AC 113.
25. [1938] AC 415.
26. Ibid., p. 426.
27. [1938] SCR 398.
28. [1949] AC 134.
29. *Tomko v. Labour Relations Board (N.S.)* [1977] 1 SCR 112, at 120.
30. [1955] SCR 454.
31. See, for example, his comment on the *Olympia* case in *Canadian Bar Review* (1955), p. 993, and his judgment in the *Tomko* case.
32. *Reference Re Quebec Magistrate's Court* [1965] SCR 772.
33. *Seminaire de Chicoutimi v. A.G. Québec* [1973] SCR 681.
34. *Re Residential Tenancies Act, 1979* [1981] 1 SCR 714, at 723.
35. Ibid. p. 728.

36. [1978] 2 SCR 638.

37. *Crevier* v. *A.G. Québec* [1981] 2 SCR 220.

38. A majority of the Canadian Bar Association's Committee on the Constitution called for a constitutional guarantee of the judicial review traditionally exercised by superior courts over officials, inferior tribunals, and statutory bodies of all kinds. See *Towards a New Canada* (Ottawa: Canadian Bar Foundation, 1978), p. 51.

39. [1982] 1 SCR 62.

40. *McEvoy* v. *A.G. New Brunswick*, [1983] 1 SCR 705.

41. *Globe and Mail* (Toronto), 14 Mar. 1983.

42. In August 1983 the federal minister of justice, Mark MacGuigan, issued a discussion paper supporting this proposed amendment. While this proposal to add s. 96B to the Constitution has been widely discussed in professional circles, it has not yet been proceeded with at the political level. *The Constitution of Canada: A Suggested Amendment Relating to Provincial Tribunals* (Ottawa, 1983).

43. In the Confederation Debates, Hector Langevin provided the only sustained defence of federal control over the appointment of provincial judges. In his view, the main advantage of such a system was that it would keep off the bench the "troublesome advocate of the second, third or fourth order of talent" who was likely to have a great influence on the local legislature. *Parliamentary Debates on the Subject of the Confederation of the British North American Provinces* (1865), pp. 387-88.

44. House of Commons, *Debates*, 1898, p. 6766; and 1900 p. 9114.

45. For an analysis of impediments to effective court administration stemming from the Constitution, see Perry S. Millar and Carl Baar, *Judicial Administration in Canada* (Montreal and Toronto: McGill-Queen's University Press with the Institute of Public Administration of Canada, 1981), ch. 3.

46. According to Peter Hogg, the idea of establishing a system of national courts does not appear to have been explicitly put forward as a rationale for s.96. See his "Federalism and the Jurisdiction of Canadian Courts," *University of New Brunswick Law Journal* (1981), p. 15, n. 15.

47. For a discussion of this factor in developing federal courts in the United States, see Henry M. Hart and Herbert Wechsler, *The Federal Courts and the Federal System* (Brooklyn: Foundation Press, 1953), ch. 1.

48. For a discussion of such a proposal, see W.R. Lederman, "Current Proposals for Reform of the Supreme Court of Canada," *Canadian Bar Review* (1979), p. 688.

49. This argument has been forcefully made by Nicole Duplé in "La reforme constitutionnelle et l'article 96 de l'Acte de l'Amérique du Nord britannique," in Stanley Beck and Ivan Bernier, eds., *Canada and the New Constitution: The Unfinished Agenda* Vol. 1, (Montreal: Institute for Research on Public Policy, 1983), p. 145.

50. For a discussion of the founding of the Supreme Court, see Frank MacKinnon, "The Establishment of the Supreme Court of Canada," *Canadian Historical Review* (1938), p. 245.

51. The principal exception is that the Court can be asked to answer questions referred to it by the federal government. See Peter H. Russell, "The Jurisdiction of the Supreme Court of Canada: Present Policies and a Programme for Reform," *Osgoode Hall Law Journal* (1968), p. 1.

52. L.F.G. Baby, in House of Commons, *Debates*, 1975, p. 922.

53. See Peter H. Russell, *The Supreme Court of Canada as a Bilingual and Bicultural Institution* (Ottawa: Queen's Printer, 1969), ch. 1.
54. *Crown Grain Co.* v. *Day* [1908] AC 504. The Supreme Court had reached a similar conclusion in *Clarkson* v. *Ryan* (1890), 17 SCR 251.
55. *A.G. Ontario* v. *A.G. Canada* [1947] AC 128.
56. Ibid., p. 154.
57. See John Willis, "Securing Uniformity of Law in a Federal System—Canada," *University of Toronto Law Journal* (1943-44), p. 352. S. 94 has never been used.
58. See ch. 14 below for an analysis of the Supreme Court's workload.
59. Statutes of Canada 1974-75-76, c. 18.
60. See, for example, Albert S. Abel, "The Role of the Supreme Court in Private Law Cases," *Alberta Law Review* (1965), p. 39.
61. Special Joint Committee of the Senate and House of Commons on the Constitution of Canada, *Final Report*, recommendation 46, p. 39.
62. The Quebec Liberal Party, *A New Canadian Federation* (Montreal), 1980, p. 58, and Task Force on Canadian Unity, *A Future Together* (Ottawa: Supply and Services, 1979), pp. 100-101.
63. The Canadian Bar Association's Committee on the Constitution reported that in 1975 the Supreme Court heard thirty-one predominantly civil law cases; in 1976, sixteen; in 1977, only six. See *Towards a New Canada*, p. 58.
64. Peter W. Hogg, *Canada Act 1982 Annotated* (Toronto: Carswell, 1982), pp. 92-94.
65. Ronald Cheffins, "The Constitution Act, 1982 and the Amending Formula: Political and Legal Implications," in Edward P. Belobaba and Eric Gertner, eds., *The New Constitution and the Charter of Rights* (Toronto: Butterworths, 1983), p. 53.
66. *McNamara Construction* v. *The Queen* [1977] 2 SCR 654, and *Quebec North Shore Paper* v. *C.P. Ltd.* [1977] 2 SCR 1054.
67. *Farwell* v. *The Queen* (1893) 22 SCR 553.
68. *McNamara Construction*, p. 658.
69. For a critical appraisal of these cases, see Peter W. Hogg, "Constitutional Law—Limits of Federal Jurisdiction—Is There a Federal Common Law?" *Canadian Bar Review* (1977), p. 550.
70. *The Queen* v. *Thomas Fuller Construction* [1980] 1 SCR 695.
71. John B. Laskin and Robert J. Sharpe, "Constricting Federal Court Jurisdiction: A Comment on Fuller Construction," *University of Toronto Law Journal* (1980), p. 295.
72. Zelman Cowan, *Federal Jurisdiction in Australia* (Melbourne: Oxford University Press, 1959).

CHAPTER 4
JUDICIAL INDEPENDENCE AND THE SEPARATION OF POWERS

At the beginning of chapter 3 we pointed out that Canada's original Constitution did not explicitly treat the judiciary as a third and separate branch of government. The Constitution Act, 1867, in contrast to the US Constitution, does not begin with articles on the legislative and executive branches and then follow with Article III on the judicial branch. Judicial institutions in the Canadian Constitution appear to be essentially creatures of the legislature not of the Constitution. The one important feature of judicial independence expressly provided for was the security of tenure of superior court judges. In 1982, for the first time, explicit reference was made to the concepts of judicial independence and impartiality in Canada's formal Constitution. Section 11(d) of the Charter of Rights and Freedoms gives any person charged with an offence the right "to be presumed innocent until proven guilty according to law in a fair and public hearing by an independent and impartial tribunal."

The explicit "guarantee" of judicial independence, it must be noted, applies only to courts which try criminal cases. In this chapter we will take a closer look at the extent to which judicial independence and the separation of powers are part of Canada's constitutional system and consider the consequences of including a more explicit enunciation of these principles in the formal Constitution.

The Importance of Constitutional Convention

To begin with, it is important to bear in mind that the Canadian constitution does not consist solely of the Constitution Acts, 1867 to 1982. As with virtually all constitutional democracies, the corpus of constitutional rules in Canada includes, in addition to the formal "written" Constitution, organic statutes, judicial decisions, and constitutional conventions. In the Canadian system, constitutional conventions play a particularly important role in regulating the relationships among the different branches of government—including the relationship of the judiciary to the legislature and the executive. In this respect the Canadian Constitution draws heavily from the British constitutional tradition. "In Britain," wrote S.A. de Smith, "the independence of the Judiciary rests not on formal constitutional guarantees and prohibitions but on an admixture of statutory and common-law rules, constitutional conventions and parliamentary practice, fortified by professional tradition and public opinion."[1]

To some extent, de Smith's words continue to apply to Canada. Although there are sections of the formal Constitution that deal with judicial independence (namely, the guarantee of tenure for superior court judges in section 99 of the original Constitution and the reference to "an independent and impartial tribunal" in section 11(d) of the new Charter of Rights and Freedoms), it would be a serious mistake to regard these provisions as the sole or even primary constitutional basis for judicial independence in Canada. In the words of Professor Hogg, "The independence of the judiciary has become such a powerful tradition in the United Kingdom and Canada that there may be little point in a fine analysis of the language of the provisions by which it is formally guaranteed."[2] Nevertheless, times are changing and judges, like virtually every other group in Canadian society, are becoming less inclined to rely on informal tradition to protect their interests. As we shall see, they too are seeking more formal legal protection. Of course, when judges do this they tend to turn to themselves—the judiciary—to settle disputes about their own rights and powers.

The most important constitutional convention concerning judicial independence requires that the judge not be interfered with by public or private forces in making his decision. Shimon Shetreet in his classic study of the English judiciary has given a succinct formulation of this element of the independence of individual judges: "In the making of judicial decisions and in exercising other official duties they are subject to no authority but the law."[3] At least the first part of this statement applies in Canada. In performing their adjudicative functions judges must not be directed as to how they should decide by any authority other than the law. They should not even be subject to direction by other judges, including the judges of higher courts, except to the extent that the decisions of such judges serve as authoritative precedents. The freedom of the judge from interference in his decision-making, especially interference by members of the executive branch of government, is a crucial requirement of adjudication. If the judge is to serve as a third party settling a dispute about the legal rights of two other parties, one of which is often the executive branch of government, he must be independent and not under instructions or subject to the direct pressure of supporters of one of the parties to the dispute. The Universal Declaration unanimously adopted by representatives of the twenty-eight countries represented at the World Conference on the Independence of Justice in Montreal in 1983 expressed this essential element of judicial independence this way:

> Judges individually shall be free, and it shall be their duty, to decide matters before them impartially in accordance with their assessment of the facts and their understanding of the law without any restrictions, influences, inducements, pressures, threats or interferences, direct or indirect, from any quarter or for any reason.[4]

Recently, in a decision on the Charter of Rights, Chief Justice Brian Dickson stated that "the complete liberty of individual judges to hear and decide the cases that come before them" is the core of judicial independence.[5]

The second part of Shetreet's dictum concerning judges exercising official duties other than adjudication is more problematic. In England and Canada judges have been subject to the direction of senior judges and, in some circumstances, of officials from the executive branch, on a variety of administrative matters. The contentious aspect of this practice is the involvement of the executive branch in court administration. While there is as yet no clear consensus among Canadian judges on this question, there is increasing support for the view that the executive branch should have no authority over administrative matters that directly impinge on adjudication. Most politicians and citizens would support the proposition put forward in 1981 by Jules Deschênes, that "the independence of the judiciary requires absolutely that the judiciary and it alone manage and control the movement of cases on the trial lists and the assigning of the judges who will hear these cases."[6] Certainly all Canadian judges would agree with this proposition.

It should be noted that what is at stake here is not so much the independence of the individual judge as the collective independence of the judiciary as a branch of government. It seems to be generally conceded that chief justices, chief judges, and their associates may give administrative direction to members of their courts, especially with regard to what is referred to as "case flow management." But there is still considerable dispute about the extent to which *all* aspects of court administration, including the hiring and firing and supervision of court support staff and the determination of court budgets, should be under the judicial branch of government.

In *R*. v. *Valente*, the first case in which the courts were called upon to consider what is meant by the reference to "an independent and impartial tribunal" in the Charter of Rights, one of the many issues considered was whether the general responsibility exercised by the provincial attorney general over court administration violated the new constitutional guarantee of independence for criminal courts. The Ontario Court of Appeal found that the attorney general's responsibilities with respect to Ontario's Provincial Court (Criminal Division) did not violate this section of the Charter. The court took the position that while "the Executive must not interfere with, or attempt to influence the adjudicative function of the judiciary," some executive involvement in court administration was acceptable. As an example of "reasonable management constraints," Chief Justice Howland cited the executive's responsibility for providing court rooms and court staffs. On the other hand, "the assignment of judges, the sittings of the courts, and the court lists," he said, "are all matters for the judiciary." He acknowledged that the distinction between what is acceptable and what is unacceptable may not always be easily made: "There may be a fine line between interference with adjudication and proper management controls."[7] The Supreme Court upheld Howland's handling of this issue. Justice Le Dain, who wrote for a unanimous court, stated that judicial independence required "judicial control over the administrative decisions that bear directly and immediately on the exercise of the judicial function"; but the administrative autonomy beyond this which many judges were seeking, while it "may well be highly desirable," was not legally required by section 11(d) of the Charter.[8]

An episode which occurred in British Columbia in 1979 shows how the "fine line" referred to by Chief Justice Howland may be breached. In 1979 Judge

Govan adjourned a case in the Richmond, British Columbia family court because he found the legislation giving him jurisdiction in the case—the recently amended Family Relations Act expanding the family law jurisdiction of provincially appointed judges—*ultra vires*. Subsequently Judge Govan received a telephone call from the deputy attorney general of the province, Richard Vogel, suggesting that Judge Govan should consider not sitting in the Richmond family court so that other judges with a different view of the legislation's constitutional validity could deal with the case load in that area. While Justice P.D. Seaton of the BC Court of Appeal who conducted an inquiry into this affair found no evidence of "sinister conduct" or "improper motive," he did conclude that the conduct of Mr. Vogel and of several members of his staff was "inappropriate."[9] Justice Seaton's report emphasized the threat to judicial independence that results from the fact that the same ministry which is responsible for court administration is also responsible for prosecutions. In British Columbia the executive's notion of working out case-load problems through a "teamwork" approach with the judiciary showed insufficient respect for the judiciary (or at least for its provincially appointed component) as a separate branch of government.

The Judges Affair of 1976

The closest Canada has come in modern times to experiencing a serious breach of the principle of non-interference in judicial decision-making occurred in 1976, when four federal cabinet ministers were accused of interfering with the judiciary. Bearing in mind that the principle of non-interference is primarily a matter of constitutional convention and that the sanctions for violating convention are administered in the political arena, it is important to observe how the Canadian political community handled this affair.[10]

The event that triggered the "judges affair" was the citation of André Ouellet, minister of corporate and consumers affairs in the Trudeau government, for contempt of court—an episode that, in itself, indicates the considerable legal power Canadian judges have to sanction those who publicly criticize the judiciary. In December 1975 Ouellet was cited for contempt by Justice Kenneth MacKay of the Quebec Superior Court. Ouellet had referred to Justice MacKay's acquittal of three sugar companies on charges of price fixing (charges initiated by Ouellet's department) as "completely unacceptable," "silly," and "a complete disgrace." In January 1976 the citation for contempt was upheld by Justice James Hugessen of the Quebec Superior Court. The prosecution in this case was conducted by Richard Holden, a prominent Conservative lawyer who had been appointed by Justice MacKay. When the federal minister of justice, Ron Basford, refused to pay Holden's fee on the grounds that it was the responsibility of the provincial government, Justice MacKay wrote him a letter in which he referred to a warning he had given Ouellet "to refrain from interfering with the course of justice, a practice that seems to be all too prevalent amongst your colleagues." Basford replied that he was at a loss to understand this phrase. MacKay wrote back describing three separate incidents, involving Marc Lalonde, Jean Chrétien, and Bud Drury, all federal cabinet ministers. In Justice MacKay's view these incidents constituted "unwarranted attempts to interfere with the judicial process." These letters were published in the Toronto *Globe and Mail* on 3 March 1976 and immediately became the focus of a major parliamentary row.

Instead of appointing a royal commission of inquiry, as was urged by the opposition parties, the government referred MacKay's allegations to the chief justice of Quebec's Superior Court, Jules Deschênes. Deschênes did not think it appropriate for him to conduct an inquiry into the activities of ministers; however, he did obtain statements from the judges who had been the targets of the alleged interference. These statements were included in a letter from Deschênes to Basford tabled in the House of Commons on 12 March 1976. An examination of this material, together with statements made by ministers in the House of Commons, indicates the following:

– Marc Lalonde in 1969 when he was principal secretary in the Prime Minister's Office called on Justice MacKay at his home in Montreal on a Sunday morning. Justice MacKay had been conducting the trial of a number of persons from Trinidad, charged with the destruction of a computer at Sir George Williams University. On the weekend in question he was preparing his address to the jury. Mr. Lalonde informed Justice MacKay of a message received from Canada's High Commission to Trinidad which expressed concern that violent riots might occur in Trinidad if a guilty verdict was rendered at that time. Justice MacKay told Mr. Lalonde that he was about to charge the jury the next day, that there was nothing he would do to delay the decision, and that because of the complexity of the case the jury would not likely come to a decision until the end of the following week at the earliest. Lalonde repeated that the situation was one of grave concern.

– Jean Chrétien in 1971, when he was minister of indian affairs and northern development, telephoned Mr. Justice Aronovitch of the Quebec Superior Court to find out when he would render judgment in bankruptcy proceedings concerning a company in his constituency. He had been asked to do this by some of the unemployed persons affected by these proceedings. The judge told Chrétien that he would render his decision when it was ready and that Chrétien's call would have no influence on the date of judgment.

– Bud Drury, minister of public works, telephoned Justice Hugessen during the hearing of contempt proceedings against André Ouellet. Ouellet had first asked Finance Minister John Turner to do this; when rebuffed by Turner, he had turned to Drury. Drury asked Hugessen if an apology from Ouellet could terminate proceedings and whether the proceedings represented a ganging-up of the English-speaking establishment against French Canadians. Justice Hugessen told Drury that an apology and its effect on the contempt proceedings was a matter for discussion between counsel for the two sides and that the point about an anti-French Canadian conspiracy was simply ridiculous.

Not one of the three ministers who talked to the judges resigned as a result of these revelations. Drury at least recognized the impropriety of what he had done and offered his resignation, only to have it refused by Prime Minister Trudeau. André Ouellet resigned four days after the refusal of Drury's resignation but did not give as his reason an admission that his efforts to have ministerial colleagues call the judge hearing the case constituted a serious breach of constitutional convention.

The judges affair indicated that while there was universal acknowledgment on the part of all the politicians involved of the general principle of non-interference (indeed, private conversations designed to influence judges can be grounds for criminal contempt), it was not clearly recognized by ministers of the crown that ministerial conversations with judges deciding cases, even when their purported purpose was simply to obtain information about the timing of court proceedings, are improper. There is an acceptable and public means of obtaining such information through the court officials who administer court registries. When, instead of using these channels, ministers take the direct approach and telephone judges or appear on their doorstep on a Sunday morning, at the very least their conduct appears to constitute an attempt at improper influence. To clarify this matter and to ensure that there would be no doubt in the future about communications between ministers and judges, on 12 March 1976 Prime Minister Trudeau made the following statement in the House of Commons:

> In future no member of the Cabinet may communicate with members of the judiciary concerning any matter which they have before them in their judicial capacities, except through the Minister of Justice, his duly authorized officials, or counsel acting for him, nor may any member of the Cabinet communicate with quasi-official bodies which are constituted as courts of record concerning any matter which they have before them in their judicial capacities except through the minister responsible, his duly authorized officials, or counsel acting for him.[11]

Two years later there was a sequel to the judges affair which demonstrated that Mr. Trudeau's guidelines would have some force. On 7 September 1978 John Munro, minister of labour in the federal government, tendered his resignation when it was revealed that he had called a judge on behalf of a constituent the evening before the judge's decision regarding sentence.[12] In the same year a similar breach of the non-interference rule led to a resignation of an Ontario cabinet minister, Solicitor General George Kerr.[13] Kerr phoned a deputy crown attorney about charges brought against one of his constituents. At first Premier Davis decided that the matter did not justify requiring Kerr to give up his cabinet post. Instead, on 8 November 1978 he issued guidelines similar to Prime Minister Trudeau's stipulating that no member of the cabinet other than the attorney general in his capacity as chief law officer of the crown "may communicate with members of the judiciary concerning any matter which they may have before them in their judicial capacity."[14] The Davis guidelines also forbad ministerial communication with crown attorneys, assistant crown attorneys and provincial prosecutors concerning any matter before the courts. Subsequently, in the wake of mounting public protest and the report of a senior law officer indicating that Mr. Kerr had intended to influence the sentencing of a constituent, George Kerr submitted his resignation.

It is interesting to note that in the preamble to the Ontario guidelines, Premier Davis expressed his "natural reluctance" to resort to formal codification "in the light of the unwritten constitutional heritage which has served us so well." Other Canadian jurisdictions continue to rely entirely on unwritten custom and convention for the protection of this essential ingredient of the principle of judicial independence. It is to be hoped that this principle is observed just as thoroughly in these provinces and the federal territories as it now ought to be in those jurisdictions that have found it necessary to reinforce unwritten constitutional rules with written guidelines.

Formal Constitutional Guarantees

The most important condition of judicial independence explicitly stated in Canada's original Constitution is the security of tenure provided for superior court judges in section 99. Section 100 also contributes to the independence of the judges of superior, county, and district courts by providing that their salaries be fixed by Parliament, thus protecting them from possible manipulation of their remuneration by the executive. The provision in section 96 for central government control over appointments to the higher provincial courts is sometimes pointed to as another way in which the Constitution secures judicial independence.[15] But this claim seems very far-fetched. Only the staunchest believer in the superior integrity of federal politicians as compared with provincial politicians could put much faith in section 96 as a guarantee of judicial independence. The behaviour of federal ministers in the 1976 judges affair and the influence of patronage in selecting federally appointed judges does not support the thesis that a higher level of virtue prevails in Ottawa than in the provincial capitals. One other element of the original Constitution which may be viewed as implicitly recognizing the principle of judicial independence is the preamble to the Constitution Act, 1867. The preamble states that the basic purpose of the Constitution is to unite the founding colonies of British North America into a federal union "with a Constitution similar in Principle to that of the United Kingdom." It might well be argued that the principle of judicial independence was and indeed is a part of the fundamental body of principle at the heart of the British constitutional system.

The language of section 99 has a long ancestry in British and in colonial constitutional history. In England the Act of Settlement in 1701 established judicial tenure during good behaviour and provided that a judge might be removed upon an address of both Houses of Parliament.[16] The purpose of this act was to ensure that there was no return to the Stuart kings' practice of removing judges for political reasons. It was not until well into the nineteenth century that the same degree of security of tenure was extended to the judges of higher courts in Britain's North American colonies. The first statutory requirement for judicial tenure during good behaviour in British North America was provided for Upper Canada's Court of King's Bench in 1834.[17] This security of tenure was established after the removal of two King's Bench judges whose off-the-bench political activities had offended the colonial authorities. For the United Province of Canada, Lord Durham's *Report* recommended that "the independence of the judges should be secured, by giving them the same tenure of office and security of income as exist in England."[18] In the 1840s the terms of the Act of Settlement were secured for the senior judges of the colony of Canada and Nova Scotia and carried forward into the Confederation Act of 1867 for the superior court judges of all the provinces.

William Lederman in his classic study of judicial independence emphasizes that while this crucial element of judicial independence was established in colonial Canada about the same time as responsible government it should not be viewed as a by-product of responsible government but as "a distinct governmental virtue of great importance worthy of cultivation in its own right."[19] Responsible government—the convention that the crown must take direction from ministers who are accountable to and have the confidence of the elected legislature—was a response to the demand for a more popular and democratic system of government. Security of judicial tenure speaks to a different value: the *liberal* concern that government, including popular democratic government, not deprive citizens of the opportunity of having their legal disputes adjudicated by judges free from the threat of being removed if their judgments displease the government. This value is an essential ingredient of *liberal* democratic government.

To the uninitiated, the words used in the Act of Settlement and in section 99 of the Canadian Constitution may seem, on their face, to provide little protection against arbitrary or political dismissals of judges. But these terms have a technical meaning which has meant that in fact they provide quite a strong basis for security of judicial tenure. Holding office "during good behaviour" means that judges do not serve at the pleasure of the government and that they should be removed from office only if it is shown that they have rendered themselves incapable of discharging the responsibilities of judicial office. In chapter 7 we will examine more closely the meaning which has been given to "good behaviour" and the conditions governing the removal of Canadian judges at all levels. The point to emphasize here is that both in Great Britain and in Canada the tenure enjoyed by judges who enjoy this constitutional protection has indeed been secure: in Great Britain, since 1701, only one judge, Sir Jonah Barrington, an Irish judge of the High Court of Admiralty, has been removed upon an address of both Houses of Parliament[20] and in Canada no superior court judge has been removed since 1867.[21]

Important as security of tenure is as one of the necessary conditions for judicial independence, it would be a mistake to equate it with judicial independence or to consider it as a guarantee of judicial impartiality. There may well be other ways, less crude than outright removal, whereby government officials or politicians endeavour to influence the judiciary. Political considerations in the selection of judges and governmental control of promotions within the judicial system are two examples. Also, although there is a well-established convention in Canada that matters which are before the courts should not be debated in Parliament or the provincial legislatures, it is not unknown for Canadian politicians to bring public pressure to bear on judges, especially judges in the lower criminal courts, in deciding such matters as bail and sentence.[22] The political scientist concerned about ascertaining the degree of judicial independence in Canada must remain sensitive to the possibility of political influences which operate at a level more subtle than the threat of removal. These influences and pressures may come as much from the private as from the public sector.

There is some doubt about which judges in Canada enjoy the formal constitutional protection of tenure afforded by section 99. The section applies to "Judges of the Superior Courts." This term clearly embraces the judges who serve on the highest trial courts and courts of appeal in the provinces and northern territories and excludes those who serve on county and district courts, as well as all of the provincially appointed judges. But what about members of the Supreme Court of Canada and the Federal Court of Canada? The federal government appears to have acted on the assumption that these courts are not "Superior Courts." While it has provided *statutory* protection for these judges' security of office—namely, office during good behaviour subject to removal by the governor general on address of the Senate and House of Commons—on exactly the same terms as section 99,[23] it has felt free to modify these statutory provisions without formal constitutional amendment. In 1927 the statutory guarantee of tenure for Supreme Court judges was modified by requiring that members of the Court retire at the age of seventy-five. This change was accomplished simply by amending the Supreme Court Act.[24] However, when compulsory retirement at seventy-five was introduced in 1960 for the superior court judges of the provinces, a formal amendment was secured to section 99 of the Constitution Act, 1867. Professor Lederman, on the other hand, has contended that both the Supreme Court and the Federal Court's predecessor, the Exchequer Court, are superior courts and their judges are therefore subject to the constitutional protections of sections 99 and 100.[25]

Although this issue is primarily of symbolic rather than operational importance, it does seem anomalous that the judges who serve on the highest court in the land should have a constitutional status less clear, and possibly inferior, to that of the judges whose decisions they review. Similarly, it makes no sense for the Federal Court which, as we shall see, now exercises a function that has traditionally been one of the most important inherent responsibilities of superior courts—reviewing the legality of the decisions of federal administrative bodies—to be treated as constitutionally inferior to provincial superior courts.[26]

The so-called lower court judges—county and district court judges and provincially appointed judges—who constitute the majority of Canadian judges, are definitely not covered by section 99. But lack of formal constitutional protection does not mean these judges lack security of tenure. In chapter 7 we will discuss in more detail the conditions under which these judges hold office and the ways in which they can be removed. Suffice it to note here that the federal and provincial statutes governing these judges' terms of office, provide that, subject to a compulsory retirement age, these judges can be removed only for cause: that is, misbehaviour or demonstrated incapacity for office. In most cases the judge can be removed only after an inquiry conducted by a superior court judge or a judicial council. Provisions such as these pertaining to judges of Ontario's Provincial Court (Criminal Division) were reviewed in the *Valente* case. The Supreme Court repudiated the contention that the conditions of independence applicable to the Provincial Court judges should be exactly the same as those set forth in sections 99 and 100 of the Constitution for federally appointed judges. "The essence of security of tenure for purposes of s. 11(d)," said Justice Le Dain, "is a tenure, whether until an age of retirement, for a fixed term, or for a specific adjudicative task, that is secure against interference by the Executive or other appointing authority in a discretionary or arbitrary manner."[27]

Although the tenure of the vast majority of Canadian judges meets the *Valente* standard, there are still a number of situations that may fail to meet the constitutional norm. These are exhaustively explored by Jules Deschênes in his *Maîtres Chez Eux.*[28] He points to the fact that in Nova Scotia and the Yukon the executive appoints, at pleasure, officials to hear small claims cases. With respect to courts exercising criminal jurisdiction, where the constitutional guarantee of section 11(d) of the Charter applies, among the more questionable arrangements are those that give the executive the power to decide whether a judge who has reached compulsory retirement age can carry on for a few extra years as a "supernumerary." This arrangement looks invidious where a judge needs post-retirement employment as a means of adding to his pension entitlement. In the *Valente* case, the Supreme Court viewed such arrangements as unconstitutional but noted that the principal objection had been removed in Ontario by an amendment to Ontario's Courts of Justice Act that makes the reappointment of judges who had reached retirement age depend on the recommendation of the chief judge and the provincial judicial councils rather than the discretion of the executive. But other cases continue to raise constitutional shortcomings in the terms of office of lower court judges. For instance, in 1985 Justice Noel Goodridge of the Trial Division of Newfoundland's Supreme Court, on the basis of section 11(d) of the Charter, struck down statutory provisions making the tenure of probationary and supernumerary Provincial Court judges depend entirely on executive discretion.[29]

A long-standing feature of the statutory provisions relating to the judiciary that may well be unconstitutional is the section of the federal Judges Act under which the salary of any federally appointed judge may be suspended by the cabinet if on the basis of an inquiry carried out by the Canadian Judicial Council the judge is found "to have become incapacitated or disabled from the due execution of his office."[30] Granted, suspension of salary is not quite the same thing as removal; still, it comes very close and may be unconstitutional at least with respect to those judges whose tenure and salary are subject to the provisions of sections 99 and 100 of the Constitution.[31] This issue has never been put to the test because the suspension of salary has never, it would appear, been carried out.[32] There is, however, evidence that on more than one occasion the threat to use this procedure led to the resignation of a judge about whom the minister of justice had received complaints and made "discreet inquiries."[33]

The Berger Affair

In 1981-82 an event occurred that raised important questions about both the conventional and formal constitutional rules relating to the independence of the judiciary, and the separation of powers. This event was the Canadian Judicial Council's inquiry and report concerning the intervention of Justice Thomas Berger, a member of the Supreme Court of British Columbia, in the constitutional debate preoccupying the country at that time. The "Berger affair" made Canadians much more aware of a new instrument of government, the judicial council, which had come into existence at both the federal and provincial levels in the 1960s and 1970s. In Part Three we shall examine the structure and functions of these councils and the role they play in administering the judicial profession. Here, we shall concentrate on the constitutional issues associated with the Canadian Judicial Council's handling of the Berger case.

The Berger affair was triggered by two letters written by Justice G.A. Addy of the Federal Court to the Canadian Judicial Council on 18 and 19 November 1981. The letters constituted a formal complaint that certain statements made by Justice Thomas Berger and reported in the press and on television constituted grounds for removing Berger from office.[34] The statements in question criticized the constitutional accord reached by Prime Minister Trudeau and nine provincial premiers on 5 November 1981 on the grounds that Quebec was denied a veto in the amending process and the entrenchment of aboriginal rights had been abandoned. An article putting forward these criticisms appeared on 18 November on the "op-ed" page of *The Toronto Globe and Mail*. In addition, Berger's remarks on aboriginal rights made in a convocation address at Guelph University and in connection with the promotion of his book *Fragile Freedoms* were reported in the media.[35] Justice Addy alleged that these controversial pronouncements threatened "incalculable harm" to "the independence of the judiciary, the administration of justice and the maintenance of the principle of separation of powers."[36] According to Addy, Berger either did not have "the faintest idea of the position and role of a judge in the British parliamentary system today," or, if he did, then "he is guilty of misconduct which . . . would tend to cause far greater harm to the administration of justice than sleeping with a prostitute or driving whilst impaired."[37] While Addy's complaint was made formally and in private, a few days later Prime Minister Trudeau complained publicly about Berger's conduct: "I just regard that as the judiciary getting mixed into politics. . . . I hope the judges will do something about it."[38]

Under the 1971 legislation establishing the Canadian Judicial Council, the council "may investigate any complaint or allegation made in respect of a judge of a superior, district or county court."[39] The council is chaired by the chief justice of the Supreme Court of Canada and consists of the chief justice and associate chief justices of the courts staffed by federally appointed judges. The council's role in the area of discipline is to deal with allegations of serious misconduct on the part of federally appointed judges. It has no power to discipline judges itself. But on the basis of a report from the council, the minister of justice may recommend to cabinet suspension of a judge's salary, the removal of a county or district court judge, or the initiation of a joint parliamentary address to remove a superior court judge. The council receives numerous complaints, many of which emanate from the losing party in court cases. Therefore the complaints have to be screened to select those that appear serious enough to warrant a full investigation. In the Berger case, much to the chagrin not only of Berger but of the chief justice of his own court and several other members of the Judicial Council, on 8 March 1982 a majority of the council accepted a recommendation of its executive committee that Justice Addy's complaint be formally investigated. The inquiry was to be carried out by a committee of investigation consisting of three council members.

The committee of investigation found that Justice Berger's conduct, in its opinion, did constitute grounds for removing him from office. However, the committee did not recommend removal. It felt that Justice Berger and other judges may have misunderstood the constraints on judicial conduct and that it was not fair to set standards *ex post facto*. The full council, however, did not accept the committee's conclusion about the gravity of Berger's conduct. In its report to the minister of justice on 31 May 1982 the council stated that "while the Judicial Council is of the opinion that Mr. Justice Berger's criticisms were indiscreet, they constitute no basis for a recommendation that he be removed from office."

The council went on to set out a basic guideline concerning off-the-bench speeches and writing by judges: "The Judicial Council is of the opinion that members of the Judiciary should avoid taking part in controversial political discussions except only in respect of matters that directly affect the operation of the courts."[40]

What are we to make of this episode so far as the constitutional principle of judicial independence is concerned? First, we must note that there was both a charge and a counter-charge: while Berger's accusers allege that his conduct endangered the independence of the judiciary, he and his defenders claim that to concede to a judicial council the power to investigate and censure judges for conduct that does not constitute grounds for removing them from office "would truly impair the independence of the judiciary."[41] The claim that a judge's intervention in political debate jeopardizes the collective or institutional independence of the judiciary was counterposed by the claim that the "independence of individual judges" is threatened by the "general superintendence . . . over the conduct of judges" asserted by a council of judges.[42]

There may well be merit in both positions. Justice Berger's conduct, especially agreeing to have his remarks on the Quebec veto published in a leading national newspaper at the very time when this was the hottest political issue in the country, was indiscreet. Nevertheless, the decision to apply the formal investigative machinery of the Judicial Council to him, particularly in circumstances when it may appear that such a procedure was adopted under pressure from the prime minister, also showed questionable political judgment.[43]

It may be impossible to draw a precise line, but there are reasons for insisting on some limits to the off-the-bench political activities of judges in order to maintain two essential characteristics of the judicial office: impartiality and independence. In chapter 1 we acknowledged that total impartiality on the part of judges (especially with regard to the value judgments embedded in adjudication) is impossible. Further, in the Canadian system, partisanship in the appointing of judges seriously detracts from the appearance of partiality. But it is no answer to contend that public confidence in the impartiality of the judiciary does not matter and that judges should feel as free as ordinary citizens to enter the political fray. It is incumbent on judges, however appointed and however closely identified they may have been before their appointment with a particular political party or cause, to change their "lifestyle." Benjamin Cardozo, a great judicial realist who fully acknowledged the inescapable subjective element in judging, still advocated that those appointed to judicial office should do their best to cultivate a "judicial temperament" which, as he put it, "will help in some degree to emancipate [the judge] from the suggestive power of individual dislike and prepossession . . . to broaden the group to which his subconscious loyalties are due."[44] If judges openly participate in partisan politics, there is a danger that they will come to be regarded by a politically active citizenry not as third parties, but as aligned with one of the parties appearing before them. If adjudication is sustained in these circumstances, it will be primarily through force and not on the basis of consent.

The second reason for some limit to the off-the-bench political activity of judges is to preserve their independence from political attack. Judges on the bench, as this book argues throughout, exercise a great deal of political power in our system of government. Their power to check the other branches of government—the so-called political branches—when they exceed their legal and constitutional boundaries is an important element in our system of government. But it is precisely to preserve an independent source of political power within the judicial process that judges should be very careful about stepping outside that process and endeavouring to exercise power and off-the-bench influence in the politicians' arena. Politicians will fight back and attack judges who attack them on their turf. That is the nature of combat among elected politicians in a democracy. Those who criticize (or, for that matter, support) politicians in the channels of communication where public opinion is influenced, where power is won or lost, are fair game. A judiciary that engages in this kind of political combat is likely to jeopardize the advantages of being free from political inter- ference in its work—especially its work in applying constitutional limits on government. These considerations support the Judicial Council's finding that Justice Berger's political attack on Trudeau and the nine premiers was indiscreet.

The council's disapproval of judicial participation "in controversial political discussions" does acknowledge one exception: "matters that directly affect the operation of the courts." It may be necessary when the integrity of the admin- istration of justice is under attack in the political arena for judges, especially chief justices and judicial councils, to speak out and endeavour to influence public opinion.[45] Even here, however, judges might be more successful through quiet diplomacy than rabble-rousing public statements. The council's guideline is confined to participation in "controversial political discussion." This seems to leave considerable room for off-the-bench speaking and writing by judges on legal and constitutional issues, providing it is done in a reasonably low-key scholarly or professional setting. J.O. Wilson's *A Book for Judges* (written at the request of the Canadian Judicial Council) gives the following advice to newly appointed judges:

> You will be asked to make speeches to legal and other organizations and you may properly accept such invitations and comment fairly freely on the law as it is, less freely on the law as you think it ought to be. Any criticism, direct or implied, of current legislation or of delivered judgments, is generally to be avoided in state- ments made off the bench, lest your hearers infer criticism of a legislature, federal or provincial, or of a court and hence, perhaps political bias, or disrespect for other courts.[46]

It remains to be seen whether a clearer, more comprehensive set of guidelines on this aspect of judicial conduct can be drawn up. This author remains somewhat sceptical about the wisdom of endeavouring to substitute a codified set of rules for the good judgment of the judiciary.

Even though the Canadian Judicial Council's verdict on the impropriety of Justice Berger's behaviour might be supported, the procedure used by the council could be faulted as unduly heavy-handed. As the chief justice of Berger's court, Allan McEachern, pointed out, there are informal ways of dealing with indis- cretions such as Berger's. McEachern reports that other informal checks had "already played their role in this case as Berger, J. disengaged himself from the constitutional debate as soon as I spoke to him."[47] Subjecting Berger's behaviour to a formal inquiry in those circumstances was unnecessary and oppressive. The investigation was damaging to the judge's prestige and may well have had something to do with his decision a year later to retire from the bench.

Chief Justice McEachern also questioned whether the Judicial Council had exceeded its powers in conducting an inquiry into behaviour which, in his view, could not on its face constitute grounds for removal and further whether the "discipline" of judges by the Judicial Council was compatible with the constitutional independence of the judiciary. John Robinette, a leading member of the Canadian bar, wrote a memorandum for the chairman of the investigation committee on these questions.[48] On the first issue, Robinette concluded that extrajudicial conduct might well constitute valid grounds for recommending removal of a judge and that there did not need to be a prima facie case for removal before launching an inquiry. So in a strictly legal sense the council would appear not to have exceeded its powers in conducting an investigation.

Robinette's memorandum does not deal directly with the constitutional question. Interestingly, he does state that "There is nothing in section 41 which empowers the Canadian Judicial Council to recommend to the Minister of Justice any disciplinary act other than removal from office. It follows, in my opinion, that the Council has no power to recommend a formal reprimand of the Judge to the Minister of Justice."[49] So, although the council cannot recommend a reprimand, can it administer one itself? On this Robinette says only that in its report to the minister on the results of an inquiry the council can express its opinion on the conduct of the judge. Technically, negative comments such as were contained in the report of the investigation committee and the resolution of the full council which accompanied it may not constitute a "reprimand." But it is doubtful whether either the public or Justice Berger would see these comments as anything other than a public reprimand, especially when they are publicly released by the minister of justice.

The question of whether it is constitutional for the Canadian Judicial Council to "discipline" judges has not been clearly answered. Even though the constitutional waters here remain somewhat murky, at least we can conclude that overly energetic use of a judicial council's investigatory powers, especially when quieter methods of protecting judicial standards are available, does nothing to enhance the principle of judicial independence.

The Separation of Powers

The separation of powers as a principle of government requires that the main functions of government—namely, the executive, legislative, and judicial functions—be assigned to different branches and that these branches be staffed by totally separate groups of state officials. As far as executive-legislative relations are concerned, there is little room for the application of this principle in Canada with a parliamentary-cabinet system of government in which the executive is headed by the leaders of the strongest party in the legislature. However, the principle applies much more to the judiciary and its relationship with the other branches of government. Clearly, the separation of powers is a corollary of judicial independence: the judiciary would not be independent if the primary judicial and executive functions were carried out by the same officials. Short of this extreme, there may still be a considerable overlap of executive, legislative, and judicial functions.

In Canada we have in practice moved a long way toward separation of judicial personnel from the executive and legislative institutions. In colonial Canada it was not until the 1840s and 1850s that judges ceased being members of the executive and legislature.[50] As late as the 1850s, the lieutenant-governor of Nova Scotia was deciding cases as a chancery judge.[51] By the time of Confederation the formal separation of the judges of the higher courts from the executive and legislative branches was pretty well complete. However, as has been pointed out, at the lower court level, police officers and municipal councillors in some jurisdictions were empowered to adjudicate criminal cases for some time after Confederation. It is only with the judicialization of the lower criminal courts which has occurred across Canada since World War Two that this overlap of executive and judicial authorities has disappeared from the Canadian scene. Today most Canadians would vigorously object to the mixture of executive and judicial powers that existed in the past. This change in political attitudes indicates the extent to which Canadians have increasingly come to see the judiciary as a check not only on the executive but, especially with the Charter of Rights, on the legislature as well. It is utterly inappropriate for those whose function it is to enforce legal and constitutional limits on the other branches to be part of those branches.

While the separation of judges from the executive and legislature is now virtually complete,[52] there is not by any means a complete separation of functions. In the modern Canadian state a great deal of the adjudicative function—that is, deciding disputes about legal rights—is carried out by administrative tribunals which are not formally part of the judiciary. Indeed, as tribunals of first instance these federal and provincial administrative bodies have a larger case load than the regular courts. On the other side, as our analysis in chapter 1 pointed out, courts themselves do a good deal of law-making and some judges carry out important administrative responsibilities. Outside the judicial process itself, some judges participate in the legislative and executive arenas. Occasionally judges give informal advice on draft bills (and not only on bills relating to judicial institutions).[53] As we have also noted, many Canadian judges accede to requests by the federal and provincial governments to serve as royal commissioners. In this capacity they give policy advice to government. Again, as the Canadian judiciary's role in providing an independent check on the other branches increases—as it surely will with the Charter of Rights—these off-the-bench collaborative activities may well decline.

Separate as the judicial branch has become in the practice of Canadian government, there is still little recognition of this in the formal Constitution, which does not explicitly establish the judiciary as a separate branch of government. Nor has constitutional interpretation set any firm boundaries on the responsibilities that can be assigned to the judiciary. Here the Canadian Constitution differs from both the American and Australian Constitutions.

The American Constitution stipulates that the judicial power of the United States shall extend to certain "cases and controversies," while the Australian constitution gives that country's High Court jurisdiction in respect of certain "matters." On the basis of these provisions, the American and Australian courts have ruled that the constitutionally entrenched judicial power does not extend to giving advisory opinions on questions submitted to the courts by government. The judicial power is to be invoked only for settling legal disputes which arise in the normal course of litigation: the executive cannot use the judiciary as its legal advisor. Quite the opposite situation pertains in Canada. There is no language in Canada's Constitution confining the judicial power to the settlement of "cases and controversies" or to certain "matters." In 1875 a clause was inserted in the Supreme Court Act empowering the federal government to refer questions to the Supreme Court "on any matter whatsoever." Since then all the provinces have followed suit and have enacted legislation providing for references to the highest court in the province.[54] There is a right of appeal to the Supreme Court of Canada in these provincial references. For the most part the questions referred to the courts by federal and provincial governments concern constitutional issues. Many of the most important judicial decisions on the constitution have been rendered in response to reference questions.

The constitutional validity of reference questions was considered by the courts early in the century. The provinces were provoked into challenging the reference procedure when the federal government broke off negotiations with the provinces and referred to the Supreme Court a series of questions concerning jurisdiction over the insurance industry. The Supreme Court found the reference procedure constitutional, although one member of the Court, Justice Idington, wrote a remarkable dissenting opinion.[55] Idington contended that allowing the executive to obtain advisory opinions from the courts was incompatible with the principle of the separation of powers, a principle which, in his view, was incorporated in Canada's Constitution through, among other things, the phrase "a Constitution similar in Principle to that of the United Kingdom" in the preamble to the Constitution Act, 1867. But Idington's position was repudiated not only by all his colleagues on the Supreme Court, but also, on appeal, by the Judicial Committee of the Privy Council. It is interesting to note that in upholding the reference procedure, the Judicial Committee put forward the rather far-fetched notion that the answers judges give in reference cases should leave them free to decide similar issues when they arise subsequently in ordinary cases, because the answers to reference questions do not create binding legal precedents. As advisory opinions the answers "will have no more effect than the opinions of the law officers."[56] This has turned out to be a legal fiction: courts and governments have continued to accord as much weight to judicial decisions rendered in reference cases as to decisions resulting from ordinary cases.[57]

The reference case procedure gives the executive branch of government a privileged access to the judicial process. With broadened rules of standing for those who wish to litigate constitutional issues[58] and a constitution which puts the rights of citizens at least on the same level as the powers of government, the need for such a procedure and its legitimacy should be increasingly questioned. Although reference cases now constitute a much smaller proportion of constitutional cases than earlier in Canadian history, provincial and federal governments still resort to them and not only to settle division of powers issues. The Trudeau government's decision to refer questions concerning language rights in Manitoba to the Supreme Court shows how the reference procedure can be used to bring broad questions concerning constitutional rights before the courts and, further, by doing so, to influence the Liberal party's leadership contest.[59] Judges may decline to answer questions that are too vague or hypothetical.[60] However, the Supreme Court's willingness to answer questions concerning constitutional convention—questions which it acknowledged were not legal in nature—will make it difficult for Canadian courts in the future to decline to answer reference questions because they are too political.[61]

If Canadian constitutional law puts no limit on the functions that can be assigned to the courts, what about the other side of the separation of powers coin—the power to take judicial functions away from the courts? Here, as has already been explained in chapter 3, sections 96, 99, and 100 of the Constitution Act 1867 restrict the capacity of provincial legislatures to assign judicial functions to non-judicial bodies. Peter Hogg has referred to this constitutional restriction as the "little separation of powers doctrine."[62] Recently, as we have seen, a series of Supreme Court decisions has cut down provincial legislation on the grounds that functions of section 96 courts were being unconstitutionally assigned to lower courts or provincial administrative tribunals.

As long as the primary rationale for this "little separation of powers doctrine" has been maintenance of the jurisdiction of federally appointed section 96 judges, it makes sense for the doctrine to apply only to the provinces. However, once the rationale extends to a concern for maintaining the jurisdiction of those judges whose independence is constitutionally guaranteed, it is hard to see why this doctrine should not limit the federal Parliament as well as provincial legislatures. What, it might be asked, is the point of constitutionally entrenching tenure for superior court judges if Parliament is free to strip power away from these judges and assign it to adjudicators who lack this protection? This seems to be part of the Supreme Court's rationale in the *McEvoy* case for denying Parliament the power to unify all criminal jurisdiction in the lower provincial courts. Thus the Supreme Court appears to be coming around to the position long held by Professor Lederman that the constitutional entrenchment of superior court jurisdiction restricts Ottawa as much as the provinces. Among other things this may mean, given the *Crevier* case, that the Court will reverse itself and overturn federal legislation that purports to totally exclude judicial review even on jurisdictional grounds of federal administrative tribunals.[63]

The Entrenchment of Judicial Review

One kind of jurisdiction traditionally exercised by Canadian courts that may well be entrenched is judicial review of the constitutionality of government activity. The power of the courts to veto legislation or executive activities which in the judiciary's view violate the law of the Constitution is the most dramatic political role played by Canadian courts. Even though this power is not expressly established in the Canadian Constitution, it has been exercised by the judiciary since the country's earliest days.[64]

In contrast to the United States, there was no landmark decision early in Canadian history similar to Chief Justice Marshall's in *Marbury* v. *Madison*[65] justifying the power of the judiciary to overrule legislation that conflicts with the constitution. At first the rationale for judicial review in Canada was based more on imperialism than on constitutionalism. Canada's Constitution took the form of an act of Parliament of the United Kingdom. Another imperial act, the Colonial Laws Validity Act, stipulated that where colonial legislation conflicted with imperial legislation, the latter must prevail. But when Canada ceased to be a colony, legally subordinate to Great Britain—a development which crystallized in law with the passage of the Statute of Westminster in 1931—imperialism was no longer an appropriate rationale for judicial review. By then, at least at the level of political thought, federalism (the role of the judiciary as umpire of the federal system) had become the main foundation for judicial review. As the Canadian constitutional system since then has come to place as much emphasis on the rights of citizens as on the powers of government, federalism has given way to constitutionalism as the underlying rationale of judicial review. This process culminated in 1982 with the addition to the Canadian Constitution of a Charter of Rights and Freedoms and a clause which for the first time explicitly asserts the legal supremacy of the Constitution. That clause, section 52(1) of the Constitution Act, 1982, states that:

> The Constitution of Canada is the supreme law of Canada, and any law that is inconsistent with the provisions of the Constitution is, to the extent of the inconsistency of no force or effect.

This new supremacy clause, while clearly establishing the legal supremacy of the Constitution, does not state that the judiciary is the authority that must decide in disputed cases whether or not a law is inconsistent with the Constitution. Nevertheless, by now the judiciary's power to make these determinations and overrule legislation that conflicts with the Constitution is well established.

Even before 1982, on the few occasions when governments attempted to prevent the courts from reviewing the constitutional validity of legislation, the courts ruled that they could not do so. In 1935 Ontario Premier Mitchell Hepburn was determined to cancel contracts between Ontario Hydro and some Quebec power companies committing Ontario to purchase power in quantities and at prices which, in the middle of the Great Depression, the Hepburn government viewed as quite out of keeping with Ontario's needs. Accordingly, legislation was passed cancelling the contracts. There was some doubt, however, as to whether under the Constitution a province could legislate in relation to contracts creating rights in another province. To avoid any possibility of this issue being raised in the courts, the legislation included a section purporting to bar any suit against Ontario Hydro for failing to meet its obligations under the old contracts. Other legislation required the consent of the provincial attorney general for any suit against the Hydro Commission. This permission was clearly not forthcoming when the Quebec power companies attempted to bring an action against Ontario Hydro in the Ontario courts challenging the constitutional validity of the legislation cancelling the contracts. But this effort to bar judicial review failed. The Ontario Court of Appeal, in a decision which split the court three to two, ruled, in the words of Justice Masten,

> . . . that the Legislature cannot destroy, usurp, or derogate from substantive rights over which it has by the Canadian Constitution no jurisdiction and then protect its action in that regard by enacting that no action can be brought in the Courts of the Province to inquire into the validity of its legislation, thus indirectly destroying the division of powers set forth in the B.N.A. Act. In other words it cannot by such indirect means destroy the Constitution under which it was created and now exists.[66]

In 1962 the Supreme Court of Canada rejected a claim of the British Columbia government based on long-established principles of crown prerogative that would have prevented the court from hearing a constitutional challenge to the province's takeover of B.C. Electric, a provincial company whose shares were wholly owned by a federally incorporated company.[67] The Court's opinion, written by Chief Justice Kerwin, was succinct and did not explore the full constitutional implications of the issues at stake. Still, the decision did establish that crown immunity cannot be used as a barrier to judicial review of the constitutional validity of legislation. As Barry Strayer sums it up, "In the struggle between judicial review and the prerogative, judicial review has emerged supreme."[68] In *Operation Dismantle*, one of the Supreme Court's early Charter decisions, the Court repudiated any notion that certain acts of the executive in the fields of foreign and defence policy are in principle beyond judicial review. Cabinet decisions, Chief Justice Dickson pointed out, fall under section 32 of the Charter "and are therefore reviewable in the courts and subject to judicial scrutiny for compatability with the Constitution."[69]

Thus it would seem fair to conclude that as a matter of law the power of the judiciary to review the constitutional validity of legislation and acts of the executive is entrenched in the Canadian Constitution. The federal Parliament under section 101 and the provincial legislatures under section 92(14) have power over the jurisdiction of courts. But this power does not enable either level of legislature to pass legislation which is immune from constitutional review in the courts.[70] Although this very significant modification of legislative supremacy has for some time been an established precept of Canadian law, it may still not be clearly understood at the level of popular opinion. For many Canadians the principle of "parliamentary sovereignty" will likely remain part of their sense of national identity for some time, despite what judges and professors say.

Further Constitutional Entrenchment of Judicial Power

The treatment of the judicial power in the Canadian Constitution has attracted increasing criticism. Nowhere has this dissatisfaction been more eloquently or vigorously expressed than in Jules Deschênes' *Maîtres Chez Eux*, a study of court administration in Canada sponsored by organizations representing federally and provincially appointed judges. Deschênes recommended that "the Canadian Constitution should proclaim, on the federal and provincial levels, the principle of the individual and collective independence of the judicial power."[71] Similar proposals were included in the drafts of comprehensive new constitutions produced by the constitutional ferment of the late 1970s.[72] The constitutional settlement of 1982 did not include adoption of a general guarantee of the principle of judicial independence. As we have seen, section 11(d) of the Charter of Rights, guaranteeing the right to a fair trial in criminal proceedings, included the words "by an independent and impartial tribunal." It is unlikely that this will satisfy those who want the independence of the courts enshrined as a fundamental principle of the Canadian Constitution.

Interest in enshrining the general principle of judicial independence in the Constitution derives much of its support from the impulse to replace the messy collection of constitutional documents and unwritten conventions that constitute Canada's constitutional system with a comprehensive constitutional code incorporating all of the basic principles and institutions by which the country is governed. Some are struck by the nation-building advantages of such a document. Canada, it is thought, might be stronger if its citizens could hold in their hands, and school teachers could pin on the wall, a single document setting out the entire Constitution of the country. Whatever the symbolic advantages of enshrining all the principles of government and institutional relationships in the formal Constitution, it must be borne in mind that constitutional entrenchment entails judicial review of legislation or acts of government that are alleged to transgress what is constitutionally guaranteed. This is the practical—and rather unpredictable—side of constitutional entrenchment.

Why, it might be asked, should Canadians be concerned about judicial enforcement of a guarantee of judicial independence? If the politicians interfere with the courts, what's wrong with the judiciary's invoking a constitutional guarantee to overrule such actions? Putting the question this way ignores the most likely ways in which judicial enforcement of judicial independence is likely to arise. To begin with, the judiciary will have to determine which adjudicative functions must be performed by judges whose independence is constitutionally guaranteed. After all, if there is no limit on legislatures in assigning judicial functions to administrative tribunals whose members' independence is not constitutionally entrenched, what would be the point in a constitutional guarantee of judicial independence? Canada has already had a taste of judicial decisions based on this rationale in cases interpreting section 96. These cases have placed questionable and rather unpredictable restrictions on the flexibility of provincial governments in developing appropriate arrangements for administering provincial laws. A broad constitutional guarantee of judicial independence would widen and strengthen the role of judges in this field of public policy.

A guarantee of judicial independence would also call upon Canadian judges to determine the essential institutional requirements of judicial independence. In the *Valente* case, judges of Ontario's Provincial Court (Criminal Division) tried to obtain reforms of their court by intervening on the side of an accused person who was claiming that his case could not constitutionally be heard in a Provincial Court because that tribunal lacked the "independence and impartiality" required under section 11(d) of the Charter. The Provincial Court judges' senior judicial colleagues on the Ontario Court of Appeal and the Supreme Court of Canada rejected their claim and upheld the Provincial Criminal Court as having independence and impartiality. The case reveals the range of policy questions which may be brought before the courts under even a "mini-guarantee" of judicial independence. The Deschênes report, raises many more questions about the control which an independent judiciary should exercise over various phases of case flow management, over the hiring and firing of court support staff, and over court budgets. The controversy over the Canadian Judicial Council's reprimand of Justice Berger points to yet another problematic dimension of judicial independence: the independence of the individual judge from the collective sanctioning of judicial councils or from the directives of individual chief justices or chief judges.

These questions support the basic thesis about judicial independence advanced in chapter 1: in the real world there is no such thing as absolute independence. In all states, including liberal democratic states that place a high value on the ideal of judicial independence, the institutions of government and politics (of which the judiciary is a part) form an interdependent system. In a liberal democracy, direct interference by the executive in judicial decision-making—telling the judges how to decide their cases and punishing them if they disobey such directives— can readily be identified, at one end of the spectrum, as an unacceptable limitation on judicial independence. At the other end of the spectrum, judicial independence need not be taken so far as to have judges collect the revenues required for the maintenance of their institutions or command the coercive forces needed to execute their judgments. The tough questions about judicial independence lie between these extremes. The belated application of modern management techniques to court administration and the establishment of a brand new instrument of government, the judicial council, pose novel and challenging questions in this middle area. Canadian judges themselves, all of whom surely believe in the general principle of judicial independence, are clearly divided on many of these questions.[73]

Some judges, in litigation such as the *Valente* case, may provide authoritative rulings on some of these questions—at least as they relate to judges who preside in courts of criminal jurisdiction. But it is doubtful whether judicial interpretation of a constitutional guarantee is the best way of resolving the complex and contentious policy issues that exist in this field. Over more than a century the practice of judicial independence has been steadily evolving in the Canadian system of government. The most recent developments have been in connection with the courts presided over by provincially appointed judges. In recent years a virtual "judicialization" of these so-called lower courts has taken place. This process is still going on, at different paces, in the provinces and territories. Progress has been made through the interaction of responsible ministers, government officials, judges, and members of the legal profession. It is questionable how much this process benefits from a constitutional decision requiring the immediate reform of existing arrangements across the country, or alternatively, placing the good housekeeping constitutional seal of approval on the status quo.

There is a further, somewhat indelicate, thought that must be added to these reservations about a constitutional guarantee of judicial independence. In interpreting such a guarantee, judges are policing the boundaries of their own power. In doing so, their own institutional interests are involved in a manner that does not arise when they are umpiring constitutional disputes between the two levels of government or between the citizen and government. Certainly judges should continue to play a significant role in developing law and policy with respect to judicial institutions. But it may be best for their influence to flow through informal discussions and negotiations rather than through authoritative rulings in constitutional cases. Canadians might well be cautious about making changes in the Constitution which will give judges a more powerful role in defining their own power and shift power away from those who are politically accountable and represent other interests in society.

It is to be hoped that this caution does not come too late. Although the Supreme Court in *Valente* was quite restrained in interpreting the scope of the guarantee of judicial independence in section 11(d) of the Charter, the Court also noted the declining confidence in constitutional tradition as a means of protecting judicial independence. In the words of Mr. Justice Le Dain, "while tradition reinforced by public opinion may operate as a restraint upon the exercise of power in a manner that interferes with judicial independence, it cannot supply essential conditions of independence for which specific provision of law is necessary."[74]

Recent events in Quebec indicate how far Canadian judges may be prepared to go in using legal means to defend what they regard as essential to their institutional autonomy. In the spring of 1986 a group of Provincial Court judges and the chief justice of the Superior Court initiated court actions challenging budgetary cutbacks in court support staff decided upon by the attorney general of Quebec.[75] Judges of the Superior Court who dealt with the judges' request for a temporary injunction to stop the cutbacks until the main issue could be heard in the fall brushed aside the attorney general's initial argument that they might have a conflict of interest in determining this matter.[76] The Canadian public may come to have a different perspective on this issue if the judiciary are too generous to themselves in interpreting the metes and bounds of their own institutional power.

Summary and Conclusion to Part Two

Our examination of the constitutional framework has focused on two key relationships between the judiciary and other parts of the Canadian state. In chapter 3 we looked at how the Canadian judicial system is related to Canada's federal system, which divides governmental power between two levels of government. In this chapter the discussion shifted to the relationship of the judiciary to the legislature and executive.

With regard to federalism, it was pointed out that in no federation is judicial power divided in a manner exactly parallel to the division of legislative jurisdiction. In all federations there is a practical inclination to integrate jurisdiction over national and local matters within a single system. But the potential for judicial integration is much greater under the Canadian constitution than in virtually any other federal state. The key to that integration is section 96 of the Constitution Act, 1867, under which the federal government appoints the judges of the intermediate and highest courts of the provinces.

This potential for integration is threatened today as section 96 courts are being outflanked, by purely provincial courts whose judges are appointed by provincial governments, and by the recent growth of purely federal courts. The judicial system has been caught up in the power struggle between federal and provincial politicians. The disadvantages of section 96 and its incompatibility with pure federalism have become more manifest than its advantages. This has culminated in a movement among political elites to dismantle section 96. Consumers of justice should be wary of this tendency of the federal-provincial power struggle to push Canada toward the inconveniences of a more American-style dual court system.

With regard to the judiciary's relationship with the executive and legislature, the central precepts are the independence of the judiciary and the separation of powers. These norms, at least until recently, have been dealt with primarily by the informal constitution: that is, by custom, convention, and ordinary statutes. The formal Constitution does not establish the judiciary as a separate branch of government. One element of judicial independence, the security of tenure of superior court judges, is guaranteed in the Constitution, and the new Charter of Rights refers to the independence and impartiality of the criminal courts.

The judges affair of 1976 and the Berger affair in 1981-82 showed how two different facets of judicial independence were dealt with in the arena of political action. In the 1976 incident it was necessary to issue explicit guidelines to remind ministers of the most fundamental aspect of judicial independence—the principle of non-interference in the adjudicative work of judges. The Berger affair brought to light more problematic dimensions of judicial independence concerning the independence of the individual judge from the collective imposition of sanctions by senior judges through judicial councils, and the difficulty of reconciling judicial independence from political interference with judicial intervention in major political debates.

Although the judiciary is not constitutionally established as a separate branch of government, it has become increasingly separate in practice. The insistence on a stricter separation of powers has been part and parcel of the liberalization of Canada's political culture. Increasingly, the courts are perceived as a check on the other branches of government. Support for the Charter of Rights owes much to that trend. However, a legacy survives from those earlier times when there was much less concern in Canada with the separation of powers: for example, the use of judges as royal commissioners and the reference case procedure whereby the executive branch obtains "advisory opinions" from the judiciary.

One crucial ingredient of judicial power that has become constitutionally entrenched is the power of the judiciary to veto laws or executive acts which violate the Constitution. Judicial decisions and the constitutional supremacy clause in the Constitution Act, 1982 give this power of judicial review a firm basis in Canadian constitutional law.

Should the judicial power be more fully entrenched in the Constitution? Should judicial independence and the separation of powers be more explicitly provided for in the formal constitutional text? There is a considerable agitation to rely less on custom and convention and to establish a stronger charter of judicial power in the formal Constitution. We have argued that, however appealing such a move might be from a symbolic point of view, it entails a questionable increase in the power of judges to decide a wide range of issues concerning the boundaries of their own power.

Notes to Chapter 4

1. S.A. de Smith, *Constitutional and Administrative Law*, 2nd ed. (Harmsworth: Penguin Books, 1973), pp. 365-66, n. 35.
2. Peter W. Hogg, *Constitutional Law of Canada*, 2nd ed. (Toronto: Carswell, 1985), p. 120.
3. Shimon Shetreet, *Judges on Trial* (Amsterdam: North Holland Publishing Company, 1976), p. 17.
4. *Universal Declaration on the Independence of Justice*, (Montreal: World Conference on the Independence of Justice, 1983), s. 2.02.
5. *The Queen* v. *Beauregard* [1986] 2 SCR 56.
6. Jules Deschênes, *Maîtres Chez Eux* (Ottawa: Canadian Judicial Council, 1981), p. 124.
7. *R.* v. *Valente* (No. 2) (1983) 2 CCC (3d) 417.
8. *Valente* v. *R.* [1985] 2 SCR 673, at 712.

9. *Report of the Honourable Mr. Justice P.D. Seaton, Commissioner*, Victoria, BC, 23 Oct. 1979.
10. For an account of this episode, see John Saywell, ed., *Canadian Annual Review of Politics and Public Affairs, 1976* (Toronto: University of Toronto Press, 1978), pp. 13-18.
11 House of Commons, *Debates*, 12 Mar. 1976, p. 11771.
12. R.B. Byers and John Saywell, eds., *Candian Annual Review of Politics and Public Affairs, 1978* (Toronto: University of Toronto Press, 1978), p. 30.
13. Ibid., p. 132.
14. "Memorandum to Executive Council: The Communication between Members of the Executive Council and the Judiciary and Key Officials in the Judicial System," 8 Nov. 1978.
15. See, for example, Mark MacGuigan, minister of justice, *The Constitution of Canada: A Suggested Amendment Relating to Provincial Tribunals* (Ottawa, 1983), p. 1
16. Shetreet, *Judges on Trial*, pp. 10-11. Note that in England it is not clear whether judges can be removed only by means of a joint address by both Houses of Parliament or by some other procedure—for instance, by *scire facias* (removal of the grant of office before a court of law). The generally accepted view is that the joint address is exclusive in practice. See ibid., ch. 4.
17. See W.R. Lederman, "The Independence of the Judiciary," *Canadian Bar Review* (1956), pp. 1148-58.
18. Lord Durham, *A Report on Canada* (London: Methuen, 1922), p. 207.
19. Ledermen, "Independence of The Judiciary," p. 1158.
20. Shetreet, *Judges on Trial*, pp. 143-44, n. 88.
21. There have been four "attempts" at removal and some judges have resigned when faced with the prospect of going through the removal procedure. For further discussion, see ch. 7 below.
22. See, for example, evidence concerning the influence of Ontario's Department of the Attorney General on magistrates in John Hogarth, *Sentencing as a Human Process* (Toronto: University of Toronto Press, 1971), pp. 193-96.
23. See the Supreme Court Act, Revised Statutes of Canada, S-19, s. 9 and The Federal Court Act, RSC 1970, c. 10, s. 8.
24. 1926-27 (Can.), c. 38, s. 2.
25. Lederman, "Independence of the Judiciary," pp. 1175-76.
26. One practical implication of this inferior treatment is that Federal Court judges must retire at age seventy rather than seventy-five.
27. *Valente* v. *R.*, p. 698.
28. See pp. 101-24.
29. *The National*, Dec. 1985, p. 6.
30. The Judges Act, Revised Statutes of Canada, J-1, s. 34(3).
31. This is the view of Lederman, "Independence of the Judiciary," p. 1162.
32. In 1960 Lester Pearson, John Diefenbaker, and Davie Fulton (who was then minister of justice) reported that they knew of no occasion when this provision had been used. House of Commons, *Debates*, 14 June 1960, p. 4891.
33. R. MacGregor Dawson, *The Government of Canada*, 4th ed. (Toronto: University of Toronto Press, 1963), p. 439.
34. The letters are appendices B and D to the Report of the Investigation Committee

of the Canadian Judicial Council to the Hon. Jean Chrétien, minister of justice, *Re: Mr. Justice Thomas Berger*, 31 May 1982.

35. Ibid., appendices C, E, J.
36. Letter of 18 Nov. 1981.
37. Letter of 19 Nov. 1981.
38. Report of the Investigation Committee, appendix I.
39. 19-20 Elizabeth II, c. 55, s. 32(2).
40. This is in the form of a resolution of the Canadian Judicial Council accompanying the Investigation Committee's Report to the minister of justice.
41. Justice Berger's Memorandum to Members of the Supreme Court of British Columbia, 15 Mar. 1982, Report of the Investigation Committee, appendix L.
42. Letter from Chief Justice Allan McEachern, Supreme Court of British Columbia to Mr. Justice B.J. MacKinnon, associate chief justice of Ontario, and chairman of the Investigation Committee. Ibid., appendix M.
43. Chief Justice Laskin has pointed out that the complaint about Berger had become part of the Canadian Judicial Council's agenda several days before the prime minister's public statements on the issue ("Address to the Canadian Bar Association Annual Meeting," Toronto, 2 Sept. 1982, pp. 11-12). Nevertheless, the controversial decision of the council's executive committee to conduct a full investigation came after Trudeau's statements.
44. Benjamin N. Cardozo, *The Nature of the Judicial Process* (New Haven: Yale University Press, 1921), p. 176.
45. For a discussion of the chief justice as a defender of judicial independence, see Canadian Institute for the Administration of Justice, *A Compendium of Information on the Status and Role of the Chief Justice in Canada* (Montreal, 1987, pp. 245-266.
46. J.O. Wilson, *A Book for Judges* (Ottawa: Canadian Judicial Council, 1980), p. 11. Professor Leon Dion in "The Judge, Modern Citizen: More Democracy for Judges" (Address to the Canadian Association of Provincial Court Judges, 26 Sept. 1980) does not appear to go much further than Wilson. He thinks judges should not criticize laws, regulations, or the Constitution, but they should be "free to express their views on constitutional reform" (pp. 38-39).
47. Report of the Investigation Committee, appendix M, p. 12.
48. Ibid., appendix P.
49. Ibid., pp. 2-3.
50. See Lederman, "Independence of the Judiciary," for a discussion of these developments.
51. J. Murray Beck, *The Government of Nova Scotia* (Toronto: University of Toronto Press, 1957), p. 70.
52. Perhaps the most significant residue of judicial participation in the executive is the provision in the royal letters patent that designates the chief justice of the Supreme Court of Canada as administrator in the event of the death, incapacity, removal, or absence from Canada for less than a month, of the governor general. If both the governor and the chief justice are unavailable, other judges of the Supreme Court act as deputy governor general. See J.R. Mallory, *The Structure of Canadian Government* (Toronto: Macmillan of Canada, 1971), p. 58.
53. Whether or not judges should do this is a matter of debate within the Canadian judiciary. For a summary of different views and practices, see Canadian Institute

for the Administration of Justice, *Role of the Chief Justice*, pp. 200-5.

54. For a survey and analysis of federal and provincial legislation concerning executive references to the courts, see B.L. Strayer, *The Canadian Constitution and the Courts* (Toronto: Butterworths, 1983), ch. 9.

55. *A.-G. Ont.* v. *A.-G. Can.* (1910) 43 SCR 536.

56. [1912] AC 571, at 589,

57. See Gerald Rubin, "The Nature, Use and Effect of Reference Cases in Canadian Constitutional Law," *McGill Law Journal* (1959-60), p. 168.

58. See Strayer, *Canadian Constitution*, and Dale Gibson, "Enforcement of the Canadian Charter of Rights and Freedoms," in W.S. Tarnopolsky and G.-A. Beaudoin, eds., *The Canadian Charter of Rights and Freedoms* (Toronto: Carswell, 1982), pp. 453-58.

59. A cabinet decision on 22 Mar. 1984 to refer questions on Manitoba language rights to the Supreme Court put pressure on John Turner to alter his position on this issue. *See Globe and Mail*, 23 Mar. 1984.

60. See Hogg, *Constitutional Law*, pp. 15-16.

61. *Patriation Reference* [1981] 1 SCR 753 and *Quebec Veto Reference* (1982) 140 DLR (3d) 385.

62. Hogg, *Constitutional Law*, p. 130.

63. In *Pringle* v. *Fraser* [1972] SCR 821, the Supreme Court upheld federal legislation precluding review even on jurisdictional grounds of decisions of the federal Immigration Appeal Board. The *Crevier* case is discussed above at p. 59.

64. For a discussion of the views of the Fathers of Confederation on judicial review, see Jennifer Smith, "The Origins of Judicial Review in Canada," *Canadian Journal of Political Science* (1983), p. 115.

65. *Marbury* v. *Madison* 1 Cranch 137, 2 L. Ed. 60 (1803).

66. *Ottawa Valley Power Co.* v. *Hydro-Electric Commission* [1936] 4 DLR 594, at 603.

67. *B.C. Power Corp.* v. *B.C. Electric* [1962] SCR 642.

68. Strayer, *Canadian Constitution*, p. 124.

69. *Operation Dismantle* v. *R.* [1985] 1 SCR 441, at 455.

70. Under s. 33 of the Canadian Charter of Rights and Freedoms, Parliament or a provincial legislature may enact legislation that shall operate for five years, notwithstanding a conflict with s. 2 or ss. 7 to 15 of the Charter. The courts can review legislation purporting to rest on s. 33 to see whether it falls within the powers conferred by this section of the Constitution. The blanket use of this power by the Quebec legislature was struck down by the Quebec Court of Appeal on 14 June 1985 in the *Alliance des Professeurs de Montréal* v. *A.G. Québec* (1985) 21 DLR (4th) 354.

71. *Maîtres Chez Eux*, p. 16.

72. See, for instance, the federal government's Constitutional Amendment Bill (C-60) of 1978, s. 100, the Committee on the Constitution of the Canadian Bar Association's *Towards a New Canada*, p. 27, and the Quebec Liberal party's "Beige Paper," p. 60.

73. For an account of differences of opinion among Canadian judges concerning their proper role in the administration of courts, see Deschênes, *Maîtres Chez Eux*,

pp. 39-43, and Ian Greene, "The Politics of Court Administration in Ontario," *Windsor Yearbook of Access to Justice* (1982), p. 124.
74. *Valente* v. *R.*, p. 702.
75. *Le Devoir*, 30 Apr., 1 May 1986.
76. Ibid., 2, 3 May 1986.

PART THREE

THE JUDGES

CHAPTER 5
APPOINTING AND PROMOTING JUDGES

In this part we look at the personnel of the bench: the seventeen hundred and fifty men and women who serve as full-time judges in Canada. It should be recalled from chapter 3 that this complement of Canadian judges has three main components.[1] The largest group (over one thousand of the seventeen hundred and fifty) is made up of judges appointed by provincial and territorial governments. These judges preside in the limited jurisdiction trial courts of the country that handle most criminal matters, family law, and small claims. Next in size are the approximately seven hundred section 96 judges. These are the judges whose manner of appointment, qualifications, and terms of office are set out in the formal Consitution. These judges are appointed by the federal government and preside over the intermediate and highest trial courts and the courts of appeal of the provinces and territories. Thirdly, a much smaller group of federally appointed judges serve on courts established and maintained by the federal government. The most important of these are the nine judges who serve on the country's highest court, the Supreme Court of Canada. In addition, there are the judges of the two specialized federal courts: the twenty-five members of the Federal Court and the ten members of the Tax Court.

The qualities of these judges, their political and social orientation, the method of appointing, removing, disciplining, and educating them, will have a crucial bearing on the role of the judiciary in the Canadian state. Our examination of these issues begins in this chapter with the appointment and promotion of judges, for it is in these processes that the dependence of judges on other actors in the state apparatus is most manifest. Unless judges appoint themselves or are chosen by lot, as in ancient Athens, they will be chosen by others. Those others, the appointing authorities, will not be a random collection of individuals, but part of the system of political and social power in the country. This may be at odds with the traditional ideology of the liberal state with its emphasis on the neutrality of the judiciary under the rule of law. But ideological myth must confront the reality of an elite recruitment process. For that is what is involved in selecting judges: appointing judges is part of the process of recruiting a society's governing elite. The process may or may not select the best people for the job—that is another very important question—but we can be sure about one point: the process in social and political terms is never neutral.

A Comparative Perspective

In broad perspective, the Canadian system of selecting and appointing judges is based on the practice developed in England and now followed in much of the common law world. This system has two basic features: first, the judges are appointed by those who head the executive branch of government; and secondly, the judges are selected from the practising bar. There are certainly plenty of variations on this model. The Canadian system, as we shall see, differs in some important respects from ther contemporary English system and within Canada there are significant differences between federal and provincial systems and among the provinces. However, for purposes of international comparison, this basic system of executive appointment of practising lawyers should be put along-side its two main competitors in the liberal democratic world: an elected judiciary, and a career judiciary.

The direct election of judges was adopted by a majority of the American states. Its original inspiration was populist or Jacksonian democracy which flour-ished for a time in the nineteenth century. Judges were recognized in the United States as having a good deal of power. For the populist democrat, power is only legitimate when exercised by persons directly elected by the people. Ergo, judges should be elected. A majority of American states continue to elect judges, although often with significant modifications designed to overcome the weak-nesses of the electoral system. The leading reform has been the introduction of nominating commissions designed to make professional merit the prime consid-eration in selecting names for the election ballot. Where the best known of these reformed systems (the so-called Missouri Plan) operates, the only name on the ballot is that of a judge who has served a probationary year and who was appointed by the governor of the state from a list of three individuals selected by a nom-inating commission.[2] Nominating commissions similar to those used to check partisanship in the American election systems have been proposed to check partisanship in the Canadian appointive system. We shall take a closer look at these proposals later in this chapter.

Populist democracy has not been a vigorous strain in the Canadian body politic. Only when Canadians have become disgusted with the degree to which ministerial selection of judges has been infected with political patronage have they shown any admiration for the elective system. Early in this century, after a series of particularly questionable appointments by the federal goverment, Canadian lawyers began to suggest that the elected system across the border was producing better judges than Canada's appointive system. In 1904 an editorial in the *Canadian Law Journal* commented:

> The time for boasting of our system as compared with the elective system as worked out in the State of New York seems to be at an end . . . . It would seem rather a shameful thing for us that the electors of a democratic country should show more sense of responsibility in such an important matter than the Ministers of the Crown in a comparatively conservative community.[3]

But this was more of a protest than a proposal. It is not only our more conservative political culture that has kept Canadians from adopting the electoral system; the direct election of judges has been unacceptable to Canadians for reasons that have ultimately persuaded American jurisdictions to either abandon or thoroughly modify that system. The skills and associations required to win party nominations and popular elections may exclude some of the best candidates for judicial office and promote the worst. It has also been shown that the vast majority of voters in American judicial elections do not have the slightest knowledge of the persons on the ballot.[4] But perhaps the most serious reason for rejecting the election system is its threat to the independence of the incumbent judge who faces re-election and may be wary of upholding the legal rights of unpopular litigants.

The indirect election system—election by the legislature — may be somewhat more attractive to Canadians. Eight of the original American states started off with this system, and a few still use it.[5] More significantly, the two West European federations, West Germany and Switzerland, have adopted such a system of selecting members of their highest court. In West Germany each of the houses of the federal Parliament elects half the members of the Federal Constitutional Court.[6] In Switzerland the judges of the Federal Court are elected by the Federal Assembly which consists of both houses of the national legislature.[7] A milder American form of legislative participation—the advice and consent of the American Senate on presidential nominations to the Supreme Court and other federal courts—may be somewhat more congenial to Canadians. In 1978 the Trudeau government and in 1979 the Pepin-Robarts Task Force on Canadian Unity recommended that nominations to the Supreme Court of Canada be subject to review and approval by a federal upper house reconstituted to better represent the regions of Canada. Similar proposals have been endorsed by the Ontario government's Advisory Committee on Confederation, the Quebec Liberal party, the Canadian Bar Association's Committee on the Constitution and the Macdonald Royal Commission on the Economic Union and Development Prospects for Canada.[8] Canadian diffidence about advertising the political nature of judicial appointments is evident in the CBA committee's stipulation that the legislature's consideration of Supreme Court nominees take place in camera. A more recent CBA committee report rejects any kind of legislative participation in judicial appointments.[9]

Canadian interest in involving the federal legislature in judicial selection is fed by two impulses. First, there is the need in a federation to ensure that the sectional interests of the nation are adequately represented in the selection of judges who have the final say in adjudicating disputes under the federal constitution. But as the power and discretion of judges comes to be more broadly recognized, a deeper democratic urge for more openness and accountability in their selection arises. The establishment of a constitutional bill of rights coupled with judicial review gives judicial power a much higher political profile. Thus we find that in both Italy and Japan, whose postwar, American-influenced constitutions contained both of these elements, there is some domocratization of the appointment process. In Italy five of the fifteen members of the Constitutional Court are chosen by Parliament,[10] while in Japan the electorate is called upon to approve or disapprove the continued tenure of Supreme Court judges appointed since the last election.[11] The entrenchment of a Charter of Rights in the Canadian

Constitution is bound to generate greater demand for legislative scrutiny of Supreme Court nominations.

The career judiciary, the other main alternative to the Anglo-Canadian system, is followed in European civil law countries. It was not established in France until well after the Revolution; hence it was not part of the cultural legacy of the Québécois. This means that the legal profession in both French and English Canada has developed on essentially English lines, which has been decisive for judicial recruitment. In France the judiciary is one of several specialized branches of the legal profession which law graduates enter on graduation, but the legal profession in Canada, as was pointed out in chapter 2, is much more unified—even more unified than it is in England. The practice of selecting judges from the bar was adopted in Canada as soon as there were barristers available, and was incorporated in the Constitution Act, 1967 for the federally appointed section 96 judges. It has been applied by statute to the federal courts established under section 101 and, in more recent years, to the lower provincial courts. Today, aside from lay justices of the peace who hear cases involving traffic violations and other summary offences, the judges of all the provincial courts except those of Alberta and Newfoundland are required by statute to be members of the bar. Even in these two provinces it is the custom to appoint persons with experience in professional practice.

The continental career system by which judges enter judicial service at an early age and, rather like civil servants, experience their entire professional life as government employees, appears to diminish judicial impartiality and independence. The English common law system of judicial recruitment which Canada follows is thought to produce more independent-minded judges for two reasons: first, the lawyer judges spend a good portion of their career in the private sector often representing those who oppose the government; and secondly, once appointed they are not at the bottom of a career ladder and so should not be under pressure to ingratiate themselves with the authorities who control their career progress.[12]

But these points should not be pressed too hard. As we shall see when we examine more carefully the backgrounds of Canadian judges, many of the lawyers who become judges have significant political links with government. Some have served as crown attorneys and officials in justice departments. Others have been retained as private lawyers to represent government. Besides political and professional links there are more informal social and family connections. As a group, the lawyers appointed to preside over Canada's courts are not exactly disconnected from the most powerful groups in Canadian society. It would be a miracle were it to be otherwise. Also, while there is no regular career ladder within the Canadian judicial system, promotions certainly occur, particularly at the higher court levels. Governments also appoint judges to perform non-judicial functions on such governmental bodies as regulatory boards and royal commissions. Guy Bouthillier's study of Quebec judges shows that the judicial career is far from being one of complete immobility: 43 of the 126 judges who served on Quebec's

Court of Sessions of the Peace (the provincial criminal court) between 1915 and 1975 received some further appointment after their initial appointment to the bench.[13]

Another factor narrowing the differences between the continental civil law system and our traditional system is recognition of the need for judicial education and training. In contrast to the English situation, the pool of lawyers from which Canadian judges are recruited is not only much larger but includes many who have little or no courtroom experience. The law itself has become so voluminous and complex that confidence in the capacity of the generalist judge to do justice to the issues raised in any area of law is no longer well placed. Thus we find a number of Canadian writers calling for a more systematic approach to the education of the Canadian judge. E.A. Tollefson, for example, proposes a system of examinations for candidates for judicial vacancies, followed by a year of instruction and in-service training for the successful candidates.[14] Two Quebec scholars, Jean de Montigny and Pierre Robert, after taking a close look at the French system, recommend an École de la Magistrature, modelled on L'École Nationale de la Magistrature in Bordeaux, to which judges would go for two months after their appointment and at intervals thereafter.[15] While no Canadian jurisdiction has gone this far, increasing attention is being given to judicial education at both the federal and provincial levels. The Canadian Judicial Council since its establishment in 1971 has played a leading role in this area, organizing seminars for federally appointed judges from all parts of Canada.[16] Provincial judicial councils and associations of provincial court judges have also entered the field of judicial education.[17]

The establishment of judicial councils at both the federal and provincial levels represents a major development in the organization of the judicial branch of government in Canada, although it has received very little public notice. This new instrument of judicial self-government will be examined in more detail later in this part. Here we wish only to draw attention to the tendency of these councils, emphasizing as they do the judiciary as a distinct profession, to draw us closer to the continental model. Another mark of this tendency is the establishment of professional associations of both federally and provincially appointed judges.[18] In some provinces, judicial councils have come to play an important role in the appointment of judges. A strong desire to curb political interference in the selection of judges may encourage other provinces or federal reformers to move in this direction. Canada may thus move closer to the postwar Italian system, where concern for judicial independence in the appointing process inspired constitutional provisions vesting responsibility for the appointment of judges in a High Judicial Council, a majority of whose members are elected by career judges.[19] Lest Canadians should conclude that this is the surest way to eliminate politics from the appointment system, it should be pointed out that it has promoted an intense political struggle between younger and older judges to control the judicial hierarchy.[20]

In considering the future of Canada's judicial appointment system, democracy and professionalism should be marked down as concerns that will have to be taken into account. To some extent, these are competing values. The professional urge is to emphasize a technical, apolitical appreciation of judicial merit and to question the participation of anyone who is not a lawyer or judge in the selection process. The democratic urge, on the other hand, is to require accountability and popular participation in selecting judges who appear to have so much discretionary authority. Increasingly there will be a demand for adequate representation of the political and social diversities of the country within a judiciary which appears to have so much influence in determining the rights of citizens and the powers of government. While it will not be easy to accommodate the concerns of both professionalism and democracy, reforms that are either insensitive or overly responsive to one or the other will not likely be acceptable to the Canadian community.

The Federal Appointing System

Having sketched in the broad features of the Canadian system of judicial recruitment and compared that system with its main alternatives in the western democracies, it is time to take a closer look at how the Canadian system works, first at the federal and then at the provincial level. In doing so it is useful to distinguish three stages in the appointing process: the selection of candidates, the screening of candidates, and the final appointment.

The last of these stages is obviously the least important in determining who become judges. At both the federal and provincial levels the formal appointment is made by the representative of the crown and the cabinet: the governor general or the lieutenant-governor in council. It is what goes on at the two earlier stages that is of most interest to the political scientist. Most of the contemporary effort to reform the system has concentrated on the second stage, the screening and assessing of candidates. However, it is often at the first stage, the identification and elimination of serious candidates, that the most significant choices are made.

At the federal level the minister of justice and the prime minister play the most important role in appointing judges. The minister of justice is responsible for bringing forward to cabinet the names of persons to fill most of the judgeships at the disposal of the federal government.[21] The main exceptions are the chief justiceships, which are within the prerogative of the prime minister.[22] There are quite a few of these: in addition to the chief justices of the Supreme Court of Canada and the Federal Court, there are two chief justices (one for the superior trial court and one for the Court of Appeal) for all of the provinces except Prince Edward Island (which has only one) plus some associate chief justiceships for the larger provinces.

In contrast to the English system, where the recommendations of the prime minister (for the Lord Chancellor, the law lords and chief justices) and of the Lord Chancellor (for the ordinary judges) go directly to the Queen, in Canada the ministerial recommendations are submitted to the cabinet.[23] This, of course, increases the political forces that can be brought to bear on the selection of judges. As William Angus has pointed out, ''Behind the closed door of a cabinet meeting, the considered recommendation of the Minister of Justice or Attorney General may go for nought in the face of local, ethnic, partisan, personal or other considerations.''[24] This involvement of the cabinet also means that individual ministers, especially the minister in charge of patronage for the province in which an appointment is to be made, have frequently intervened in the appointment process, sometimes to the point of having a veto over appointments.[25]

The prime minister's role in judicial appointments extends well beyond recommendations for chief justice positions. By appointing strong justice ministers and exhibiting a deep concern for the quality of judicial appointments, a prime minister can do much to improve the quality of the judiciary. R.B. Bennett and Pierre Trudeau were particularly keen to make some progress in reducing the influence of patronage in the appointment of judges. In 1914 Bennett had been a founding father of the Canadian Bar Association which was established in large measure as a means of bringing the legal profession's weight to bear on the struggle for an improvement in judicial appointments. He was president of the association when he became prime minister in 1930. As prime minister, Bennett was able to make some progress at least in the selection of Supreme Court justices.[26] Trudeau, perhaps because he was less of a party man than most prime ministers, was able to accomplish more, particularly in the first half of his prime ministership. Although the reforms introduced during his era were relatively modest and were undermined by his return to blatant patronage appointments at the end of his regime, they represented the most substantial effort up to that time to modify partisanship by considerations of merit.

The filling of all Supreme Court vacancies, not just the chief justiceship, is of particular concern to the prime minister. The archival research of Professors Snell and Vaughan has shown how much prime ministers have been involved in Supreme Court appointments.[27] This is not surprising. The political stakes are much greater in making appointments to this court; no other judicial positions can have such a decisive influence on the direction of the country's legal development. In filling the vacancy on the Supreme Court bench created by Chief Justice Laskin's death, Trudeau must have been very conscious of the significance of this appointment for the interpretation of the new Charter of Rights. Supreme Court appointments receive much more publicity than any other appointments, and much more today than in the past. The symbolic consequences of Supreme Court appointments must be carefully calculated. Regional, ethnic, religious, (and nowadays gender) considerations must be taken into account. With so much to lose through a bad appointment and so much to gain through a good one, and perhaps with only one or two openings to fill during their incumbency, prime ministers are not inclined to leave the selection of Supreme Court justices entirely to the justice minister.

The judicial positions at the disposal of federal politicians are a remarkable source of power. A federal minister of justice can have an enormous influence on the quality of Canadian justice. During Otto Lang's three and a half years as justice minister, for example, there were 161 new appointments and 29 promotions.[28] Not only do federal politicians fill a large number of judicial positions, they appoint the most powerful judges in Canada. The judges of the highest provincial courts as well as the judges of the federal courts and the Supreme Court of Canada are all appointed by the central government. In no other federal state is there such a centralization of control over judicial appointments. In the United States, the president's appointing power extends to roughly the same number of judicial positions—between seven and eight hundred—but these federally appointed judges represent only about 5 per cent of the American judiciary whereas federally appointed judges account for about 40 per cent of the Canadian judiciary.[29] The American president plays no role in choosing the judges of the highest state courts who have the final say in deciding issues of state law. Further, in appointing the federal judiciary he is subject to more checks and balances (especially the tradition of senatorial privilege) than apply to the federal appointing authorities in Canada. The judicial appointing power of federal political leaders is impressive even when compared with that of their counterparts in unitary states. In the United Kingdom, even though the population is more than twice as large as Canada's, there are approximately half as many senior judgeships as in Canada for the national government to fill.[30] On the continent, the centrally appointed judiciaries of countries such as France and Italy are much larger than the Canadian, but political leaders must share their appointing power with judicial councils.[31]

In the past both federal Liberals and Conservatives have not been reluctant to favour supporters of their own party in selecting lawyers for judicial appointment. Perhaps R.B. Bennett said it all when he told the House of Commons in 1932 that "there has been too much political patronage concerned in appointments to the Bench."[32] The two scholarly studies that have been done of the federally appointed judiciary confirm the extent to which partisan political considerations have influenced appointments. But both studies also indicate that patronage may have significantly declined over the years. Guy Bouthillier investigated the careers of the seventy-four persons appointed to the Quebec courts of appeal from 1867 to 1972 and found that forty of them (54 per cent) had been cabinet ministers or members of the legislature at the federal or provincial level.[33] However, the proportion overtly involved in politics declined from 78.5 per cent between Confederation and World War One to 22 per cent for the period since World War Two. Similarly, Bouthillier's study of Quebec's Superior Court revealed that while 34 per cent of the judges appointed to this court between 1849 and 1974 had been elected politicians, the proportion declined to just under one-eighth for those appointed since 1962.[34] William Klein's research on the careers of judges appointed by the federal government to the courts of Manitoba, Ontario, and Quebec from 1905 to 1970 took into account (wherever possible) judges who had lost elections as well as those who were successful.[35] Klein found that one-third of the judges had contested elections, although the percentage was considerably higher (42 per cent) for the Quebec judges.[36] Most of these appointments followed party lines: 94.8 per cent of the former politicians appointed by Liberal governments to Ontario courts were Liberals, while 81.4 per cent of the Conservative appointees were Conservatives.[37] Like Bouthillier, Klein recorded a decline in overt partisanship over time: whereas 43 per cent of Laurier's appointees had contested elections, only 21 per cent of those appointed under Trudeau up to 1970 had done so.[38] The same trend is evident with regard to appointments to the Supreme Court of Canada. Whereas 22 (55 per cent) of the forty Supreme Court judges appointed before 1949 had at some point in their career been elected politicians, only one of the twenty-two judges appointed since then had been elected to public office, and only one other judge appointed since 1949 had been an unsuccessful candidate.[39]

The data reviewed above take into account only the most overt political activity of judicial appointees: running in elections. Many of the lawyers who have been appointed to the bench have been behind-the-scenes supporters of the government party. This kind of political activity is much more difficult to identify. What evidence we have suggests that this less overt political patronage may still be a considerable factor in judicial appointments. In the early 1950s, Gilbert R. Schmitt contacted leading lawyers in every province to ask about the political involvement of federally appointed judges. Schmitt reported that in six of the provinces all of the judges then serving were supporters of the party in power in Ottawa at the time of their appointment. In the four other provinces, the percentage of party supporters ranged from 87 per cent for Ontario and 85 per cent for Alberta and British Columbia to a low of 70 per cent for Quebec.[40] In 1966 another survey carried out for the annual meeting of the Association of Canadian Law Teachers revealed that "all but a few of the judges appointed during the period were affiliated with the party in power at the time of their appointment, and most were actively engaged in politics."[41]

Sir Robert Megarry, an English judge, identifies four historical stages in the part played by politics in appointments to the bench:

> In the first stage, party politics may play so large a part that some of those appointed fall short of the standards that the office demands. In the second stage, political claims do no more than give some preference amongst those who are fully qualified for appointment . . . . The third stage comes when the political opponent has prospects of appointment which, other things being equal, are on a par with those of a political supporter, or nearly so. At the fourth stage politics have ceased to play any real part. Appointments are made very largely from the ranks of those who have made law and not politics their life.[42]

It is when patronage appointments are at Megarry's first stage that they are most clearly objectionable. Being a supporter of the party in power or having served in elected office certainly should not disqualify lawyers for the bench. On the contrary, experience in public life can be an important asset for the judge. However, when partisan political considerations lead to the appointment of poorly qualified persons or the elimination of superior candidates because of their political affiliations, an unacceptable method of judicial selection exists. According to Megarry (and other commentators on the English judicial scene[43]), England has for some time passed the grubby first stage and since 1946 has been at the fourth stage.

In Canada the first stage had certainly not been passed midway through the 1960s. Research conducted by the Canadian Bar Association's Committee on the Appointment of Judges indicates that, while recent reforms at both the federal and provincial levels have had some effect, they have not by any means eliminated the influence of patronage.[44] The committee found that "political favouritism" was still a "dominant consideration" in federal appointments to the section 96 courts in the Maritime provinces and Saskatchewan, as well as to the Federal Court, and was a "significant factor" in county and district court appointments in Alberta, Manitoba, Newfoundland, and Ontario. Similarly, for provincial appointments the committee found party patronage to be a dominant factor in the Maritimes and a significant factor in Ontario, Manitoba, and Saskatchewan. It would appear that for a great many judicial appointments Canada, in 1985, was still somewhere between Megarry's stages one and two.

Aside from its impact on the quality of the judiciary, the political nature of judicial appointments at the federal level is also of interest to the political scientist because of the power it enables the federal political elite to exercise. There are two principal dimensions of this power. First, there is the pure patronage element: the availability of a very large number of judicial vacancies for purposes of party management. As part of the orgy of patronage appointments which occurred in 1984 to facilitate the change in leadership of the federal Liberal party from Pierre Trudeau to John Turner, two cabinet ministers, three MPs (two of whom were former cabinet ministers) and a defeated Liberal candidate received judicial appointments.[45] These appointments demonstrated that a willingness to use judicial appointments as a mechanism for managing the affairs of the governing party was, unfortunately, far from dead at the federal level.

The second dimension of political power in the political control of judicial appointments is the opportunity this gives the governing party in Ottawa to influence the political orientation of judicial power in Canada. Until now there is little evidence of conscious ideological selection in federal judicial appointments. This is so even with regard to attitudes to Canadian federalism, the one area in which the federal government might be thought to have had a clear interest in the policy orientation of judges. In the early days the federal government was not above ensuring that the person chosen to fill a Supreme Court vacancy was reliably centralist. As John A. Macdonald put it, "We must endeavour to get a good man who will not throw Dominion rights away."[46] But in the modern epoch this criterion does not appear to have been a major factor in Supreme Court appointments. Most of the lawyers and judges appointed to the Court have not had a discernible position on federal issues. Bora Laskin's writings on the Canadian constitution indicated that he had strong centralist leanings. But his appointment by the Trudeau government was more than balanced by the appointment of justices Pigeon and Beetz, both of whom, as professors, had been strong defenders of provincial rights.

On issues other than federalism, at least until the advent of the Charter of Rights, federal appointing authorities have not perceived the judiciary as a threat to their policy or ideological interests. It is unlikely that there has been any conscious search for judges of the "right" ideological persuasion. Partisanship in recruiting the federal judiciary has, to be sure, systematically excluded supporters of third parties. This has meant, for example, that lawyers identified with the New Democratic party have rarely been appointed to judgeships even in provinces where that party holds power. While the exclusion of strongly committed socialists from the higher echelons of the Canadian judiciary no doubt significantly affects the policy direction of judicial decision-making in Canada, it is doubtful that this exclusion is primarily due to partisanship in the appointing process. It is more likely the general effect of recruiting judges from the ranks of upper middle class lawyers. In England, where a democratic socialist party has frequently held power but where partisanship in judicial appointments has been greatly reduced, Professor Griffith describes the spectrum of political opinion represented on the bench as ranging "from that part of the centre which is shared by right-wing Labour, Liberal and 'progressive' Conservative opinion to that part of the right which is associated with traditional Toryism—but not beyond into the reaches of the far right."[47] This characterization probably also fits the Canadian judiciary pretty well.

The Charter of Rights may well make the politicians who control judicial appointments more interested in the policy orientations of the persons they appoint. Here American experience is instructive. In that country Democrats and Republicans do differ in their orientation to the civil liberties issues involved in interpreting a constitutional Bill of Rights.[48] Despite several much heralded examples of Supreme Court justices disappointing the ideological expectations of the presidents who appointed them, the evidence is overwhelming that the party affiliation of the appointing president has a significant influence on the decision-making of the judges they appoint. John Gottschall's study of decisions rendered by the circuit courts of appeal in the United States showed that the judges appointed by Democratic presidents were significantly more supportive of the rights of the criminally accused and prisoners and of claimants of gender discrimination than the judges appointed by Republican presidents.[49] Republican presidential candidates promised to reverse what they regarded as the excessively liberal tenor of judicial decisions by appointing judges of their own ideological persuasion. The Republican platform in 1980 called for the appointment of judges who had "the highest regard for protecting the rights of law-abiding citizens."[50] A similar infusion of party ideology into the judicial recruitment process is likely to occur in Canada if Liberals and Conservatives differ significantly in their approach to the policy issues arising from judicial interpretation of the Charter of Rights.[51]

Reform of the Federal Appointing Process

In 1967, when Pierre Trudeau became minister of justice, there was a modest breakthrough in reforming the federal appointment process. Mr. Trudeau adopted the practice of seeking the opinion of a committee of the Canadian Bar Association before appointing any judge.[52]

This was the culmination of many years of agitation by the CBA for an improvement in the method of appointing judges. In 1949 the association had passed a resolution calling for consultation with a committee consisting of the provincial chief justices and representatives of the legal profession before appointing judges to the courts of a province. In 1957 it took a different tack and called for a system which would concentrate responsibility for judicial appointments in the hands of the minister of justice, minimizing the role of the prime minister and eliminating participation by other cabinet ministers. The reform that was finally put into practice in 1967 was modelled closely on the American Bar Association's Committee on the Federal Judiciary, established in 1946, and which, from the Eisenhower era to the Reagan administration, played a major role in the appointment of federal judges in the United States.[53] At its annual meeting in 1966 the CBA established a National Committee on the Judiciary. It is this committee which from 1967 on has been consulted by the minister of justice on most of the judicial appointments made by the federal government.

The role of the Canadian bar's judiciary committee is based on an informal arrangement.[54] It has no statutory basis, and its composition evolved considerably over the years. By 1985 it had twenty-three members with representation from all the provinces and territories. The committee comes into play in the middle of the selection process: after candidates for appointment have been identified by the minister of justice but before the minister makes his recommendations to cabinet. The names of prospective appointees are given to the chairman of the committee, together with whatever background information is available. The names are circulated to all members of the committee, but the chairman will rely primarily on members of the committee from the region in which the appointment is to be made. Typically, members make several telephone calls to obtain the views of other members of the legal community on the suitability of nominees. Questions are asked about legal ability, temperament, character, and health. Committee members report individually to the chairman, who may check back with members if there appears to be a serious disagreement among the appraisals. The committee does not vote on nominees, nor does it compare candidates for a particular vacancy or rank them. In each case the chairman, on the basis of members' reports, arrives at a determination of whether a candidate is "qualified," "highly qualified," or "not qualified." For a time in the early 1980s the category "qualified with reservations" was also used. The chairman's report is given to the minister on a confidential basis. The report may include more detailed comments about a candidate's qualifications: for instance, information that his or her practice has been confined to a particular field or that he or she has had limited court experience.

Unlike its American counterpart, the CBA committee has not attempted to insert itself in the early part of the selection process when the names of possible candidates are first being considered. This means that a political filter has continued to apply to the pre-selection process. As G.M. Stirling, a lawyer who served on the committee, acknowledged, "None of us would be naive enough to think that the names that are submitted are not prompted, in most instances, by some political considerations."[55] The American Bar Association's committee found that it could be much more effective when it was able to carry out an informal investigation before the government becomes strongly committed to a candidate. As Joel Grossman describes it,

> This is the period in the selection period when the choice is most likely to be open for discussion, and the chairman, who is in constant contact with the Deputy Attorney General, has a real opportunity to use the information he receives . . . to either block the nominations of someone considered not qualified or enhance the chances of someone considered well qualified. The chairman is able to do more than simply file a report; he becomes, in effect, the confidant of the Attorney General.[56]

In comparing American and Canadian procedures, it is important to bear in mind that in the United States the convention of senatorial courtesy and the Senate's ratification role produce a heavy overlay of politics at both the beginning and end of the judicial appointment process. In the United States a number of appointments have been made despite negative assessments by the ABA committee. While the Canadian committee has obtained no influence in the early part of the selection process, there is only one known instance of a person being appointed whom it considered to be "not qualified." In Canada, it would seem, the political dimension of the appointing process is less public while deference to professional authority is greater.

The vetting of federal government nominees by a committee of the CBA has been at best a first step in improving the judicial appointment process at the federal level. The most it has achieved is the establishment of a minimum level of competence for appointments. In Canada, where the pool of professionals from which the central government selects judges is much more widely dispersed than is the case in England, it is clearly advantageous to be able to consult with the bar in all parts of the country. But even within this limited context the use of the bar committee has some problematic features. Research on the ABA committee indicates that in both membership and contacts it is far from representative of professional opinion in that country. It tends to express the outlook of that small phalanx of lawyers who rise to positions of prominence in professional organizations. The Canadian committee may have similar limitations and, of course, even if it represents the legal profession adequately, it does not represent the perspectives of the wider community. As long as we know so little about what lies behind the committee's verdicts of "not qualified" and "qualified," it is difficult to judge the fairness or appropriateness of its assessments. Again

American research suggests that the criteria on which these assessments are made may be overly narrow.[57] There is also the danger that professional gossip and politics may unfairly eliminate candidates.

Another development in the federal selection process has had the potential for raising the quality of judicial appointments rather than simply maintaining a threshold of minimal competence. John Turner, during his term as justice minister, is credited with introducing a more systematic approach to collecting information about possible candidates for judicial office.[58] Instead of relying on the names put forward by cabinet ministers, members of Parliament, or a lawyer's friends, Turner took the initiative of seeking out experienced, able lawyers whose names might not be pushed by any politicians or interest group.

When Otto Lang succeeded Turner as justice minister in 1972 he institutionalized this process by establishing the position of special advisor to the minister of justice. The special advisor's function is to assist the minister in collecting information from a wide variety of sources about possible judicial appointees. The aim is to establish a bank of names and a good deal of information about availability and professional and personal qualifications so that, in Mr. Lang's words, "the best possible choice can be made."[59] It is through the special advisor that provincial chief justices are sometimes consulted about candidates for appointment to their courts.

These changes introduced by Turner and Lang in the 1970s were certainly a step in the right direction. In the contemporary world, with ever-increasing levels of technical complexity and professional sophistication, organizations in the private and public sectors cannot be content with minimal levels of competence for their leading personnel. For far too long the politicians in charge of recruiting judges for the federal judiciary in Canada put the interests of their party above the pursuit of excellence. Most observers of the appointment process in Canada would agree that there was a noticeable improvement in the quality of appointments during the Turner-Lang period. But they should also be struck by the fragility of this improvement in that it was very dependent on the personal commitment and strength of a few ministers. It is not at all clear that federal justice ministers in more recent years have all been as keen on following a merit approach or as successful in resisting the political pressures of their cabinet colleagues. Nor have all the minister's special advisors had the stature and ability of Ed Ratushny, the first incumbent in that office.

Let us not forget that in mid-summer 1984, at the end of the Trudeau era, six Liberal politicians were appointed to the bench. While one or two of these appointments could be defended on their merits, it is doubtful that anyone would say that each of these meets Lang's standard of the "best possible choice." For the first time since 1967 the name of one of the appointees was not submitted to the CBA's committee. The vulnerability of the appointing process to the personalities and whims of the governing party which this episode so vividly demonstrates is a strong part of the case for a more enduring institutional reform: that is, for the establishment of true nominating commissions. We will look more closely at such proposals after examining the provincial appointing process and reforms instituted at that level.

Consultation with the Provinces on Federal Appointments

Before turning to the methods used by provincial governments in appointing judges, it is important to consider the role of provincial governments in the federal appointing process. It would certainly not be unreasonable for provincial governments to be consulted on a great many federal appointments. After all, most of the judges Ottawa appoints—the section 96 judges—staff the higher courts of the provinces. These are courts which it is the constitutional responsibility of the provinces to establish and, save for the appointment and payment of the judges, to maintain. The chief justices and chief judges of these courts play an important role in administering the judicial systems in each province. In addition, of course, the staffing of the Supreme Court of Canada is of great interest to the provinces, given that it has the final say in adjudicating constitutional disputes and settling issues of provincial law. Indeed, of all the federally appointed judges, it is only with regard to the handful of judges appointed to the purely federal courts, the Federal Court of Canada and the Tax Court of Canada, that the provinces do not have a clear and legitimate interest. Not only do the provincial governments have a legitimate interest in most federal judicial appointments, but their proximity to the provincial bar and the fact that they are often controlled by political parties different from the party in power in Ottawa, should enable them to augment the information available to the appointing authority about good candidates for judicial office.

And yet, as logical as it may be for the provinces to be consulted on federal judicial appointments, there is certainly no constitutional or statutory requirement for such consultation, nor has it been an established practice or convention. The influence of provincial attorneys general or other members of provincial governments on federal judicial appointments has been spasmodic and uneven. It has depended primarily on personal or political connections between the governments. The Canadian Bar Association's Committee on the Appointment of Judges found that "lack of consultation by the minister of justice with the attorneys general and chief justices of the various provinces has been a chronic weakness of the selection and appointment systems."[60]

Provincial governments and legislatures do control the number of vacancies to be filled on section 96 courts. It is provincial legislation which determines the size (i.e., the number of judges) of these courts and alters their structure—for instance, by creating a court of appeal separate from the superior trial court or merging the country or district courts with the superior trial court. When provincial legislatures make these changes in the size or structure of their section 96 courts, the legislation cannot take effect until the federal Parliament makes matching changes in the federal Judges Act providing for the appropriate number and distribution of judicial salaries. Federal co-operation in these situations, over the years, has been by no means automatic, and often involves consultation.[61] But this consultation is about numbers and structure, not about prospective appointees, although on occasion provincial governments have tried to use their control over numbers as a means of forcing the federal government to take their advice on appointments.[62]

There appears to be no difference in the case of appointments to the Supreme Court of Canada. Former provincial premiers have served on the Supreme Court: New Brunswick's George King and Prince Edward Island's Sir Louis Davies. But their appointment owed nothing to contacts with the provincial governments. In special circumstances federal leaders have communicated with their provincial counterparts about impending appointments. In 1932, for instance, Prime Minister Bennett wrote to the premier of New Brunswick to explain how difficult it was to find anyone in that province of the calibre he was seeking to fill a Supreme Court vacancy.[63] And in 1979 apparently there was some discussion with the Ontario government when Ottawa decided to break with the customary regional distribution of Supreme Court places and appoint Justice McIntyre of British Columbia to a vacancy created by the retirement of an Ontario justice. But these occasional contacts with the provinces are far from constituting a practice of consultation on Supreme Court appointments.

The difficulties that may arise through the absence of consultation with the provinces were dramatically brought to light by recent events in Saskatchewan. In 1982, shortly after coming to power, a Conservative government led by Grant Devine passed an order-in-council decreasing the Saskatchewan Court of Appeal from seven to five judges.[64] The Court of Appeal had been expanded from five to seven a few months earlier but the two new positions had not been filled when the Devine government took office. The new Conservative administration was determined to check what it regarded as unrestrained Liberal patronage in filling section 96 judgeships and chose the tactic of closing off vacancies until the federal minister of justice agreed to consult with the government of Saskatchewan on appointments. The minister of justice, Mark MacGuigan, refused to succumb to this pressure. In 1983 he appointed William Vancise, a Regina lawyer, to the province's Court of Queen's Bench. Saskatchewan's District Court had recently been merged with the Court of Queen's Bench. To keep the merged court relatively decentralized, provincial legislation required that there be a resident Queen's Bench judge in a number of the province's smaller cities. The provincial government intended that the judge filling the vacancy to which Vancise was appointed should reside in Swift Current. But the federal authorities did not consult Saskatchewan before the appointment. This created an embarrassing situation, as Mr. Justice Vancise was not keen about moving to Swift Current. The immediate denouement of this situation was the elevation of Vancise to a vacancy on the provincial Court of Appeal and the appointment of another Regina lawyer, Mr. Ian McLellan—again without consultation—to the position on the Court of Queen's Bench.

That was by no means the end of the affair. During 1983 and 1984 there was open warfare between the provincial and federal governments over judicial appointments in Saskatchewan. The provincial cabinet passed an order-in-council which would close each vacancy on the Court of Queen's Bench until its strength fell from thirty to twenty-four judges.[65] The intention was to block any further appointments by the Trudeau government to the Saskatchewan courts. A group of Saskatchewan trial lawyers, frustrated by the effect this cutback on judicial manpower was having on the processing of cases, challenged the legality of this manoeuvre. Justice Wimmer of the Court of Queen's Bench ruled that while there is no doubt about the constitutional power of the provincial legislature to alter the size of the courts, the statute governing the Court of Queen's Bench with its provisions requiring judges in specific locations did not permit the cabinet by order-in-council to eliminate positions on that court.[66]

This unfortunate Saskatchewan situation did not end until the election of a federal Conservative government in the fall of 1984. The Saskatchewan cabinet then passed orders-in-council reinstating two positions on the province's Court of Appeal and four on the Court of Queen's Bench. John Crosbie, the then federal justice minister, agreed to consult with both the provincial attorney general and the relevant chief justice and seek their suggestions before filling vacancies in section 96 courts.[67]

If this sorry episode does nothing else, it may at least demonstrate that good will and good sense cannot be counted on to ensure that the appropriate kind of intergovernmental co-operation takes place in the appointment of section 96 judges. There is a real danger that this episode, despite the minister of justice's commitment to provincial consultation, will strengthen the resolve of provincial leaders to dismantle section 96 and eliminate the federal appointment of provincial judges. That would not be an entirely unreasonable response. But, as we argued in the previous chapter, it would be a tragedy—at least for us consumers of justice—to move in this direction; in effect, it would mean abandoning all the advantages of our integrated court system and moving decisively in the direction of the American dual court system. To avoid this outcome it is essential to find an effective way of accommodating provincial demands for a guaranteed role in staffing their higher courts.

Australian developments throw some interesting light on the need for federal-provincial co-operation in maintaining an integrated judicial system. The Australian constitution did not contain anything like Canada's section 96 as the basis for an integrated, national system of courts. Instead, its courts of general jurisdiction were entirely state institutions with the judges appointed by state governments. The federal legislature could establish specialist courts in areas of federal jurisdiction. In recent years as federal legislation increasingly conferred jurisdiction on these federal courts, notably in the fields of family and business law,[68] Australians became much more aware of the inconvenience resulting from a dual system of courts. To avoid these problems, a committee of the Australian Constitutional Convention, made up of government and opposition politicians from the Commonwealth and state levels, has proposed a constitutional amendment which would make it possible to confer jurisdiction in both state and federal matters on a single set of courts and judges.[69] What is instructive about this proposal is the clear recognition that if Australia is to enjoy the benefits of an integrated judicial system, both levels of government must be involved in the appointment of judges. Thus, for the proposed Australian Court of Appeal which would serve as an intermediate court of appeal between the state superior courts and the High Court of Australia, it is proposed that the judges be appointed by the Commonwealth government subject to consultation with state and territorial governments and that the latter governments appoint the judges of the state and territorial superior courts subject to consultation with the Commonwealth.

In 1979 the Australians took the step of making consultation with the appropriate state attorney general a statutory requirement in the appointment of judges to their highest court, the High Court of Australia.[70] For some time there has been acceptance in principle among the federal and provincial political leaders in Canada of at least this much provincial involvement in federal judicial appointments. Federal and provincial constitutional proposals, beginning with the Victoria Charter in 1971, have included provisions for provincial input into appointments for the Supreme Court of Canada. These proposals have given the attorney general of the province from which the Supreme Court vacancy is being filled a power of veto over federal nominations and, in some cases, an opportunity to bring forward names. Some of these proposals have called for ratification by a reformed Senate on top of this participation by provincial governments.[71] The two levels of government would appear to be close enough to agreeing on provincial government involvement in Supreme Court appointments to make such an amendment a distinct possibility in the next few years.[72]

Intergovernmental negotiations along classic "executive federalism" lines may not be the best way of facilitating federal-provincial co-operation in the selection of judges. The trouble with requiring simply that one level consult with the other or obtain the agreement of the other is that each may confront the other with patronage selections or prevent the appointment of anyone with the slightest political ties. An approach which will do more to remove partisan politics from the centre of the selection power is the use of nominating commissions designed to identify the most able candidates. Professor Lederman has proposed such a federal-provincial commission in the context of Supreme Court of Canada appointments.[73] Such commissions have perhaps even more relevance in connection with the appointment of section 96 judges and have, as we shall soon see, been recommended by organizations representing legal academics and the bar. Some of the ingredients of the nominating commission approach can already be found in reforms in the selection of provincially appointed judges recently introduced in several provinces.

Provincial Appointing Systems

The majority of Canadian judges are appointed by the governments of the ten provinces and two territories. Although the courts presided over by these judges are sometimes referred to as lower courts or inferior courts, they are the courts in which most Canadians will have their only first-hand encounter with the justice system. These courts are the courts of first instance in most criminal cases. In addition, many of them have an extensive jurisdiction in the area of family law and in hearing civil disputes involving limited amounts of money.

No doubt the selection process in each of the provinces and territories has its own idiosyncracies. But they all share one basic feature: the appointing authority is vested in the provincial or territorial executive. More precisely, it is vested in the lieutenant-governor in council (i.e., the cabinet) in the nine common law provinces, in the "gouvernement" of Quebec, in the commissioner of the Northwest Territories and in the commissioner in executive council in the Yukon. This common feature provides a much more centralized control over lower court appointments than existed in earlier years when local officials often served as "police magistrates" in many of the provinces. Professionalization and provincialization have been hallmarks of the judicialization of Canada's lower courts which has taken place in the modern era.[74] As a result, control over recruitment to these courts is much more centralized than it is in the United States, where considerable municipal involvement in appointments at the lower court level survives, or in England and Wales, where local committees advise the Lord Chancellor on the appointment of lay magistrates.[75]

Control of judicial appointments by the provincial cabinet has meant, of course, that there has been a good deal of political patronage in appointing judges at this level. Just how important political factors have been is hard to say as these appointments have been subjected to less scrutiny by researchers than federal appointments. In 1968 Ontario's Royal Commission of Inquiry into Civil Rights, headed by Chief Justice James McRuer reported:

> There has been a tradition in Ontario that there should be a strong political influence in the selection of magistrates. This has not been peculiar to any political party nor does the influence differ substantially from that which has been brought to bear on the appointment of judges by successive federal governments. There have been isolated cases where one who has not been a supporter of the party in power has been selected for the office, but such cases are unusual.[76]

McRuer's analysis of the situation in Ontario would probably have applied to other provinces at that time. Guy Bouthillier's study of the judges who have served on Quebec's Court of the Sessions of the Peace, Quebec's provincially appointed criminal court, shows that the proportion of former politicians among the judges who have served on this court is much smaller than among the judges appointed by Ottawa to Quebec's section 96 courts: 16.5 per cent as opposed to 54 per cent for the Court of Appeal and 30 per cent for the Superior Court.[77] As with the latter two courts, the appointment of former politicians to the Court of the Sessions of the Peace diminished markedly over time. Indeed for the period from 1970 to 1974 the percentage was down to 3.7 per cent. Although Bouthillier reports that a relatively low proportion of these provincially appointed judges had earlier in their career been elected to the provincial or federal legislatures, he also shows that many others had been involved in politics in less formal ways. He concluded that until recent years few of them had remained completely out of politics.

Bouthillier's findings confirm what common sense would suggest. Judicial appointments at the provincial court level have not been very attractive to elected politicians. Compared with federal appointments not only is the remuneration lower but, probably of even greater importance, the provincial appointments are of much lower status. The party supporters who obtain provincial appointments are more likely to have been campaign workers or defeated candidates. And yet it is not unheard of for a provincial cabinet minister to be appointed to the Provincial Court. In 1983, for example, a Nova Scotia cabinet minister, Harry How, had been pressing for a reform of the province's labour laws designed to limit the right to strike. "The day after announcing his latest plan to save Nova Scotia from creeping unionism . . . [he] was moved from right wing to the bench, as chief Provincial Court judge."[78]

The How appointment in Nova Scotia points up the ideological colouring of the provincial bench which may result when a single party is in power for an extended period of time. Generally speaking, provincially appointed judges do not affect public policy by developing the law: unlike federally appointed judges, their decisions do not become rules of law binding on other courts. It is more through the basic orientation of their day-to-day handling of the masses of cases that come before them—particularly sentencing in criminal cases and the treatment of family and youth problems in family courts—that the policy implications of their work will be felt. As John Hogarth points out in his study of sentencing in Ontario, it is significant that nearly all the magistrates then serving in Ontario were supporters of the Conservative party.[79] A "right of centre" provincial bench could make its weight felt in determining the extent to which prison is selected among the alternative sanctions for those convicted of crimes.

Since the 1960s all the provinces have restructured their lower courts. Instead of "magistrates" we now have Provincial Courts presided over by "judges." Quebec had a provincial criminal court staffed by legal professionals for many years, and established a Provincial Court for civil matters in 1965. Ontario led the way for the common law provinces with the enactment of its Provincial Courts Act in 1968 implementing many of the recommendations of the McRuer report.[80] Over the next ten years, in a remarkable demonstration of Ontario's influence on provincial public administration, the other common law provinces all passed legislation judicializing their magistracy and establishing Provincial Courts.[81] This was much more than a nominal change. No doubt it was part of the general province-building of the period which witnessed the modernization and structural sophistication of provincial institutions.[82] It also reflected a new awareness on the part of provincial authorities of the serious adjudicative function performed by the provincially appointed judiciary. Even in the northern territories, where the institutions of government retain some colonial characteristics, the magistrates have become judges serving on Territorial Courts.

The judicialization of the magistracy has nearly eliminated the lay judge in Canada. In most provinces it is a statutory requirement that to be eligible for appointment to the provincial court a person must be a practising lawyer. Even where, as in Alberta and Newfoundland, it is not a legal requirement, the practice nowadays is to appoint experienced lawyers. "Grandfather clauses" in the new legislation enable a few non-lawyers to survive on the provincial bench; but they will soon disappear. The only place where lay persons continue to perform an adjudicative role is in those provinces and territories that use justices of the peace to try minor offences. Modern awe of professionalism has meant that the tendency to rely exclusively on the legal profession to staff the provincial judiciary is generally regarded as a major reform. However, it is far from clear that the qualities needed for the various functions performed by these Provincial and Territorial Courts are uniquely to be found among those with a law degree.[83] Be that as it may, the transition to a greater professional emphasis has been accompanied by some significant refinements in the method of recruiting provincial judges.

The minister of justice and attorney general has the responsibility for bringing recommendations for judicial appointments before the provincial cabinet.[84] In five provinces (Alberta, British Columbia, Newfoundland, Ontario, and Saskatchewan) the minister is now assisted in performing this function by provincial judicial councils, and in Quebec by nominating committees. In the Yukon and the Northwest Territories judicial councils play the primary role in recommending nominees for appointment to the Territorial Courts. It is only in the three Maritime provinces and Manitoba that the judicial appointment process is based on the unfettered discretion of the provincial attorney general.

The involvement of judicial councils and nominating commissions in the selection of Provincial and Territorial Court judges is the most significant reform that has been made in the Canadian system of appointing judges. This type of reform may serve as a prototype for reforming the appointing process at the federal level. Earlier in this chapter we noted how the establishment of judicial councils has been part of the movement toward a more professional judiciary in Canada. Here we are concerned with the role of judicial councils in the appointing process—a role performed by only seven of the twelve judicial councils which have been established in Canada.[85] The council established at the federal level, the Canadian Judicial Council, is involved only in discipline and education. Similarly, the judicial councils of Manitoba, New Brunswick, Nova Scotia, and Quebec play no part in judicial appointments. The seven judicial councils which are involved in the appointing process all include judges, lawyers, and lay persons in their membership. The same tripartite membership is present in the ad hoc nominating committees Quebec has chosen to employ in the selection process rather than that province's Conseil de la Magistrature.

British Columbia has gone further than any other province in establishing through legislation a strong role for its judicial council.[86] The Provincial Court Act stipulates that the cabinet may appoint only persons who have been recommended by the British Columbia judicial council. Although this legislation was introduced by an NDP government in 1975 it has won the support of all parties. In the British Columbia system the judicial council acts as a true nominating commission: the council, not the minister, has the primary responsibility for collecting names and establishing a bank of good prospects for the provincial judiciary. With appointments to the provincial bench, much more than with appointments to the federal bench, it is more normal for lawyers to put their name forward and, in that sense, apply for a judicial appointment. In British Columbia these "applications" are directed to the judicial council, not to the minister. Lawrence Goulet, who as chief judge of the Provincial Court chaired the BC judicial council in its formative years, has given the following description of the council's processing of applications:

> The Council is completely unaware of any contact this person may have had with the Government, if any. The Council will interview each applicant who meets the statutory requirements and provides a recent photograph, a medical certificate and additional personal information as required. Pending the interview, Council gathers information from the Law Society of British Columbia and the Canadian Bar Association on a formal basis and informally as well from justices, judges and other persons who are likely to have knowledge of the applicant's suitability. [87]

The council approves considerably more names than there are actual vacancies so that the list it submits leaves the minister with some discretion in deciding which name to bring forward to cabinet. However, in this system the minister must choose a person who has passed through the judicial council's filter—a filter designed to test personal aptitude and professional ability rather than political affiliation.

It is perhaps not without significance that the BC judicial council is the only one of the councils involved in appointing provincial judges whose membership contains no federal appointees. In the other common law provinces and in the territories judges appointed by Ottawa serve on the council and, except in Alberta, chair it. British Columbia's willingness to give such a powerful role to its judicial council may, in part, reflect the greater control the provincial government has over appointments to the council.

In some provinces the judicial council's role in appointments has been much more passive, closer to the screening function performed by the Canadian Bar Association's National Committee on the Judiciary in federal appointments. This basically has been the role of Ontario's judicial council, the first to be established, and would also appear to be the role of Saskatchewan's.[88] Councils do not collect information about candidates in the same way as the bar committee. They rely more on the personal, first-hand knowledge which members, especially judicial members, may have of the nominee, and, at least in Ontario, on an interview. In the Ontario system it is the attorney general not the council who comes up with most of the names. Before submitting a name to the judicial council the minister consults with the chief judge of the court to which the individual is to be appointed and the chief judge may interview the prospective appointee. The attorney general will take his own soundings, both professional and political. With appointments to the provincial bench there is an expectation that a position will be filled by a lawyer practising in the area where the vacancy occurs. Consequently, the names that are brought to the minister's attention as well as the pressures to which he is subjected will in large measure emanate from a particular municipality. It is at this early, informal stage in the selection process that political considerations are apt to come into play. As at the federal level, in this passive judicial council system there is a danger that the names which finally reach the "independent" screening body will pass through a fairly tight political filter, unless a strong and committed minister consistently puts the needs of the bench ahead of those of his party.

In Alberta, although the legislation governing the judicial council was modelled closely on Ontario's, since its establishment the council has come to play a role much more like British Columbia's in the appointing process.[89] The names of most applicants are forwarded by the minister to the council. The attorney general takes most of his appointments to cabinet from the list of names generated by the council, even though he is not legally required to do so. The judicial councils of Newfoundland and the territories also appear to be closer to the British Columbian than to the Ontario model. In Newfoundland the judicial council invites suitable persons to apply, interviews candidates, and the cabinet usually appoints persons recommended by the council even though it is not legally obliged to do so. In the Northwest Territories the judicial council's recommendations go straight to the commissioner. This is the only council empowered to make recommendations for the position of chief judge. The Yukon council's role in appointments is similar to British Columbia's in that the commissioner in council is required to appoint "on the recommendation of the judicial council."[90]

Quebec has established a distinctive method of recruiting judges for its provincial courts. Just before the Parti Québécois came to power in 1976, Jérôme Choquette, the minister of justice in Robert Bourassa's Liberal government, had recommended that a judicial council be established and given the function of advising the government on judicial nominations.[91] However, when a Conseil de la Magistrature was created in 1978, the PQ government did not give it a role in appointments. Instead, the minister of justice, Marc-André Bédard, experimented with a system of nominating committees. When vacancies occurred a committee was struck consisting of the chief judge of the court in which the position was to be filled, a lawyer designated after consultation with the bar, and a non-lawyer appointed by the government. A remarkable feature of this system was the advertising of vacancies in the newspaper of the Quebec bar. The publicizing of vacancies was designed to ensure that "any lawyer meeting the requirements could let his availability be known in an apolitical manner."[92] The committee would meet with applicants and recommend the best candidates to the minister. After a trial period legislation was enacted in 1978 authorizing the establishment of this system by regulation, and the procedure came into force the following year.[93] The minister is still not bound by law to select judges from the names recommended by nominating committees, although Mr. Bédard, who served as justice minister until 1984, committed himself to choosing only persons recommended by a committee.

The arrangements discussed above represent the first moves in Canada toward the use of judicial nominating commissions which have become so popular in the United States. Only the Quebec committees are pure nominating committees; the judicial councils combine a discipline function with their appointing function. The combination of these two functions in a single body might be questioned, although it is difficult to see that there is anything inherently wrong in having the same body that selects judges receive complaints about these judges. Indeed, the exposure to public dissatisfaction with judges may give these councils a shrewder insight into the characteristics they should be looking for in judicial recruits.

Thus far this reform has been confined to the lowest level of the judiciary. But there is much to be gained in moving to a system that gives priority to aptitude and ability rather than political affiliation in filling judicial positions at this level. Not only does the work of these judges have a great impact on the ordinary citizen but also, given the lower status and remuneration of these positions, it is a challenge to recruit outstanding lawyers to them. Through interviews conducted in jurisdictions that have adopted this type of reform, the CBA's Committee on the Appointment of Judges in Canada found that among lawyers familiar with the lower courts in these provinces there was a "consensus that the system has improved the quality of appointments and is working well."[94] The committee was most favourably impressed with the activist type of council such as British Columbia's and Quebec's nominating committees. It recommended that all the provinces bring their selection procedures up to the standards established by these two provinces.[95]

Nominating Commissions for Federal Appointments

For some time it has been clear that reform of the judicial appointing process is most urgently needed at the federal level. It is the federal government, after all, that appoints judges to all the higher courts in the country, both federal and provincial, trial and appellate. Reforms introduced by the Trudeau government (vetting by a committee of the Canadian bar and data collection by a special advisor to the minister of justice) and by the Mulroney government (consultation with the provinces) have no doubt improved the process. But, in the opinion of most observers, these reforms have not gone nearly far enough. The spate of patronage appointments by Trudeau and Turner in the summer of 1984 was a stark reminder of how vulnerable the federal system is to partisan manipulation.

The approach to reform most frequently favoured is the nominating commission. As noted earlier, as far back as 1949 the Canadian Bar Association called for the establishment of a nominating committee in each province. In the

1960s and 1970s similar proposals were put forward by practising lawyers and law professors. These more recent proposals move closer to the "Missouri Plan" nominating commissions that have been so widely acclaimed in the United States. They also reflect reforms in the Canadian provinces by including representatives of the general public in the membership of the proposed commissions. And they have incorporated a feature specially designed for Canada's section 96 judiciary: both levels of governments must be represented on the commissions.

This reform movement received some vigorous stimulation from the advent of the Charter of Rights, which exposed and expanded the power of the judiciary in the Canadian system of government, and from the patronage appointments which re-advertised shortcomings in the system of selecting the senior members of the Canadian judiciary. In 1985 the Canadian Bar Association and the Association of Canadian Law Teachers both issued reports calling for the establishment of judicial nominating commissions at the federal level. The bar committee proposed that an advisory committee on federal judicial appointments be established in each province and territory. These committees would be composed as follows:

- the chief justice of the province or territory, or his delegate, who would act as chairman
- one person appointed by the federal minister of justice
- one person appointed by the provincial or territorial attorney general
- two lawyers, one appointed by the governing body of the legal profession and one by the branch of the Canadian Bar Association in each province or territory
- two lay people representative of the public to be appointed by majority vote of the other committee members.[96]

A somewhat similar committee is proposed for appointments to the Federal Court, the Tax Court, and any additional courts the federal Parliament may create, except that this committee would not include a provincial government representative. This advisory committee on appointments to federal courts would be chaired by the chief justice of the Federal Court and, in addition to the minister of justice's appointee, would include two lawyers (to be named by the CBA and the Federation of Law Societies) and three members (two of whom must be lay persons) selected by the others in a manner that takes into account regional representation.[97] It is proposed that these committees have the primary responsibility for developing lists of suitable candidates for all federal judicial appointments.

The proposals of the Association of Canadian Law Teachers' special committee on judicial appointments closely parallel those of the CBA.[98] The Law Teachers call their nominating bodies judicial nominating councils. Their membership would have the same five components as the bar association's advisory committees. The Law Teachers are more flexible about numbers, so that the representation of the bench, the bar, and the public could be enlarged in the more populous provinces with the bar representatives being elected by regional sections of the provincial bar. These councils would be chaired by the federal minister of justice's nominee, not by the provincial chief justices. In submitting lists of suitable candidates for each vacancy, councils would list up to five names in order of merit.

Both sets of proposals recognize that section 96 of the Constitution, which vests appointing authority in the governor general, may preclude legislation binding the minister of justice to recommend appointments from lists submitted to him by these nominating bodies. However, while the CBA Committee was content to put its faith in the evolution of a constitutional convention that would constrain the minister to select from the advisory committees' lists, the Law Teachers would have the minister required by statute to give written reasons for appointing judges not recommended by a judicial nominating council.

Structurally, the main difference between the two sets of proposals is in relation to the Supreme Court of Canada. Whereas the CBA proposed simply that the same advisory committee(s) used for section 96 appointments in the province (or provinces in the region) from which the appointment is to be made be asked to make recommendations on Supreme Court vacancies, the Law Teachers recommended a special Supreme Court of Canada judicial nominating council. This council would be composed of the chief justice of the Supreme Court, a nominee of the Canadian Judicial Council, nominees of the minister of justice and provincial attorney(s) general of the province or provinces from which the candidate is to be selected, two members of the bar chosen by the Canadian Bar Association and the Federation of Law Societies, and one member of the public chosen by the other members of the council. This is an interesting addition to the myriad of proposals considered over the years for reforming the system of appointing Supreme Court justices. The proposal entails a much broader formal participation in the process than has been contemplated in the proposals considered by federal and provincial governments in the past.

A system of advisory bodies along the lines of these proposals has much to recommend it. Such a reform could improve both the recruiting and screening functions. The minister of justice might retain the Office of Special Advisor on Judicial Appointments to ensure that the names of good prospects are considered by the relevant committees. But nominations could be sought and received from a much wider variety of sources. The presence of a chief justice on each committee should provide better assurance that the needs of the court for which a vacancy is being filled are always taken into account. A widening of the talent pool for judicial recruitment should also occur simply by virtue of having a publicly known agency for assessing candidates for judicial office. One of the key faults which the CBA report identified in the existing system is the mystique of secrecy that envelops it.

Nominating commissions should also be in a position to be more thorough and penetrating in assessing the qualifications of candidates. The screening carried out since 1967 by the Canadian Bar Committee's National Committee on the Judiciary, while perhaps better than nothing, was done in a rather unprofessional manner. Frequently the committee was required to check out long lists of names in a few days through a haphazard system of long distance, and often gossipy, phone calls. The 1985 CBA report sees the broader-based advisory committee system as a distinct improvement over its national committee. The inclusion of non-lawyers would add popular legitimacy and strengthen the nominating bodies' capacity for assessing personal qualities such as patience and good citizenship, which are as essential for an effective judiciary as technical proficiency.

The main alternative to be considered is the strengthening of the justice minister's support staff along English lines. In 1973 the British section of the International Commission of Jurists recommended a nominating commission to improve the system of appointing judges in Great Britain.[99] Instead of adopting that proposal, the British developed a different means of strengthening the capacity to identify and assess candidates for judicial office. In the office of Lord Chancellor, who is the officer in government with the prime responsibility for advising the Queen on judicial appointments, a number of senior staff positions have been established to assist in gathering information about prospective candidates.[100] A permanent secretary (equivalent to a deputy minister) and a judicial appointments division carry out extensive consultations on a regular basis with the bench and the profession. Compared with this, the Canadian justice minister's staff resources are meagre: he has only his special advisor, a relatively unknown and junior member of the profession who usually comes and goes with each minister. And bear in mind that the Canadian minister is responsible for many more appointments each year than is his English counterpart, and that the judges he selects will have considerably more power in our society than English judges have in theirs.

There are two factors which probably rule out the English system as an alternative means of reforming the Canadian process. First, the Canadian legal profession is organized very differently from the profession in England. It does not produce the small pool of identifiable judicial talent that the division of the profession into barristers and solicitors and the QC system does in England. Secondly, the English Lord Chancellor is a distinctly less political functionary than the Canadian minister of justice. The wonderful illogic whereby the Lord Chancellor's office combines executive, legislative, and judicial responsibilities is not for export and is probably crucial to insulating him from the political pressures to which a Canadian justice minister is subjected. It must be remembered that in England recommendations for judicial appointments are not taken to cabinet but are submitted by the Lord Chancellor or the prime minister directly to the Queen. So far as section 96 appointments are concerned, although it is only convention that requires the justice minister to submit recommendations to cabinet, it is a convention that would be very difficult to change.

Politics, of course, cannot and should not be removed from the appointing process. Glen Winters, who as executive director of the American Judicature Society was a leading exponent of nominating councils in the United States, put the point well when he wrote: ''The practical difficulties of complete and utter insulation of judicial selection from all political influence are probably at least as great as those found by the mother of Achilles in her effort to dip her son completely in the river.''[101]

Nominating commissions will have their politics, but it is reasonable to believe that their politics will be broader and more representative than the political influences that are now brought to bear on federal appointments. The federal minister of justice and his cabinet colleagues could still bring forward the names of promising candidates who happen to be party stalwarts. But this particular group of politicians would no longer dominate the networks through which names come to the attention of the appointing authorities. Opposition party leaders, provincial governments, the bar, the bench, and members of the public could also submit names with some assurance they would receive equal consideration. A political dynamic would no doubt develop within the nominating committees and would also be at work in the processes whereby professional organizations select members for these committees.[102] Inevitably, there will be efforts to lobby members of the committees on behalf of candidates. But, again, these political forces would be less susceptible to control by the governing party in Ottawa.

There is the opposite danger that nominating commissions will be too balanced. They may be so balanced that only candidates who offend no one—who are, indeed, champions of blandness—can survive commission scrutiny. An Australian writer, James Crawford, gives this as the major reason for rejecting the nominating commission for his country: "The danger of an 'independent' Commission is that it would produce 'safe,' uncontroversial appointments . . . ."[103] Crawford suggests that, under such a system, Bora Laskin might not have been appointed in Canada, nor Felix Frankfurter in the United States. In West Germany the careful balancing of party influence in appointing members of the Constitutional Court has favoured middle-of-the-roaders in the selection process. Carl Baar has argued that if "professional concerns" operate to the exclusion of overt policy concerns "an appointing authority would be opting for the status quo and creating a judiciary less inclined to respond to new developments in government."[104] It would be unfortunate if political balance and prevailing professional norms systematically excluded from the Canadian judiciary individuals with a sharp political profile or an innovative approach to jurisprudence. Our discussion of the paradox of adjudication in chapter 1 demonstrated that judges inescapably make law in deciding disputes about the law. This is especially so with the higher appellate courts and above all with the Supreme Court of Canada. The collegial interaction of judges on these courts would be much impoverished if they all came out of the same professional and ideological mould.

One way of preventing this tendency would be to make the nominating committees publicly accountable for their selection policies. Under the systems that have been proposed, the minister of justice and cabinet remain responsible for judicial appointments in that they would not be legally bound to choose from the lists presented by the committees. Indeed, it is arguable that ministerial responsibility and accountability will be more effectively secured when the justice minister or prime minister can be asked to justify the appointment of persons not recommended by a nominating committee. But it is also possible that a justice minister may hide behind a faceless unaccountable nominating committee.

If these committees are required to disclose the names of those recommended for appointment, it would be easier to tell whether they are dominated by the bias of blandness. This measure of accountability would better balance the democratic and professional concerns which, at the beginning of this section, we argued must be served in reforming the appointing system.

The establishment of nominating commissions for appointments to section 96 courts would help to maintain Canada's uniquely integrated judicial system. If provincial governments are not given greater assurance that appointments to the provinces' section 96 courts are not dominated by the interests of the party in power in Ottawa, they will cease to regard these courts as the linchpins of the Canadian judicial system and will seek to control appointments to these courts themselves. The establishment of nominating committees to which both levels of government make appointments could arrest this process. Also, by establishing the same standard of professionalism and non-partisanship at the federal level as a number of the provinces have established for provincial appointments, this reform might make more provinces willing to abandon the hierarchy of trial courts and unify jurisdiction at the superior court level, thereby strengthening the basis for a truly national judiciary. As we shall see in Part Four, this approach to reforming the structure of Canada's trial courts has much to recommend it.

The Promotion of Judges

In the Canadian judicial system, unlike the French, a lawyer does not enter the judicial service immediately following graduation at the bottom of the judicial ladder and gradually work his way toward the top. In this sense there is no regular career path through the various levels of the judicial hierarchy. A system in which promotions are an expected feature of a judicial career has been looked upon as undermining the independence the judge should have of the appointing authorities. In Lord Denning's words, "There is the security of tenure, . . . but the hope for promotion and the favouritism which is thereby accorded, and the influence of a decision, as such, to suit the powers in authority, mean that there is great danger in introducing into this country a ladder of promotion."[105] James McRuer, a former chief justice of the High Court of Ontario, cast similar aspersions on a promotion system when he wrote that "it would be a corrupting thing for a magistrate or a judge to be in a position in which he could use his judicial office politically to advance his own promotion."[106]

Although there is no regular system of promotions within the Canadian judicial system, promotions do occur. They are not usually referred to as such; the less indelicate term "elevation" is favoured. The least frequent kind of promotion or elevation is from the provincially appointed lower courts to the higher, section 96 courts. William Klein found that only thirty (4 per cent) of the 749 judges who served on the section 96 courts of Manitoba, Ontario, and Quebec between 1905 and 1970 had begun their judicial careers as magistrates or judges in provincially appointed courts.[107] Throughout most of that period, outside of

Quebec, there were no professional qualifications for provincial court appointments. Consequently it is not surprising that promotions to the higher courts were so rare. But this should change now that there has been such an upgrading of the provincially appointed judiciary. There is much to be gained by promoting outstanding judges from the lower courts of the provinces and territories. Today they constitute a valuable reservoir of talent and experience which should not be overlooked in staffing the higher trial courts. Moreover, the recruitment of able lawyers to the provincially appointed courts will be impeded if appointments at that level are regarded as a dead-end beyond which promotion is virtually unheard of. When we bear in mind that in Canada the party in power nationally has often been different from the party in power provincially, we can recognize how partisan political influence on judicial selection may impede the promotion of able lower court judges to the county, district, or superior courts of a province. This is yet another argument for developing a merit selection system for both levels of the provincial court system.

It is within the section 96 courts that most promotions occur. Traditionally, in all provinces except Quebec there were three rungs within the federally appointed provincial judiciary: county and district courts at the bottom, the superior trial court in the middle, and the provincial court of appeal at the top. In six provinces the county and district courts have now been merged with the superior courts. The three levels remain only in British Columbia, Nova Scotia, and Ontario. Very little use has been made of judges with trial experience at the county and district court level for staffing the superior courts. Klein's study shows that less than 1 per cent of the judges who served on county courts in Manitoba and Ontario between 1905 and 1970 were promoted, whereas nearly one-fifth of the superior court judges received promotions.[108] Canada follows the English and American pattern of drawing heavily on judges from the superior trial courts for appointments to courts of appeal. Bouthillier's study of the Quebec judiciary, for example, shows that nearly half (thirty-four out of seventy-four) of the judges who have served on Quebec's Court of Appeal were promoted from the Superior Court.[109]

As might be expected, it is the highest court in the land, the Supreme Court of Canada, which has filled the highest proportion of its vacancies by promoting judges from lower courts. In table 5.1, the fourth column shows that thirty-six of the sixty-two justices who have served on the Supreme Court since its founding in 1875 have had previous judicial experience on the highest provincial trial court, a provincial court of appeal, or the Federal Court of Canada. The tendency is particularly marked in recent years: eight of Trudeau's ten appointments and Clark's only appointment (Chouinard) were "promoted" from lower courts. All of the present incumbents were "elevated" from positions in lower courts.

This pattern of promotions to the highest court is also found in other common law countries. In England Shetreet reports that "the Law Lords are normally promoted from the Court of Appeal or, in the case of Scottish Law Lords, from the Court of Session."[110] Henry Abraham's data on the 101 appointees to the US Supreme Court between 1789 and 1979 show that the percentage with previous judicial experience is 58.4 per cent—almost exactly the same as Canada's 58.1 per cent.[111]

Some might question this heavy reliance on judicial experience in staffing the Supreme Court. With a constitutional Charter of Rights increasing the political significance of the Supreme Court's work, political experience may seem more salient than ever before. However, as table 5.1 demonstrates, judicial experience and experience in public life are not mutually exclusive: most of the Supreme Court appointees with judicial experience also had some other experience in public life as government or university officials, in the governance of their profession, or as candidates for elected office. Those who had not held official positions may have had a considerable involvement with public issues through their law practice. While Abraham is surely correct when he states that "experience in the courts below . . . should not become a *requirement* for qualification for the Supreme Court," it is equally true that holding elected office is not the only kind of experience in public life that provides a valuable background for Supreme Court justices. What we expect, above all, from our Supreme Court justices is an ability to write clear and wise opinions about disputed issues of law. The ingredients of that ability include both a deep knowledge of law and a sensitivity to how the developing edge of the law will affect society. Today our legal system is so complex and professional legal standards are so much higher that it is increasingly difficult to develop and retain the legal skills required for a Supreme Court justiceship while pursuing a successful career in politics. Hence, we should expect a marked decline in the appointment of former politicians to the Supreme Court and a tendency to appoint persons who combine professional and community leadership with distinction as appellate court judges.

This review of promotions has shown that, unlike some European countries, Canada cannot be said to have a career judiciary with a regular ladder of promotions. Nevertheless, judicial promotions are not that infrequent, especially from the superior court to the court of appeal level and from the latter to the Supreme Court of Canada. The question that arises is whether promotions on this scale endanger judicial independence. Surely it is rather far-fetched to envisage Canadian judges shying away from deciding cases against the government because they are afraid of jeopardizing their chances for a promotion. Still, it must be admitted that the risk is there and is apt to become greater under the Charter of Rights when there is more at stake for government in the work of the courts. Apparently promotions within the federally appointed judiciary were not

TABLE 5.1 SUPREME COURT JUSTICES 1875-1984

JUSTICE	YEARS	CHIEF JUSTICE OF CANADA	PROVINCE	PREVIOUS COURT EXPERIENCE*	POLITICAL EXPERIENCE OR PUBLIC OFFICE
1. Richards, W.B.	1875-79	1875	Ont.	C.J.	A.G. Canada West
2. Ritchie, W.J.	1875-92	1879	N.B.	C.J.	Member, House of Assembly
3. Strong, S.H.	1875-02	1892	Ont.	C.A.	
4. Taschereau, J.T.	1875-78		P.Q.	S.C.	
5. Henry, W.A.	1875-88		N.S.		A.G., N.S., Father of Confed.
6. Fournier, T.	1875-95		P.Q.		Min. of Justice
7. Taschereau, H.E.	1878-06	1902	P.Q.	S.C.	Member, Leg. Assembly
8. Gwynne, J.W.	1879-02		Ont.	S.C.	
9. Patterson, C.S.	1888-93		Ont.	C.A.	
10. Sedgewick, R.	1893-06		N.S.		Dep. Min. of Justice
11. King, G.E.	1893-01		N.B.	S.C.	Premier of N.B.
12. Girouard, D.	1895-11		P.Q.		Conservative M.P.
13. Davies, L.H.	1901-24	1918	P.E.I.		Premier of P.E.I., fed. cabinet
14. Mills, D.	1902-3		Ont.		Min. of justice
15. Armour, J.A.	1902-3		Ont.	C.J.	
16. Nesbitt, W.	1903-5		Ont.		President Canadian Bar
17. Killam, A.C.	1903-5		Man.	C.J.	Member, prov. legislature
18. Idington, J.	1905-27		Ont.	S.C.	Crown attorney
19. Maclennan, J.	1905-9		Ont.	C.A.	
20. Fitzpatrick, C.	1906-18	1906	P.Q.		Min. of Justice
21. Duff, L.	1906-44	1933	B.C.	S.C.	
22. Anglin, F.A.	1909-33	1924	Ont.	S.C.	
23. Brodeur, L.P.	1911-23		P.Q.		Fed. cabinet
24. Mignault, P.B.	1918-29		P.Q.		
25. Malouin, A.C.	1924-24		P.Q.	S.C.	Liberal M.P.
26. Newcombe, E.L.	1924-31		Ont.		Dep. Min. of Justice
27. Rinfret, T.	1924-54	1944	P.Q.	S.C.	Defeated Lib. candidate
28. Lamont, J.H.	1927-36		Sask.	S.C.	A.G., Sask.
29. Smith, R.	1927-33		Ont.	S.C.	Liberal M.P.
30. Cannon, L.A.	1930-39		P.Q.	S.C.	Member, Leg. Assembly
31. Crocket, O.A.	1932-48		N.B.	S.C.	Conservative M.P.
32. Hughes, F.J.	1933-35		Ont.		
33. Davis, H.H.	1935-44		Ont.	C.A.	President, Canadian Bar Assoc.
34. Kerwin, P.	1935-63	1954	Ont.	C.J.	
35. Hudson, A.B.	1936-47		Man.		A.G., Man

TABLE 5.1 SUPREME COURT JUSTICES 1875-1984—*Continued*

JUSTICE	YEARS	CHIEF JUSTICE OF CANADA	PROVINCE	PREVIOUS COURT EXPERIENCE*	POLITICAL EXPERIENCE OR PUBLIC OFFICE
36. Taschereau, R.	1940-67	1963	P.Q.		Member, Leg. Assembly
37. Rand, I.C.	1943-59		N.B.		A.G., N.B.
38. Kellock, R.	1944-58		Ont.	C.A.	
39. Estey, J.W.	1944-56		Sask.		A.G., Sask.
40. Locke, C.H.	1947-62		B.C.		Treasurer, Law Society
41. Cartwright, J.R.	1949-70	1967	Ont.		Bencher Law Society
42. Fauteux, J.H.	1949-73	1970	P.Q.	S.C.	Chief crown prosecutor
43. Abbott, D.C.	1954-73		P.Q.		Min. of Finance
44. Nolan, H.G.	1956-57		Alta.		
45. Martland, R.	1957-82		Alta.		Bencher, Law Society
46. Judson, W.	1958-77		Ont.	S.C.	Bencher, Law Society
47. Ritchie, R.A.	1959-85		N.S.		V.P., Barristers Society
48. Hall, E.	1962-73		Sask.	C.J.	Chairman, Royal Commission
49. Spence, W.	1963-79		Ont.	S.C.	Wartime Prices & Trade Board
50. Pigeon, L.P.	1967-80		P.Q.		Advisor to Que. P.M.
51. Laskin, B.	1970-84	1973	Ont.	C.A.	Pres. Can. Assoc. Univ. Teachers
52. Dickson, R.G.B.	1973-	1984	Man.	C.A.	
53. Beetz, J.	1974-		P.Q.	C.A.	Dean of law, special counsel to P.M.
54. de Grandpré, L.P.	1974-77		P.Q.		Pres., Canadian Bar
55. Estey, W.Z.	1977-		Ont.	C.J.	Bencher, Law Society
56. Pratte, Y.	1977-79		P.Q.	C.J.	
57. McIntyre, W.	1979-		B.C.	C.A.	
58. Chouinard, J.	1979-		P.Q.	C.A.	Cons. candidate, sr. prov. official
59. Lamer, A.	1980-		P.Q.	C.A.	Chairman, Federal Law Reform Comm.
60. Wilson, B.	1982-		Ont.	C.A.	
61. Le Dain. G.E.	1984-		Ont.	F.C.	Dean of law
62. LaForest, G.V.	1985-		N.B.	C.A.	Dean of law, Dept. of Justice

*This column indicates the highest judicial position held prior to appointment to the Supreme Court: S.C. = a provincial superior court; C.A. = a provincial court of appeal; C.J. = chief justice of a provincial or colonial court; F.C. = Federal Court of Canada.

usually referred to the Canadian Bar Association's National Committee on the Judiciary. However, the bar's recent reform proposals recommend that judges proposed for elevation to a higher court should not be treated differently from other candidates.[112] Their names should be submitted to the appropriate advisory committee. This certainly makes good sense. Reducing both the appearance and reality of partisan political influence on judicial promotions will make them more compatible with judicial independence.

As we have contended throughout, judicial independence cannot be treated as an absolute. To pursue a purist policy and eliminate all judicial promotions because of a potential threat to independence would do great damage to the quality of the Canadian judiciary. Such a policy would eliminate a pool of talent— certainly not the only pool, but an extremely valuable source for staffing the country's higher courts. Further, making appointments to the lower and inter-mediate courts final has a deleterious effect on recruitment at this level. There should be more not fewer promotions from these courts.

There is one other kind of judicial promotion that has long been accepted in Canada: the promotion of ordinary judges, or puisne judges as they are called on the higher courts, to the position of chief judge or chief justice. As was noted earlier in this chapter, there are now a great many of these positions in the federal and section 96 courts. The chief judges, associate chief judges, senior judges, and administrative judges of the Provincial and Territorial Courts would bring the total number of judgeships carrying administrative responsibilities close to one hundred. The proliferation of leadership positions in the Canadian judicial system results from more than simply a growth in the judiciary. It also reflects a greater interest in court administration and a policy of retaining in judicial hands responsibility for those aspects of court administration that have a direct bearing on adjudication.

Given the nature of the chief justice's role, it is to be expected that these positions will most frequently be filled by promotion within a court. The administrative responsibilities of the chief justice or chief judge, especially the assigning of judges to cases and to courtrooms or circuits, will be exercised best when the chief knows his colleagues well and has their respect. As a recent study of the chief justice in Canada puts it, "Whenever a particular Chief Justice does not acquire, over a period, the confidence and willing collaboration of his colleagues, the operation of the court suffers and there is a real possibility that he will have to face unpalatable measures from the government such as a request for his early retirement."[113] That study reported that of the eighteen chief justices appointed during John Turner's and Otto Lang's period as justice minister (1968-75) fourteen came from within the court (or the bench at another level) and only four came directly from practice.[114] One of the more spectacular occasions when one of these senior positions was filled from outside the judiciary altogether occurred in 1906 when Charles Fitzpatrick went directly from being federal minister of justice to the chief justiceship of the Supreme Court of Canada. More recently James Jerome, Speaker of the House of Commons, was made associate chief justice of the Federal Court. Sometimes a chief justice will be appointed from another court. In Ontario four successive chief justices of that province's superior trial court, the High Court—McRuer, Gale, Wells, and Estey—moved to that position from the Court of Appeal. A much more unusual promotion occurred when Alan Gold, the chief judge of Quebec's Provincial Court, replaced Jules Deschênes as chief justice of Quebec's Superior Court. This was the only time in Canadian history that a provincially appointed chief judge was chosen to be chief justice of a federally appointed court.

Very little is known about the process of selecting chief justices or chief judges. At the federal level, as has been pointed out, the appointment of chief justices is a prerogative of the prime minister. Provincial chief judges are appointed by the cabinet. No doubt at both levels the minister of justice and attorney general plays an important role in identifying candidates. Soundings are taken, especially of the judges on the court in question. These may soon reveal that there is a logical successor to a retiring chief justice. But sometimes the choice may be more difficult. A court, like a university department, might be found to be so divided that a distinguished outsider is considered the best solution. Partisanship may be a factor in the selection: the Fitzpatrick and Jerome appointments are clear examples. Appointments to chief justiceships are not vetted by the CBA's National Committee on the Judiciary.

Both the Canadian Bar Association and the Canadian Law Teachers think it is as appropriate for nominating committees or councils to be involved in the selection of chief justices and chief judges as it is for them to be concerned with the appointment of puisne judges. However, it might be questioned whether nominating commissions really would provide the most effective means for sounding out judges on the administrative skills of their colleagues or the personal relationships within a court. Ministers and well-qualified deputies may be in a better position to do that. It is essential that the appointing authorities always consult members of the court directly affected by their choice and, in the case of section 96 appointments, ascertain the views of their provincial counterparts. A more radical alternative which Justice Deschênes has put forward for consideration is that the chief justice be selected by the ordinary judges on the court in question.[115] It is likely to be a long time before any Canadian government is likely to agree to this much judicial autonomy.

Notes to Chapter 5

1. See table 3.2, p. 52.
2. See Glen R. Winters and Robert E. Allard, "Judicial Selection and Tenure in the United States," in Harry W. Jones, ed., *The Courts and the Public Law Explosion* (Englewood Cliffs, N.J.: Prentice Hall, 1965).
3. Quoted in William H. Angus, "Judicial Selection in Canada—The Historical Perspective," *Canadian Legal Studies* (1967), p. 233.
4. Allen T. Klots, "The Selection of Judges and the Short Ballot," in Glen R.

Winters, ed., *Judicial Selection and Tenure: Selected Readings* (Chicago: American Judicature Society, 1967), p. 108.

5. E. Blythe Stason, "Judicial Selection Around the World," in ibid., p. 25.

6. Donald P. Kommers, *Judicial Politics in West Germany* (Beverly Hills: Sage, 1976), ch. 4.

7. Fred I. Morrison, "The Swiss Federal Court: Judicial Decision Making and Recruitment," in Joel Grossman and Joseph Tanenhaus, eds., *Frontiers of Judicial Research* (New York: John Wiley, 1969), p. 133.

8. For a review of these and other proposals, see Peter H. Russell, "Constitutional Reform of the Judicial Branch: Symbolic vs. Operational Considerations," *Canadian Journal of Political Science* (1984), p. 227.

9. *Report of the Canadian Bar Association Committee on the Appointment of Judges* (Ottawa: Canadian Bar Foundation, 1985), recommendation 10.

10. J.C. Adams and P. Barile, *The Government of Republican Italy* (Boston: Houghton Mifflin, 1961), p. 128.

11. David J. Danelski, "The People and the Court in Japan," in Grossman and Tanenhaus, *Frontiers of Judicial Research*, p. 45.

12. This view of the disadvantages of the career system is put forward, for instance, by R.M. Jackson, *The Machinery of Justice in England*, 7th ed. (Cambridge: Cambridge University Press, 1977).

13. Guy Bouthillier, "Profil du juge de la Cour des sessions de la paix," *Revue du Barreau* (1978), p. 13.

14. E.A. Tollefson, "The System of Judicial Appointments: A Collateral Issue," *University of Toronto Law Journal* (1971), p. 162.

15. Jean de Montigny and Pierre Robert, *Analyse Comparative des Législations et des Perspectives de Réforme* (Montréal: Université de Montréal Centre internationale de Criminologie Comparée, 1973), pp. 157-58.

16. For a description of the council and its activities see Jules Deschênes, *The Sword and the Scales* (Toronto: Butterworths, 1979).

17. For a brief overview of provincial judicial councils see Jules Deschênes, *Maîtres Chez Eux* (Ottawa: Canadian Judicial Council, 1981), pp. 172-82.

18. Most federally appointed judges belong to the Canadian Judges Conference. Provincially appointed judges belong to the Canadian Association of Provincial Court Judges.

19. See Mauro Cappelletti, John Merryman, and Joseph Perrilo, *The Italian Legal System* (Stanford: Stanford University Press, 1965), pp. 103-107.

20. For an analysis of this conflict, see Ezio Moriondo, "The Value System and Professional Organization of Italian Judges," in V. Aubert, ed., *Sociology of Law* (Harmsworth: Penguin Books, 1969).

21. The legal authority for this responsibility appears to stem from the general provisions of the Department of Justice Act (RS 1970, c. 71, s. 4(c)). See Ed Ratushny, "Judicial Appointments: The Lang Legacy," in A.M. Linden, ed. *The Canadian Judiciary* (Toronto: Osgoode Hall Law School, 1976), p. 32.

22. This is based on an order-in-council that goes back at least until 1920. See R.M. Dawson, *Constitutional Issues in Canada* (London: Oxford University Press, 1933), p. 125. Recommendations for chief judges of county and district courts are made by the minister of justice.

23. This is not a legal requirement in the case of section 96 judges as that section of the Constitution vests the appointing authority in the governor general, not the governor-in-council. Professor Hogg also notes that the recommendation of a chief justice is one of the prime minister's powers which he "may by convention exercise independently of his colleagues if he chooses." See *Constitutional Law of Canada* (Toronto: Carswell, 1985), p. 146.

24. William H. Angus, "Constitutional Reform: The Judiciary," paper presented to annual meeting of the Association of Canadian Law Teachers, Calgary, 6 June 1968.

25. *Report of the Canadian Bar Association Committee on the Appointment of Judges* (Ottawa: Canadian Bar Foundation, 1985).

26. The improvement in the quality of Supreme Court appointments under Bennett is described in James G. Snell and Frederick Vaughan, *The Supreme Court of Canada* (Toronto: The Osgoode Society, 1985), ch. 6. William Angus, however, suggests that generally Bennett was not able to practise what he preached. See Angus, "Judicial Selection in Canada," p. 241.

27. See Snell and Vaughan, *The Supreme Court.* A case study of the pressures and cross-pressures on a prime minister in making a Supreme Court appointment is provided in James Snell, "Frank Anglin Joins the Bench: A Study of Judicial Patronage, 1897- 1904," *Osgoode Hall Law Journal* (1980), p. 664.

28. Ratushny, "Judicial Appointments," p. 33.

29. Henry J. Abraham, *The Judicial Process* (New York: Oxford University Press, 1980), reports that in 1979 there were roughly 710 federally appointed judges and 14,000 judges of state and local courts.

30. According to a recent account, there are 9 law lords, 20 members of the Court of Appeal, 75 high court judges and 300 circuit court judges. See Alec Samuels, "Appointing the Judges," *New Law Journal* (1984), p. 85. In addition, of course, the Lord Chancellor is responsible for the appointment of all the lower court judges, including over 20,000 lay magistrates.

31. The Italian Council is discussed above at p. 111. In France a High Council of the Judiciary (made up mainly of presidential appointees) chooses the judges of the highest courts. See Abraham, *Judicial Process*, ch. 2.

32. House of Commons, *Debates*, 1932, p. 2999.

33. Guy Bouthillier, "Matériaux pour une analyse politique des juges de la Cour d'appel," *La Revue Juridique Thémis* (1971), p. 563. Throughout most of this period this court was known as the Court of King's Bench.

34. Guy Bouthillier, "Profil du Juge de la Cour Superieure du Québec," *Canadian Bar Review* (1977), p. 436.

35. William J. Klein, "Judicial Recruitment in Manitoba, Ontario, and Quebec" (Ph.D. thesis, Deptartment of Sociology, University of Toronto, 1975).

36. Ibid. table v-46.

37. Ibid. table v-44.

38. Ibid. table v-46.

39. For a summary of biographical detail on Supreme Court justices, see George Adams and Paul J. Cavaluzzo, "The Supreme Court of Canada: A Biographical Study," *Osgoode Hall Law Journal* (1969), p. 61.

40. Gilbert R. Schmitt, "Canadian Politicians and the Bench," *Saturday Night*, 19 Jul. 1952, p. 7.

41. John Willis, "Methods of Appointing Judges—An Introduction," *Canadian Legal Studies* (1967), p. 217. The survey was carried out by Professor R.B. Risk.
42. "A Symposium on the Appointment, Discipline and Removal of Judges," *Alberta Law Review* (1973), p. 308.
43. Professor J.A.G. Griffith, who is perhaps a more objective observer than Megarry, in his book on the English judiciary writes that "Today, being an active member of a political party seems to be neither a qualification nor a disqualification for appointment." *The Politics of the Judiciary* (London: Fontana/Collins, 1977), p. 24. For a discussion of the earlier highly partisan approach to judicial appointments in England, see Harold J. Laski, *Studies in Law and Politics* (New Haven: Yale University Press, 1932), ch. 7.
44. *Report of the Canadian Bar Association Committee on the Appointment of Judges*, ch. 6. The committee collected data on all judges appointed between 1978 and 1985 through provincial branches of the Canadian Bar Association and its own interviews.
45. On 29 June 1984, Pierre Trudeau on his last day as prime minister appointed Justice Minister Mark MacGuigan to the Federal Court of Appeal, and Privy Council president Yvon Pinard to the trial division of the Federal Court. Ten days later, in fulfilment of a written pledge to take care of some Trudeau loyalists, Prime Minister Turner appointed MP Bud Cullen, a former minister, to the trial division of the Federal Court, MPs Paul Cosgrove and Robert Daudlin to the county court in Ontario, and Joseph Mullally, a defeated Liberal candidate, to the Manitoba Court of Queen's Bench.
46. Quoted in Snell and Vaughan, *The Supreme Court*, p. 46.
47. Griffith, *Politics of the Judiciary*, p. 31.
48. See Herbert McCloskey and Adela Brill, *Dimensions of Tolerance: What Americans Believe About Civil Liberties* (New York: Russell Sage, 1983).
49. Jon Gottschall, "Carter's Judicial Appointments: The Influence of Affirmative Action and Merit Selection on Voting in the U.S. Court of Appeals," *Judicature* (Oct. 1983), p. 164. For an earlier study showing the influence of party affiliation on the decision-making of state and federal judges across a wide range of issues, see Stuart Nagel, "Political Affiliation and Judges' Decisions," *American Political Science Review* (1961), p. 313.
50. W. Gary Fowler, "Judicial Selection under Reagan and Carter: A Comparison of their Initial Recommendation Procedures, *Judicature* (Dec./Jan. 1984), p. 267.
51. The Liberal party has dominated the federal political scene for so long in Canada that there has not been a sufficient number of judges appointed by Conservative governments to test for differences between Liberal and Conservative appointees. My own study of the Supreme Court's decisions in civil liberties cases in the 1950s showed a marked division between Quebec francophone judges and the rest of the Court, a difference which I attributed to the relatively conservative strata of Quebec society from which the Liberal party selected judges. See Peter H. Russell, *The Supreme Court of Canada as a Bilingual and Bicultural Institution* (Ottawa: The Queen's Printer, 1969), pp. 188-206.
52. Trudeau announced this practice at the September 1967 meeting of the Canadian Bar Association and explained it in the House of Commons. House of Commons, *Debates*, 30 Nov. 1968, pp. 4895-96.

53. The classic study of the work of the American committee is Joel B. Grossman, *Lawyers and Judges* (New York: John Wiley, 1966).

54. An early account of the committee was provided by Ed Ratushny, a former special advisor on judicial appointments to the minister of justice, in his article in Linden, ed., *The Canadian Judiciary*. For a more up-to-date account see *Report of the Canadian Bar Committee on the Appointment of Judges*, ch. 4. For a description of the committee's function from a minister of justice's perspective, see Otto Lang, "Judicial Appointments," *Law Society of Upper Canada Gazette* (1974), p. 121.

55. "Symposium on the Appointment, Discipline and Removal of Judges," p. 286.

56. Grossman, *Lawyers and Judges*, pp. 93-94.

57. Ibid., pp. 111-13. The committee does not consider a candidate qualified if he is over sixty-four and does not recommend a candidate without trial experience for the district court.

58. Both Turner's and Lang's efforts are discussed in Ed Ratushny's article on the Lang legacy, in *Canadian Judiciary*.

59. *Canadian Bar Bulletin*, June 1973, p. 2.

60. *Report of Canadian Bar Association Committee on the Appointment of Judges*, p. 68.

61. These consultations have increased in the modern era. In 1965 Justice Minister Guy Favreau committed the federal government to more systematic consultations with the provinces on these matters. House of Commons, *Debates*, 13 Jul. 1965, p. 5428.

62. Davie Fulton, justice minister in the Diefenbaker government, reported that Premier Smallwood of Newfoundland tried to influence the selection of a judge before implementing legislation proclaiming an additional judgeship in the province's Superior Court. Ibid., 1 Aug. 1960, p. 7368.

63. Snell and Vaughan, The Supreme Court, pp. 146-47.

64. Order-in-council 748-182. For an account of these events, see Edward Greenspan, "Row Blows Up on How Ottawa Appoints Judges," *Financial Post*, 10 Dec. 1983.

65. Order-in-council 244/84.

66. *Saskatchewan Criminal Defence Lawyers Association* v. *The Government of Saskatchewan* (1984) 11 DLR (4th) 239.

67. *Minutes of Proceedings of the House of Commons Standing Committee on Justice and Legal Affairs*, 4 Dec. 1984, p. 3:10.

68. See James Crawford, *Australian Courts of Law* (Melbourne: Oxford University Press, 1982).

69. Australian Constitutional Convention 1982, Standing Committee "D," *Fourth Report to Executive Committee*, vol. 1, pp. 17-18.

70. High Court of Australia Act 1979, s. 6. Crawford notes that until 1979 regional distribution had not been a factor in High Court appointments. *Australian Courts of Law*, p. 156.

71. Both elements were contained in the "Best Efforts" draft tentatively agreed to by federal and provincial ministers in the summer of 1980. In this proposal a deadlock would be broken by the chief justice of Canada or a person designated by him.

72. A constitutional amendment on the method of appointing Supreme Court judges requires the approval of the federal Parliament and the legislatures of seven provinces representing 50% of the population. However, such an amendment is likely to be tied to an amendment concerning the Supreme Court's composition which would require the agreement of all the provinces.

73. W.R. Lederman, "Current Proposals for Reform of the Supreme Court of Canada," *Canadian Bar Review* (1979), p. 687.

74. For a summary of developments, see Marek Debicki, "Courts," in David. J. Bellamy, Jon H. Pammett and Donald C. Rowat, eds., *The Provincial Political Systems* (Toronto: Methuen, 1976), ch. 25.

75. For information on the appointment of lay magistrates in England, see Elizabeth Burney, *J.P.: Magistrates, Court and Community* (London: Hutchinson, 1979), ch. 4.

76. Royal Commission of Inquiry into Civil Rights (Ontario), *Report No. 1*, vol. 2 (1968) p. 539.

77. Bouthillier, "Profil du juge de la Cour des sessions de la paix," p. 13.

78. *Globe and Mail*, 7 Nov. 1983.

79. John Hogarth, *Sentencing as a Human Process* (Toronto: University of Toronto Press, 1971), p. 64.

80. 1968 (1st session) c. 17.

81. In Nova Scotia the court is called the Provincial Magistrate's Court, even though its members are called judges, whereas members of Newfoundland's Provincial Court are called Magistrates.

82. For a discussion of province-building, see Alan Cairns, "The Government and Societies of Canadian Federalism," *Canadian Journal of Political Science* (1977), p. 695.

83. For a vigorous critique of exclusive reliance on lawyers for the provincial judiciary, see A. Falzetta, "The Appointment of Magistrates," *Canadian Journal of Corrections* (1967), p. 137.

84. In Newfoundland, Nova Scotia, Ontario, and Saskatchewan the minister's role in submitting recommendations to cabinet is prescribed by statute. In Nova Scotia, the family court and its judges come under the minister of social services.

85. For a brief overview of the provincial councils, see Deschênes, *Maîtres Chez Eux*, pp. 172-82. For a more empirical account of the councils, see Peter McCormick, "Judicial Councils for Provincial Judges: A Comparison of the Experience of the Five Western Provinces," paper presented at the annual meeting of the Canadian Political Science Association, Montreal, June 1980.

86. RS BC, c. 341, s. 5(1).

87. Lawrence S. Goulet, "The B.C. Experience in the Appointment Process," paper delivered to annual meeting of the Association of Canadian Law Teachers, Montreal, 30 May 1985.

88. See *Report of Canadian Bar Committee on the Appointment of Judges in Canada*, ch. 2.

89. McCormick, "Judicial Councils for Provincial Judges," pp. 18-21. According to McCormick this evolution has not been completely smooth: "For some time the council was following the B.C. practice while the Attorney General was still following the Ontario practice." SYT 1983, c. 10, s. 4(1).

90. Ibid.
91. Jérôme Choquette, *Justice Today* (Québec: Gouvernement du Québec, 1975), p. 142.
92. Letter of Quebec minister of justice, Marc-André Bédard, to Robert H. McKercher, president of the Canadian Bar Association, 6 Dec.1983.
93. oc 1641-79, 6 June 1979.
94. *Report of the Canadian Bar Association Committee, on the Appointment of Judges in Canada*, p. 16.
95. Ibid., recommendation 21.
96. Ibid., recommendations 11, 12.
97. Ibid., recommendation 19.
98. Association of Canadian Law Teachers Special Committee on Judicial Appointments, *Recommendations for Consideration at the Annual Meeting*, Montreal, 1 June 1985.
99. JUSTICE, *The Judiciary* (London: Stevens, 1972). JUSTICE is the British section of the International Commission of Jurists.
100. See Samuels, "Appointing the Judges."
101. "The Judicial Nominating Committee," in Winters, ed., *Judicial Selection and Tenure*, p. 129.
102. For an analysis of the bar politics affecting nominating councils in Missouri, see Richard A. Watson, Rondal G. Downing and Frederick C. Spiegel, "Bar Politics, Judicial Selection and the Representation of Social Interests," *American Political Science Review* (1967), p. 54.
103. Crawford, *Australian Courts of Law*, p. 53.
104. Carl Baar, "Judicial Appointments and the Quality of Adjudication: The American Experience," *La Revue Juridique Thémis* (1986), p. 13.
105. Quoted in Shimon Shetreet, *Judges on Trial*, (Amsterdam: North Holland Publishing Co., 1976), p. 78.
106. Royal Commission Inquiry Into Civil Rights (Ontario), *Report*, p. 540.
107. Klein, "Judicial Recruitment," p. 312.
108. Ibid., table vi-59. Klein's figures include promotions to chief justiceships.
109. Bouthillier, "Materiaux pour une analyse politique des juges de la Cour d'appel," p. 580.
110. Shetreet, *Judges on Trial*, p. 79.
111. Abraham, *Judicial Process*, pp. 54-58.
112. *Report of the Canadian Bar Association Committee on the Appointment of Judges in Canada*, recommendation 16.
113. Canadian Institute for the Administration of Justice, *A Compendium of Information on the Status and Role of the Chief Justice in Canada* (Montreal, 1987). pp. 198-9.
114. Ibid., p. 9.
115. Deschênes, *Maîtres Chez Eux*, pp. 190-92.

CHAPTER 6

REMUNERATION AND QUALIFICATIONS

The appointing process discussed in the previous chapter is only one of the key variables in determining the composition of the third branch of government. Equally important are the level of remuneration and the formal and informal qualifications which shape the pool from which judges are chosen. These factors are examined in this chapter.

We begin with remuneration for a variety of reasons. In our rather materialistic modern societies (both capitalist and socialist) the level of remuneration has much to do with the incentives for entering the judicial occupation. Levels of remuneration also tend to reflect both the internal stratification of the judicial branch and the judiciary's position in the social hierarchy of the broader society. Finally, like every other occupation, judges are drawn into political activity in order to secure their economic interests.

Remuneration of Federally Appointed Judges

A recurring issue with regard to Canada's federally appointed judiciary is whether the level of remuneration is high enough to attract excellent lawyers to the bench. Parliamentary debates are strewn with speeches of politicians lamenting the low level of judicial remuneration. In 1932 we find Prime Minister Bennett telling the House of Commons that "the inadequacy of the salary makes it impossible to attract to the bench the best legal minds we have."[1] Nearly fifty years later we find Jean Chrétien as minister of justice making much the same point: "Some members tell me that I should seek the best minds available to become judges. However, the best people will not always accept these assignments because it involves many sacrifices."[2]

Of course there are certainly voices to be heard on the other side. A glance at table 6.1 showing the salaries paid to federally appointed judges over the years will make it clear that for the "ordinary Canadian" an appointment to the bench would not at any time have involved much of an economic sacrifice. Representatives of the CCF and NDP have often pointed this out. However, as long as we look to the ranks of experienced and successful lawyers to staff our courts, comparisons with ordinary Canadians are irrelevant. The comparison that counts is with professional legal incomes in a competitive capitalist economy.

To recruit "the best legal minds" to the judiciary it is not necessary to match the incomes of the best lawyers. A judicial position has some advantages which partially offset the economic opportunities that are lost when a lawyer gives up private practice in his or her peak earning years. Judges can become eligible for a pension and benefits for their surviving spouse and children which are very

TABLE 6.1 CHANGES IN SALARIES[1] OF FEDERALLY APPOINTED JUDGES, 1868-1985

JUDICIAL POSITION	1868	1886[2]	1906[2]	1920	1946	1951	1955	1963	1967	1971	1975	1978	1979	1980	1983[4]	1985[5]	1986
Chief Justice, Supreme Court of Canada	8000	10 000	15 000	20 000	25 000	27 500	35 000	42 000	50 000	68 000	72 000	80 000		88 000	106 000	135 000	
Judge, Supreme Court of Canada	7000	9000	12 000	16 000	20 000	22 500	30 000		45 000	63 000	67 000	74 000		81 000	98 100	124 000	129 168
Chief Justice, Exchequer Court, Federal Court, Provincial Supreme Court	5000	6000	8000	10 000	13 333	16 000	18 500	25 000	32 000	42 000	58 000	62 000		69 000	76 000	92 100	113 900
Judge, Exchequer Court Federal Court Provincial Supreme Court	4000	5000	7000	9000	12 000	14 400	16 900	21 000	28 000[3]	38 000	53 000	57 000		63 500	70 000	84 900	105 000
Chief judge, County and District Courts										30 000	51 000	55 000	63 000	71 000	87 000	108 900	109 200
Judge, County and District Courts	2600	3000	3500	4000	6666	8000	10 500	16 000	21 000	28 000	46 000	50 000	57 500	65 000		100 000	

[1] The source for these salaries is federal legislation. Since 1906 the salaries of all federally appointed judges have been provided for in the Judges Act.
[2] Figures for these years are maximum salaries: uniform federal rates for section 96 were not established until 1920.
[3] Exchequer court judges were paid $2000 more.
[4] The 1983 salaries incorporate the automatic increases made in 1981 and 1982 in accordance with the 1981 amendment to the Judges Act. The source for these figures is the Report of the Commission or Judges' Salaries and Benefits. That report does not contain data on the 1983 salaries of county and district court judges.
[5]. These salaries incorporate increases in Bill C-48.

expensive to purchase in private practice. The judge's work, while often arduous, seldom involves the nervous strain which so often is a feature of a leading practitioner's life. Certainly the work and income of the judge are more secure. In Canada considerable social prestige attaches to the position of a judge, especially on the federally appointed bench. In addition, there is the satisfaction of performing an important civic function. Those who derive no satisfaction from public service should not become judges.

There are negative factors that must be weighed against these positive aspects of judicial service: the tiresome and repetitive character of judicial workloads, the abandonment of participation in active political life and of close association with colleagues in the legal profession; the physical uprooting to a new city which so often goes with the acceptance of a judicial appointment in Canada, and the constant travelling which is a feature of service on the Federal Court and several of the provincial superior courts. It is difficult to attach precise values to these non-monetary dimensions of income. In Canada the prestige attached to a position in the federally appointed judiciary, while considerable, is not yet as great as with positions on the higher English or American courts. Still, experience suggests that outstanding lawyers in Canada will sacrifice some monetary income as a condition of accepting a judicial appointment. The key to a sound salary policy for judicial remuneration is gauging the differential between judicial salaries and private lawyers' income that will still permit the recruitment of "above average lawyers" to the bench.[3] It is only in the last few years that an approach to setting judicial salaries at the federal level has been adopted that has some promise of yielding such a policy.

Section 100 of the Constitution Act, 1867 requires that "the Salaries, Allowances, and Pensions of the Judges of the Superior, District and County Courts . . . shall be fixed by the Parliament of Canada." This constitutional requirement has meant that settling the level of remuneration for section 96 judges cannot be left to executive discretion, as it is in the provinces of Canada and in many other democratic countries. The salaries, allowances, and pensions of all federally appointed judges are established by act of Parliament. Traditionally this has been done by periodic amendments to the Judges Act. (table 6.1 presents a summary of these amendments).

From a democratic perspective the legislative method of determining judicial remuneration has the advantage of exposing the process to public scrutiny and discussion. Debates on amendments to the Judges Act have indeed been the occasion of lively parliamentary discussions on the judicial branch. On the other hand this process has had the disadvantage of being all too periodic. Amendments to the Judges Act must compete for attention with many other items on the crowded parliamentary timetable. When prices are stable this is not a serious problem. But in a period of high inflation it could result, as it did for a time in the 1970s, in a significant decline in the real income of judges. A remedy to this inflexibility was introduced in 1981 when the Judges Act was amended to provide for automatic annual adjustments equal to the increase in the industrial composite index of prices or 7 per cent, whichever is lower.[4]

The other change introduced in 1981 was the establishment of a Review Commission to examine the adequacy of judicial compensation every three years.[5] The first commission was appointed by the minister of justice, Mark MacGuigan, in April 1983. It consisted of Otto Lang, a former justice minister, as chairman and two others. The commission, as required, reported six months later. Its report, recommending substantial increases in compensation over and beyond the automatic increases provided for in 1981, was sent to the House of Commons Standing Committee on Justice and Legal Affairs. In 1984 Mr. Lang appeared before the committee and his recommendations were discussed. But, despite representations on behalf of the judges requesting immediate implementation, no legislative proposals came forward at that time.[6] It was not until 1985 under the Mulroney government that the Judges Act was amended to raise the base salaries of the federally appointed judiciary. But the changes effected by Bill C-48 in November 1985 (and made retroactive to April 1985), although substantial, fell considerably short of those proposed by the Lang commission. Whereas the Lang proposals called for increases ranging from 27 per cent to 33 per cent, the changes actually implemented range from 12 per cent to 15 per cent.[7]

Much concern has been expressed about the failure to automatically implement the recommendations of the Review Commission. Marcel Lambert, a Conservative MP, has repeatedly called for adoption of the "negative resolution" system used in the Australian state of New South Wales, whereby a remuneration tribunal's recommendations automatically become law unless within a specified time period specific objection is made to its recommendations by 50 per cent of the legislature. According to the Lang Report, section 100 of the Constitution Act, 1867 precludes such a procedure. However, the commission recommends that consideration be given to a constitutional amendment that would permit the Australian procedure, a procedure that in the commission's view "would in no way derogate from Parliament's overall control."[8]

The negative resolution procedure preserves only a shred of parliamentary control over judicial salaries. Now that automatic inflationary increases of up to 7 per cent have been built into the Judges Act, it is difficult to see any pressing reason for adopting such a procedure. This procedure would further undermine parliamentary government in Canada. The recommendations of the Lang Report involved significant changes in the basic level of judicial salaries, in judicial pensions, and in the application of taxation to judicial incomes. The rationale for changes of this kind should be publicly reviewed.[9] The Canadian judiciary is strong enough to take the buffeting which may be associated with periodic discussions of its level of compensation on the floor of the House of Commons. Legislative debate on the remuneration of judges provides one of the few opportunities for public review of judicial performance. It would be a shame to eliminate this ounce of accountability. If the Review Commission's recommendations are to be the basis of adjusting judicial remuneration, it should be by the affirmative resolution procedure requiring a positive vote of Parliament before the commission's proposals become law, as has been done since 1965 in England, with orders-in-council increasing the salaries of the higher judiciary.[10]

The salary increases recommended by Lang were designed to restore the real income of judges to their 1975 level. If implemented in 1985 they would have raised the salary of provincial superior court judges (the largest cadre of federally appointed judges) from $93 800 to $119 000. Many Canadians would find it difficult to accept a salary increase of this magnitude at any time and least of all during a period of budgetary cutbacks. Indeed, it was fiscal restraint that Justice Minister John Crosbie gave as the reason for not implementing the Lang proposals.[11] Others might question the rationale for the Lang proposals. One reason for selecting 1975 as a satisfactory base year was that in 1975 there was a restoration of the historic relationship between the salaries of the most senior civil servants and the salaries of federally appointed judges. In 1985 Mr. Crosbie assured the House of Commons that the much more modest increases in Bill C-48 would restore the "relativity" that existed in the past between judicial salaries and those of the most senior classification of deputy minister. But it is still not clear why this historic relationship (which also pertains in the United Kingdom) should be followed. Members of Parliament and the public might be equally concerned about how much judicial incomes exceed those of members of the elected branch of government. In 1983 a federal MP received $67 100 (indemnity plus expense allowance) as compared with the $84 900 salary of the superior court judge. The 1985 increases will substantially widen that gap.[12]

A more cogent argument for the salary level recommended by Lang is the relationship between judicial salaries and the income of lawyers in private practice. On the basis of data that may understate professional income levels, the commission found that there was a wide gap between the income of lawyers in the third quartile (i.e., above average) and judicial salaries. The third quartile of lawyers who had been practising for ten years had a before-tax income of $95 269 in 1981 as compared with a 1981 salary of $74 900 for superior court judges. Bearing in mind that ten years of professional practice is the *minimum* required for a federal appointment and that most judges are appointed after twenty to twenty-five years of practice, it is more relevant to take the differential for lawyers called to the bar in the years 1960 to 1964. The above-average lawyers in that age group were earning $126 750 in 1981—70 per cent more than a superior court judge. This is indeed a large differential, even when the value of judicial annuities is taken into account. The commission was convinced that, despite all the increases made in recent years, "the level of compensation has increasingly stood in the way of some top quality lawyers agreeing to become judges."[13]

In assessing the appropriate level of remuneration for federally appointed judges, Canadians might also consider, as the Lang Commission did not, judicial salaries in the United States. No doubt foreign comparisons are often misleading, but economic conditions and the circumstances of professional life are not so different in the United States as entirely to rule out American comparisons. Canadian salaries at current levels do not compare badly with American ones. For instance, in 1982 the *average* salary of judges in the general jurisdiction trial courts of the states (whose work most resembles that of a superior court trial judge in Canada), was $48 058 (or approximating $58 000 in Canadian dollars) as compared with $80 100 in that year for a superior court judge in Canada.[14] This difference reflects the fact that there is a uniform national salary scale for Canada's general jurisdiction judges. However, in the more prestigious U.S. federal courts, salaries appear to be higher: as of January 1987 the salary of an American Supreme Court judge was $107 200 ($149 008 Canadian), while U.S. district court judges earned $81 000 ($112 729 Canadian), and circuit court of appeal judges $85 700 ($119 123 Canadian).[15]

In the final analysis, the crucial test must be the effect of salary levels on recruitment. While the Lang Report states that some top-quality lawyers have rejected judicial appointments because of the remuneration, federal justice ministers (including Mr. Lang when he held that office) have boasted of their emphasis on professional merit in selecting judges. Unquestionably there have been some outstanding appointments from the private bar over the last ten years. More evidence is needed of the extent to which existing compensation levels impede the recruitment of a high-quality judiciary before implementing the salary proposals in the triennial commission's report.

Besides salary levels, two other dimensions of judicial compensation have become policy issues at the federal level in recent years: income tax and pensions. Both are dealt with in the triennial commission's report. These issues were examined in the 1979 Dorfman Report on judicial compensation,[16] while pensions were the focus of a 1981 Committee on Annuities, headed by Jean de Grandpré.[17] And both issues have been pursued through lobbying efforts of the Canadian Bar Association and the Canadian Judges Conference.

Since 1921 judges have paid income tax on their salaries on the same basis as other citizens. But the tax reform legislation enacted in 1971 and its interpretation by the Department of National Revenue greatly increased the tax burden in the year of appointment for those judges who were winding up their private practice. This caught many newly appointed judges by surprise and for many lawyers became a deterrent to accepting a judicial appointment. The Dorfman and Lang reports both contained proposals for eliminating this obstacle to recruitment by introducing special tax provisions in the Judges Act that would significantly reduce tax liability in the year of appointment. The case for making this change in judicial remuneration is more compelling than the proposal for higher salary levels. But if this modification of the application of taxation to judicial incomes is introduced, it should apply equally to all Canadian judges, including those appointed by the provinces.[18]

In 1975 Parliament made a significant change in the pension arrangements of federally appointed judges which had, to use the words of the Dorfman Report, "a disquieting effect" on the judges.[19] Henceforth judges would be required to contribute to their pensions and their survivors' benefits. The change was not quite that simple: a grandfather clause was included. Judges appointed before 17 February 1975 were required to contribute at the rate of 1.5 per cent of salary (to cover the cost of improvements in the level of survivors' benefits), while those appointed after that day were required to contribute at the rate of 7 per cent.[20]

Prior to 1975 the annuities payable to federally appointed judges upon their retirement and to their surviving spouses and children were non-contributory. This package of benefits, certainly when non-contributory, and even when contributions are required, is an inducement to lawyers to accept an appointment to the bench. The judge's pension is equal to two-thirds of salary at the time he or she leaves the bench and it is indexed. A judge becomes eligible for it at age sixty-five after fifteen years of service or at the mandatory retirement age, which is seventy-five for Supreme Court of Canada and provincial superior court judges, and seventy for Federal, county and district court judges providing he or she has served for ten years.[21] A surviving spouse receives half the pension, but must give it up on remarrying. Dependent children are eligible to receive one-fifth of the surviving spouse's annuity and this is doubled if there is no surviving spouse.

The introduction of a contributory element into this attractive benefit package raised a tremendous hue and cry from the legal profession and from judges. It was attacked as a violation of the principle of judicial independence. We are told that within the judiciary the change created an "unhealthy degree of malaise."[22] The primary source of grievance was the differing annuity contributions resulting from the grandfather clause. This agitation led to review of the 1975 change by the Dorfman and de Grandpré committees, both of which have called for a return to non-contributory pensions and a refund with interest of the contributions made by judges appointed since 1975. Dorfman would have all judges contribute just 1.5 per cent of salary to the supplementary benefits account. Both the Clark and Trudeau governments appeared to look with favour on these proposals but took no action.

In the meantime one judge was not content with normal lobbying and resorted to the judicial arena. This court challenge has been unsuccessful. In *Beauregard v. The Queen*, the Trial Division of the Federal Court ruled that the introduction of contributory pensions violated section 100 of the Constitution. This judgment was upheld by the Federal Court of Appeal.[23] The reasoning behind this decision was that section 100 of the Constitution states that pensions "shall be fixed and provided by the Parliament of Canada" and that this language does not contemplate Parliament charging judges for their pensions through a contributory scheme. The political scientist cannot refrain from remarking on the amount of self-discipline required by judges to remain "impartial" in deciding such a case. It is gratifying to report that the Supreme Court of Canada in a unanimous decision rejected the specious line of reasoning that had prevailed in the lower courts. In the Supreme Court's opinion, "Canadian judges are Canadian citizens and must bear their fair share of the financial burden of administering the country."[24]

Canadian citizens must find it difficult to understand why judges should not contribute to their pensions. Because judges are appointed in mid-career or later it is clear that an adequate pension cannot be fully financed by contributions.

Nevertheless, contributions at the rate most of us must pay into our own pension plans would help fund these benefits and make judges appear less like a privileged class. The Lang Commission agreed with proposals of the two earlier advisory committees to repeal and refund contributions to pensions because it disapproved of the inequity in the differential level of payments by the two classes of judges. But this differential could, of course, be eliminated by requiring all judges in the future to pay the same 7 per cent rather than 1.5 per cent. The Lang Commission stressed that annuities and salary deductions should be treated as part of overall compensation.

The Lang Report states that "we do not consider the issue of contributions to annuities as in any way affecting the independence of the judiciary."[25] Surely this view is correct. The judges' independence from government interference in adjudicating cases is not affected by Parliament mandating contributions to retirement income. Contributions to pensions and other benefit schemes are required in other democratic jurisdictions, including most of the Canadian provinces.[26] The invocation of judicial independence introduced a large red herring into this issue.

Judicial independence was reinforced by the establishment of the Office of Commissioner for Federal Judicial Affairs in 1977.[27] The commission took over from the Department of Justice the administration of personnel matters with respect to all federally appointed judges except the judges of the Supreme Court of Canada; the registrar of the Supreme Court became responsible for the latter. In addition to the payment of salaries and annuities, many details of personnel management must be worked out with individual judges. These include travel and conference allowances, leaves of absence, moving expenses and opting for early retirement or supernumerary status. It was felt that judges should not be negotiating these matters with officials from a government department which frequently appears in cases before them. The commissioner acts as a deputy of the minister but he and his staff are not part of the Department of Justice. The commissioner is appointed by the cabinet after consultation with the Canadian Judicial Council.

The establishment of the Commissioner for Federal Judicial Affairs moves Canada closer to both England and the United States. In England, these aspects of personnel administration for the judiciary are the responsibility of the Lord Chancellor, who is the country's highest judge as well as a member of the cabinet and Speaker of the House of Lords. In the United States, at the federal level, they come under the Judicial Conference of the United States headed by the chief justice of the Supreme Court. The federal commissioner also has responsibility for budgetary management of the Federal Court and the Canadian Judicial Council and for ensuring that the physical plant, equipment and staffing needs of these bodies are met.

Remuneration of Provincially Appointed Judges

Traditionally there has been a large gap between the remuneration of provincially and federally appointed judges. Provincially appointed judges have been paid on a much more modest scale. During the 1970s, as part of the overall reform of the Provincial Courts, the gap did narrow. Indeed, when the salaries of Provincial Court judges in several provinces approached and even surpassed the salaries paid to county and district court judges, the federal minister of justice used this as an argument for raising the salaries of section 96 judges.[28] However, a report prepared for the Canadian Association of Provincial Court Judges in 1981 indicates that the compensation of the provincially appointed judiciary has not kept pace with improvements in the compensation of the federally appointed judiciary.[29] That report showed that the salaries paid to judges of the Provincial and Territorial Courts at the end of 1980 ranged from a low of $38 000 in Newfoundland to a high of $57 400 in Quebec, when the lowest salary among the federally paid judiciary was $65 000. The overall compensation package does not change the picture: except for Prince Edward Island, these judges' pensions are contributory and in most jurisdictions they are not available on as favourable terms as the pensions of the federal judiciary.

The traditional practice of paying judges of the so-called lower courts much less than the judges of the intermediate and superior courts of the provinces may appear logical when the judicial system is viewed as a hierarchy. But the problem with translating this hierarchy of courts into a hierarchy of salaries is that we do not want the quality of justice to be hierarchically arranged. The quality of adjudication is likely to bear some relationship to the remuneration of the adjudicator. Commentators on our judicial system never tire of observing that most Canadians who experience the quality of justice at first hand do so in the lower courts. Accepting lower standards here in the courts used most often by Canadians from lower income brackets, is a significant source of social injustice in Canada.[30]

Some time ago Canada departed from the British practice of using unpaid lay members of the local community to administer justice in the lower courts. We now require a much higher level of professional competence on the part of those who serve as judges on the Provincial and Territorial Courts. The federal Parliament has given these judges extremely important functions in the field of criminal justice and the provinces have done the same in the area of family and civil law. All together the responsibilities of these courts are considerably greater than those of the English magistrates' courts. In these circumstances, it is essential to recruit very good lawyers to serve on these courts. The recruitment challenge becomes clear when you consider that in 1981 the median income of lawyers who had been in practice fifteen to twenty years (the professional cohort from which most provincial and territorial judges are recruited) was $89 400, up to twice as much as was then paid to judges on these courts.[31] Of course, professional income is not the only measure of the lawyer who will make a good judge, and many fine lawyers have accepted appointments to these courts despite the income. This is particularly true outside of the big cities where a Provincial Court judgeship may be an attractive way of capping a successful legal career. Still, the systematic differential between the remuneration of provincially and federally appointed judges remains highly questionable.

One barrier to removing this differential is the combination of routine and minor matters with extremely important adjudicative responsibilities in the work of the Provincial and Territorial Courts. The processing of traffic violations does not call for the same skills and character required for the adjudication of serious criminal and civil cases. As the provincial justice systems are restructured so that the legally qualified judges concentrate their energies on more serious disputes, the courts presided over by these judges will appear less as lower courts and more as the major trial courts they now, in part, are. As this occurs the two-class system of trial courts we now have should be less tolerable and Provincial Court judges should be accorded the same status and remuneration as federally appointed trial judges. The logical end of this process is an adjudicative service for the settlement of disputes about important legal rights and duties that is neither federal nor provincial, upper or lower, but of a uniformly high quality throughout the nation.

The two-class system is reflected not only in the lower compensation levels of the Provincial and Territorial Court judges but also in the administration of their personnel arrangements. There is nothing like the Commissioner for Federal Judicial Affairs to serve as a buffer between these judges and the executive branch. Provincial legislatures have delegated to the cabinet power to fix the salaries of provincially appointed judges by regulation. In the *Valente* case, the Supreme Court of Canada rejected the argument that this arrangement violated the guarantee of judicial independence in section 11(d) of the Charter. Justice Le Dain viewed it as "far from clear that having to bring proposed increases to judges' salaries before the legislature is more desirable from the point of view of judicial independence, and indeed adequate salaries, than having the question determined by the Executive alone, pursuant to a general legislative authority."[32]

Recent events in Ontario, however, throw into question the constitutional seal of approval given by the Supreme Court of Canada to the Ontario and other provincial systems. It is ironic that these events occurred in Ontario, which has gone further than other jurisdictions in endeavouring to establish an independent mechanism for determining judicial salaries. Since 1980 it has had a Provincial Courts Committee made up of an appointee of the provincial and family court judges' associations, a government appointee and a chairman chosen by the first two.[33] In the *Valente Case*, Justice Le Dain said that the existence of this committee was "assurance that proper consideration will be given to the adequacy of judicial salaries," although he also stated that it was not an essential condition of judicial independence. In the fall of 1985, when the government of Ontario rejected a recommendation from the committee that salaries be increased from $71 855 to $80 000 and announced a 4.4 per cent increase to $75 000, Edward Greenspan, a lawyer representing the judges on the committee, resigned. Greenspan accused the government of bargaining in bad faith. His resignation was followed by a publicized request from the Provincial Court (Criminal Division) judges to the lieutenant-governor for an independent inquiry, and a speech by Chief Judge Andrews of the family court at the opening of courts early in 1986 suggesting that Ontario's Provincial Court judges might find it difficult to deal impartially with the government in the courtroom because of their displeasure with the government's treatment of the salary issue. Andrews's speech elicited an immediate response from Ontario's attorney general, Ian Scott, to the effect that judges who feel diminished in their capacity for impartiality should resign.[34]

This ugly episode does not inspire confidence in a system that makes judicial salaries so dependent on executive discretion. Nor does it serve as a good advertisement for the collective-bargaining approach to settling disputes. Collective bargaining implies that both sides may resort to economic or political sanctions when the bargaining breaks down. The Ontario experience gives just a taste—a very bad taste—of the political sanctions that both sides might use. The better model would appear to be that now in operation at the federal level. The triennial commission there is not structured on labour relations lines. It does not purport to be a bargaining process but rather a reasonably objective inquiry into the salary level needed to produce a high-quality judiciary. Given executive domination of the legislature in Canada's parliamentary system, the cabinet will have the last word whether salaries are fixed by legislation or regulation. But, there is more accountability and less likelihood of continual political rancour when a public statute like the Judges Act fixes the basic salary level and provides for periodic reviews and automatic annual increases. However, the key problem for Provincial Court judges is not procedural but a failure to persuade provincial governments that the work they do is as challenging, as important to society and as deserving of the same level of remuneration as that of the federally appointed trial judges.

If differences between the personnel arrangements of provincially and federally appointed judges are questionable, the treatment of the lowest locally appointed adjudicator, the justice of the peace, is even more dubious. Throughout Canada lay justices of the peace continue to perform adjudicative functions. Ontario is one jurisdiction where the significance of their judicial work has actually increased as a result of the judicialization of the magistracy. As provincial judges' responsibilities for cases involving serious criminal offences increased, the JPs have been given a primary role in hearing cases involving provincial offences. In some of these cases quite significant penalties can be meted out. For instance, in the case which provoked the first major constitutional review of the JPs status, the accused, Charles Currie, was liable to a fine of up to $10 000.[35] Notwithstanding the important judicial functions performed by justices of the peace, they held office at the pleasure of the cabinet, their salary increases were determined by the deputy attorney general, their salary could be suspended by that same official, and many worked on a fee-for-service basis under which their income depended on the amount of business brought to them by the police.[36]

The *Currie* case produced a scathing judicial indictment of the JPs position in Ontario. The constitutional issue in the case was whether an accused person is deprived of his right under section 11(d) of the Charter of Rights to be tried "by an independent and impartial tribunal" if he is tried by a justice of the peace. Justice Ewaschuk of the Ontario High Court ruled, emphatically, that the Ontario JPs did not have the independence required by the Constitution. While the judge found the JPs' terms of office totally lacking in independence, he was particularly critical of the fee-for-service system and the executive-dispensed salary increases.

Currie, like *Valente* and *Beauregard*, is yet another instance of members of the judiciary turning to their own arena to obtain improvements in their conditions of office which they had not been able to obtain by making direct representations to the government. The Metropolitan Toronto Association of JPs which had been agitating for reforms was an intervenant in the *Currie* case. Under pressure of this litigation the Ontario government scrambled to avoid what could have been a chaotic situation if justices of the peace, who play such a vital role in Ontario's criminal justice system were deemed to be unconstitutional. While the *Currie* case was before the courts, amendments to the Justices of the Peace Act were enacted which put fee-for-service JPs on a judicially administered roster system and established some security of tenure JPs.[37] The day after the Ewaschuk decision, the cabinet passed regulations removing the deputy attorney general's power to suspend salaries or approve increases. A few days later, the province's attorney general was successful in obtaining a court order to have JPs continue hearing cases until the Ontario Court of Appeal could rule on the matter. Unlike Justice Ewaschuck, the Court of Appeal considered their situation in the light of the reforms so hurriedly introduced by the Ontario government and found that there was no breach of the Charter.[38] Still, the *Currie* case established that justices of the peace who perform significant judicial functions are not to be treated like minor bureaucratic functionaries but must enjoy at least the minimal conditions of judicial office.

Professional Qualifications

Membership in the legal profession is a formal legal condition of eligibility for appointment to most judicial positions in Canada. For judges of the section 96 provincial courts (the superior, county and district courts) membership in the bar is a constitutional requirement. Sections 97 and 98 of the Constitution that provide for this contain an element of special status for Quebec. Whereas section 98 requires that federally appointed judges in Quebec must always come from the bar of that province, section 97 imposes a similar requirement on the selection of judges for the common law provinces only until such time as these provinces agree to the adoption of uniform laws in relation to property and civil rights and to court procedure. This, however, has turned out to be a meaningless distinction. The day has never come, and probably never will, when the common law provinces agree to exercise the opportunity they have under section 94 of the Constitution to abandon their power of making distinctive laws concerning property and civil rights and court procedure and turn over jurisdiction in the these fields to the federal Parliament. The judges of the section 96 courts continue to be drawn from the bars of the provinces in which they serve.[39]

The Constitution is silent on the years of professional experience required for appointment to the section 96 courts. There was no requirement for years of experience in federal legislation until 1912 when the ten year rule was introduced for superior, county and district court judges.[40] Until then the provinces had legislation concerning the professional qualifications of these judges, some of which was carried over from pre-Confederation days. The new federal requirement in a few instances was more demanding than that which pertained in some provinces. At the time, the federal minister of justice expressed doubt as to the constitutional validity of provincial laws on this subject.[41] The ten-year rule has stood since 1912 with one minor modification: a 1977 amendment permits years served as a Provincial Court judge to count toward meeting the professional requirement.[42] A ten-year rule has also been applied to the other federally appointed judgeships. Eligibility for the Supreme Court of Canada requires experience on a superior court of a province, or ten years' standing at the bar of a province.[43] It is interesting to note that there is no such professional requirement *in law* for appointment to the United States Supreme Court or, for that matter, to the other American federal courts.[44] Appointees to the Federal Court and Tax Court must either have served on a section 96 court or have ten years' standing as professional lawyers.[45]

Professional legal standing as a requirement for provincially appointed judges arrived much later. But, as we have seen, it is now a statutory requirement in eight of the provinces and the Northwest Territories, and even where it is not legally prescribed it is the practice to appoint qualified lawyers. In Newfoundland, without a law school and with a relatively low lawyer-to-population ratio, there has been a program of spotting potential provincial magistrates in the police ranks and sending them to the Dalhousie Law School for their legal education.[46] Only Ontario and Quebec have matched the ten years required for federally appointed judges, and Ontario did this as recently as 1984.[47] Most other jurisdictions have been content with a formal requirement of five years.[48]

To contemporary Canadians it must seem eminently logical to require that judges have a formal education in law and some professional legal experience. As the country's largest mass circulation newspaper, the *Toronto Star*, put it, "real judging" should be left to judges "trained in law."[49] This popular view is fundamentally sound. Adjudication—the *raison d'être* of courts of law - is the function of settling disputes about legal rights and duties. To perform this function well, knowledge of the law is essential. Of course, "the law" is not, as popular discourse sometimes implies, simply a set of rules that can be looked up in a book. It includes all that it is appropriate to take into account in making decisions about disputed points of law. Law is as much a decision-making craft as a fixed body of knowledge. That craft may be called into play even in a parking ticket case when, for instance, an accused person claims the protection of the Charter of Rights. At this stage in our history, with the ever-increasing complexity of our legal system and the expansion and improvement of legal education, Canadians would be foolish not to insist that their courts of law be staffed by professional lawyers. With a legal profession which has more than doubled in size since 1970, Canada certainly has enough lawyers for all of its judicial positions!

Such a thorough-going professionalization of the judiciary may, however, have some drawbacks. It means that the non-lawyer—the "ordinary citizen"— becomes basically a subject of the judicial branch rather than a participant in it. This process is intensified by the declining use of juries in the higher trial courts of Canada: they are rare in civil cases and are used in only the most serious criminal cases. The elitist implications of this trend are modified in that as the legal profession has expanded it has become more accessible to all sections of society. Still, the monopoly of participation in the judicial branch of government by a profession, particularly one already so heavily represented in the other two branches, must be a source of concern in a democratic society, even when the profession itself is relatively democraticized. Empowering lay justices of the peace who are often political appointees with little education of any kind to sit as single judges to try even minor cases is a poor way of meeting this concern. It is unlikely to increase the legitimacy of the courts. More promising are proposals, such as Thomas Berger's royal commission recommendations for family courts in native communities, designed to give the professional judge access to panels of lay assessors drawn from local communities in determining dispositions involving families and young offenders.[50] Traditional forms of public participation could also be strengthened: the decline in the use of the jury trial might be arrested; witnesses should be treated with civility and properly remunerated.[51] We have also noted the need for lay participation in the appointment of judges. Later on we will examine other possibilities for lay participation in judicial discipline.

Recruitment Patterns

It must be stressed that the professional requirements set down in statutes are minimum standards. In practice, the appointing authorities, both federal and provincial, usually appoint lawyers who have practised many more years than the legal requirement. Most federally appointed judges have been over fifty when appointed and provincially appointed judges only slightly younger.[52] Today there may be a trend toward appointing lawyers who are somewhat younger, but few are appointed in their thirties when they meet the minimum age requirement. When he was minister of justice, John Crosbie reported that the average age of federally appointed judges at the time of appointment had come down to forty-nine.[53] A shift to appointing lawyers in their early forties rather than their early fifties should still provide a long enough period of performance to serve as a basis for assessing merit and, at the same time, bring to Canadian courts the outlook of a younger generation. In British Columbia, where thirty of the seventy-one Provincial Court judges appointed between 1973 and 1983 were under forty years of age, Judge Goulet reports that this break from tradition was "overwhelmingly successful."[54] On the other hand professional "burn-out" might become more of a problem with younger appointments. Retirement ages of seventy and seventy-five could result in thirty-five to forty years in office—a long time to retain one's interest in any job!

There is a great deal of variety in the professional backgrounds of Canadian judges. It is here that we find the most marked contrast between the Canadian and English judiciaries. In England the higher courts are staffed exclusively by barristers who live their professional lives in the courts and who constitute less than one-tenth of the legal profession. Justice Megarry estimates that at any given time only about one hundred and fifty to two hundred barristers have attained the level of professional success and are of the right age to be eligible for appointment.[55] In Canada the legal profession is not organized into separate branches of solicitors and barristers. Plenty of lawyers who have specialized in solicitors' work and have had little or no courtroom experience have been appointed to the bench. This is as true of the lower trial courts as of the higher. Indeed, John Hogarth in his study of Ontario magistrates (before they became Provincial Court judges), found that while all of the legally trained magistrates had at least ten years' experience at the bar prior to appointment, very few of them had specialized in criminal court work.[56] Again, in contrast to Britain but like the United States, legal academics are occasionally appointed to the judiciary—to trial courts as well as to courts of appeal.

Earlier we noted a trend away from appointing lawyers who had been elected politicians. The demands of political and professional life are such today that it is increasingly difficult to be accomplished and successful in both realms. The two major sociological analyses that have been made of the Canadian judiciary demonstrate some further trends of interest to the political scientist. What stands out in Guy Bouthillier's studies of the Quebec judiciary is the large number of judges whose legal career involved government work. For example, of 161 lawyers who have served on Quebec's Superior Court, 77 did legal work for either the federal or provincial government and 30 per cent had been crown prosecutors.[57] A similar trend can be seen in the significant number of lawyers from the federal Department of Justice and other branches of the federal public service recently appointed to the Federal Court and the Ontario superior courts. William Klein's study draws attention to a different tendency: the importance of involvement in professional organizations, especially the Canadian Bar Association. He shows that while the proportions of benchers (who govern the professions in each province) and law teachers who received appointments in Manitoba, Ontario and Quebec diminished slightly between 1905 and 1970, the frequency with which executive members of the Canadian Bar Association went to the bench increased by leaps and bounds. In the 1960s, 78 per cent of CBA executives in the provinces studied became judges as compared with 2 per cent in the 1920s.[58] Bouthillier's and Klein's research suggest that government service and involvement at the national level in professional activities are transcending electoral politics as the most frequented roads to the bench.

These patterns bring into question how close we are getting to a system of judicial recruitment based on general criteria of merit rather than particular connections with the appointing authorities. But what is "merit" in this context? To this question there is surely no simple answer. Definitions of the good judge usually produce a profile of some God-like creature, a paragon of all the virtues. At least we can be confident that being good at judging involves some combination of personality and knowledge. For trial courts in our system, where the judge sits alone and must conduct a fair trial in which professional adversaries are the prime players, the former may be even more essential than the latter. Some years ago, when Maurice Rosenberg surveyed American trial judges for their views on the qualities they found most important in their work, he found that they ranked personality traits—moral courage, decisiveness, a reputation for fairness, patience, good health (both mental and physical), and consideration for others—ahead of any professional skills.[59] For courts of appeal, where decision-making is a more collective activity, there is room, and indeed a need, more diversity in professional backgrounds and personalities.

Should the Judiciary Be Socially Representative?

Is there also a need for a more representative mix of social backgrounds among members of the Canadian judiciary? In terms of social class, there can be no doubt about the unrepresentative character of the Canadian judiciary. Nearly all of Canada's judges are recruited from the ranks of moderately successful lawyers who have reached at least mid-career. A moderately successful, middle aged lawyer, while not necessarily rich is certainly not poor. There is a similar class bias in the parental background of the lawyers who become judges. This is true whether one looks at the top or the bottom of the judicial hierarchy. Adams and Cavaluzzo in their biographical study of the first fifty Supreme Court of Canada judges, found that only two of them were born into working-class families.[60] John Hogarth, in his study of Ontario magistrates, reports that "more than half the magistrates come from business or professional families, while not many more than one in ten of the general population are drawn from these occupational groups."[61] Bouthillier's research on the Quebec judiciary yields similar results. In particular he draws attention to occupation inheritance: the high number of judges raised in the families of judges and lawyers.

The unrepresentative character of the Canadian judiciary in a social class sense is a fact. But is it also a problem, something that in a liberal democracy we should be seeking to change? I think not. It is important that social and economic barriers to legal education be removed, but to a large extent this has been done in Canada. Admission to law school now depends on academic marks and aptitude tests, not social connections. But, advantages of birth do remain: it helps a lot to grow up in an environment that nurtures an interest in the legal vocation or, more generally, an environment that makes the affluence and prestige of the lawyer the expected standard of success. Only the most fiendishly authoritarian regime would try to eliminate such advantages. Nor is there reason to believe that if more lawyers with working-class backgrounds were appointed to the bench, our courts would treat members of that class more fairly or leniently. Some very tough attitudes may be engendered in the person who has had to struggle and "make it the hard way." In his study of sentencing, Hogarth found that magistrates from working-class families were rather more punitive in their attitudes and beliefs.[62]

The uniformity in the class backgrounds of Canada's judges does not constitute, as Dennis Olsen has suggested, a "contradiction . . . between liberal-democratic ideology and practice."[63] The ideal of liberal democracy is not a classless society without structure. The pluralism valued by liberals is not a wide-open, limitless pluralism in which truly all things are possible. As we argued in the opening chapter, the judiciary as part of the governing structure in any society will be supportive of its prevailing ideology. Through their legal education and professional experience, judges absorb the values and accommodate the interests that have shaped the law. That law—the law they must as judges interpret and apply—is no more neutral than it is fixed or certain. We should not expect judges in Canada to believe that private ownership of the means of production or exchange is evil or that poverty should be accepted as a defence for robbery. But within this common *Weltanschauung* there can be many grounds for differing with the outlook and sensitivities of the government of the day. It is here that political pluralism is needed in staffing the judiciary of a liberal state. We should be concerned about recruitment policies that favour partisan supporters of the government or crown attorneys over defence lawyers. As long as judges are recruited entirely from the ranks of successful lawyers (and that policy, as we have seen, is now well established in Canada) the bourgeois orientation of the Canadian judiciary is unavoidable. This may very well mean that when class issues are clearly at stake in adjudication, the Canadian judiciary is not impartial. R.M. Jackson, in his study of the English judiciary, notes how the class bias of English judges has been reflected in a series of questionable decisions concerning the rights of trade unions. But the remedy, Jackson suggests, is not to seek out working-class judges but to recognize that, given this limitation of the judiciary, industrial disputes should as far as possible be kept out of the courts and resolved by joint bodies representing employers and workers.[64]

There are, however, some other ways in which the Canadian judiciary is unrepresentative, about which we should be more concerned. Aboriginal persons have not been appointed to the bench above the position of justice of the peace. Indeed, there are very few non-Caucasians among Canadian judges. Also, less than 5 per cent of Canadian judges are women. The under-representation of women is worse on the higher courts: in 1980 Pauline Jewett told the House of Commons that only twenty (3 per cent) of the 657 federally appointed judges then serving were women and all but two of these had been appointed since

1971.[65] At that time there were no women on the Supreme Court of Canada or the superior courts of six provinces. Under-representation in these areas has more than a symbolic significance. It also means that insights and knowledge needed for intelligent adjudication are often lacking. Native Canadians who become judges are likely to be much better informed than Canadian judges have been up to now about the meaning and significance of aboriginal rights—rights which are now entrenched in the Canadian Constitution.[66] Black judges might call into question the harsher sentences given black youths in the Halifax Provincial Court.[67] Through their first-hand experience of "the deprivations of person-hood," to use Pauline Jewett's phrase, women judges should be able to help Canadian courts respond more intelligently to claims of sex discrimination. It would surely be ridiculous to aim for a judiciary that precisely mirrored the diversity of the Canadian population. Without approaching that extreme, there is still much that could be done and much to be gained in moving the Canadian judiciary away from the vertical mosaic that John Porter described a generation ago.[68] Access to legal education has now been broadened to the point that it should be possible to appoint more members of under-represented groups without sacrificing quality. This is certainly true in the case of women, who by now constitute a significant proportion of the lawyers with ten years of practice.[69] Research on the results of President Carter's affirmative action approach to judicial appointments concludes that this policy, far from undermining merit selection, on balance improved the quality of appointments.[70]

Linguistic and Regional Representation

The need to reflect the constitutional ideal of official bilingualism in Canada's judicial process poses a distinctive representational challenge to the Canadian judiciary. The Constitution has always provided the right to use English or French in courts established by the federal Parliament and in the courts of Manitoba and Quebec.[71] In 1982 a similar requirement was added for the courts of New Brunswick.[72] The scope of this constitutional right has been broadly interpreted by the Supreme Court of Canada. In 1979, in the *Blaikie* case, the Court held that the right applies to administrative tribunals exercising judicial or quasi-judicial powers as well as to the regular courts, and is available to corporations as well as to individuals.[73] In provinces where the constitutional right does not apply, the need to resist Quebec separatism has created political pressure to provide bilingual court services. This is particularly true of Ontario which has the largest French minority. In 1984 that province inserted a clause in its Courts of Justice Act declaring English and French to be the "official languages" of its courts.[74] The act identifies areas of Ontario in which there is a significant francophone population and in these designated areas gives the litigant the right to require a hearing "before a judge who speaks both the English and French language."[75]

Bilingual judges (and juries), although not the only way, are certainly the most effective way of providing judicial services in English and French. In Quebec, because most francophone lawyers have been bilingual, it has not been difficult to staff a bilingual judiciary. Thus, even though anglophones, in the modern period, have been under-represented on the Quebec bench,[76] members of Quebec's English-speaking community have always been able to have their cases heard by judges proficient in their language. The same has not been true for the French-speaking minority outside of Quebec, although in recent years Ontario has made an impressive effort in a practical, if not a symbolic, way to meet the Quebec standard. In other provinces a good many judges are taking advantage of the language training available under the auspices of the Canadian Judicial Council. However, in Manitoba and New Brunswick, where court service in French and English are constitutionally mandated, it would appear that not enough judges are proficient in French to give reality to the constitutional right to use French in court proceedings. While the Supreme Court of Canada in 1986 in the *Société des Acadiens Case* held that the language guarantee itself does not require that the judges hearing cases pleaded in French be able to understand French, it did refer to the common law requirement that parties in judicial proceedings be heard and understood.[77]

At the federal level, the Federal Court Act requires that at least eight of the Federal Court's twenty-five judges come from Quebec.[78] There is no such requirement in the act establishing the Tax Court of Canada, although that court too is constitutionally obliged to hear cases in both languages. The Supreme Court Act of 1875 required that two of the Court's judges come from Quebec. This requirement was not changed when the Supreme Court was expanded to seven judges in 1927 but was increased to three Quebec judges when the Court was increased to nine in 1949.[79] Of course, the rationale for this provision was not so much language as the need to provide judges with a background in Quebec's distinctive civil law. Indeed, the constitutional right to be heard in French in the Supreme Court of Canada was scarcely a reality until the 1960s. No translation services were provided and a majority of the judges could not understand spoken French.[80] As a result, Quebec lawyers appearing before the Court jeopardized their chances of winning if they chose to argue in French. Much has been done since then to remedy the situation. Instantaneous translation is available and newly appointed English-speaking justices take French immersion courses. Francophone lawyers may still feel that they will communicate more effectively if they argue in English. Nonetheless, it is interesting to observe how much more frequently in recent years bilingual Quebec lawyers will make a point of exercising their constitutional right to use French in the Supreme Court.

A representational pattern that has assumed the status of a constitutional convention is the representation of the major regions of Canada on the Supreme Court of Canada. This convention, like many others, cannot be stated with mathematical precision. Table 6.2 shows that while there has been some variation over the years in the number of judges from each region, for all but four years

TABLE 6.2 REGIONAL REPRESENTATION ON THE SUPREME COURT OF CANADA, 1875-1982

YEAR*	QUEBEC	ONTARIO	ATLANTIC PROVINCES	WESTERN PROVINCES
1875	2	2	2	0
1888	2	3	1	0
1893	2	2	2	0
1903	2	1	2	1
1905	2	2	2	0
1906	2	2	1	1
1927	2	3	1	1
1949	3	3	1	2
1979	3	2	1	3
1982	3	3	1	2

* The years listed are years in which appointment to the Supreme Court altered the pattern of regional representation.

of this century the Supreme Court has included justices from Ontario, Quebec, the Atlantic provinces and the Western provinces. A prime minister who departed from this degree of regional representation would likely suffer serious political consequences. Thus geography is the most important representational factor in staffing the Canadian Supreme Court. Some attention has been paid to religion in that at least one-third of the Court has been Roman Catholic and it has usually included a Catholic from English-speaking Canada. However, until the appointment of Bora Laskin in 1970, no person of a non-Christian faith had served on the bench. The Court has been quite unrepresentative in terms of ethnicity and gender.[81] Except for Laskin no person of a non-British or non-French heritage has been appointed. In 1982, Bertha Wilson became the first woman to serve on the Court.

The fact that regional representation looms so large in appointments to the Supreme Court reflects the politics of the Canadian federation. Geography has been a consideration in appointments to the u.s. Supreme Court but no greater than religion and, in the modern era, not as crucial a factor as ideology.[82] The justification for this emphasis in the Canadian case is primarily symbolic. Justices do not function on the Court as representatives of their regions. The participation of the Quebec judges in Quebec appeals ensures that expertise in Quebec's civil law can be brought to bear on these cases. Regional expertise is much less salient for cases coming from common law Canada and there is much less of a regional pattern in panels of the Court dealing with these cases. Now that the Court's docket is concerned mostly with issues of federal law and constitutional law, the functional rationale for regional representation is weaker than ever. But at the same time the strains in the Canadian federation are such that it has become more essential than ever before to secure the allegiance of political elites in the various regions of Canada for national institutions such as the Supreme Court. Thus, for the foreseeable future the principle of regional representation will be observed and is likely to be recognized in any agreement reached by the current generation of political leaders on entrenching the Supreme Court in the Constitution.[83]

Notes to Chapter 6

1. House of Commons, *Debates*, 17 May 1932, p. 2999.
2. Ibid., 18 Dec. 1980, p. 5897.
3. This is the objective of judicial salary policy as stated in the first *Report of the Commission on Judges' Salaries and Benefits* (Lang Report) (Ottawa: Minister of Justice, 1983).
4. 29-30 Elizabeth II, c. 50, s. 19(2).
5. Ibid., s. 19(3).
6. J.J. Robinette appeared before the committee on behalf of the Joint Committee on Judicial Benefits of the Conference of Chief Justices and the Canadian Judges Conference. See *Proceedings of the Standing Committee on Justice and Legal Affairs*, 31 Jan., 7 Feb. 1984.
7. *The National*, Oct. 1985, p. 31.
8. *Report of the Commission on Judges' Salaries and Benefits*, p. 14.
9. All the more so since the salaries of other public officials such as the auditor general and the commissioner of official languages, as well as judicial salary scales in some of the provinces, have been tied to federal judicial salaries.
10. Shimon Shetreet, *Judges on Trial* (Amsterdam: North Holland Publishing Company, 1978), p. 33. Until 1965 salaries of the higher judiciary could be increased only by statute.
11. House of Commons, *Debates*, 11 Oct. 1985, p. 7601.
12. *Report of the Commission to Review Salaries of Members of Parliament and Senators* (Ottawa: Minister of Supply and Service, 1985), p. 22.
13. *Report of the Commission on Judges' Salaries and Benefits*, p. 6.
14. National Center for State Courts, *Survey of Judicial Salaries*, May 1982. There is a great deal of variation in state court salaries: in some states, such as New York, judicial salaries are comparable to those of Canada's section 96 judges. The Lang report calls for the elimination of the extra $3000 which some provinces pay to their section 96 judges but recommends that the next triennial commission consider the question of whether the salaries of section 96 judges should be uniform across the country. For an American judge's discussion of how much better off Canadian judges are, see Lois G. Forer, "Oh Canada! Where Judges Go First Class," *Judges' Journal* (Summer 1986), p. 14.
15. Bulletin of the Federal Court, *The Third Branch*, Feb. 1987, p. 4.
16. *Report and Recommendations of Advisory Committee as Judicial Compensation and Related Matters* (Dorfman Report) (Ottawa: Minister of Justice, 1979).
17. *Report and Recommendations of Advisory Committee on Judicial Annuities* (de Grandpré Report) (Ottawa: Minister of Justice, 1981).
18. Thus it would be best to make the change in the Income Tax Act rather than in the Judges Act which applies only to federally appointed judges.

19. Statute Law (Superannuation) Amendment Bill, Statutes of Canada, 1974-75-76, s. 81.
20. From 1975 to 1977 these judges would contribute only 6.5%. The full 7% came into effect in Jan. 1977.
21. Under an 1983 amendment to the Judges Act a judge who has served less than ten years and retires before the mandatory retirement age receives a proportionate pension. A judge may also receive the annuity if he resigns or is removed as a result of becoming afflicted with a permanent disability.
22. *De Grandpré Report, p. 15.*
23. *Beauregard* v. *The Queen* [1984] 1 FC 1010; dismissing appeal from Addy, J. in *Beauregard* v. *The Queen* [1981] 2 FC 543.
24. *The Queen* v. *Beauregard* [1986] 2 SCR 56, at 76.
25. See Lang Report, pp. 5-10.
26. For a review of arrangements in other jurisdictions see de Grandpré Report, pp. 5-10.
27. 25-26 Elizabeth II, c. 25, ss. 44-48.
28. House of Commons, *Debates*, 15 May 1975, p. 5831.
29. Canadian Association of Provincial Court Judges, *Judicial Compensation in Canada as of January 1, 1981.*
30. For a vigorous presentation of this argument, see Denis Olsen, *The State Elite* (Toronto: McClelland and Stewart, 1980), ch. 3.
31. The professional income figure is based on the data in the *Lang Report*, and the age of lawyers at the time of appointment to Provincial Courts in Guy Bouthillier, "Profil du juge de la Cour des sessions de la paix," *Revue du Barreau* (1978).
32. *Valente* v. *R.* [1985] 2 SCR 673, at 706.
33. The committee is now established under s. 88 of the Courts of Justice Act. Originally it was established by Order-in-council 643/80.
34. See *Ontario Lawyers Weekly*, 20 Dec. 1985, and *Globe and Mail*, Jan. 1986.
35. *Re Charles Currie* v. *The Niagara Escarpment Commission*, (1984) 46 OR (2d) 484.
36. For an examination of the JPS office in Ontario, see Allan W. Mewett, *Report to the Attorney General of Ontario on the Office and Function of the Justice of Peace in Ontario* (Toronto: Ministry of the Attorney General, 1981).
37. An Act to Amend the Justices of the Peace Act, SO 1984, c. 8.
38. *Reference re Justices of the Peace Act and R.* v. *Currie* (1984) 48 OR (2d) 609.
39. When new provinces were formed in a frontier area the requirement of s. 97 must have been a bare formality, as judges were recruited from established provinces. See Dale and Lee Gibson, *Substantial Justice: Law and Lawyers in Manitoba, 1670-1970* (Winnipeg: Pegius, 1972).
40. Statutes of Canada 1912.
41. House of Commons, *Debates*, 25 Mar. 1912, pp. 6014-15.
42. 25-26 Elizabeth II, c. 25, s. 1. In some provinces the law provides that a provincially appointed judge (who may be appointed with less than ten years standing) ceases to be a member of the provincial bar upon such appointment.
43. The Supreme Court Act, s. 5.
44. Although Abraham states that "custom would automatically exclude" anyone who did not have a law degree. Henry J. Abraham, *The Judicial Process*, 4th ed. (New York: Oxford University Press, 1980), p. 53.

45. Federal Court Act, s. 5(3).
46. See Geoffrey L. Steele, *Report of Royal Commission to Enquire Into the Magistry of Newfoundland and Labrador* (St. John's, 1973).
47. Courts of Justice Act, so 1984, c. 11, s. 52.
48. In the Northwest Territories the requirement is only for three years. A number of provinces make provision for other legal or judicial experience.
49. *Toronto Star*, 25 June 1984. The *Star* was commenting on the *Currie* case discussed above.
50. *British Columbia Royal Commission on Family and Children's Law* (Berger Commission) (Vancouver, 1974).
51. For an examination of the mistreatment of witnesses in Canadian courts see John Hagan, "Victims Before the Law: A Study of Victim Involvement in the Criminal Justice Process," *Journal of Criminology* (1982), p. 371.
52. William J. Klein, "Judicial Recruitment in Manitoba, Ontario, and Quebec" (Ph.D. thesis, Department of Sociology, University of Toronto, 1975), shows a mean initial appointment age of 53.6 for the federally appointed judges he studied and an average "professional age" (i.e. years at the bar) of 25.4 years for judges serving in 1969. Bouthillier, in his article on the provincially appointed judges of the Quebec Court of Sessions of the Peace, shows an average age at the time of appointment of 48 as compared with 51 and 55 for the Superior Court and Court of Appeal respectively.
53. House of Commons, *Debates*, 11 Oct. 1985, p. 7601.
54. Lawrence S. Goulet, "The B.C. Experience in the Appointment Process," paper delivered to annual meeting of the Association of Canadian Law Teachers, Montreal, 30 May 1985, p. 9.
55. "A Symposium on the Appointment, Discipline and Removal of Judges," *Alberta Law Review* (1973), p. 304.
56. John Hogarth, *Sentencing as a Human Process* (Toronto: University of Toronto Press, 1971) pp. 60-61.
57. Guy Bouthillier, "Profil du juge de la Cour Supérieure du Québec," *Canadian Bar Review* (1977), p. 465.
58. Klein, "Judicial Recruitment," p. 152.
59. Maurice Rosenberg, "The Qualities of Justice—Are They Strainable?" *Texas Law Review* (1966), p. 1.
60. George Adams and Paul J. Cavaluzzo, "The Supreme Court of Canada: A Biographical Study," *Osgoode Hall Law Journal* (1969), p. 84.
61. Hogarth, *Sentencing as a Human Process*, p. 54.
62. Ibid., p. 212.
63. Olsen, *State Elite*, p. 52.
64. R.M. Jackson, *The Machinery of Justice in England*, 7th ed. (Cambridge: Cambridge University press, 1977), pp. 474-75.
65. House of Commons, *Debates*, 18 Dec. 1980, p. 5890.
66. For a critique of the Canadian judiciary's treatment of aboriginal rights issues, see Brian Slattery, "The Hidden Constitution: Aboriginal Rights in Canada," in Menno Boldt, Anthony J. Long and Leroy Little Bear, *The Quest for Justice* (Toronto: University of Toronto Press, 1985).
67. See K.E. Renner and A.H. Warner, "The Standard of Social Justice Applied to

an Evaluation of Criminal Cases Appearing Before the Halifax Courts," *The Windsor Yearbook of Access to Justice* (1981), p. 62.

68. John Porter, *The Vertical Mosaic* (Toronto: University of Toronto Press, 1965).

69. Pauline Jewett estimated in 1980 that women with ten years' professional experience constituted 15% of the total number of lawyers practising in Canada. House of Commons, *Debates,* 18 Dec. 1980, p. 5892.

70. Sheldon Goldman, "Carter's Judicial Appointments: A Lasting Legacy," *Judicature* (Mar. 1983), p. 343.

71. Constitution Act, 1867, s. 133; Manitoba Act, 1870, s. 23.

72. Constitution Act, 1982, s. 19(2).

73. *A.G. Quebec* v. *Blaikie* [1979] SCR 1066.

74. SO, 1984, c. 11, s. 135(1).

75. Ibid., s. 136(2). S. 136(3) establishes a right to bilingual juries when jury trials are held in districts designated in the statute. In Dec. 1986 this right was extended to the whole of Ontario, but in the superior court the demand for this service has been largely in Ottawa, Prescott, Cornwall, and Cochrane.

76. Bouthillier, "Profil du judge de la Cour Superieure," reports that in 1973, 15% of Quebec's Superior Court judges were English as compared with 19% of the population and 25% of the provincial bar, and overall only 5% of the provincially appointed Court of Sessions judges have been English.

77. *Société des Acadiens* v. *Minority Language School Board No. 30* [1986] 1 SCR 549.

78. SC 1985, c. 38, s. 11.

79. The Supreme Court Act, s. 6.

80. See *Peter H. Russell, The Supreme Court of Canada as a Bilingual and Bicultural Institution* (Ottawa: Queen's Printer, 1969).

81. For an analysis of these features of the first fifty appointments to the Supreme Court, see Adams and Cavaluzzo, "The Supreme Court."

82. For an analysis of the representational aspects of Supreme Court appointments in the United States, see John R. Schmidhauser, "The Justice of the Supreme Court: A Collective Portrait," *Midwest Journal of Political Science* (1959), pp. 1-56. Abraham, *Judicial Process*, provides data on appointments since 1959.

83. This is more fully developed in Peter Russell, "Constitutional Reform of the Judicial Branch: Symbolic vs. Operational Consideration," *Canadian Journal of Political Science* (1984), p. 227.

CHAPTER 7

RETIREMENT, REMOVAL, DISCIPLINE, AND EDUCATION

In discussing the judiciary's term of office, the focus traditionally has been mainly negative: how to protect judges from interference or pressure that might undermine their independence and impartiality. In this chapter we will certainly be concerned with these issues but not to the exclusion of the positive side of the ledger: how to ensure that judges are responsible to the society they serve and are professionally competent.

In considering the ways in which judges leave the bench these two countervailing concerns come into play. Security of tenure is certainly an essential condition of judicial independence. The influence which leaders of the political branches may have on the judiciary in controlling the appointing process becomes more tolerable to the extent that judges, once appointed, cannot be removed when their decisions displease those who appointed them. But tenure can be so secure that judges are insulated from any kind of accountability to the public they serve and hold office regardless of their capacity to perform their function well.

By Confederation, as we noted in chapter 4, security of tenure was reasonably well established for federally appointed judges in Canada. However, it was not until well into this century that the provincially appointed, lower court judges began to acquire a modicum of the security of tenure required for judicial independence. Although the judicialization of the magistracy has included a substantial reform of the terms on which these judges hold office, there is still considerable room for improvement. While the concern for security of tenure has been progressively addressed, until quite recently very little attention has been given to the other side of the coin: ways and means of protecting society from judicial incompetence or arrogance.

Mandatory Retirement

An important change in the terms of office of Canadian judges has been the introduction of compulsory retirement. Traditionally judges were appointed for life. They gave up their position only through voluntary retirement—often at a very advanced age—or death. Judges of the United States Supreme Court and federal constitutional courts are still appointed for life. But in Canada compulsory retirement was introduced early in the century for federally appointed judges whose tenure was deemed by the government not to be entrenched in the formal constitution. A mandatory retirement age of eighty was established for county and district court judges in 1903. Since then it has been lowered to seventy. The Supreme Court Act was amended in 1927 to require that Supreme Court judges retire at seventy-five. Exchequer Court judges also had a mandatory retirement age of seventy-five but the newly appointed judges of the Federal Court which in 1971 replaced the Exchequer Court were required to retire at seventy. It was considered necessary to amend the Constitution in order to establish a mandatory age for the provincial superior court judges. This was done by a 1960 amendment to section 99 of the Constitution setting the retirement age at seventy-five.

The introduction of compulsory retirement has undoubtably been of benefit to society. It removes the danger of a senile judiciary and allows more room for the rejuvenation of a branch of government which is always in danger of being a generation behind in its outlook. When the retirement age is as high as seventy-five it minimizes the loss of experienced judges at the peak of their ability. However, the variation in retirement ages for different kinds of judges is arbitrary and unjustifiable. There is no reason to believe that Federal and county court judges are less able at age seventy than superior or Supreme Court judges. The Federal Court has already ruled that mandatory retirement at seventy for its members violates the equality guarantee in the Charter.[1]

The picture looks even worse when we take into view the retirement ages established for the largest cadre of Canadian judges, those appointed by the provinces and territories. In most jurisdictions the age is sixty-five; in Alberta and Quebec it is seventy. Compulsory retirement provisions which exist in many fields of public employment will likely be challenged in the courts as violating the guarantee in section 15 of the Charter of Rights against discrimination based on age. New Brunswick, in legislation designed to meet the requirements of the Charter of Rights, repealed the section of its Provincial Court Act setting the compulsory retirement age for judges at seventy.[2] It will be interesting to see how the justices of the Supreme Court of Canada whose own employment is guaranteed to age seventy-five assess the reasonableness of laws which require retirement at a considerably earlier age.

The difference between the ages at which provincial court judges and superior court judges leave the bench is reduced when account is taken of the post-retirement service of provincial court judges and the inducement for early retirement or reduced responsibilities before retirement introduced for federally appointed judges. Five provinces and the Northwest Territories have provisions that enable some provincial and territorial judges to carry on for a few years after reaching the retirement age. However, in all of these except Ontario this post-retirement opportunity, which can often significantly increase the value of the judge's pension, is at the pleasure of the executive branch of government. The Supreme Court's ruling in The *Valente* case, as we have seen, probably makes this situation unconstitutional. At the federal level in 1971 the Judges Act was amended so that after fifteen years on the bench a judge could retire at age sixty-five with full pension.[3] The same legislation made it possible for a superior court judge after ten years' service and on reaching age seventy to become a "supernumerary judge" with a reduced workload.[4] The availability of this option to a judge does not depend on executive discretion but does require complementary provincial legislation creating supernumerary positions on the relevant courts.

This venture in "co-operative federalism" appears to have worked well. The supernumeraries provide chief justices with a pool of experienced judges to assist in special cases of long duration and in meeting peak workload situations. The ability of experienced judges is thus not completely lost to the system while many new places are opened up. By 1975 the supernumerary option had been extended to county and district court judges and was available to all section 96 court judges at age sixty-five after fifteen years of service.[5] Thus far only British Columbia among the provinces has followed the federal example and permits provincially appointed judges after twenty years' service or at age sixty, whichever comes first, to serve as supernumeraries. The supernumerary semi-retired judge, with responsibilities determined by senior judges, seems much the best way of balancing judicial independence with the practical needs of the judicial system.

Removal

In Canada judges have been reasonably well protected from removal by political authorities who might be displeased by their decisions. This, of course, is the central concern in providing security of tenure for judges. Such security is an essential ingredient of judicial independence in any society. Without such independence judges are not free to perform the adjudicative function properly, especially when the cases before them bear directly on the interests of those who can remove them. A basic degree of security of tenure for the federally appointed senior judiciary has been provided for in law since Confederation. Although the legislation protecting the lower court judges' security of tenure came in much later, and in some jurisdictions still falls short of an acceptable standard, it is important to bear in mind that political constraints are probably more important than legal rules in preventing politicians from interfering with the judiciary. A government that removed a judge as a means of countering decisions it did not like would be in great difficulty with the Canadian electorate.

In terms of legal protection, the most unsatisfactory situation has been that of justices of the peace. It was only in 1984, when threatened by the Charter litigation already referred to, that Ontario introduced legislation establishing that JPs can be removed only for cause after an investigation by the Justices of the Peace Review Committee.[6] Justice de Weerdt of the Supreme Court of the Northwest Territories has ruled that territorial JPs must be deemed to have security of tenure for life even though a territorial ordinance states that they serve "at pleasure."[7] This was the only way he could avoid ruling that the entire JP Ordinance, because of its incompatibility with the Charter of Rights, was of no force or effect. Justices of the peace who try cases continue to serve "at pleasure" in a number of other jurisdictions. Although a judge of Saskatchewan's Court of Queen's Bench has found that this should not impair their ability to engage in independent and impartial adjudication, higher courts are likely to disagree.[8] Where JPs discharge adjudicative functions it is essential that their security of tenure be equivalent to that enjoyed by other members of the provincial or territorial lower courts.

When we go further up the judicial ladder and consider the laws governing the removal of judges, there are two features to be considered: the grounds for removal and the mechanism of removal.

Most Canadian judges hold their office "during good behaviour." Section 99(1) of the Constitution establishes this condition of office for "Judges of the Superior Courts"—a phrase which includes the provincial and territorial courts of appeal and the highest trial courts. The same condition has been set down in statute for all other federally appointed judges[9] and for provincially appointed judges in British Columbia, Manitoba, New Brunswick, and Quebec.[10] Legislation in Newfoundland and Nova Scotia has given provincially appointed judges office on good behaviour after one "probationary" year.[11] This probationary arrangement, as previously noted, has been ruled unconstitutional. The statutes of other provinces and the territories do not explicitly state that judges hold office during good behaviour but refer to "misbehaviour" as grounds for removal.[12]

The term "during good behaviour"(*quamdiu se bene gesserint*) has its roots in English common law. Originally it referred to an office created for life which could be terminated only by the death of the grantee or upon breach of good behaviour. "Breach of good behaviour" as a common law precept has a very narrow meaning. Generally it is confined to an improper exercise of the office, neglect or refusal to perform the duties of the office, or conviction for a serious criminal offence involving moral turpitude. Note that this common law meaning does not embrace inability to perform the office because of age or mental or physical illness, nor scandalous behaviour off the bench short of conviction for a crime.[13] However, the grounds for removing judges have been considerably widened to include circumstances beyond the common law meaning of misbehaviour.

The parliamentary concept of the behavior which could justify the removal of a judge has traditionally been wider than the common law.[14] In Canada, as in England, Parliament plays a pivotal role in the removal of judges, as it is an address by both Houses of Parliament that leads to the removal of the judges of the highest courts. While only one judge has actually been removed by this method in the United Kingdom and no Canadian judge has as yet been so removed, proceedings directed toward this form of removal have been initiated against a number of judges in both countries. In several instances the conduct complained of occurred in the judge's private life and involved behaviour which tarnished the judge's reputation for probity and integrity but was not criminal in a strictly legal sense.

This was certainly the case with Mr. Leo Landreville who, in 1966, was the last superior court judge to be subjected to removal proceedings.[15] The charges against Landreville were based on activities he was involved in as mayor of Sudbury just before he was appointed to the bench in 1956. It was alleged that he had been given shares in the Northern Ontario Natural Gas Company in return for using his influence as mayor to assist the company in obtaining the franchise for the distribution of natural gas in Sudbury. Although criminal charges against Landreville were dismissed at a preliminary hearing in 1964, the Law Society of his province (the governing body of the legal profession) found that his behaviour was "inconsistent with the reputation for probity required of one of Her Majesty's Judges." Subsequently, a royal commission of inquiry conducted by Ivan Rand, a retired justice of the Supreme Court of Canada, and a select committee of Parliament concurred with this finding and recommended removal by joint address of both Houses of Parliament. When the minister of justice, Pierre Trudeau, announced his intention to introduce a resolution to adopt a joint address requesting the governor general to remove Landreville, the judge submitted his resignation.[16]

At one point during the Landreville episode, Mr. Trudeau's predecessor as justice minister, Lucien Cardin, took the position that there were no limits to the grounds on which Parliament could base an address for removal. In 1965 in a letter to Mr. J.J. Robinette, Landreville's legal counsel, Cardin asserted that the power to remove on address "extends to any ground and it is open to Parliament to make an address for the removal of a judge on any ground it sees fit, whether it constitutes misbehaviour or not."[17] In a strict legal sense this may be correct: Parliament is not restricted to the common law meaning of misbehaviour and its actions in this area are not reviewable by the courts.[18] But in terms of constitutional convention, there surely are limits. On numerous occasions leading British and Canadian statesmen have expressed views similar to those of Lord John Russell, who in 1843 said, "Independence of judges is so sacred that nothing but the most imperious necessity should induce the House to adopt a course that might weaken their standing or endanger their authority."[19]

In 1883, Edward Blake gave this account of the outer limits of Parliament's power to review the conduct of judges:

> What was the cause, then, which could properly bring the Judge's actions under our consideration? It was a charge of partiality, of malfeasance of office—not that the Judge erred, for all may err in judgment, but that he degraded his office, betrayed his trust, wilfully and knowingly did a wrong thing, perverted justice and judgment—that is the nature of a charge which would alone make it proper to have been brought here.[20]

It would be a breach of constitutional convention to initiate removal proceedings against a judge because the government regarded a judge's decisions as being in error or at odds with its policies. Also, as we saw in chapter 4, the Canadian Judicial Council concluded that the kind of impropriety committed by Thomas Berger in his off-the-bench political pronouncements did not constitute grounds for removal.

The federal Parliament and provincial legislatures have endeavoured to provide more precise statutory definitions of the reasons which could justify removal of a judge. In 1971, when Parliament established the Canadian Judicial Council and gave it the responsibility of investigating complaints that might lead to the removal of a county or superior court judge, it inserted in the Judges Act the following four grounds upon which a recommendation for removal might be based:

    (a) age or infirmity
    (b) having been guilty of misconduct
    (c) having failed in the due execution of his office
    (d) having been placed, by his conduct or otherwise, in a position incompatible
        with the due execution of his office.[21]

These terms may strike the reader as very broad and general. But, as Jules Deschênes has said, "It is well-nigh impossible to put into words just what is not 'good behaviour'. The unpredictability of human conduct will always confound statutory criteria, however carefully drafted."[22] Still, statutory language can be overly broad and Deschênes is right to criticize the inclusion of the phrase "or otherwise" in the fourth of the grounds listed above. This open-ended phrase was not carefully considered by Parliament.

The grounds set out in provincial and territorial statutes for the removal of lower court judges resemble those in the federal Judges Act. Although no two jurisdictions have exactly the same wording, the grounds that are covered include physical and mental infirmity, neglect of duty, and scandalous conduct or, to use the language of Quebec's Courts of Justice Act, "an act derogatory to the honour, dignity or integrity of the magistracy."[23] The Quebec statute provides for a more precise "code of judicial ethics" to be drawn up by the province's judicial council which would eventually replace the more general language of the statute. Nova Scotia's legislation uses some questionable language where it refers to execution of the office "in a manner contrary to the public interest" as grounds for removal.[24] This language has the unfortunate connotation that a judge could be removed if the government found the judge's decisions contrary to the government's conception of "the public interest."

More important than the wording of the statutory criteria for removal are the mechanisms through which these terms are applied, and the judgment of those who operate these mechanisms. For judges who serve in the upper echelon of Canadian courts (the courts included in the Judges Act definition of superior courts, namely the Supreme Court of Canada, the Federal Court, the provincial and territorial courts of appeal and the superior trial courts), the removal procedure involves a most intricate system of checks and balances in which all three branches of government participate. The judiciary is now involved at the beginning of the process: the Canadian Judicial Council (which is made up of the chief justices and associate chief justices of the superior courts) is responsible for investigating any alleged wrong which may lead to removal.[25] Under the Judges Act, the Council *must* investigate if requested to do so by the minister of justice and *may* do so in response to a complaint from any other source. The council may (and in most cases probably would) establish a committee to carry out the investigation. When the investigation has been completed, the full council reports its conclusions to the minister of justice, as was done in the Berger affair. Should the council find a judge's behaviour constitutes grounds for removal, the minister might proceed with a resolution in Parliament to have a select committee consider the Judicial Council's report and conduct its own inquiry; alternatively, he might immediately proceed with a motion for a joint address of Parliament requesting the governor general to remove the judge.[26] In response to such a request presumably the governor general would remove the judge.

I say "presumably" because this complex removal procedure has never been taken to the final stage. The Landreville case in 1966 was as close as we have come to removing such a judge. Prior to that only four cases reached the parliamentary stage, all of them in the last century. The first, involving the chief justice of Nova Scotia, William Young, proceeded no further than the receipt of a petition by the House of Commons.[27] Select committees were established to investigate petitions concerning two Quebec judges, Lafontaine in 1868 and Loranger in 1876. The Lafontaine Committee appears to have simply dropped the matter[28] and the Loranger Committee found the complaint was not substantiated.[29] The final case involved Chief Justice Edmund Burke Wood of Manitoba. Wood, who was constantly in difficulty for his injudicious conduct on and off the bench, was the subject of a lengthy petition to Parliament in 1881. Before Parliament could establish a select committee to investigate these complaints, the chief justice suffered a stroke while hearing a case and died.[30]

The use of a judicial inquiry in the Landreville case was an innovation, although it had been advocated as early as 1868 by Sir John A. Macdonald.[31] In 1966 some members of Parliament attacked the judicial inquiry as "a forum substituted improperly for this high court of parliament."[32] The minister of justice, Lucien Cardin, defended the procedure on the grounds that judicial independence would be better served if the government's decision to bring an allegation of judicial misconduct before Parliament was based on an independent judicial inquiry. The constitutional validity of using a judicial inquiry as the first stage in the removal procedure for judges whose tenure is secured by section 99 of the Constitution was considered by the Federal Court of Canada in one of several cases initiated by Mr. Landreville following his resignation.[33] In 1977 Justice Collier of the Federal Court found that section 99 does not preclude a judicial inquiry prior to joint address proceedings in Parliament. However, Justice Collier went on to find that Ivan Rand, who conducted the Landreville inquiry, had erred procedurally by failing to give proper notice, as required under the Inquiries Act, of the charge that Landreville had committed "gross contempt" in giving evidence to the Ontario Securities Commission and as a witness in a perjury trial. This decision was of assistance in enabling Landreville, in 1981, after yet another Federal Court decision in his favour,[34] to obtain an ex gratia payment of $250 000 from the Liberal cabinet in lieu of the pension it had refused him when he resigned in 1967.[34]

The Rand inquiry in the Landreville case did not provide an impressive precedent for the use of a single-judge royal commission in removal proceedings. Rand's report is replete with irrelevant comments about Landreville's lifestyle. Its treatment of evidence concerning his alleged wrongdoing as mayor of Sudbury is rambling and incoherent. The creation of the Canadian Judicial Council in 1971 and the statutory role it now has in the removal process is a distinct improvement over the one-judge ad hoc inquiry. The advantage of its collegial judgment has already been experienced in the Berger affair where, it will be recalled, the full council's view that Justice Berger's political indiscretions did not constitute grounds for removal prevailed over the opinion of its investigating committee. Some may fear that the injection of this large council of senior judges into the removal process will provide too strong a shield against the removal of judges. But here it should be borne in mind that under our constitution the right of a member of Parliament, including a minister, to initiate proceedings in Parliament to remove a superior court judge continues and could be exercised regardless of whether a report recommending removal has been received from the Canadian Judicial Council.[35]

County and district court judges, the lowest level of federal appointees, have always been subject to a simpler removal procedure. They can be removed by the federal cabinet on the recommendation of the minister of justice after the receipt of a report from the Canadian Judicial Council.[36] Before the establishment of the council, a judicial inquiry had to take place before the cabinet could make a decision to remove. A removal order and the report on which it is based must be laid before Parliament. The absence of an active role for Parliament in the removal of county court judges has been a sore point with many of these judges. The Deschênes report, *Maîtres Chez Eux*, recommends that "no federally- or provincially-appointed judge should be removed from office without a vote of Parliament or of the provincial legislature concerned."[37] Ontario's county and district court judges recently pointed to the anomaly of providing the full joint address of Parliament treatment for judges of the new Tax Court of Canada while denying it to members of their court whose jurisdiction comes so close to that of a superior court.[38]

While this slight to the status of country and district court judges is objectionable, it does not follow that their tenure is rendered unacceptably insecure by the absence of an active role for Parliament in their removal procedure. Only four judges at the county and district court level have actually been removed.[39] One of these did involve politics: the removal of Lewis St. George Stubbs, a Manitoba county court judge in 1933. Stubbs, embittered against capitalism by the economic suffering he was witnessing during the Great Depression, took to delivering rabble-rousing speeches on and off the bench, often denouncing parties appearing before him.[40] But while some might question Stubbs's removal, it does not demonstrate the need for an active parliamentary role. Parliament is apt to be even less tolerant of judges who use their position as a platform from which to denounce the prevailing economic system. The World Conference on the Independence of Justice in 1983 did not find that judicial independence required a role for the legislature in removal proceedings. What it insisted upon was an inquiry by judges or a judicial council as a pre-condition of removal.[41] Similarly, in the *Valente* case, it will be recalled, it was held that the Ontario Provincial Court judges' independence was not undermined by the fact that a joint address of the Legislative Assembly was not required to remove them.

Interestingly, as the *Valente* case was proceeding through the courts, Ontario became the only province requiring a vote of the provincial legislature to remove Provincial Court judges. This is the final step in a procedure initiated by the provincial judicial council followed by a judicial inquiry.[42] In all other provinces and territories except British Columbia the cabinet has the power to remove following an inquiry by a judge or judicial council. British Columbia has gone the furthest in judicializing the entire removal procedure. There the attorney general may order an inquiry, but the tribunal of inquiry which, depending on the preference of the judge under investigation, may be the provincial judicial council or a judge of the province's Supreme Court, has the power to order removal. There is an appeal from the tribunal's decision to remove but it is to the Court of Appeal, not to the legislature.[43] Quebec is the only province that requires participation by the Court of Appeal in the removal process.[44] If the Conseil de la Magistrature, after an inquiry by a committee comprised of five of its members, recommends removal, the minister of justice may file a motion requesting the Court of Appeal to review the case.[45] The government may remove the judge upon receiving a report from the Court of Appeal.

The requirement of an inquiry by judges or a judicial council as a pre-condition of removal meets the basic institutional requirement for judicial independence. The Deschênes Report recommends that judicial independence would be even better secured by requiring that the provincial executive and federal executive (in the case of county court judges) be bound "by the conclusion of exoneration pronounced by the judicial authority." Deschênes is concerned that without this protection judges will be "given over, bound hand and foot as it were, to the total discretion of executive power."[46] Deschênes surely exaggerates this danger and ignores the opposite risk that judges inquiring into complaints about fellow judges might be too lenient and prevent responsible ministers from doing anything about judges who are woefully intemperate or neglectful of their duties. Deschênes is more reasonable in calling for the removal of the executive discretion which now exists in a number of jurisdictions over the decision to suspend a judge during the course of an inquiry and over the decision to open an inquiry to the public.[47] Both of these matters should be left to judicial authorities. To go beyond this and permit the judiciary to tie the hands of responsible ministers on the removal decision itself is to give too high a priority to judicial independence over the principle of accountability in our system of democratic government. But to ensure that ministers are accountable it is essential that the government's actions and the judicial reports which precede them all be reported and tabled in the legislature. Regrettably, in a majority of legislatures this is still not a statutory requirement.[48]

Discipline Short of Removal

Society is inadequately protected from judicial misconduct if the removal process is the only way of sanctioning judges. As Glenn Winters and Robert Allard have observed in their review of American procedures, removal is "unsuitable for dealing with the most common types of judicial misconduct, which warrant some form of discipline short of removal."[49] If a judiciary is to be reasonably accountable to the society it serves, there must be ways and means of responding to complaints other than the "death penalty" of removal. As universities have found with tenured professors, if removal is the only sanction there will frequently be no effective response to legitimate complaints. "Discipline" is hardly the right word to describe this intermediate range of remedies, as it connotes an authoritarian regimentation of conduct which is as out of keeping with the independence of the judge as it is with the academic freedom of the professor. A more appropriate phrase is "professional responsibility," for the aim is to ensure that those who enjoy security of tenure live up to the standards of professional conduct that justify such a privilege.

It is only in the last fifteen years or so that a formal mechanism has been established in Canada for responding to complaints about judges. That mechanism is the judicial council. Judicial councils now exist in every province except Prince Edward Island, in both northern territories, and at the federal level. While the functions performed by this new instrument of government vary considerably from jurisdiction to jurisdiction, one function common to all of the councils is the investigation of complaints. Before the arrival on the scene of the judicial council, there was a variety of informal means of dealing with complaints. Lawyers and, less frequently, members of the public, might complain to an attorney general or chief justice about mistreatment by a judge. In response, a chief justice, if he found the complaint had merit, might speak to the offending judge or, in more serious cases, assign him to different or fewer cases, or sometimes even urge the judge to resign.[50] Occasionally questions have been asked in the legislature about a judge's conduct—for instance a delay of many years in rendering judgment in a case—and critical comments have appeared in the press on the rudeness or overbearing manner of a judge. But given the conventions of parliamentary government and the law of contempt in Canada, these public checks on judicial misconduct have been used infrequently. In addition, of course, where the judicial conduct at issue involves a point of law—for instance, a judge's failure to disqualify himself from hearing a case where there is a reasonable apprehension of bias—aggrieved litigants can and have appealed the judge's decision to a higher court.[51]

The introduction of the more formal institutionalized procedures of judicial councils has been part of the judicialization of the Canadian magistracy which we have been tracing through this chapter. Establishing a systematic and accessible process of responding to the full range of complaints was, in a sense, a quid pro quo for giving the lower court judges security of tenure. For lawyers, litigants, jurors or witnesses who feel they have been mistreated by a judge, the judicial council should provide a more visible and accessible agency for dealing with their complaints. For politicians, too, it is, usually a more appropriate and effective means of responding to constituents' complaints than debate in the legislature. In 1984, for example, Ontario NDP leader Robert Rae requested the Canadian Judicial Council to review what he regarded as appalling comments by a county court Judge belittling the seriousness of a rape offence.[52] At the same time the judicial council protects the collective independence of the judiciary by relieving the executive branch of any obligation to carry out its own investigation of judicial misconduct. The rights of the individual judge are also better protected in that most of the statutes establishing judicial councils provide judges who are under investigation with the right to a fair hearing.[53]

By virtue of the fact that it has jurisdiction over all federally appointed judges who constitute over 40 percent of the Canadian judiciary, the Canadian Judicial Council is the most important of the twelve judicial councils which now exist in Canada. Unlike the provincial and territorial councils, the Canadian Judicial Council is entirely judicial in its composition. It is composed of the chief justice of the Supreme Court of Canada as chairman and the chief justices, senior associate, and associate chief justices of the federal, provincial, and territorial superior courts. The county and district court chief judges are not members of the council, although some of them serve on a county court committee which is advisory to the council. Because the council is so large (its membership numbered thirty-seven at the end of 1983),[54] most of the work in relation to complaints is done by a small executive committee. This committee considers all complaints and identifies those which are serious enough to merit a formal inquiry. The full council votes on whether a formal inquiry should take place. As we saw earlier, Justice Thomas Berger's off-the-bench political comments were the occasion of one of these rare inquiries. As of 1983, the council had voted to conduct investigations in only three other cases and in two of these the judge resigned before the inquiry could be carried out.[55]

The small number of formal inquiries conducted by the council should not be taken as a measure of its effectiveness. Its very existence and the judges' knowledge that their behaviour might be reviewed by it should have some effect in promoting their own sense of professional responsibility. The council's report on its 1983 activities indicates the range of complaint activity. The executive committee received thirty-four complaints—significantly up from the eighteen it had handled in each of the two previous years.[56] Many of these involved losing parties (eight of them in divorce cases) who were, mistakenly, trying to use the council as a Court of Appeal. Some were downright frivolous: one complainant wanted members of the Supreme Court of Canada removed because of their participation in the 1981 *Patriation Reference* case. But four or five were more serious. One of these was lodged by jurors who after the conclusion of the trial were told by the judge that "you either did not understand the law that I gave you or you are unwilling to accept it." They complained that they were "humiliated" by this outburst. The council reports that the judge in reviewing this incident with his chief justice admitted he had been indiscreet and "was told that he could communicate this to the members of the jury and it was hoped that they would accept his explanation."[57] In another case the council noted that a judge who had signed an anti-abortion, right-to-life petition acknowledged that he was wrong to have done so. The council concludes that "it was satisfied that the views expressed would not improperly influence the Judge in the discharge of his judicial functions."[58]

As a disciplinary body, the Canadian Judicial Council relies primarily on admonitions and informal conciliation. The only sanction provided for in the Judges Act, aside from removal, is termination of a judge's salary. The cabinet must suspend a judge's salary if the Canadian Judicial Council so recommends. Originally this sanction was to be used only against judges who were found to be "incapacitated" by reason of age or infirmity and refused to resign. When the Canadian Judicial Council was established in 1971 this limitation was removed, so that now the Judges Act purports to make this sanction applicable when a judge is found to be incapacitated or disabled from the due execution of office for any reason. As we noted in chapter 4, it is doubtful that this sanction could be applied to superior court judges whose tenure is constitutionally secured and whose removal requires a joint address by both Houses of Parliament. In any event, the sanction has not been used. In dealing with conduct which is serious enough to be questioned and reviewed but not serious enough to justify removal, the Judicial Council has found it more appropriate to adopt "sanctions" that are more educational and conciliatory in nature. The furor that arose over its handling of the Berger affair should strengthen its commitment to this policy.

Judicial councils have also become the principle means of dealing with complaints about Canadian judges who are appointed by provincial and territorial governments. There are some interesting differences between these provincial and territorial councils and the Canadian Judicial Council. Their composition is considerably more diverse. As table 7.1 shows, all of them include representatives of the legal profession and all but Nova Scotia's have provision for non-lawyers.[59] This better protects the public interest than a system which relies entirely on judges to respond to complaints about fellow judges. Even though the chief judges on these councils will normally play the lead role in screening and following up complaints, the presence of non-judges on the councils provides more assurance of an adequate response. On the other hand, it is only in British Columbia and Quebec that the judges' interest in fair treatment is served by the inclusion of judicial representation other than the chief judge of their court.[60] Quebec, as may be appropriate for Canada's civil law province, has charged its council with the responsibility of drawing up a code of judicial ethics to indicate "in particular which acts or omissions are derogatory to the honour, dignity or integrity of the judiciary."[61] As for alternative sanctions to removal, a number of provinces provide for an official reprimand by the judicial council and most provide for the suspension of the judge during the course of an inquiry that might

TABLE 7.1   COMPOSITION OF PROVINCIAL AND TERRITORIAL JUDICIAL COUNCILS

	JUDGES	LAWYERS	OTHER	TOTAL
Alta.	3	1	2	6
B.C.	3	2	4	9
Man.	1	2	2	5
Nfld.	3	1	2	6
N.B.	2	1	2	5
N.S.	4	1	0	5
Ont.	6	1	2	9
Que.	9	2	2	13
Sask.	3	1	2	6
NWT	2	1	1	4
Yukon	3	2	2	7

lead to removal. But it is likely that these councils, like their federal counterpart, rely primarily on informal methods for dealing with judges who fail to maintain a proper standard of professional conduct.

The establishment of judicial councils in Canada has probably succeeded in establishing a better reconciliation of security of tenure and accountability. One must say "probably" because the performance of these councils has not been systematically studied. We know little about how satisfactory these councils are from the point of view of either the complainants or the judges. While in fairness to judges who are often unfairly maligned it is essential to maintain confidentiality concerning the details of the cases the councils screen, more could be done to provide a public account of the work of the councils. At the very least all of them should make available to the public annual reports of the kind prepared by the Canadian Judicial Council.[62] If the Canadian judiciary is to continue to exercise great power over Canadians and yet enjoy the security of tenure which is so vital to its independence, it must be accountable to Canadians for the way it governs itself.

Education and Professional Development

Traditional concerns about the quality of the judiciary have focused on improving the appointment system, insistence on a minimal level of legal competence, and security of tenure. The prevailing assumption seems to have been that if political favouritism is eliminated from the selection process and experienced, respected lawyers are appointed to the bench and protected from government interference, we will have as high a quality of justice as can be expected. Increasingly, this assumption is being called into question. Some years ago, in a seminal article, E.A. Tollefson argued that "even if the best possible appointments are made, we will not get the quality of justice which we are entitled to expect, because

the system itself substantially prevents the attainment of judicial excellence."⁶³
Tollefson went on to advocate a set of reforms designed to improve the competence of the Canadian judiciary featuring a training program and a system of
continuing education.

Since 1971, when Tollefson wrote his article, there has been increasing
recognition of his basic contention that "apart from rare exceptions, our judges,
at the time of their appointment are not prepared for the duties which society
expects them to perform."⁶⁴ Although there is still nothing like the year-long
program of instruction and in-service training which he advocated for all judicial
recruits, more attention has been given than ever before to judicial education
and professional development. No longer is it assumed that all that is required
for a quality judiciary is to appoint able lawyers and hope that they will grow
with the job.

Some key institutional developments have done much to foster judicial education
in Canada. One of the prime responsibilities of the Canadian Judicial Council,
established "to promote efficiency and uniformity and to improve the quality of
judicial service," is "the continuing education of judges."⁶⁵ Under the aegis of
the CJC there has been a significant expansion of educational opportunities for
federally appointed judges. The council sponsors an annual seminar for superior
court judges and another for county and district court judges from all parts of
the country, and a week-long orientation seminar for all newly appointed federal
judges. In 1974 the Canadian Institute for the Administration of Justice (CIAJ)
was founded by a group of law professors and judges to carry out research on
the administration of justice in Canada and to develop educational programs in
Canada for judges and for those performing adjudicative functions on administrative tribunals. The membership of CIAJ has grown to include many of Canada's judges (both federally and provincially appointed) as well as academics,
lawyers and interested citizens. With its roots in the university (the CIAJ began
at the Osgoode Hall Law School, York University, moved to the faculty of law,
University of Alberta in 1977, and to the faculty of law, University of Montreal
in 1986), the institute has been well placed to provide instructional services for
judicial seminars. The CIAJ, for example, contracts with the Canadian Judicial
Council to provide the instruction at the annual seminar for newly appointed
judges. Again, it was the institute which brought together an international group
of experts at its 1983 annual conference to assist members of the Canadian
judiciary in examining problematic aspects of interpreting Canada's new Charter
of Rights and Freedoms. At the provincial level, judicial councils in British
Columbia and Quebec were assigned statutory responsibility for developing educational programs for Provincial Court judges. In other provinces associations
of Provincial Court judges have played the leading role in organizing seminars,
while in some jurisdictions chief judges have taken the initiative in developing
orientation programs for newly appointed judges.

All of this constitutes a beginning, an essential first stage, in developing the
skills and knowledge needed for a high level of performance of the adjudicative

function in the late twentieth century. But it is no more than that—just a beginning. Chief justices and chief judges have devised various ''mentor'' schemes for enabling newly appointed judges, many of whom as lawyers or professors had little if any courtroom experience, to be in close contact with experienced colleagues for their first few months on the bench. While many of the federally appointed judges attend the annual seminar for newly appointed judges, it often occurs months after they have begun sitting. But there is still no systematic program of instruction laid on for all those, including justices of the peace, who must conduct trials for the first time. In recent years seminars on opinion-writing have been conducted on an ad hoc basis (the current chief justice of Canada, Brian Dickson, has been a leading instructor) but, again, no regular program of instruction in this craft has been established for newly appointed members of the higher courts. The seminars that are now frequently held tend to focus on new laws, such as the Charter, or the Young Offenders Act; they do not provide much of an opportunity for judges to explore in an intensive way developments in the human sciences that would better equip them to deal with the issues they confront in such matters as criminal sentencing, the resolutions of family disputes, or deciding questions of social equality under the Charter. No jurisdiction has established a program of judicial sabbaticals that would enable a judge at least once in his or her career to have an extended study leave.

A project which would make it possible to move on to the second stage of professional judicial development is the establishment of a national judicial centre. This idea has been under discussion for a good many years.[66] In November 1985 Justice William Stevenson, of Alberta's Court of Appeal, was asked to carry out a study of the possibility of establishing such a centre. The responses he received from a survey of seventeen hundred Canadian judges demonstrated a high level of support for improvements in the educational services available to judges. Justice Stevenson has recommended the establishment of a judicial centre whose primary role in judicial education would not be the delivery of instructional programs but the setting of national standards and the evaluation and co-ordination of programs.[67] The centre would also have a research and development function: for instance the production of standard jury instructions such as those developed by the Federal Judicial Centre in Washington, D.C.

If a Canadian judicial centre were to be established, it is essential that it serve the entire Canadian judiciary and not be confined to federally appointed judges. In this respect Canada should not follow the American approach. In the United States the Federal Judicial Center is concerned only with the federal judiciary; there is a separate centre for state courts. Such a set-up is appropriate for that country's dual court system. But it would be a serious mistake to take that approach here in Canada; to do so would commit Canada to a continuous evolution in the direction of the American dual court system. One of the difficulties in moving forward with the judicial centre proposal in Canada is that for some time the Canadian Judicial Council has been put forward as the instrument for implementing the proposal. The council already exists, has a mandate for judicial education and research, and has some space in Ottawa. However, the CJC has one crucial shortcoming: it is made up entirely of the chief justices and associate chief justices of the section 96 and federal courts. Thus, it excludes the majority of the Canadian judiciary: the provincially and territorially appointed judges. To serve as a resource for the professional development of a national judiciary in Canada a judicial centre must represent the needs and interests of all levels and branches of the judicial system. Fortunately, the centre recommended by Justice Stevenson is very much along these lines.

If a Canadian judicial centre is established, it would be the ideal agency to investigate two possible innovative devices for enhancing judicial quality; one that has been developed in Britain and the other in the United States. Because they both have implications that may appear to threaten judicial independence, the possibility of adopting them in Canada would be best studied by an independent judicial centre rather than by the executive branch of government.

The British device is the practice of having lawyers serve as part-time judges before their permanent appointment to the bench. Practising barristers are frequently appointed as "recorders" or "assistant recorders" to conduct jury trials in various parts of the country for a few weeks each year. This use of part-time judges was greatly expanded when the Courts Act of 1971 empowered the Lord Chancellor to appoint practising barristers to serve for stipulated periods as deputy High Court judges. In England today most judges before their appointment to a full-time position have had some judicial experience as either a deputy High Court judge or an assistant recorder.[68] Sir Robert Megarry claims that this system, besides the assistance it provides in responding to case-load problems, is of great assistance to the appointing authorities in that "predictability of performance as a judge is vastly increased for candidates who have acted as judges and so have had trial runs."[69] And, as Megarry points out, this experience also gives the barrister an opportunity "to find out what life as a judge will be like" before taking the plunge into a career change that is very difficult to reverse.[70]

The Canadian Bar Association's Committee on the Appointment of Judges has recommended that the federal and provincial governments explore means to give practising lawyers some experience as part-time judges.[71] The guarantee of security of tenure for superior court judges in Canada's written Constitution may be a constitutional bar to adopting the English system at the federal level. The probationary year for initial appointees to Newfoundland's Provincial Court has already been found to violate the guarantee of judicial independence in section 11(d) of the Charter. These provisions are condemned in the Deschênes Report as "inconsistent with the independence necessary to the judicial function."[72] While Deschênes perhaps overdoes it when he refers to this probationary status as "a sword of Damocles" hanging over the head of a new judge, it must be acknowledged that a more genuine threat to independence is posed by a system of probationary or part-time appointments in a country where judges are charged with the responsibility of applying a constitutional Charter of Rights. At a more practical level there is also the observation of another English writer that "litigants and lawyers do not much care for substitute or probationary judges feeling that they are being fobbed off with second class justice.''[73]

It may be that the American device — the review of judges' performance by lawyers who appear before them — is a more promising possibility for Canadians to consider. Such a proposal will not be joyously embraced by most Canadian judges. Twenty-five years ago when the idea of having student appraisals of professors was first promulgated among Canadian academics there were howls of outrage: it would only encourage professors to pander to the mob, it could never be done in a fair and responsible manner, it would undermine academic freedom, and so on. Since then, student assessments of the teaching performance of their professors have become standard practice in Canadian universities. In the evolution of appraisal instruments certainly some mistakes were made. But through a process of trial and error student appraisals have developed to the point where they have become a useful form of feedback to the professor and an important source of information to those responsible for tenure and promotion decisions. The very fact that professors know their teaching efforts will be appraised each year is a spur to conscientiousness in this area of their professional responsibility.

Performance review and consumer appraisal are essential ingredients of modern management techniques. While performance evaluation of judges has flourished in the United States, as Carl Baar has pointed out, it has received little consideration in Canada.[74] It is difficult to understand why judges whose work can have such a direct effect on our lives and yet who are virtually irremovable, should not be subjected to some such form of appraisal. It would be especially appropriate for trial judges whose individual rudeness, impatience, or incompetence can have such deleterious effects on the administration of justice.

Much has been done in the United States to develop fair and accurate methods of appraisal.[75] If lawyers are to be polled, it is essential to identify those practitioners whose exposure to the judge has been sufficient to provide a sound basis for assessment. Clear and concise questionnaires have been developed by several American bar and judicial organizations focusing on such topics as courteousness to litigants and lawyers, attentiveness to arguments of counsel, punctuality, judicial demeanour, courtroom discipline, and knowledge of the law. In some states with elected judiciaries the results of these appraisals are published when judges are running for re-election.

The first Canadian proposal for reviewing judicial performance has come from the Law Union, a group of reform-minded Ontario lawyers. They propose to produce a commentary on judges based on a survey of the profession, possibly analyses of reported decisions and biographical data, including the judge's area of practice and political background. The primary purpose of this manual would be to guide lawyers who are taking cases before the Ontario judiciary.[76] There is a danger that this kind of public appraisal, if not well done, might deteriorate into an opinionated labelling of judges by a biased sample of lawyers. There may be greater value in a more discreet appraisal of performance by lawyers with appropriate experience. Such appraisals have a better chance of being sufficiently respected by judges to be used for their own self-development and to be used by judicial councils for discipline purposes and nominating commissions in considering judges for "elevations." The important point is that a well-conceived system of performance review could serve Canadians' interests in building a judiciary that is both more professional and more accountable—and do so without endangering the judicial independence essential to a liberal democracy.

Systematic performance review by professional lawyers and the consideration of public complaints by judicial councils, while worthwhile means of enhancing judicial accountability, are no substitutes for a widening of public scrutiny and discussion of the judiciary. Canadians are not likely, and for good reasons, to opt for an elected judiciary. But they need not be so reserved in expressing their views on the quality of the justice they receive from their judges. One factor that has contributed to this reserve is the law of contempt. Here we are concerned not with that branch of contempt that has to do with keeping order in the courtroom or with the enforcement of court orders but with that aspect of contempt which has to do with punishing people for saying nasty things about judges—for "scandalizing the court." This aspect of the law of contempt has flourished in Canada through judge-made common law long after its abandonment in other liberal democracies. Canadians in the contemporary era have been found guilty of contempt for calling a court a "mockery of justice," or for accusing a court of "iron curtain" tactics, or for saying, as André Ouellett did, that a judicial decision was "silly" and could not have been made by a sane judge. In 1986 an Ontario lawyer, Harry Kopyto, was convicted of scandalising the court for stating that "the courts and the RCMP are so close together you'd think they were put together with Krazy Glue." Many Canadians will agree with the Toronto *Globe and Mail* that Kopyto's case "should be the last case under this scandalous law."[77]

Professor Robert Martin maintains;

> At the very least, the existing law of contempt imposes a substantial degree of caution on writers and publishers. Canadian journalists, to put it simply, are afraid to write stories which are critical of the judiciary. They are afraid of contempt proceedings.[78]

Martin points out how the law of contempt appears to conflict with numerous clauses in the Charter of Rights. However, as he also demonstrates, judges may not be the most detached group to decide whether the law of contempt is a reasonable limit on these rights. Here Canadians may have to look to the legislative branch for clear and decisive relief of this constraint on their right to criticize their judges.[79] In "Charterland," with its emphasis on equality and with so much power in the hands of judges, it certainly makes sense to give judges no less but no more protection from unfair public criticism than the law of libel and defamation provides for the rest of us. Judicial independence will not be a victim of such a reform. In the contemporary age the judiciary should earn public respect through quality performance rather than with criminal sanctions.

Summary and Conclusions to Part Three

Throughout these three chapters in examining the various issues which relate to staffing the Canadian judiciary we have drawn attention to two concerns: professionalism and democracy. Increasingly in recent years there has been a concern that the bench be staffed by highly qualified legal professionals and that its interests be under the aegis of judicial councils and associations in which senior members of the judiciary play the dominant role. On the other hand, the Charter of Rights has significantly raised public awareness of judicial power so that there is an interest in a judiciary that is more representative of the community it serves and whose security of tenure leaves some room for a measure of accountability.

In the past, political patronage has had a substantial influence in appointing judges in Canada. The consequences of patronage have been most severe at the federal level where the minister of justice and the prime minister control appointments to all the senior positions in the courts of the provinces and in the federal courts. In no other western nation does the system of appointing judges concentrate so much power in so few hands. During the Trudeau era some modest reforms were instituted: nominees were screened by a committee of the Canadian Bar Association, and a special assistant to the minister of justice expanded the recruitment networks. But these reforms did not do much to diminish the domination of the selection process by the party in power in Ottawa.

More significant reforms of the appointing process were achieved in a number of the provinces, which gave judicial councils the central role in the selection of nominees for appointments made by the province. These councils, comprised of judges, lawyers, and lay persons, have made aptitude and ability the prime considerations in the recruitment process. Among the common law provinces British Columbia has led the way, while Quebec has accomplished much the same thing through the use of ad hoc nominating committees. While an improvement in the quality of the provincially and territorially appointed judiciary is evident in those jurisdictions that have instituted this type of reform, the improvement is limited by the status and salary of these lower court judges. The remuneration of judges appointed at this level has not kept pace with the salaries of federally appointed judges, nor with the income of lawyers.

The Charter of Rights, by making Canadians more aware of judicial power, has increased interest in the quality of judicial appointments. There is now concern that partisan domination of the appointing process can lead to the kind of ideological manipulation of the bench which the United States has witnessed. The spate of partisan appointments by prime ministers Trudeau and Turner in 1984 was a spur to reform of the federal appointing process.

The approach to reform that seems to have the widest support is the advisory nominating council. Proposals of this kind, modelled in part on Missouri Plan reforms in some of the American states and on judicial councils and nominating committees in the Canadian provinces, were brought forward in 1985 by the Canadian Bar Association and the Association of Canadian Law Teachers. Both called for advisory councils made up of judges, lawyers, and lay persons to produce short lists of approved nominees for all appointments to the section 96 and federal courts, including the Supreme Court of Canada.

A distinctive feature of these proposals, tailor-made for the Canadian situation, is the representation of both the federal and provincial governments on the nominating councils. Canada's integrated judicial structure (provincial courts of appeal and higher trial courts staffed by federal appointees) calls out for close co-operation between the two levels of government in making appointments to these section 96 courts. In the past, this co-operation has been at best spotty and reached an all-time low when the Saskatchewan government in the early 1980s closed down judicial positions rather than have any more appointments by the Trudeau Liberals in Ottawa. While the Mulroney government has promised to consult with the provinces on judicial appointments, the representation of the provinces on nominating commissions would provide a more secure institutional basis for this consultation. Securing provincial participation through membership on a broad-based nominating council would also avoid a system of federal-provincial patronage trade-offs.

The nominating council approach is more likely to win approval in Canada than the other reform proposal which has been promulgated: legislative ratification of judicial appointments. Legislative ratification threatens to politicize the appointment process too openly for Canadian tastes. On the other hand, there is a possibility that the nominating council approach as a consequence of the very balance of political forces it contains will have a more subtle yet nonetheless distinct bias, favouring a bland, middle-of-the-road professionalism. Here democracy requires at least some form of accountability on the part of nominating councils if they are to become so influential in selecting our judges.

Even though Canada, like the rest of the common law world, does not have a career judiciary with a regular ladder of promotions, still promotions frequently occur within the Canadian court system, particularly at its higher echelons. The Supreme Court of Canada in recent years has been staffed exclusively by "elevations," as they are so delicately termed, from provincial courts of appeal and the Federal Court. Many superior trial court judges are appointed to courts of appeal. Below this level, promotions are relatively rare. Promotions would appear to be more consonant with judicial independence if they were dependent on a less partisan appointment system. Under the proposed nominating councils judges proposed for promotion would be treated no differently than other candidates.

The judicialization of the provincial magistracy means that virtually all of Canada's judges are now professional lawyers. This degree of professionalization has probably been, on balance, beneficial, but it has left very little opportunity for the ordinary Canadian to participate in the administration of justice. The practice in some jurisdictions of using lay justices of the peace to try "minor" criminal cases does not seem a very promising way of facilitating participation by non-lawyers. Review of the independence and impartiality of the justices of the peace through Charter challenges has revealed how inappropriate their terms of office are for those performing adjudicative functions. Arresting the decline of the jury, the better treatment of witnesses and the use of lay assessors may be better ways of providing opportunities for lay participation in Canada's justice system.

Reliance on reasonably successful lawyers to staff the bench inevitably produces a judiciary that is unrepresentative in a class sense of the Canadian community. This class bias, it is argued, is not incompatible with the principle of liberal democracy. It does suggest, however, that the judiciary may not be the most appropriate instrument for settling industrial disputes involving working-class interests.

There are ways in which the Canadian judiciary is unrepresentative of the community it serves that could and should be remedied. The under-representation of women and native Canadians is a prime example. Also, there is still some way to go in recruiting a judiciary with the language skills that can make bilingualism a reality in the courts of Canada for the country's French-speaking minority. Recruitment programs designed to meet these defects, far from conflicting with a merit selection system, would contribute to the development of a judiciary that can serve all Canadians more effectively.

Once appointed, Canadian judges have a high degree of security in their tenure of office. Indeed, no superior court judge has ever been removed. Compulsory retirement has been introduced in this century—with a bewildering and arbitrary range of age limits for various types of judges. But some of these limits will now be challenged under the equality provisions of the Charter.

Preoccupation with security of tenure as a condition of judicial independence has left little room for consideration of judicial accountability. The establishment of judicial councils in nine of the provinces, both northern territories, and the Canadian Judicial Council at the federal level has begun to remedy this situation. All of these councils are involved in judicial discipline and reviewing complaints against judges. Except for Nova Scotia, the provincial and territorial councils include lay persons in their membership. The role of the Canadian Judicial Council in investigating complaints against federal judges is a distinct improvement over the ad hoc style one-judge inquiry used in the Landreville affair in 1966. Still, its exclusively judicial composition makes it a less credible instrument of accountability than its provincial counterparts. They too could become more accountable by reporting annually to the legislature on their response to complaints.

The removal of patronage from the appointment process, maintaining levels of remuneration and working conditions capable of attracting outstanding legal professionals to all levels of the judiciary, widening recruitment networks, and establishing responsive complaint procedures are necessary but by no means sufficient steps toward establishing the standards of professionalism and accountability Canadians should expect of their judiciary in the next century. The process of establishing programs and resources for the education and professional development of judges has just begun. The creation of a judicial centre capable of serving a national judiciary would provide the logical institutional basis for the next step in this process. Under the aegis of such a centre, consideration should be given to innovations such as performance reviews which, however radical they may seem to today's judges, may be necessary to justify judicial power to future generations.

Finally, an important ingredient of judicial accountability is public discussion of the performance of judges. In Canada this element of accountability has been unreasonably restricted by a law of contempt fashioned by the judges themselves.

Notes to Chapter 7

1. *Addy* v. *The Queen in Right of Canada* (1985) 22 DLR (4th) 52. A bill is to be introduced in 1987 to make uniform the retirement age for all federally appointed judges at seventy-five.
2. SNB 1983, c. 4, s. 18(1).
3. 19-20 Elizabeth II, c. 56, s. 7.
4. Ibid., s. 20.
5. In 1984 data obtained from the commissioner of federal judicial affairs indicated that there were eighty supernumerary judges serving in eight of the provinces and on the Federal Court of Canada.
6. The Justices of the Peace Review Committee is made up of the chief judges of the criminal and family divisions of the Provincial Court and one other senior Provincial Court judge.
7. *Walton* v. *Hebb*, judgment rendered 11 Oct. 1984.
8. *Re Heagle and the Queen* (1983) 7 CCC (3d) 562.
9. Supreme Court Act, s. 9, Federal Court Act, s. 8. An act passed in 1882 stated that county court judges hold office "during good behaviour," but this provision seems to have been dropped in subsequent revisions of the Judges Act.
10. RSBC, c. 341, s. 10(1), RS Man., c. P148, s. 2(3)(a); RSNB c. P-21, s. 6(1); RSQ, c. T-16, ss. 80, 110, 127.
11. SN 1974, c. 77, s. 19; RSNS, c. J-1, s. 6.
12. See, for example, Alberta's Provincial Courts Judges Act, s. 11, RSA, c. P-20.1, s. 11(1).
13. See Shimon Shetreet, *Judges on Trial* (Amsterdam: North Holland Publishing Company, 1976), pp. 88-89.
14. See W.R. Lederman, "The Independence of the Judiciary," *Canadian Bar Review* (1956), p. 788.
15. For a succinct account of the Landreville affair, see *Landreville* v. *The Queen* (No. 2), (1977) 75 DLR (3d) 380.
16. House of Commons, *Debates*, 31 May 1967, p. 793, 8 June 1967, p. 1281.
17. *Landreville* v. *The Queen* (No. 2), p. 391.
18. Shetreet, *Judges on Trial*, pp. 108-109.
19. Quoted in Ibid., p. 105.
20. House of Commons, *Debates*, 9 Apr. 1883, p. 522. Blake's statement concerned a county court judge but is equally applicable to a superior court judge. For other Canadian statements, see R.M. Dawson, *The Principle of Official Independence* (London: P.S. King & Son, 1922), ch. 2.
21. 19-20 Elizabeth II, c. 55, s. 33(2). This is now s. 41 of the Judges Act.

22. Jules Deschênes, *Maîtres Chez Eux*, (Ottawa: Canadian Judicial Council, 1981), p. 116.
23. sq 1978, c. 19, s. 33. This is now s. 271(c) of Quebec's Courts of Justice Act.
24. sns 1976, c. 13, s. 6(4)(c).
25. 19-20 Elizabeth ii, c. 55, s. 32. This is now s. 40 of the Judges Act.
26. Dawson writing in 1922 indicated that an inquiry by a select committee of the House was part of the established procedure (p. 36). Shetreet, however, shows that in England a select committee has not always been used and instead the matter may be referred to a committee of the whole House (p. 131). With an inquiry by the Canadian Judicial Council now inserted into the Canadian process, there is even more reason to retain the option of omitting a select committee inquiry and having the matter referred directly to a committee of the whole House.
27. House of Commons, *Journals*, 1867-68, p. 26.
28. Ibid., p. 722.
29. House of Commons, *Debates*, 19 Feb. 1878, p. 369.
30. For a full account, see Dale and Lee Gibson, *Substantial Justice* (Winnipeg: Peguis, 1972), p. 138.
31. House of Commons, *Debates*, 1868, p. 685.
32. Ibid., Richard Bell, 3 Feb. 1966, p. 669.
33. *Landreville* v. *The Queen* (No. 2).
34. *Landreville* v. *The Queen* [1981] 1 fc 15.
35. It would require a constitutional amendment to s. 99 to restrict or qualify Parliament's role.
36. Judges Act, s. 41(5).
37. *Maîtres Chez Eux*, p. 123.
38. Brief of the County and District Judges' Association of Ontario to the Honourable Mark MacGuigan, Minister of Justice, with Respect to the Discussion Paper Entitled "The Constitution of Canada: A Suggested Amendment Relating to Provincial Administrative Tribunals," p. 19.
39. Gerald L. Gall, *The Canadian Legal System*, 2nd ed. (Toronto: Carswell, 1983), pp. 187-88.
40. Dale and Lee Gibson, *Substantial Justice*, pp. 258-65.
41. *Universal Declaration on the Independence of Justice*, s. 2.33, Montreal, 1983.
42. so 1984, s. 56.
43. rsbc, c. 341, ss. 18-20.
44. Courts of Justice Act, s. 85.
45. sq 1978, c. 19, adds Part vii to the Courts of Justice Act and establishes the Conseil de la Magistrature.
46. Deschênes, *Maîtres Chez Eux*, p. 123. Deschênes is not opposed to the executive retaining discretion to be merciful and refuse to act on a judicial report recommending dismissal.
47. Ibid., pp. 117-20. Six jurisdictions do not provide for temporary suspension. Four of those that do (New Brunswick, Newfoundland, Prince Edward Island, and the Yukon) give the executive some or all of the power to suspend. Under federal legislation and in British Columbia, New Brunswick, and Saskatchewan, the executive can order an open hearing.
48. Only New Brunswick, Newfoundland, Ontario, and the federal Judges Act require that the report of the judicial inquiry be tabled in the legislature. Tabling provides

the occasion for members of the legislature to question the government about its response to the report.

49. Glen R. Winters and Robert E. Allard, "Judicial Selection and Tenure in the United States," in Harry W. Jones, ed., *The Courts, the Public and the Law Explosion* (Englewood Cliffs, N.J.: Prentice-Hall, 1965).

50. Canadian Institute for the Administration of Justice, *A Compendium of Information on the Status and Role of the Chief Justice in Canada* (Montreal, 1987).

51. For a discussion of judicial rulings on bias, see J.O. Wilson, *A Book for Judges* (Ottawa: Canadian Judicial Council, 1980), pp. 23-31.

52. *Globe and Mail*, 24 Jan. 1984.

53. The one exception appears to be Nova Scotia. That province's legislation leaves it to the judicial council to establish its rules of procedure. RSNS, c. J-1, s. 13C(4).

54. *Report on the Activities of Council for 1983* (Ottawa: Canadian Judicial Council).

55. Interview with Pierre Chamberland, executive secretary to the Canadian Judicial Council.

56. *Report on the Activities of Council for 1983*, p. 8.

57. Ibid., p. 12.

58. Ibid., p. 13.

59. Only Quebec stipulates that members of the council who are not judges or representative of the bar must not be lawyers. SQ 1978, c. 19, s. 256(g).

60. In Quebec two judicial members of the council are truly representative in that they are appointed on the recommendation of a body representative of the provincially appointed judges. Ibid., s. 256(e).

61. Ibid., s. 270.

62. The Canadian Judicial Council's annual reports are not tabled in Parliament. They are available on request through the chief justice of Canada.

63. E.A. Tollefson, "The System of Judicial Appointments: A Collateral Issue," *University of Toronto Law Journal* (1971), p. 162.

64. Ibid., pp. 168-69.

65. Judges Act, s. 39.

66. For an early reference, see Mr. Justice Willard Estey, "Who Needs More Courts?" *Windsor Yearbook of Access to Justice* (1981), p. 279.

67. W.A. Stevenson, *Canadian Judicial Centre Project Report* (Edmonton, 1986).

68. Alec Samuels, "Appointing the Judges," *New Law Journal* (1984), p. 86.

69. R.E. Megarry, "The Anatomy of Judicial Appointment: Change But Not Decay," *University of British Columbia Law Review* (1984), p. 127.

70. Ibid., p. 129.

71. *Report on the Appointment of Judges*, p. 100.

72. Deschênes, *Maîtres Chèz Eux*, p. 105.

73. Samuels, "Appointing the Judges," p. 129.

74. Carl Baar, "Judicial Appointments and the Quality of Adjudication: The American Experience," *La Revue Juridique Thémis* (1986), p. 24.

75. For a review of these developments, see Dorothy Linder Maddi, *Judicial Performance Polls* (Chicago American Bar Foundation, 1977).

76. Cristin Schmitz, "Ontario Law Union will rate judges on performance, biases," *Lawyers Weekly* (20 June 1986).

77. *Globe and Mail*, 7 Nov. 1986.

78. Robert Martin, "Criticizing the Judges," *McGill Law Review* (1982), p. 20.

79. For some proposals on legislative reform of the law of contempt, see Law Reform Commission of Canada, *Contempt of Court: Offences Against the Administration of Justice* (Ottawa, 1977). Professor Martin does not think these reforms go far enough, and I am inclined to agree.

THE COURTS

LOWER CRIMINAL COURTS

Basic Structure of Canadian Courts

In Part Four we will look at the seven basic types of court operating in Canada today. The figure below depicts in a simplified way the place of these courts in Canada's judicial structure.

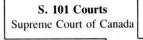

```
                        ┌──────────────────────────┐
                        │      S. 101 Courts       │
                        │  Supreme Court of Canada │
            ┌───────────────────────────────┐──────────────────────┐
            │         S. 96 Courts          │ Federal Court of Canada │
            │   Provincial Courts of Appeal │    Appeal Division      │
            │ Trial Courts of General Jurisdiction │  Trial Division  │
            │  (superior, county, and district) │
      ┌─────────────────────────────────┐
      │ The Provincial and Territorial Courts │
      │ Criminal                              │
      │ Family and Youth                      │
      │ Small Claims                          │
```

FIGURE 1 BASIC STRUCTURE OF CANADIAN COURTS

At the top and on the right are the section 101 courts, the two principal courts established and maintained by the federal Parliament and government: the Supreme Court of Canada and the Federal Court of Canada. The Supreme Court is of course the highest court in the land, the final court of appeal for all matters of law. The Federal Court, established in 1971, absorbed the old Exchequer Court and operates in a number of special areas of federal law. On the left are first the section 96 courts of the provinces and territories, which for the Fathers of Confederation were to be the foundation of Canada's judicial system. All the provinces and territories have a court of appeal and a superior trial court of general jurisdiction. Only three provinces (British Columbia, Nova Scotia, and Ontario) have retained county or district courts as locally based trial courts with a criminal and civil jurisdiction slightly lower than that of superior courts. Finally, at the bottom on the left, are the three main types of provincial "lower court": criminal, family and youth, and small claims. By no means do all of the provinces and territories maintain a separate court for each of these three purposes, but cases dealing with criminal, family and youth, and small claims matters constitute the business of the so-called lower courts across the country.

It must be stressed that this is a functional way of looking at the court system. Canada's courts do not come neatly packaged in these seven forms. The judicial systems of the provinces and territories display a great deal of structural diversity and a bewildering variety of court names. Indeed, there would almost seem to be a conspiracy within the legal profession to complicate judicial structure and the names of courts so that the ordinary citizen will be sure to feel the need for a professional guide to the court system. It is not the function of this book to provide a road map for this complex terrain. Rather, the aim is to help the political scientist and the citizen understand the various functions performed by different types of court and recognize both the practical and political implications of structuring the courts in different ways.

Each of the seven types of court discussed in this chapter has its own peculiar institutional history. Some, like the superior trial court and lower criminal court, have roots deep in British and colonial history. Others, like the family court and the Federal Court, are relative newcomers representing responses to contemporary social problems and political values. If all seven can be said to "administer justice," the justice they provide comes in very different forms. They operate in quite distinct settings with different methods of decision-making, serve different clienteles, and perform a variety of functions within Canadian society. It may seem that the only thing some of them have in common is that they are called courts and are presided over by judges. And yet, as we shall be at pains to point out, all seven to some extent perform the essential judicial function of adjudication—that is, the resolution of disputes about legal rights and duties.

One reason for beginning the discussion of the work of the courts at the bottom of the structure rather than the top is that traditionally the political scientist has been too mesmerized by the Supreme Court. To the extent that students of politics have given any attention to the judicial branch, their gaze has been fixed almost exclusively on the apex of the judicial pyramid. This preoccupation with the Supreme Court fosters the illusion that all power in the judicial system is concentrated at the top. By beginning with the lower courts we hope to correct this unbalanced perception of judicial power.

In this chapter we examine the lower criminal court. This is the court in which all criminal cases begin and most of them end. Thus in Canada it is in the lower criminal court that most citizens will have their only first-hand experience with the judicial system.

Structural Variations

In the common law provinces the principal lower criminal court function is performed by judges appointed to Provincial Courts.[1] In the Northwest Territories and the Yukon this function is performed by judges of the Territorial Courts. Criminal proceedings with respect to adults are by no means the only business of these Provincial and Territorial Courts. In some jurisdictions they also perform the function of youth courts, family courts, and small claims courts. Ontario has the most specialized structure with its Provincial Court divided into Criminal, Family, and Civil divisions. Nova Scotia has a Family Court which is quite distinct from its Provincial Court and for administrative purposes is under the aegis of the minister of social services rather than the attorney general. In other provinces there are Provincial Court judges, especially in heavily populated urban areas, who specialize in criminal matters or in family court or small claims court work. But in other parts of these provinces and in the northern territories, where population is too sparse to justify the presence of several specialist judges, the Provincial or Territorial Court judge often must be a jack of all trades. While many of the Provincial and Territorial Courts are multi-functional, it is only their role in criminal justice that is under consideration in this chapter.

Quebec, as might be expected, has quite a distinctive lower court structure. After Confederation Quebec, unlike Ontario, retained the Court of Sessions of the Peace and built it into the major provincial criminal court.[2] In the late 1800s, beginning in Montreal and Quebec City there was a transition from the English-style Quarter Sessions of lay justices, to a professional single-judge criminal court. By the early 1900s the judges of this court had a security of tenure and professional qualifications commensurate with those of federally appointed judges.[3] The development of Quebec's Court of Sessions of the Peace reflects the fact that the responsibilities of federally appointed judges did not extend as deeply into Quebec's judicial system as they did in other provinces; Quebec has preferred to retain more control over its own judicial institutions. There were never any county or district courts in Quebec. Most of the criminal jurisdiction exercised by county and district courts in common law Canada was absorbed by the Court of Sessions of the Peace in Quebec. The main exception is jury trials. Quebec's Court of Sessions of the Peace today exercises not only much of the jurisdiction handled by Provincial Court judges in other provinces but also the jurisdiction under Part XVI of the Criminal Code to try those charged with indictable offences (other than offences reserved for the exclusive jurisdiction of a superior court) who elect to be tried by a judge sitting alone without a jury.

Although the Court of Sessions of the Peace expanded steadily through this century and by 1982 had seventy-two judges, it by no means performs all the lower court criminal functions in Quebec. Beside it are two other provincial courts which have significant criminal jurisdiction: the municipal courts and the Provincial Courts. Quebec's municipal courts are descended from recorders courts, which in an earlier era enforced municipal by-laws and heard actions involving local taxes and licence fees. Their establishment is governed by Quebec's Cities and Towns Act. One hundred and thirty-eight Quebec communities operate municipal courts.[4] For the most part they function as traffic courts, except in Montreal, Laval, and Quebec City where they have a much more extensive criminal jurisdiction.[5] Quebec's Provincial Court evolved from district magistrates' courts. Unlike the Provincial courts of other provinces, Quebec's Provincial Courts have a major civil jurisdiction. However, its judges are vested with the criminal jurisdiction traditionally assigned to magistrates and now exercised by Provincial Courts in the common law provinces. Generally, the criminal work of the Quebec Provincial Court is only important where there is neither a court of sessions nor a municipal court.

The Wide Jurisdiction of the Lower Criminal Court

In 1971 John Hogarth, commenting on the jurisdiction of Canadian magistrates, pointed out that it was broader and covered a wider range of offences "than that given to any lower court of criminal jurisdiction in Europe, the Commonwealth, or the United States."[6] The Provincial Court judges of our day, the successors of the magistrates, continue to exercise a vast criminal jurisdiction which appears to be unmatched by the lower criminal courts of any other liberal democracy.

In Canada the more serious crimes are referred to as indictable offences, the less serious as summary offences. Mixed or, as they are called, "hybrid" offences are those in which the prosecution can choose to proceed either by summary or indictable procedures. The Criminal Code, enacted by the federal Parliament in 1892, determines how the different categories of offences are to be tried. Indictable offences are divided into three classes. The most serious are reserved for the exclusive jurisdiction of a superior court judge.[7] There are very few offences in this category: the main ones are murder and the most serious "political" crimes such as treason, intimidating Parliament, and sedition. At the other end of the spectrum are indictable offences reserved exclusively for trial by a Provincial Court judge sitting alone.[8] These include such offences as theft and driving while disqualified. In the middle are offences which give the accused the opportunity to "elect" the mode of trial. For this category, covering the majority of indictable offences, the accused has three choices: trial by a section 96 judge and jury, trial by a section 96 judge sitting alone, or trial by a Provincial Court judge sitting alone. Thus we can see that with the exception of those few offences reserved exclusively for trial by superior court judge and jury, the Provincial Court judge's criminal jurisdiction covers the full ambit of serious offences, including some for which there is a maximum penalty of life imprisonment. Even for those cases which are tried in a higher court, the Provincial Court judge is involved, for it is this judge who conducts the preliminary hearing to determine whether there is sufficient evidence to justify putting the accused on trial in a higher court.

The Provincial Court judge also deals with most summary conviction offences, which cover the vast majority of prosecutions in Canadian courts. They include a number of the lesser offences in the Criminal Code such as common assault and creating a disturbance in a public place, as well as all provincial offences and violations of municipal by-laws. As the responsibilities of provincial and territorial court judges with respect to indictable offences has expanded, increasing use is being made of lay justices of the peace to try summary offences. Ontario appears to have gone the furthest in this direction and uses justices of the peace sitting alone as a Provincial Offences Court to hear nearly all cases involving violations of provincial and municipal laws.[9] These cases include most of the minor traffic offences as well as more policy-related matters such as violations of zoning and planning laws. For some years a traffic court presided over by a single lay justice of the peace has operated in the city of Vancouver. Justices of the peace conduct preliminary hearings and hear minor offence cases (in some instances with at least one fellow JP) in several other common law provinces and in both of the northern territories.[10] Quebec also has a Court of the Justice of the Peace which is active mainly in the more remote areas where no other courts sit.[11]

The contemporary use of the lay justice of the peace as an adjudicative officer has very different connotations from the role of JPs earlier in Canadian history. Many parts of colonial Canada followed the British practice whereby members of the local elite served as justices of the peace, exercising a combination of judicial and local government functions. The legacy of this approach is still to be found in sections of the Criminal Code which empower two or more justices of the peace to exercise some of the jurisdiction of a magistrate. But during the nineteenth century Canada moved decisively away from the British model of local justice. Whereas in England, outside of London and one or two other metropolitan centres, banks of lay justices of the peace assisted by a legally trained clerk continue down to the present day to function as the lower criminal court, Canada opted for the paid, "stipendiary" or "police" magistrate.[12] By the late twentieth century the Canadian magistrate had evolved into the Provincial Court judge. In the contemporary Canadian context the lay justice of the peace sitting alone to try cases, far from being a pillar of the local society and the mainstay of the local criminal justice system, is much more at the margin both of society and of the judicial system.

Ironically, the next stage of reform of Canada's lower criminal court system may see more rather than less use of lay justices of the peace. At its worst, the practice of using JPs beyond their traditional pre-trial functions may be just a means of providing a cheap version of justice. We saw in the last part how the Charter of Rights prompted a long overdue review of the working conditions and terms of office of JPs who conduct criminal trials. But in northern Canada an adaptation of the British practice of using panels of respected members of the local community to adjudicate cases may provide a basis for a system of local justice that is not only less costly but is also more socially responsive.[13] Elsewhere, the very expansion of the Provincial Court judge's jurisdiction to cover everything from the most routine parking offence to crimes carrying a penalty of life imprisonment points to the need for a richer mix of backgrounds and aptitudes in the criminal justice system. The highly educated, experienced lawyer who is well equipped to conduct a serious criminal trial is not likely to be the most appropriate type of person to deal with routine driving offences.

An experimental traffic court in metropolitan Toronto provides a good example of the effective use of JPs. Cases are heard by justices of the peace who, although not lawyers, are usually individuals with extensive experience as court clerks.

Motorists have the option of pleading guilty, not guilty, or guilty with an explanation. Those who take the third option discuss their driving record with the justice and, instead of paying the fine (or at least the full fine) are given some professional instruction on good driving practice. This court is primarily engaged not in adjudication but in driver education, a function which lawyer-judges are not the most appropriate persons to perform.

Young Offenders

There is one other branch of criminal justice which can be distinguished from the normal work of the lower criminal court: offences committed by juveniles or, to use current terminology, by "young offenders." In 1908 the federal Juvenile Delinquents Act established the "Juvenile Court" for hearing cases involving any "child" who violated federal or provincial laws or was "guilty of sexual immorality or any similar form of vice."[14] In 1982 the Juvenile Delinquents Act was replaced by the young Offenders Act and the "Juvenile Court" by the "Youth Court."[15]

A literal reading of these acts might lead one to believe that the federal Parliament has actually created a distinct system of courts across Canada. But such a belief would be quite mistaken. All Parliament really did in passing this legislation is establish the *concept* of a special kind of court. It is left to the provinces, exercising their authority under s. 92(14) of the Constitution, to give flesh and blood to the concept: to provide the institutions, the personnel, and the services which can translate the concept into reality. In 1982, as in 1908, the federal government proceeded with its legislative concept without much consultation or co-ordination with the provinces. But that is another story.

What we want to describe here is the institutional form which the provinces gave first to the Juvenile Court and then to the Youth Court. After 1908 it was the provincial magistrate courts that began to exercise juvenile court jurisdiction. In those days municipalities bore the main responsibility for the provision of lower court facilities and only a few felt keenly enough about the Juvenile Delinquents Act to establish a specialized juvenile court with a full-time magistrate. The development of the juvenile court, for at least the first half of the century, was very haphazard indeed.[16] Later in the century, when a number of provinces began to develop family courts as a specialized branch of their Provincial Court systems, juvenile court jurisdiction was given to these institutions. This pattern was particularly marked in British Columbia, Nova Scotia, Ontario, and Quebec. There were good reasons for this merger of responsibilities. The families whose interspousal disputes, neglected children, and truancy problems are before the family court are often the same families whose children are in trouble with the police. The diagnostic approach and close interface with social services maintained by the family court made it a more appropriate institution for fulfilling the objectives of the Juvenile Delinquents Act than the regular provincial criminal court.

The Young Offenders Act represents more than a change in nomenclature. In the words of George Thomson, a judge of the Ontario Provincial Court (Family Division):

> Clearly the Act represents a substantial shift from the juvenile court philosophy of the early twentieth century to one which stresses much more strongly the rights of young offenders as well as accountability for one's behavior, responsibility of the individual and the protection of society.[17]

The act focuses on the adolescent age group from twelve to eighteen and creates a special, adult-like, criminal justice regime for this age group. Children under twelve are removed from any form of criminal prosecution. By way of contrast, the Juvenile Delinquents Act treated all those between seven and sixteen as children (extended to seventeen in British Columbia and Newfoundland and to eighteen in Manitoba and Quebec) and subjected them to a highly paternalistic criminal justice system.

In the Young Offenders Act we can see yet another effect of the rights-oriented liberalism referred to in Part One. Adolescents are to enjoy the due process rights of adults. In this respect the act establishes for Canada what was mandated for the United States by that country's Supreme Court in *Gault* and subsequent decisions,[18] and anticipates changes that would likely be mandated by Canadian courts under the Charter of Rights.[19] No longer can there be institutional confinements of indeterminate length. Young offenders must be charged with specific offences and not simply some form of "vice." There are to be full hearings and the right to representation by counsel at every stage of proceedings. Indeed, a young offender's right to counsel is extended beyond that of an adult in that the Youth Court judge must ensure that counsel is appointed for any young person who requests it, even where legal aid has been refused under a provincial legal aid plan for reasons of financial eligibility or the minor nature of the charge.[20] On the other hand, the punitive aspects of the adult system are modified for young offenders. Unless the young person is transferred to adult court (and it is easier to do this under the YOA than it was under the JDA), the maximum period of incarceration is three years. A much wider range of sanctions and treatments is available, with a clear statutory direction to minimize the deprivation of liberty.

The Young Offenders Act, like the act it replaced, leaves it to the provinces (and territories) to designate the judges who will exercise youth court jurisdiction.[21] Provinces which have been relying on family courts to deal with juvenile delinquents would logically designate their family court judges as youth court judges. That is certainly the case in Quebec, as that province had transformed its social welfare court into the youth court well before the Young Offenders Act.[22] In Ontario an interesting situation has developed whereby the Family Division of the Provincial Court serves as the Youth Court for twelve to fifteen year-olds, while the Criminal Division of the Provincial Court deals with those between sixteen and eighteen.[23] This division of responsibility is highly questionable. The Young Offenders Act attempts to strike an exquisitely delicate balance between the rights and responsibilities of adulthood and the special circumstances of youth. It imposes some challenging responsibilities on the judges who administer it and it directs that every effort should be made to reinforce family responsibilities rather than having the state, as *parens patriae*, become the surrogate parent. It is unlikely that judges and courts normally concerned with applying the procedures and sanctions of the Criminal Code are well suited for these youth court responsibilities. In this case the provincial institutional response seems almost designed to subvert the federal legislative objective.

Judicialization of the Magistracy

The liberal mutation which has occurred in Canada's political culture and can be seen at work in the transformation of juvenile courts into youth courts has also influenced modern reform of the adult criminal court. That reform was referred to earlier in this book as "the judicialization of the magistracy." It has involved the transformation of magistrates' courts into Provincial and Territorial Courts—a change that occurred in the common law provinces and territories in a span of years running roughly from the late 1960s to the early 1980s.

Much more has been involved here than merely a change in name and titles. Behind the improvements in the selection and terms of office of the provincially appointed judiciary (described in Part Three) was a much stronger emphasis on the role these judges should play in protecting the rights of those who appear before them—a clearer recognition of these judges as independent adjudicators.

As an institution of government the lower criminal court inevitably combines judicial and executive functions. It serves as an instrument of both justice and order. That is one reason why it is the court which is physically closest to the people. It is the institution which sanctions the application of the coercive powers of the state to its own citizens. The exercise of these coercive powers under the mantle of a judicial institution gives them legitimacy. As one looks back on the magistrates who preceded today's Provincial Court judges and back beyond the magistrates to the municipal officials, police officers, Hudson's Bay employees, or captains of militia who performed the lower criminal court function in eighteenth- and nineteenth-century Canada, it is apparent how much more thoroughly intermeshed were the judicial and executive functions in these earlier versions of the lower criminal court. Indeed, the very title "magistrate" connotes this combination of functions: the dictionary defines magistrate as "one clothed with public civil authority; an executive or judicial officer."[24] One of the most vivid and recent accounts of the magistrate's office is to be found in the 1973 report of Mr. Justice Geoffrey Steele which led to the judicialization of Newfoundland's magistrates. Steele reported that, particularly in non-urban areas, the magistrate "was the only legal advisor, judicial officer and law enforcement representative in the community." The crux of his report was "to recommend that the Magistracy of Newfoundland be made an essential part of the Judicial Branch of our Government."[25]

The Provincial Court and Territorial Court judge of today both in name and in practice is much more like a judge than a magistrate. Much has been done to disentangle the Provincial court judge from the police and the crown prosecutor who are, after all, one of the parties in most of the cases the judge hears. It is no longer the norm for the police and the lower criminal court to share the same physical facilities—what in the West and the Maritimes were often referred to as "public safety buildings."[26] The provincialization of administrative and fiscal responsibility for these courts (a crucial element in the judicialization of the magistracy) has provided the basis for a higher standard of court facility. Where, for reasons of convenience, new provincial court buildings include police facilities, they are much more segregated from the judges' chambers and the courtrooms. While still very much in evidence in the corridors and waiting rooms of Provincial Courts, the police seem less in charge of these institutions. British Columbia has established a separate organization of uniformed court personnel to perform the security and many of the other court functions traditionally performed by the police. In few jurisdictions do police now function as prosecutors. However, this practice, which still survives on a significant scale in Newfoundland, has been unsuccessfully challenged as a violation of the guarantee of a fair trial in the Charter of Rights.[27] The modernization of court administration has meant that in some jurisdictions the police and prosecuting attorneys no longer control the scheduling of cases in the lower criminal court.[28]

The changes described above are, as yet, by no means uniform throughout the country. The legacy of the old order can still be felt. In several provinces, for instance, Provincial Court (as well as some higher court) judges serve on police commissions—a carry-over from the days in which the magistrate supervised the police.[29] Even where the various structural and institutional reforms are more fully accomplished, there will continue to be a close relationship between law enforcement officials and lower court judges. Police court liaison officers and crown attorneys who appear in court every day develop a familiarity with judges which will be matched by only a few of the counsel appearing for the accused. These prosecuting officials become, to use Marc Galanter's phrase, "repeat players" in the courtroom drama and, as such may enjoy, or at least appear to enjoy, a distinct advantage over the "one-shotter."[30] But while it would be too much to expect a complete severing of the nexus between the coercive and judicial arms of the state, there is still much to be gained by way of striking a better balance between liberty and order by continuing with the reforms directed toward the judicialization of the basic criminal trial courts.

When we consider how relatively recent this effort at reforming the lower criminal court has been, the question arises as to why it took so long to judicialize this branch of our justice system. The answer to this question is complex and involves a great many factors. But a class explanation would seem to be the best way of accounting for the indifference shown to the judicious qualities of the lower criminal court. The clientele of the lower criminal court has been predominantly lower class: individuals with low income and low social status constitute the majority of accused.[31] Of course, this is true of accused who are tried in higher courts. But the higher trial courts—the superior, county, and district courts—have also been much involved in adjudicating disputes about the property and civil rights of the middle and upper classes. If members of these classes had been more involved as litigants in the lower criminal courts, it is unlikely that their shoddy and unjudicial condition would have been tolerated for so long. The vast extension of the criminal sanction, in particular its use in regulating automobile offences, has widened the clientele of these courts in this century and has fostered public interest in their reform.[32] But the deeper and more important factor has been the egalitarianism of the modern welfare state and its philosophy of providing a decent level of public service to all sections of society. It is still the more marginal members of our society who, in terms of personal liberty, have the most at stake in the quality of justice administered in these courts.

One welfare state program that has contributed significantly to the judicialization of the lower court is legal aid. Prior to the mid-1960s the only legal representation available to the indigent accused was that performed on a charitable basis by civic-minded lawyers. The great majority of those processed by the lower courts went without professional legal assistance even when charged with indictable offences.[33] The advent of publicly funded legal aid programs in all the provinces and territories has changed this situation. Now accused who satisfy a means test (set close to the poverty level) have a legal right to a publicly funded lawyer if a gaol sentence or loss of livelihood is likely to result from a conviction.[34] Many jurisdictions have full-time duty counsel at the courts to assist accused persons when they are first brought before the court on arraignment. Although persons charged with minor offences frequently appear without counsel, most of those charged with indictable offences are now represented by counsel.[35] The lower criminal court has become more of an adverserial arena pitting crown counsel against defence lawyers. This should mean that the balance of power is tilted somewhat less to the advantage of the state.

The Court's Role in the Criminal Justice System

Even with the judicializing reforms we have noted, it would be quite misleading to portray the lower criminal court in Canada as an adjudicative chamber in which the judges spend most of their time deciding disputes about the guilt or innocence of accused persons. Anyone who has spent some time around the criminal division of a provincial court will attest to the fact that it is more like a three-ring circus. It is in this court, or at least under the mantle of its authority, that most of the formal preliminary steps in the criminal justice system are performed. It is in this court that all those who are charged and convicted first appear, where questions of bail are settled, and where those who decide not to contest the charge against them register their guilty plea and are sentenced. A detailed study of the Provincial Court (Criminal Division) in downtown Toronto showed that most appearances before a judge involve requests for remands.[36] When trials occur—and this, remember, is where most criminal trials in Canada do take place—they are not like thrilling Perry Mason dramas unfolding before judge and jury, but rather perfunctory affairs, usually over in a few minutes, often impossible for all but the participating professionals to follow amidst the general hubbub of courtroom activity.

Like other modern industrial societies, Canada has come to rely increasingly on the criminal sanction as a means of maintaining social order. In this setting the lower criminal court operates within what has been aptly termed an ''assembly line system of criminal justice.''[37] Within such a system the role of the judge becomes marginal. The quality of justice depends more on what is done before trial or without trial. Of the hundreds of thousands of cases entering the system each year, the majority are terminated in some way other than a trial. Data reproduced by Griffiths, Klein, and Verdun-Jones from British Columbia demonstrate this clearly.[38] In that province in 1978, 114,354 criminal cases flowed into the court system. Of these, 98 per cent were ultimately disposed of within the lower Provincial Court. Forty per cent were settled by a guilty plea; in 25 per cent the crown terminated the proceedings by withdrawing the charges, staying the proceedings, or some such device; and 29 per cent went to trial. In the end 6.5 per cent resulted in a dismissal of the charges or a verdict of acquittal. Empirical research in other Canadian jurisdictions reports even fewer trials and a higher incidence of guilty pleas. Richard Ericson's longitudinal study of criminal cases in the County of Peel, near Toronto, for example, reported a guilty plea rate of 80 per cent.[39]

In many cases the guilty plea or withdrawal of charges results from informal negotiations between the accused, or more likely the accused's lawyer, and the crown attorney or sometimes the police. In the locality Ericson studied, ''the production of court outcomes took place backstage in discussions among detectives, lawyers and crown attorneys. . . . In the process, the judge serves more as an agent of ratification than adjudication.''[40] These negotiations are often loosely and euphemistically referred to as plea-bargaining. Strictly speaking a plea bargain occurs when an accused person agrees to plead guilty in return for either a reduction or withdrawal of charges or the prospect of a more lenient sentence. Empirical research on plea-bargaining is still rather scanty so it is not easy to say exactly how much of it goes on throughout the country. What evidence we have indicates that it most likely occurs in relation to indictable offences where multiple charges are laid and the accused is represented by a lawyer.[41]

We should not be concerned that disputes are settled informally without trial. In both civil and criminal proceedings if both parties are well informed about the facts and their rights we should expect matters to be settled without a trial. But we should be concerned if accused persons are induced to abandon a good defence or the crown to abandon a serious and well-supported charge simply to reduce the case-load burden of the court system or for the personal convenience of the professionals involved. It is also of concern if the opportunity to settle informally is available primarily to hardened criminals who have a lot to "sell," or to those represented by lawyers who are friendly with local prosecutors, or is systematically withheld from a racial group such as native Canadians.[42]

It is unlikely that the most effective way of dealing with abuses of the plea negotiation process is to follow the earlier advice of the federal Law Reform Commission and simply prohibit it.[43] That recommendation does not fully take into account the positive function of negotiated settlements in a justice system. A more promising approach may be to increase judicial surveillance of the process. In the Canadian legal tradition judges have stuck closely to the role of the judge in the adversarial system and have been reluctant to become involved in what takes place outside the courtroom. They have relied on crown counsel to pursue a just prosecutorial policy and defence counsel to represent the interests of the accused. With so much of the "justice" in the criminal justice system depending on the discretion exercised behind closed doors by prosecutors and defence counsel, it may be time to move in the direction of the continental "inquisitorial" system and provide an independent check on these early stages of criminal proceedings. As Verdun-Jones and Cousineau point out:

> . . . the lack of a requirement under Canadian law that a judge ferret out the critical factors that may have led to the defendant's decision to plead guilty has effectively created an environment in which it is possible for Crown and defence counsel to enter into plea bargains behind the inscrutable veil of secrecy.[44]

They urge that consideration be given to adopting the policy enshrined in rule 11 of the United States federal courts under which any plea agreement must be disclosed to the trial judge. In this system the trial judge is not a party to the negotiation but has a responsibility to ensure that the plea agreement was fair and to give the defendant an opportunity to withdraw it if in the judge's opinion it was not.

Sentencing

Sentencing is one dimension of the criminal justice system in which the decisions of the lower court judge are the dominant factor. Judges in the higher trial courts sentence too, but they deal with only a small fraction of criminal cases. Although prison authorities, parole boards, and probation officers have much to do with the implementation of the sentence once it is made, the judge is the key decision maker as to what the proper sentence should be. For most crimes Parliament has set only maximum penalties. It has given little direction as to the circumstances in which sentencing options such as restitution, probation, absolute and conditional discharges should be used. The sentences meted out by lower court judges can be appealed: for summary conviction offences to a judge of a higher trial court, for indictable offences to a provincial court of appeal. But the appeal courts in various jurisdictions have been slow to develop a clear and consistent set of sentencing guidelines.[45] Unless the lawfulness of a sentence is in dispute, sentences cannot be appealed to the Supreme Court of Canada. Consequently there is no national jurisprudence on sentencing policy. Indeed, it is not too much to say that if Canada has a penal policy it is primarily the cumulative result of the decisions made by Canada's lower criminal court judges.

These decisions can scarcely be described as adjudicative. The prosecution and defence may make submissions as to what they think is an appropriate disposition—and indeed, through a plea bargain may agree to make a joint submission. But these submissions are not binding on the judge. Nor is the judge's role here to resolve a dispute as to the accused's legal rights or duties. The judge's function in sentencing is to assess the gravity of the offence and the nature of the offender and to determine which of an often wide range of alternatives is the appropriate disposition in the circumstances. These determinations can have a major impact on the liberty and security of Canadians and on the cost of maintaining their penal institutions. The research of Canadian criminologists indicates that while for a long time there may have been an over-reliance on imprisonment, more recently there has been a move away from incarceration. Canada's overall imprisonment rate now appears to be considerably lower than that of the United States.[46]

Much of the literature on sentencing focuses on disparities and inconsistencies in sentencing practices. There is plenty of evidence of variations in sentencing practices in John Hogarth's *Sentencing as a Human Process*, the major empirical study of sentencing in Canada. Hogarth, for instance, reported that among the Ontario lower courts he studied in 1967, "one court used probation in nearly half the cases coming before it, while another never used this form of disposition."[47] Hogarth attributed most of the differences to the penal philosophy of the individual judge. Others emphasize the availability of alternative services and facilities, local community sentiment, and the contribution of other actors in the system, such as the probation officers who prepare pre-sentence reports. There is also some disturbing evidence of the influence of race prejudice.[48]

In the United States there has been a powerful movement to diminish the discretion of the sentencing judge by having the legislature prescribe a more precise "tariff" of penalties. This approach has the attraction of replacing the uncertainty and vagaries of judge-made sanctions with a code of definite and uniform penalties prescribed by a democratic legislature.[49] Given that most American innovations eventually find a following in Canada, this approach to reform is bound to be taken up here. But Canadians should not be too quick to plunge in this direction. Over several generations the fashion in penal philosophy has swung from retribution to rehabilitation and back to retribution.[50] It may be aggravating that our judges do not share a common philosophy of punishment, but we should recognize that our society has not reached a clear consensus on the purpose of punishment, on whether the prime objective should be deterrence, retribution, or reform. We may get closer to "justice" in our sentencing practices by improving the selection of judges and the quality of information available to them. It is interesting that this is where Hogarth ends up after his massive study of sentencing disparities.

Decriminalization

To advance significantly beyond the improvements made over the last twenty years in the lower criminal court, reform must move in two directions. One is to reduce our society's massive reliance on the criminal sanction; the other is to remove the invidious distinction between inferior and superior courts in the trial of serious offences. While these two types of reform may appear to be unrelated, they actually complement one another. They are both paths for moving away from a bureaucratic, sausage-machine approach to criminal justice toward a system that has a better prospect of delivering something recognizable as "justice": the first by rationing the frequency with which the system must deliver justice, the second by eliminating the double standard of justice.

As long as Canadian legislatures insist on making so many activities crimes it will be very difficult to move away from an assembly-line system of criminal justice. As Professor Baum points out, we have long passed the point where criminal law deals with the most serious violations of society's norms:

> Canadians are presumed to know the 700 sections that constitute the Criminal Code. (Each section of that code is a separate offence.) Add to this the 20,000 offences on the books of the federal government, and another 20,000 offences punishable by fine or imprisonment by the provinces. Left uncounted are the thousands of laws on the books of municipalities. In Ontario alone in a twelve-month period in 1977, the court system received more than four million charges— approximately two charges for every three residents of the province.[51]

This contagion of criminalization stems in part from a growing tendency to equate the moral with the legal. While we should expect the law to conform to our moral standards, we should not expect it to comprehensively embrace our morality. So long as we try to outlaw everything of which we disapprove, be it pot, liquor, pornography, abortion, or monopolies, we will have a justice system in which the most crucial decision-making is not by judges determining guilt or innocence but by the police deciding which of the myriad laws to enforce.

One approach to decriminalization which was all the rage a decade or so ago was diversion. This has proved to be something of a false start. Diversion programs were to focus on reported crimes involving persons with continuing relations: for instance in neighbourhoods, the work place, or the family.[52] The aim was to mend the breach in the social fabric through some form of settlement and restitution, rather than having the accused charged with an offence and sentenced by a judge. While diversion schemes have provided some useful alternative sanctions, they are not really a move away from the coercive application of criminal law. The accused person diverted, for instance, to some form of community service is presumed to be guilty and is under a form of compulsion. But the decision to divert has been made by prosecutorial officials beyond the purview of an independent judge. The maxim cited by Norval Morris—"the guilty we convict; the innocent we divert"—points to the most troubling aspect of diversion.[53]

Professor Peter Solomon has put forward another proposal which, while not actually amounting to decriminalization, at least has the merit of relieving the courts of processing masses of routine cases. He proposes the limited adoption of a system of "penal orders" used in West Germany for seventy per cent of criminal matters. A penal order

> . . . describes the wrongdoing the accused is alleged to have performed, cites the evidence at hand, indicates the applicable provision of the *Criminal Code*, and specifies the punishment to be imposed upon conviction. The accused has one week in which to object in writing or call for a trial on the merits; otherwise, the order takes effect and has the status of a conviction. Conviction by penal order cannot result in imprisonment; the usual punishment is a fine and, where appropriate, the suspension of a driver's licence.[54]

In some ways the penal order resembles the offence notice used in some provinces for driving offences, except that instead of being issued by the police, it is prepared by a legally qualified prosecutor who reviews the police evidence and approved by a judge who signs the order only if the record raises no doubt about the accused's guilt. Solomon would apply this system only to minor crimes such as some driving offences, possession of cannabis, property offences involving small amounts of money, and public order offences such as causing a disturbance. Even with regard to these offences he would apply it only to persons who have few, if any, previous convictions and are not associated with more serious crimes.

Such a system would at least cut down on the extent to which the lower criminal courts are bogged down with the burden of going through the motions of processing routine cases. In the jurisdiction studied by Solomon and his colleagues 37 per cent of the cases flowing through the court system fitted Solomon's description of a minor crime.[55] Under the penal orders system these cases would still require some prosecutorial and judge time but would save courtroom time and the attendance of all the officials, including police witnesses on overtime who typically are involved in the routine guilty plea. But the major beneficiary might be the accused. As Malcolm Feeley has shown in his study of a lower criminal court in the United States, often the process involved in the court appearances associated with a routine minor crime is much more of a punishment than the sentence finally handed down by the judge.[56]

Toward a Single Criminal Court

Even if we make some progress in relieving the massive case-load burden on the criminal courts, the need for an extensive high-quality adjudicative service to determine guilt or innocence and impose sentence will remain. But a strong case can be made for the proposition that Canada will not have such a service for the trial of all serious criminal offences until we abandon the hierarchical system of inferior and superior trial courts which has long been a hallmark of the judicial branch of government in Canada.

Over the years a number of scholars and analysts of Canada's criminal justice system have called for a restructuring of the court system which would remove the "lower court" stigma from the primary provincial criminal court. Writing when this court was still presided over by "magistrates," Professor M.L. Friedland put the case in these terms:

> Whatever may have been the justification for the grades of trial courts in the past (when the magistrate was, in fact, dealing with minor cases, as in England where to a great extend he still does), it has long since disappeared in Canada where the magistrate deals with many serious offences for which an accused can be sentenced by the magistrate to life imprisonment.[57]

A few years later, in an examination of this issue carried out for the Law Reform Commission of Canada, Darrell Roberts came to the same conclusion as Friedland. "Our whole criminal process," wrote Roberts, "is debased by the system of various grades of courts when its most important court is looked upon as inferior and subordinate."[58]

The judicialization of the magistracy which we have been tracing throughout this book has done much to improve the quality of the lower criminal court. But the unacceptable stigma of being a lower court dispensing an inferior brand of justice remains. And it is such an unreasonable stigma:—it suggests that a judge who is not competent to conduct a jury trial is competent on his own to try a case which can result in a life sentence. Despite all the reforms of the provincially appointed judiciary, the lower court image continues to restrict recruitment possibilities. And the Criminal Code's classification of offences which determines the court in which cases may be tried makes little sense and unduly complicates our criminal justice system. Ejann MacKaay's study of the labyrinthine paths of justice in the Montreal criminal courts reveals the games lawyers play with the accused's option to elect to be tried in a higher or lower court—games which have nothing to do with the prospects of obtaining justice.[59]

Proposals to unify the criminal trial court recognize that it would not make sense to have the same kind of judge, applying the same procedures, hear every case from the most serious murder trial to a parking violation. Both Friedland and Roberts would have a minor offence tribunal which could be staffed by lay personnel, providing its jurisdiction is confined to what is truly minor. The existing distinction between summary and indictable offences would not be a sound basis for establishing such a jurisdiction: some offences classified as summary can lead to significant fines or six-month jail terms. If the aim of a traffic court is primarily driver education, then from a functional point of view it may make sense to have a specialized institution for these cases. But the key objective of the unified criminal court proposal is to move away from an hierarchically organized system of trial courts. Where the prime function is to determine guilt or innocence and the appropriate sentence, there should not be an inferior and superior form of justice. The prime need, as Noel Lyon has put it, is

> to work toward an end to the deep division that exists in our courts between superior courts and so-called courts of inferior jurisdiction . . . but substituting for the hierarchical model now entrenched in our thinking a functional model in which all judges belong to an integrated judiciary but are specialized as to function and noted for their competence as judges rather than their position in a hierarchy of ascending power and importance.[60]

This is very much in line with the basic objective of reform advocated throughout this book: the concept of a trial centre staffed by a national judiciary which is neither federal or provincial, higher or lower, serving every major Canadian community.

Already a major step has been made toward this kind of restructuring in those provinces which have eliminated the intermediate trial court, the county or district court, and merged it with the superior court. Chapter 11 will examine this development more closely and the political resistance it has encountered. But to go further and, at least for serious criminal cases, eliminate the distinction between lower and higher trial courts involves surmounting constitutional as well as political obstacles. The Supreme Court of Canada's decision in *McEvoy* rules out the approach to criminal court unification favoured by some commentators and the province of New Brunswick: assigning full criminal jurisdiction on either an exclusive or concurrent basis to provincially appointed judges.[61] Now it would require a constitutional amendment to give the Provincial Court judges the jurisdiction traditionally exercised by a superior court.

A more viable approach would be for the federal government to agree to elevate the provincial and territorial court judiciary to superior court status, as it has already done with county and district court judges in six provinces. Reform of the federal appointing process along the lines proposed in the previous chapter would probably be necessary to secure provincial agreement for this kind of reorganization. The provinces would have to be convinced that federal political patronage is not such a dominant factor in the appointment of superior court judges. On the other hand, there might be some reluctance to go ahead with such elevations in provinces that have given little evidence of reforming their methods of appointing judges. Also, the federal government which pays the salaries and pensions of all superior court judges, not unreasonably, might wish to consider some compensatory adjustment in federal-provincial transfer payments before assuming responsibility for the remuneration of hundreds of provincial court judges.

No doubt there are formidable problems to be worked out in the realms of political-economy and personnel management before Canadians can enjoy the benefits of a unified criminal court. But the logic of the case for moving in this direction is strong.[62] It may be that progress will best be made on a province-by-province basis beginning with those provinces that have a carefully worked out reorganization scheme and in which court structure policy is not unduly influenced by the views of the senior judiciary.

Notes to Chapter 8

1. For an overview of all aspects of Canada's criminal court system, see Curt T. Griffiths, John F. Klein and Simon N. Verdun-Jones, *Criminal Justice in Canada* (Toronto: Butterworths, 1980), ch. 5.
2. For an account of the Quebec system, see Gerard Trudel, "Le Pouvoir judiciaire au Canada," *Revue du Barreau* (1968), p. 194.
3. In 1908 the judges were required to have practised law for ten years. The requirement was reduced to five years after 1908 but restored to ten in 1946. Courts of Justice Act, sq, c. T-16, s. 80.
4. Monique Giard and Marcel Proulx, *Pour comprendre l'appareil judiciaire québécoise* (Sillery: Presses de l'Université du Québec, 1985), pp. 25-27.
5. For an analysis of how accused and their counsel take advantage of the option of using the Court of Sessions or the Municipal Court in Montreal, see Ejann MacKaay, *The Paths of Justice: A Study of the Operation of the Criminal Courts of Montreal* (Montréal: Faculté de droit, Université de Montréal, 1976).
6. John Hogarth, *Sentencing as a Human Process* (Toronto: University of Toronto Press, 1971), p. 35.
7. Criminal Code of Canada, s. 427, 429(1). Until 1985 offences in this category had to be tried by a superior court judge and jury. The jury is now optional.
8. Criminal Code of Canada, s. 483.
9. Provincial Offences Act, rso 1980, c. 400.
10. A study of the role of the jp in Canada is currently being carried out under the direction of Dr. Anthony Doob at the University of Toronto's Centre of Criminology.
11. Courts of Justice Act, ss. 158-213. Jérôme Choquette reported in 1976 that four full-time jps were used in Montreal to hear minor criminal cases. *Justice Today* (Québec: Gouvernement de Québec, 1976), p. 96.
12. For an account of the historical evolution of the office of jp see Esther Moir, *The Justice of the Peace* (Harmsworth: Penguin Books, 1969). For an account of the jps' function in contemporary Britain see Elizabeth Burney, *Magistrates, Court and Community* (London: Hutchinson, 1979).
13. An inquiry conducted by W.G. Morrow into the administration of justice in Hay River in the Northwest Territories indicates some of the drawbacks in single members of native communities hearing cases. *Report of Inquiry re: Administration of Justice in one Hay River Area of the Northwest Territories* (Ottawa: Queen's Printer, 1968).
14. Juvenile Delinquents Act, sc 1908, c. 40, s. 2(1).
15. Young Offenders Act, 1980-81-82-83 (Can.), c. 110.
16. Jeffrey S. Leon, "The Development of Canadian Juvenile Justice," *Osgoode Hall Law Journal* (1977), pp. 101-104.
17. "Commentary on the Young Offenders Act," *Provincial Judges Journal* (1984), p. 27.

18. *In Re Gault* (1967) 387 U.S. 1.
19. Between 1982 and 1984 before the Young Offenders Act came into force Canadian judges overruled a number of sections of the Juvenile Delinquents Act on the grounds that they conflicted with the Charter of Rights.
20. Young Offenders Act, s. 11(4).
21. The act also leaves it to the provinces to decide whether the YOA applies to provincial offences.
22. Courts of Justice Act, ss. 109-23.
23. The YOA came into force in two stages: on 1 Apr. 1984 for the 12 to 15-year-olds, on 1 Apr. 1985 for the 16 and 17-year-olds. For an analysis of Ontario's difficulties in implementing the Act, see John Gault, "Political Delinquency," *Toronto Life*, May 1984, pp. 15-17.
24. Funk and Wagnall Standard Dictionary.
25. *Report of Newfoundland Royal Commission into the Magistracy of Newfoundland and Labrador* (St. John's, 1973), pp. 2 and 50.
26. M.L. Friedland, "Magistrates Courts: Functioning and Facilities," *Criminal Law Quarterly* (1968), p. 55.
27. *R. v. Hart* (1986), 26 C.C.C. (3d) 438. The trial judge found the system of police prosecutors unconstitutional, as did one of the three judges on the Court of Appeal.
28. For a description of the major role played by police officers and prosecutors in one Canadian province, see H.R. Poultney, "The Criminal Courts of the Province of Ontario and Their Process," *Law Society of Upper Canada Gazette* (1975), p. 192.
29. Philip Stenning, *Police Commissions, their development, composition, duties and powers, contracted study for Royal Commission on Certain Activities of the R.C.M.P.* (Ottawa, 1980).
30. Marc Galanter, "Why the 'Haves' Come Out Ahead: Speculation on the Limits of Legal Change," *Law and Society Review* (1975), p. 75.
31. For a lucid account of the lower-class consumers and middle-class observers of the lower criminal court in Victorian Toronto, see Paul Craven, "Law and Ideology: The Toronto Police Court 1850-80," in David H. Flaherty, ed., *Essays in the History of Canadian Law* II. (Toronto: The Osgoode Society, 1983).
32. For an analysis of the importance of automobile offences in the adult court of the mid-twentieth century, see Stuart Ryan, "The Adult Court," in W.T. McGrath, ed., *Crime and Its Treatment in Canada* (Toronto: Macmillan of Canada, 1965).
33. See *Report of the Canadian Committee on Corrections* (Ouimet Report) (Ottawa, 1969), p. 136.
34. For a suvey of legal aid in Canada today, see Canadian Centre for Judicial Statistics, *Legal Aid in Canada 1985* (Ottawa, 1985).
35. See, for example, Larry Taman, "The Adversary Process on Trial: Full Answer and Defence and the Right to Counsel," *Osgoode Hall Law Journal* (1975), p. 251. It is possible that the right to a fair trial in s. 11(d) of the Charter of Rights will be interpreted to extend access to publicly funded legal representation beyond what is now provided by statute.
36. Robert G. Hann, *Decision Making in the Canadian Criminal Court System: A System Analysis* (Centre for Criminology, University of Toronto, 1973), tables 5.6 and 5.7.

37. For an analysis of the assembly-line features of the system, see Daniel Jay Baum, *Discount Justice: The Canadian Criminal Justice System*, (Barrie: Burns and MacEachern, 1979).
38. Griffiths *et al*, *Criminal Justice in Canada*, pp. 146-47.
39. Richard V. Ericson, *Making Crime: A Study of Detective Work* (Toronto: Butterworths, 1981), p. 198.
40. Ibid., p. 221.
41. For an examination of existing research, see Simon N. Verdun-Jones and F. Douglas Cousineau, "Cleansing the Augean Stables: A Critical Analysis of Recent Trends in the Plea Bargaining Debate in Canada," *Osgoode Hall Law Journal* (1979), pp. 251-54.
42. D.F. Wynne and T.F. Hartnagel, "Race and Plea Negotiations: An Analysis of Some Canadian Data," *Canadian Journal of Sociology* (1975), p. 147.
43. Law Reform Commission of Canada, *Working Paper 15: Criminal Procedure: Control of the Process* (Ottawa, 1975). The commission's position is based largely on Gerald Ferguson and Darrell Roberts, "Plea Bargaining: Directions for Canadian Reform," *Canadian Bar Review* (1974), p. 498.
44. Verdun-Jones and Cousineau, "Cleansing the Augean Stables," p. 237. For a more far-reaching proposal to modify the English adversarial system along European lines, see Patrick Devlin, *The Judge* (London: Oxford University Press, 1979), ch. 3.
45. See J.V. Decore, "Criminal Sentencing: The Role of the Canadian Courts of Appeal and the Concept of Uniformity," *Criminal Law Quarterly* (1964), p. 324.
46. See the evidence summarized in John Hagan, *The Disreputable Pleasures* (Toronto: McGraw-Hill Ryerson, 1977), pp. 166-69.
47. Hogarth, *Sentencing as a Human Process*, p. 12.
48. Evidence of discrimination against non-Caucasians is presented in K.E. Renner, and A.H. Warner, "The Standard of Social Justice Applied to an Evaluation of Criminal Cases Appearing Before the Halifax Courts," *The Windsor Yearbook of Access to Justice* (1981), p. 62.
49. "Criminal Sentencing in Transition," *Judicature* (Oct.-Nov. 1984).
50. For an account of these fluctuations, see Martin L. Friedland, *A Century of Criminal Justice* (Toronto: Carswell, 1984), esp. ch. 8.
51. Baum, *Discount Justice*, p. 18.
52. For the philosophical rationale for diversion, see John Hogarth, "Alternatives to the Adversary System," in Walter Tarnopolsky, ed., *Some Civil Liberties Issues of the 1970's* (Toronto: Osgoode Hall Law School, 1975). For a set of diversion proposals, see Law Reform Commission of Canada, *Working Paper 7: Diversion* (Ottawa, 1975).
53. Norval Morris, *The Future of Imprisonment* (Chicago: University of Chicago Press, 1974), pp. 10-11.
54. Peter H. Solomon, Jr., *Criminal Justice Policy, From Research to Reform* (Toronto: Butterworths, 1983), p. 74.
55. This is Peel County in Ontario, the same jurisdiction on which Richard Ericson's study, *Making Crime*, is based.
56. Malcolm Feeley, *The Process Is the Punishment* (New York: Russell Sage, 1979).
57. Friedland, "Magistrates Courts: Functioning and Facilities," p. 72.
58. Darrell Roberts, "The Structure and Jurisdiction of the Courts and Classification

of Offences,'' paper prepared for the Law Reform Commission of Canada, 1973, p. 23.

59. MacKaay, *Paths of Justice*.
60. As quoted in Perry S. Millar and Carl Baar, *Judicial Administration in Canada* (Montreal and Toronto: McGill/Queen's University Press with the Institute of Public Administration of Canada, 1981), p. 101.
61. This case is discussed in chapter 2.
62. For a more detailed consideration of these reorganization proposals comparing them with court unification in the United States, see Millar and Baar, *Judicial Administration*, ch. 4.

CHAPTER 9
THE FAMILY COURT

Unlike the lower criminal courts which as an instrument of order have deep roots in colonial and British history, the family court is a distinctly modern, twentieth century institution. Its social genesis is the disintegration of the social bonds of family and community which has accompanied industrialization and urbanization. In the words of Judge Allard, "Family Courts have attempted to reflect the concern of the State for marriage and family life."[1]

The family court represents the effort of the modern state to do what it can to preserve the family and when that effort fails, as it increasingly does, to provide a fair adjudication of disputes over the rights and duties of those directly affected. It is, then, at the centre of a fundamental revolution taking place in our society: the shift away from the nuclear, patriarchal family as the basic unit of the social fabric. The family court stands astride this river of social change. Its diagnostic and therapeutic services are dedicated to reducing conflict in deteriorating family relationships; its adjudicative services impose the sanctions of the state when traditional family responsibilities are not fulfilled.

Emergence of the Institution

The family court itself has become an instrument of social and political change. The patriarchal power structure within the traditional family is increasingly challenged by the values of a more egalitarian era. As the interests of wives and children gain the status of legally enforceable rights, the courts become the arenas for adjudicating disputes among family members. An Ontario family court judge, Stewart Fisher, makes the point eloquently:

> In my role as a Family Court judge it is not an unusual sight to see fathers whose backgrounds are patriarchal (and most are) stare in disbelief and often rage when I tell them what they can do and can't do within their own families. Recently in Ontario a man burst into tears and said "I can't believe that it has come to this, that a man can't beat his wife any more."
>
> In the past, the politics of the family predated and shaped the politics of the state. Today it seems that the egalitarian politics of the state have become the politics of the family.[2]

In many respects today's family court and the social agencies attached to it are attempting to fill the vacuum created by the erosion of the traditional basis of family order.

Behind the emergence of the family court as a tribunal specializing in family-related disputes is a recognition of the limits of adjudication. Adjudication is concerned with establishing who is legally right and who is legally wrong with regard to a single issue. But disputes that arise within families that are or were living together usually are not the result of the wrongdoing of a single individual. The welfare of those involved will not be greatly enhanced simply by obtaining a verdict on a legal point in dispute. Family-related conflicts are likely to be prototypes of what Lon Fuller called polycentric disputes. Hence there is an assumption that the institution which deals with these disputes should be able to consider and, indeed, to treat not just the delinquent's crime, or the inter-spousal assault, or the father's failure to provide maintenance, but the whole situation. The family court, ideally, should deal with family-related disputes in a holistic manner so as to provide both justice and welfare. While this may be an ideal for family court enthusiasts, it is anathema to many members of the legal profession who are sceptical of the welfare professions and treasure the adversarial defence of legal rights.

It is much easier to discuss the family court ideal and the controversy surrounding it than it is to describe the institutions which have developed around that ideal. Among Canada's ten provinces and two territories there is great variety in the judicial institutions which handle the civil and criminal aspects of family-related conflict. Indeed, no two jurisdictions have identical arrangements. Graphic evidence of this diversity is provided by the Canadian Centre for Justice Statistics' 1984 publication, *Family Courts in Canada*.[3] Appendix B of that report contains a chart showing the courts given jurisdiction in each of the provinces and territories over fifteen selected family matters: marriage, divorce, matrimonial property, maintenance custody, guardianship, adoption, and so on. This grid displays not only the institutional diversity, but also the fact that fragmentation rather than unification still characterizes the judicial branch of government in this field.

The juvenile court was the focal point for the first attempt to cluster together certain aspects of family-related law in a single tribunal. Ontario legislation passed in 1916 empowering municipalities to establish juvenile courts extended the jurisdiction of these courts to all cases under the Children's Protection Act, the Truancy Act, and the Industrial Schools Act. The magistrates who presided over the juvenile court could also hear cases involving deserted wives and the enforcement of maintenance payments. Out of this amalgamation of jurisdiction grew the first family courts. By 1934 Ontario had passed legislation reconstituting its juvenile courts as juvenile and family courts. Gradually other provinces followed the Ontario example of extending the jurisdiction of Juvenile Court magistrates to such matters as deserted wives and neglected children.[4] Family courts were established on this basis in Vancouver in 1943, in Winnipeg in 1947, in St. John's, Newfoundland, in 1951, and in Calgary and Edmonton in 1952. In the early 1960s Quebec and Nova Scotia created separate and distinct province-wide networks of courts with much the same jurisdiction. Quebec established its social welfare courts (which later became youth courts) in 1960 for cities with at least 50 000 inhabitants, and Nova Scotia established its family courts in 1963.

Up to this point the Canadian family court was modelled fairly closely on

English lines. In the nineteenth century English magistrates had been given jurisdiction by a number of acts designed to protect deserted wives and children. These same magistrates dealt with inter-spousal assaults and most criminal complaints involving children. There was a clear class orientation to the Canadian family courts based on this English model. The clientele of the English and Canadian magistrate was mostly the poor. Complaints involving deserted or assaulted wives, truancy, and juvenile delinquency almost always were directed against members of lower-income families. The domestic-relations disputes of the propertied classes (contested divorces, alimony, the custody of children, and so on) were kept in the higher trial courts. In the juvenile and family court probation officers and welfare officials, not lawyers, were the dominant professionals. The facilities and court services in most provinces depended on municipal support and were generally of low quality. In some localities these courts were "poor cousins" to the magistrates' courts.[5]

In the 1960s interest began to be expressed in moving beyond the police magistrate's model of a domestic relations court to a more comprehensive family court with "competence to deal with all major aspects of family litigation."[6] Here the model which Canadian writers had in mind was the comprehensive American family court which had been established in a number of cities[7] and had long been advocated by American reformers.[8] These courts combined the traditional superior court jurisdiction over disputes involving marriage, divorce, and its ancilliary issues with the traditional lower court jurisdiction relating to delinquent children, broken homes, and abandoned wives. A few of the American courts had developed quite extensive counselling, conciliation and investigative services to assist in providing a holistic treatment of family problems and to minimize adjudication and the enforcement of legal sanctions.

Movement Toward a Unified Family Court and Its Constitutional Obstacles

Given the egalitarian and functional attractions of the American model, it might be expected that the provincial family courts would evolve in that direction and acquire a comprehensive family law jurisdiction. Certainly there was increasing pressure to move in this direction, especially as the provinces moved more decisively away from the English lower court and began to judicialize their magistrates. With the provincial governments taking over administrative responsibility for the provincial family courts, staffing them with full-time professional judges, often carefully selected on the basis of their background and interest in family law matters, connecting them to provincial social services and extending legal aid to all kinds of domestic disputes, a much stronger case could be made for vesting all aspects of family law jurisdiction in the provincial family courts. This type of reform was advocated by a number of submissions to a committee of Parliament considering amendments to the Divorce Act in 1967.[9] But the committee felt that the provincial family courts at that time were not yet ready to exercise a full jurisdiction in family law matters. It concluded:

> Some Family Courts may be competent but . . . at present, such courts are in a minority. In the future, as the Family Courts develop, the problem may be worthy of further consideration, but at present your Committee is opposed to jurisdiction in divorce matters being given to Family Courts.[10]

Although the parliamentary committee left open the possibility of unifying family-related jurisdiction in family courts presided over by provincially appointed judges, this development has not occurred. Resistance to moving in this direction stems in part from the low esteem in which the provincial courts tend to be held by influential members of the legal profession, and the sceptical attitude of many lawyers toward the welfare disciplines which are so much in evidence in the family courts. Also, to be fair, it reflects the uneven development of family courts across and within the various Canadian jurisdictions. But, perhaps more than anything else, the failure to continue on what seemed to many to be the logical path toward an effective and comprehensive family court reflects the difficulties of operating Canada's federal constitution.

Legislative jurisdiction over the package of legal relationships referred to as family law matters is divided in a complex and somewhat obscure manner between the provinces and the federal Parliament.[11] The federal government under section 91(26) has exclusive jurisdiction over "Marriage and Divorce," while the provinces under section 92(12) have exclusive jurisdiction over the "Solemnization of Marriage." Issues of custody and access to children, maintenance, and alimony can be legislated on by Parliament when they are ancillary to divorce, but are under provincial legislation when they are associated with marriage break-up or separations outside of divorce. Laws concerning the status of family members, the division of matrimonial property, adoption, the guardianship and protection of children, and the civil obligations of husbands and wives all come under provincial jurisdiction over "property and civil rights in the Province" (section 92(13)). Criminal sanctions pertaining to young people and family disputes fall within federal jurisdictions over criminal law and procedure (section 91(27)). Thus neither level of government on its own has the constitutional leverage to regulate all aspects of family-related disputes. The federal Parliament in Canada lacks the jurisdiction to establish a comprehensive national system of family courts and the provinces lack the jurisdiction which enables state governments in the United States to establish comprehensive unified family courts. The unification of family law jurisdiction in Canada requires co-operative federalism of the highest order.

Even if this level of co-operation were forthcoming, there is yet a further constitutional difficulty: the judicature sections of the Constitution. In chapter 2 we reviewed how section 96 (which gives the federal government the power to appoint the superior, county, and district court judges of the provinces) together with sections 97 to 100 (governing the qualifications, tenure, and remuneration of these judges) have been interpreted as entrenching the jurisdiction exercised exclusively by section 96 judges at the time of Confederation. While the Supreme Court in the *Adoption Reference* of 1938[12] was willing to uphold provincial legislation giving provincially appointed magistrates jurisdiction over adoption and the maintenance of deserted wives and children, it seems most unlikely that it would uphold provincial legislation reorganizing the provincial courts so as to give family courts presided over by provincially appointed judges jurisdiction over divorce and all of its ancillary issues. Further, as we have seen, the contemporary Supreme Court in the *McEvoy* case has ruled that constitutional entrenchment of the core jurisdiction of superior courts limits Parliament as well as the provincial legislatures.[13] Thus, even if the federal Parliament were persuaded (as it was not in 1967) to amend the provision of the Divorce Act (which gives the superior trial courts exclusive jurisdiction to entertain divorce petitions) and give provincially appointed family court judges jurisdiction in this field, such legislation would in all probability be found to be unconstitutional.

The Supreme Court has shown little inclination to interpret the Constitution in a way which would permit more flexibility in the institutional arrangements for dealing with family disputes. In the *British Columbia Family Relations Act* case[14] (discussed in chapter 3), the courts ruled that while provincially appointed judges of a family court could exercise jurisdiction concurrently with supreme court judges in matters of guardianship, custody, and access to children, they could not make orders concerning the occupancy and entry of the family home. The Court showed little interest in the argument that the family law functions traditionally discharged by superior courts would be dealt with in an entirely different policy setting in a modern family court and therefore should not be considered part of the entrenched core jurisdiction of superior courts.[15]

The *B.C. Family Relation Act* decision was a serious setback for family court unification. British Columbia's experimental unified family court project in the suburbs of Vancouver grew out of the Berger Royal Commission on Family and Children's Law. In its use of family counsellors, children's advocates, and lay assessors it represented some of the most imaginative thinking in this field. The unification aspect of the project involved superior court judges exercising their jurisdiction in a provincial family court building. A crucial ingredient of the project was the use of family counsellors at the intake stage of all proceedings entering this joint provincial court/superior court operation. The Supreme Court's decision had "the immediate effect of severely restricting the role of family court counsellors in the conciliation and mediation of custody disputes in the provincial Court."[16] The shift from an NDP to a Social Credit government in British Columbia may have put an end to the possibility of going forward with the Berger Commission proposals, but the Supreme Court's decision put a crimp in the plans any other provinces may have had to consolidate family services in their Provincial Courts.

The Consequences of Fragmentation

The adverse consequences of fragmented family law jurisdiction have been fully documented in a number of Canadian studies. In the 1970s, besides the British Columbia royal commission discussed above, inquiries into family law problems were carried out in Alberta, Ontario, Quebec, and Newfoundland.[17] While these reports did not all support the same solution to the problem, they all disclosed the practical inconvenience of the existing fragmentation of jurisdiction over family-related issues. The problem was compounded in provinces that had county and district courts as well as superior trial courts. In some provinces, in the course of having a domestic dispute dealt with a family could find itself bounced around among five different courts. Alberta's Institute of Law Research and Reform describes the kind of situation that can arise all too often:

> Under the present system there are many cases in which no one court can do all that is needed and the litigants must move from court to court to obtain complete relief. Custody and maintenance may be dealt with by the Family Court until divorce is sought, when the whole proceeding must be moved to another court (the trial division of the province's superior court); but the maintenance order will often go back to the Family Court for more effective enforcement. There, however, is no jurisdiction to vary the order so that it may have to go back to the Trial division. Wardship may start as a temporary wardship in the Family Court and move to the District Court for permanent wardship.[18]

A nation-wide study of the family court conducted by the Law Reform Commission of Canada emphasized the hardship inflicted on Canadian families by the jurisdictional maze:

> The most distressing effect of the present state of affairs is the despair, confusion and frustration it causes to the participants. It should not be necessary nor even feasible to apply to one court for maintenance upon desertion, another for custody, a third for wardship, and yet another for divorce.[19]

The pernicious effects of fragmentation are felt most frequently in disputes concerning maintenance payments. Quantitatively actions involving the enforcement of support payments dominate the dockets of family courts. Although no nation-wide statistics on family court business are available, an analysis of the records of Calgary's family court showed enforcement actions to be over 80 per cent of total family court applications.[20] When support payments are not associated with divorce, the provincially appointed family court judge has jurisdiction to make and adjust the orders. However, when support payments are part of a divorce settlement, these judges are in a most unenviable position. Only a judge with superior court jurisdiction can make and adjust these orders—but in many provinces disputes over their enforcement come before family court judges who are unable to vary them. Thus the judges who order the support have no role in overseeing its enforcement, and the judges responsible for enforcing the order play no role in either determining or modifying the level of support. It would be difficult to design a more ridiculous system for adjusting the arrangements

appropriate for the fluctuating economic circumstances of former marriage part-
ners. As one disgruntled litigant exclaimed when told by a family court judge
that he had to return to a higher court, "If I had the money to go to another
court, I'd give it to my kid."[21]

Unification at the Level of Section 96 Courts

There is one way in which it is possible to unify family court jurisdictions under
the present Constitution: by abandoning the family courts presided over by
provincially appointed judges and giving all the jurisdiction to the federally
appointed judges of section 96 courts. In the 1970s the federal government
encouraged this approach by offering to enter into cost-sharing agreements with
provinces willing to unify family law jurisdiction in a single section 96 court on
a pilot project basis. The first of these pilot projects was established in Hamilton-
Wentworth district of Ontario in 1977. The judges of this court were given the
status of county court judges but were able to exercise the full family law
jurisdiction of superior courts by being designated local judges of the High Court
(Ontario's superior trial court). Unified family courts organized as divisions of
the superior trial court were subsequently established as pilot projects in Saskatoon, Saskatchewan, St. John's, Newfoundland, and Fredericton, New Brunswick. Prince Edward Island, on its own and quite apart from this program, in
1975 consolidated all jurisdiction over the civil aspects of family matters in a
division of the province's Supreme Court. This was part of the restructuring and
simplification of Prince Edward Island's court system which eliminated county
courts.

Unification at the section 96 level has not turned out to be a viable solution
for the country as a whole, or even for most of the provinces that participated
in the pilot project program. New Brunswick was the only province to extend
its pilot project into a province-wide system. In 1979 it created the Family
Division of the Court of Queen's Bench (New Brunswick's superior trial court)
with full jurisdiction in all the civil aspects of family law and a concurrent
criminal jurisdiction with its provincial court in summary conviction offences
related to family disputes.[22] By 1983 the Family Division of the New Brunswick
Court of Queen's Bench was operating in six of the province's cities. The
relatively small size of New Brunswick and Prince Edward Island, and the fact
that neither had done much to develop a family court under provincially appointed
judges, were factors that made this approach to unification an attractive option
for these two provinces. Larger provinces with well-developed systems of family
courts staffed by their own appointees and working in close association with
provincial social services would not be readily persuaded to pack their institutions
up and rely on federally appointed judges in more formal, more expensive courts
located in fewer centres to provide the same service. Ontario, for instance, went
along with the Hamilton-Wentworth unified family court project because the
province had a major say in selecting the Provincial Court (Family Division)

judges who would be elevated to the status of county court judges and formally appointed to the court by the federal government. But, given the deficiencies of the federal system of appointing judges, it was highly unlikely that this degree of provincial participation could be sustained for a province-wide system of unified family courts at the section 96 level. Manitoba, on the other hand, in 1983 unified family court jurisdiction in the Family Law Division of its Court of Queen's Bench.[23] But this unified court as yet operates only in the eastern district of the province (Winnipeg, St. Boniface, and Selkirk).

Confronted with the dilemma of not being able to unify family law jurisdiction in their own family courts, and not being willing to entrust the courts presided over by federally appointed judges with delivery of a full family court service, several provinces considered constructing a hybrid unified family court which would involve bringing together provincial family court judges and superior court judges under the same roof and linked to the same social services. Proposals along this line were put forward by Ontario's Law Reform Commission and Quebec's Civil Code Revision Office. As we have seen, a British Columbia experimental project established two courts of this kind, one of which is still functioning at Richmond. This compromise approach to unification is not a satisfactory solution. It involves an awkward kind of institutional restructuring in which higher court judges are circulated through a lower family court whose services and orientation are often quite alien to them.

Current Family Court Patterns

The very diverse reactions of the provinces to the fragmentation problem has meant that by the mid-1980s there is no coherent pattern of family court development across Canada. Four different patterns can be discerned in the arrangements adopted by the provinces and territories.[24] These are as follows:

1. *Unification at section 96 level.* New Brunswick and Prince Edward Island have unified family law jurisdiction in a family division of their superior courts (the New Brunswick Court of Queen's Bench and the Prince Edward Island Supreme Court). Except for youth court responsibilities and some family-related criminal offences, provincially appointed judges perform no family court functions. Manitoba is also in this category. Although its unified section 96 family court is territorially limited, the province is committed to extending it to the whole province.[25]

2. *Mixed systems with well-developed and distinct provincial family courts.* Ontario with its seventy-three Provincial Court (Family Division) judges serving 118 localities, Quebec with its forty-four youth court judges sitting in every judicial district of the province, and Nova Scotia with a family court administered by the Department of Social Service consisting of twelve judges in seven permanent locations clearly fall under this category. This system contrasts with the first pattern in the prominence of provincially appointed judges in performing family court functions. Nova Scotia and Quebec have

not gone as far in this respect as Ontario. Their provincially appointed judges have no jurisdiction over the guardianship of children. Nova Scotia's family court judges have no jurisdiction over adoption, while Quebec's youth court judges lack jurisdiction with respect to issues of support and maintenance. Even in Ontario where the provincially appointed family court judge has the widest jurisdiction, the High Court and district court have exclusive jurisdiction in the fields of divorce, issues ancillary to divorce, and the division of matrimonial property.

3. *Mixed systems with no distinct or extensive provincial family court.* Alberta and the two northern territories fall into this category. Alberta has established specialized family divisions of its Provincial Court in a few major centres, but not on a province-wide basis under its own chief judge. Outside of these centres some family law functions are performed by judges who also exercise the criminal jurisdiction of the Provincial Court. In the Northwest Territories and Yukon there are no specialized family courts. The Territorial Court judges combine the criminal and family jurisdiction of the provincial lower court.

4. *Mixed systems with one unified family court.* The arrangements in the remaining jurisdictions are much like the previous pattern except that each has a unified family court in one centre: British Columbia's unified family court in Richmond, Newfoundland's in St. John's, and Saskatchewan's in Saskatoon.

At this point there is no indication of any convergence in the further evolution of family courts in Canada. Convergence is unlikely until there is a clear consensus on the function and nature of the family court. Also, as we shall argue, the prospects for overcoming the fragmentation problem and unifying family law jurisdiction at the superior court level would be enhanced by reforming the method of appointing section 96 judges.

Adjudication versus Therapy

There is an emphasis in the work of family courts on treating the source of conflict and endeavouring to find resolutions to disputes which are best calculated to promote the welfare of those involved. Even where formal adjudication takes place, welfare is likely to be a primary consideration in determining legal rights. In child welfare cases, for instance, where the state contests the right of parents to keep their children, the family court judge's findings on the needs of the children will be crucial in determining the rights of the parents. In domestic disputes concerning maintenance, custody, and access, court workers and judges are often predisposed toward making formal adjudication a last resort. In this setting the efforts of many judges are directed more toward facilitating and ratifying mediated settlements rather than rendering authoritative determinations of the litigants' rights.

The therapeutic objective of the family court is manifest in the relative informality which often characterizes its procedures, as well as in the cluster of support services usually associated with these courts. While there is a good deal of variation in the styles of family court judges, many are inclined to intervene in the hearing, question the litigants, and suggest compromise solutions. Some of these judges adopt this activist role even when, as increasingly is the case these days, both parties are represented by counsel.[26] Most family courts have at least a minimal intake service to counsel complaining spouses on the appropriate course of conduct when they first make contact with the court.[27] In a few of the larger courts, family counselling and conciliation services are available on the premises; elsewhere there is usually a referral system to outside counselling services. Family court judges often steer litigants and their children to clinics for psychiatric assistance and ask these clinics for information and advice when writing out dispositions. Probation officers, child welfare officials, and representatives of the social services ministry are frequent participants in court hearings.

In the contemporary debate about the family court the adjudicative and therapeutic dimensions of these courts are perceived to be in tension with one another. In the words of Judge Allard,

> Increasingly, it is seen that there are two pressures. There is pressure to formalize court procedures, to define roles and purposes in a precise manner, and in a more rigid way seek enforcement of traditional family duties. This position is supported by concern for traditional duty, for due process and a belief that the adversary type of proceeding best leads to a full and fair disposition of facts and, as a consequence, an appropriate decision. The other pressure is to avoid adversary approaches and to emphasize diagnosis and treatment to seek what is best for the family, to enquire as to the causes and cures and to make orders only where treatment fails.[28]

This tension transfers into the debate over family court structures. Among those whose priority is formal adjudication and due process of law, there is a tendency to favour unification at the higher court level. The informality of the lower court and the intervention of their support services are looked upon with suspicion as paternalistic threats to the rights of the individual litigant. On the other hand, many who are accustomed to working in the setting of a provincial family court are wary of transferring jurisdiction upward to a superior court dominated by the legal profession and the adversary process. There is a fear that in this setting little use will be made of counselling and investigative services and that the concern for arriving expeditiously at practical solutions to domestic disputes and child welfare problems will be the victim of adhering rigorously to the requirements of formal litigation.

It is doubtful whether there is a single structural solution to establishing a proper balance between the therapeutic and adjudicative functions of a family court. In an examination of judicial technologies sponsored by the National Institute of Justice in the United States, three basic court processes are identified: procedural adjudication (the traditional trial process with its emphasis on due process); decisional adjudication (the handling of a large volume of routine matters); and diagnostic adjudication (the attempt to diagnose problems and prescribe effective remedies).[29] While the report observes that diagnostic adjudication may be the emphasis of a court exercising family law jurisdiction, it concludes that "no court employs one process to the exclusion of all others" and that "a certain amount of tension among the three processes may be critical to ensuring that the multiple purposes of the courts are served." It would be unfortunate if the family court in Canada was to be captured by the ideology of either the overly confident social worker or the disputatious lawyer.

Fortunately, in the evolution of both the lower provincial family court and the higher section 96 court exercising family law jurisdiction, there is a convergence which suggests that either institution is capable of striking the balance needed in a well-functioning family court. The up-grading of the quality of judges appointed to the lower provincial courts, improvements in their physical and reporting facilities, the extension of legal aid to family law matters, and the establishment of official guardian's officers or children's advocates to represent children caught in the middle of domestic disputes have done much to make the provincial family court, where it exists, an appropriate forum in which to dispute complex issues of family law. On the other hand, among judges sitting on the higher trial courts there is increasing interest in alternative forms of dispute resolution, including procedures that facilitate pre-trial settlement.[30] Superior courts in a number of jurisdictions have established mediation services to promote mutually agreeable solutions to disputed points of custody, access, support, and property ancillary to divorce proceedings. There is no reason in principle why courts at this level cannot maintain the diagnostic and counselling services required for the effective discharge of family court functions.

Elevation as the Best Path to Unification

One point on which there is a clear consensus concerning family- and child-related adjudication in Canada is the need for unification. Opinion has been divided on whether unification should be upward or downward—upward in the higher trial courts presided over by federally appointed judges, or downward in provincial family courts presided over by provincially appointed judges. Almost all the unification achieved thus far has been of the upward variety. The province-wide system of unified family courts in New Brunswick and Prince Edward Island, the development of such a system in Manitoba, and the unified family court pilot projects in Newfoundland, Ontario, and Saskatchewan have all been at the section 96 court level. One reason for this is the constitutional bar to complete unification in the downward direction.

It is possible, of course, to amend the Constitution and remove this barrier to downward unification. In chapter 3 we noted the 1980 constitutional proposal supported by nine of the provinces which would virtually eliminate section 96 and give provincial governments the power to appoint all provincial court judges. This proposal failed to find a place in the Trudeau government's 1981 constitutional initiative which led to patriation and the Constitution Act, 1982. In 1983 consideration was given to a more modest amendment to add a section 96A to the Constitution which would simply permit the provinces to give any aspect of family law jurisdiction to provincially appointed judges. However, when Trudeau's justice minister, Mark MacGuigan, published his discussion paper on amending section 96, section 96A was dropped and only 96B—an amendment which would remove any limits on the jurisdiction which could be given provincial administrative tribunals—was put forward. Since 1983 the provinces have not shown any interest in reviving the section 96A proposal.

For a province such as Ontario, with a well-developed province-wide system of family courts presided over by provincially appointed judges, the section 96A proposal makes a good deal of sense. But by moving in the direction of expanding the jurisdiction which can be given to provincially appointed lower court judges there is a danger of perpetuating the hierarchical system of trial courts. Throughout this book we have argued against a judicial system in which some of the important matters requiring adjudication are tried by lower court provincially appointed judges while others are tried by higher court federally appointed judges. The issues at stake in family law are of great importance to the individual and to society. The judges and courts concerned with these issues should not have a subordinate status in the court hierarchy. Where family courts have a subordinate status it will be difficult to recruit the most able judges to their bench and to have the full participation of the legal profession at their bar.

In the long run, then, unification of family law jurisdiction at the section 96 court level is probably the best alternative for all the provinces and territories. But it may be difficult to gain the assent of all the provinces to move in this direction as long as the method of appointing section 96 judges is so dominated by the federal government and so patronage-ridden. Again, we see how important it is to reform the federal system of judicial selection. The nominating commissions considered in chapter 5 and advocated by the Canadian Bar Association and the Association of Canadian Law Teachers include a representative of the provincial government. These commissions would give the provinces some assurance that the selection process is not dominated by the interests of the governing party in Ottawa and that aptitude and ability would be the prime considerations in nominating lawyers for courts exercising family law jurisdiction. Once in place, these commissions could consider the qualification of judges currently serving on provincial family courts and recommend elevations to the section 96 level. In this way unification at the section 96 level could be extended from pilot projects in a few cities to a much larger number of communities.

Family court reform should converge with reform of the lower criminal court. The essential aim is to establish a comprehensive corps of trial services at every centre of population in the country. Each judicial centre should contain the support services and judges required for the different types of civil and criminal adjudication, including those appropriate for dealing with family law, child welfare, and young offender problems. The judges attached to such centres would have their different specialties but they would not be labelled as higher or lower, federal or provincial, nor would they be permanently confined to one area of specialization.

The key to this approach is to avoid equating functional specialization with hierarchical organization. Traditionally lawyers and judges have been too prone to organize special types of adjudication around special courts and then slot these courts and their judges into a complex hierarchy regulated by rigid jurisdictional rules. The organization of hospitals might provide a useful model for the restructuring of trial courts. A good hospital provides a wide range of medical services— everything from high-volume emergency services to rare and protracted surgical operations. The staff of medical practitioners who perform these services will represent a wide array of skills and aptitudes, but the doctors themselves and the specialized units in which they function are not classified as "inferior" and "superior," nor is their work encumbered by arcane jurisdictional rules.

Fortunately, as we shall see, the structure of higher courts in many parts of Canada is moving in a direction compatible with the development of comprehensive regional trial centres. The two main features of this structural change are the merger of the intermediate county and district courts with the superior courts, and the decentralization of the superior courts. But before reviewing these changes at the higher court level, we must turn to the one lower trial court function that remains to be examined: the adjudication of small civil claims.

Notes to Chapter 9

1. H.A. Allard, "Family Courts in Canada," in D. Mendes da Costa, *Studies in Canadian Family Law* (Toronto: Butterworths, 1972), p. 27.
2. F. Stewart Fisher, "Family law faces decline of patriarchal dominance,' ' *Lawyer's Weekly*, 20 June 1986.
3. Centre for Judicial Statistics, *Family Courts in Canada*, (Ottawa: Minister of Supply and Services), pp. 158-59.
4. For an account of these developments see, Allard, "Family Courts."
5. W.W. Creighton, Introduction in H.T.G. Andrews, ed. *Family Law in the Family Courts* (Toronto: Carswell, 1973), p. 10.
6. Murray Fraser, "Family Courts in Nova Scotia," *University of Toronto Law Journal* (1968), p. 169.
7. Allard points out that these model American courts are by no means typical and that "most court cases concerning delinquency and child protection are heard before municipal judges presiding over lower courts and most matrimonial disputes before superior courts." ("Family Courts," p. 3.) For a more extensive survey of family courts in the United States see Fred Reagh, "The Need for a Comprehensive Family Court System," *University of British Columbia Law Review* (1970), p. 13.
8. See, for example, Roscoe Pound, "The Place of the Family Court in the Judicial System," *National Probation and Parole Association Journal* (1959), p. 161.
9. *Proceedings of the Special Joint Committee of the Senate and House of Commons on Divorce*, submissions of Judge Peter J.T. O'Hearn, 17 Feb. 1967, and Professor Julian Payne, 21 Feb. 1967.
10. Ibid., *Final Report*, June 1967, p. 68.
11. For a more detailed analysis of the division of legislative jurisdiction in family

law matters, see Ontario Law Reform Commission, *Report on Family Law, Part V: Family Courts* (Ontario: Ministry of the Attorney General, 1974), ch. 3.

12. *Reference the Adoption Act* [1938] SCR 398.
13. *McEvoy* v. *A.G. New Brunswick* [1983] 1 SCR 705.
14. *Re B.C. Family Relations Act* [1982] 1 SCR 62.
15. For an exposition of this argument, see Stephen P. Sibold, "The Unified Family Court and Section 96 of the British North America Act," *Queen's Law Journal* (1976), p. 71.
16. John and Lorraine Waterhouse, "Implementing Unified Family Courts: The British Columbian Experience," *Canadian Journal of Family Law* (1983), p. 168.
17. Institute of Law Research and Reform, University of Alberta, *Working Paper on Courts Administering Family Law* (Edmonton, 1976); R. Gushue and David Day, *Family Law in Newfoundland* (St. John's: Government of Newfoundland, 1973); Ontario Law Reform Commission, *Report on Family Law*, Part V; Civil Code Revision Office, Committee on the Family Court, *Report on the Family Court* (Montreal, 1975).
18. *Working Paper on Courts Administering Family Law*, p. 24.
19. Law Reform Commission of Canada, *Working Paper No. 1, The Family Court* (Ottawa, 1974), p. 7.
20. Allard, "Family Courts," p. 22.
21. Norris Weisman, "On Unified Family Courts," *Reports of Family Law* (1984) , p. 277.
22. RSNB 1979, c. 36.
23. SM 1983, c. 82.
24. The data for this section are derived primarily from the reports of the Centre for Justice Statistics on *Manpower, Resources and Costs of Courts and Criminal Prosecutions in Canada 1980-82* and *Family Courts in Canada.*
25. Law Society of Manitoba, *Family Division of the Court of Queen's Bench* (Winnipeg, 1985).
26. The participation of lawyers is much greater in provinces such as Ontario and Quebec whose legal aid programs provide full coverage for family law matters.
27. There is no comprehensive survey of family court support services in Canada. For a detailed discussion of support services in Ontario which has the largest and most fully developed family court system in Canada, see Ontario Law Reform Commission, *Report in Family Law, Part V*, ch. 6.
28. Allard, "Family Courts", p. 22.
29. Cornelius Kerwin, Thomas Henderson and Carl Baar, " Adjudicating Processes and the Organization of Trial Courts," *Judicature* (Aug./Sept. 1986), p. 99.
30. See, for instance, A.H. Lieff, "Pre- Trial of Family Law in the Supreme Court of Ontario: Simplify and Expedite," *Law Society of Upper Canada Gazette* (1976), p. 300.

CHAPTER 10
SMALL CLAIMS COURTS

One of the most difficult challenges confronting contemporary justice systems is to design a mode of adjudication appropriate for settling disputes involving small amounts of money. Although the monetary value of what is at stake in such cases may seem too low to justify applying the full panoply of the normal machinery of justice with all its attendant costs, often there are important rights at issue concerning amounts of money which are significant to persons of modest means. A casual and insensitive approach to the quality of justice in this area will indicate a fundamental class bias in a society's judicial system. Until quite recently the adjudication of small civil claims was a relatively neglected component of the Canadian justice system. Simplified procedures for handling such disputes have been available since early colonial times. But throughout most of our history these arrangements have been mainly of benefit to creditors in collecting debts. It was not until the 1970s, with the rise of the consumer movement and the emergence of a more egalitarian strain in Canada's political culture, that special courts and services were established in some Canadian provinces to respond more equitably to the conflicting economic interests involved in "small claims." The institutional variations evident in these developments reflect a good deal of uncertainty about the modifications of traditional adjudication that are acceptable or desirable in dealing with disputes involving relatively small amounts of money. In no other field does the quality of justice accessible to Canadians through the judicial process vary so much across the country.

Institutional Developments

Small claim courts in Canada can trace their lineage back to the local tribunals established well before Confederation to "hear small causes." Hilda Neatby's account of the administration of justice in Quebec after the British conquest decribes the practice of commissioning several local notables to serve on a "circle" to try small civil cases.[1] In 1792, one year after Upper Canada was organized as a separate colony, a Court of Requests was established, made up of two or more justices with jurisdiction in civil cases up to forty shillings.[2] The demand for these institutions came primarily from a nascent merchant class anxious to have a convenient and inexpensive procedure for enforcing the payment of debts. Although the quality of justice administered by these "six penny chanceries" was crude, for merchants—especially those outside of the capital—the service they provided was better than waiting for the infrequent visits of the superior court judges or paying for the expensive procedures of the higher courts.

After Confederation special judicial arrangements for dealing with small claims were established in all the provinces. Some provinces followed the English system and based their small claims procedures on their county and district courts. This was the pattern in Manitoba, Ontario, and Prince Edward Island. In Ontario the small claims court presided over by a county or district court judge (or a lawyer temporarily appointed by such a judge) was known as a division court.[3] Other provinces relied primarily on provincially appointed magistrates to administer small claims procedures. In the 1880s when Quebec attempted to transfer jurisdiction over minor civil suits from Superior Court judges to provincially appointed magistrates, the federal government twice disallowed the legislation.[4] However Quebec persevered and by the mid-twentieth century had transferred all small claims work to its magistrates courts. In 1965 Quebec legislation increasing the monetary limit of the magistrates' civil jurisdiction from $200 to $500 was challenged on the grounds that it encroached on the constitutionally protected jurisdiction of superior, county, and district court judges. The Supreme Court of Canada upheld the legislation[5] and, although the decision implied that the constitution imposed some outside monetary limit on the civil jurisdiction of provincial courts, it would seem clear that "small claims" are well within that limit.

The small claims arrangements developed by the provinces generally applied to claims for debts or damages. Most provinces explicitly excluded certain kinds of cases, such as those involving title to land, defamation, contested wills, or actions against public officials. Monetary limits were originally set at well under $100, but in most jurisdictions they had risen to a few hundred dollars by the 1970s.

In the 1970s small claims procedures came in for considerably more attention by the provinces. In a number of provinces reform of the small claims courts was part of the strengthening of provincial court systems which occurred during this province-building era. Interest in this dimension of judicial reform was stimulated by a growing consumer rights movement. Empirical research on small claims courts in Canada and the United States demonstrated that to an alarming degree these tribunals were serving as judicial debt collection agencies. An overwhelming majority of suits were initiated by businesses usually represented by lawyers or experienced agents and most of the defendants were consumers. A 1974 study of small claims courts in Toronto, for example, disclosed that in 97 per cent of the cases a business was the plaintiff, in 94 per cent the plaintiff was successful, and in 74 per cent the case was disposed of by a default judgment—that is, without an appearance by the defendant.[6] While the right of businesses to collect unpaid bills was not questioned, there was increasing concern that consumers who did not pay their bills because they were dissatisfied with the product or service purchased were at a considerable disadvantage in the small claims process.

Quebec led the way in 1971 with the Act to Promote Access to Justice.[7] Under this addition to Quebec's Code of Civil Procedure, lawyers and collection agencies are banned from small claims proceedings presided over by Provincial

Court judges.[8] The judges are free to develop their own procedures for handling cases and are directed to attempt a reconciliation of the parties wherever possible. Facilities to assist plaintiffs and defendants in preparing their cases were established in the offices of court clerks. Public awareness of the new service was promoted by an extensive advertising campaign. The $300 monetary limit on suits eligible for this procedure has been increased to $1000 and the small claims court can now be used to contest provincial income tax assessments up to $1650.[9]

The shift to a more inquisitorial style of adjudication in Quebec's small claims courts is by no means the only recent development in the civil law responsibilities of Quebec's provincially appointed judges. Quebec has been more aggressive than any other province in expanding the civil jurisdiction of the provincially appointed judiciary. The civil jurisdiction of Provincial Court judges has been extended well beyond small claims. Today the Provincial Court of Quebec has exclusive jurisdiction to hear disputes where not more than $15 000 is in dispute. Quebec has also attempted to make its Provincial Court the primary court for exercising judicial review over municipalities and provincial administrative bodies. The Supreme Court of Canada has resisted these efforts in a series of cases holding that the responsibility of reviewing the legality of local by-laws and administrative agencies is part of the inherent jurisdiction of federally appointed section 96 judges.[10] These decisions have created a serious obstacle to plans for a consolidation of Quebec's lower courts into a single Court of Quebec with an extensive administrative law branch.[11]

Ontario has also taken steps to give the Provincial Court a larger role in small civil suits. The division court's name was changed to the small claims court in 1970, but at that time no basic change was made in the judiciary responsible for small claims work. Nominally small claims adjudication was still primarily the responsibility of federally appointed county and district court judges. Ontario's Small Claims Court Act empowered the provincial government to appoint small claims court judges, but only three had been appointed by 1973.[12] The act also provided for part-time judges. These ''deputy judges'' had to be lawyers and could be appointed by county or district court judges.[13] Although no statistical data on the use of these part-time judges have been published, they may have been doing the lion's share share of small claims work in the province. The Ontario Law Reform Commission's 1973 report on the small claims courts accentuated their casual nature. The commissioners reported that most of the clerks and bailiffs responsible for the staff work of these courts

> perform their duties only on a part-time basis, and many of them in rural districts conduct the court's business from their own houses. With few exceptions they are self-employed, engage their own staff, and pay for their own supplies and accommodation out of the fees they receive.[14]

Ontario has responded to this and other criticisms by moving rather haltingly toward developing the small claims courts as a division of its Provincial Court. The first step was taken in 1979 with the establishment of the Provincial

Court (Civil Division). This court, to be presided over by full-time, provincially appointed judges with the status and terms of office of Provincial Court judges, was first established on a three-year experimental basis.[15] It functioned only in Toronto and was given a jurisdiction to try civil actions involving up to $3000. This went considerably beyond the monetary limit of the small claims court which, since 1977, had been set at $1000. In 1982 this experimental court was continued and in 1984, under the general revision of the Ontario's Courts of Justice Act, the Provincial Court (Civil Division) and the small claims court were amalgamated.[16] This has left Ontario with a very hybrid small claims system. Small claims can still be heard by three kinds of appointees: judges appointed to the Provincial Court (Civil Division), district court judges (in 1984 all of Ontario's county courts became district courts), or part-time deputy judges. Currently there are twelve judges serving on the Provincial Court (Civil Division), all but three of whom sit in Metropolitan Toronto. Their work is concentrated on suits beyond the limit of small claims in the $1000 to $3000 range, so that much of the small claims work continues to be done by lawyers serving as deputy judges on short-term appointments. These deputy judges can now be appointed by a district court judge or the chief justice of the Provincial Court (Civil Division). In 1985 Judge S.D. Turner, the senior judge of the Civil Division (no chief judge has been appointed), reported that twenty-three deputy judges were hearing small claims cases.[17]

The three western-most provinces, Alberta, British Columbia, and Saskatchewan, as well as Newfoundland, have made the adjudication of small claims a Provincial Court function. The monetary limits of the civil cases which Provincial Court judges can hear in these provinces has been increased to $1000 in Newfoundland, $2000 in Alberta and British Columbia, and $3000 in Saskatchewan.[18] The northern territories have followed this model. The Northwest Territories has given its Territorial Court judges both a jurisdiction to handle small claims up to $500 by an informal procedure as well as a general civil jurisdiction to hear cases in which the claim does not exceed $5000.[19] The small claims jurisdiction of the Yukon Territorial Court is set at $1500 but can be exercised by "small claims officials" appointed by the commissioner to serve at pleasure as well as by the judges of the Territorial Court.[20]

Among the common law provinces developing their Provincial Courts as small claims tribunals, British Columbia and Ontario would appear to have been the most innovative. Both provinces have provided for the appointment of mediator/referees to work under the direction of judges. Their function is to assist the parties at working out informal settlements.[21] While none of these provinces have gone as far as Quebec in banning lawyers and corporations from their small claims courts, British Columbia, Saskatchewan, and the Yukon do not permit the recovery of costs for cases tried in their small claims courts.[22]

Nova Scotia is the only province to have established a specialized small claims tribunal outside of its Provincial Court structure. Up until 1980 Nova Scotia relied on municipal courts presided over by Provincial Court jud. adjudication of small claims.[23] This system, in the words of one academi. mentator, did "not provide a forum in which people with small claims can obt. a quick, cheap and simple adjudication of those claims, with court officials to encourage, assist and advise individuals."[24] Eventually this academic criticism received a political response. The government acknowledged that the municipal court system did not work in a practical sense because, according to the attorney general, "there were really no judges that were prepared to sit in judgment in respect of that court."[25] Legislation enacted in 1980 retained the jurisdiction of Provincial Court judges sitting in municipal courts to hear small claims up to $500, but set up along side it a small claims court to be presided over by "adjudicators" with a jurisdiction to hear cases involving debt or damage claims not exceeding $2000.[26] The adjudicators are appointed by the provincial cabinet and serve at pleasure. They are to adjudicate claims "informally and inexpensively but in accordance with established principles of law and natural justice." Lawyers and corporate plaintiffs are not excluded from these courts, but the attorney general may prescribe "days and hours during which a corporate person, its agent or solicitor shall not appear before the court as a plaintiff."[27] The availability of this new tribunal is likely to vary throughout the province as municipalities are responsible for providing and maintaining small claims court facilities.

Only three provinces, Manitoba, New Brunswick, and Prince Edward Island, continue to base small claims adjudication in higher courts presided over by federally appointed judges. In the 1970s both New Brunswick and Prince Edward Island merged their county courts into their superior courts. Instead of assigning small claims to provincial court judges, New Brunswick provided for a small claims procedure in its Court of Queen's Bench,[28] while Prince Edward Island established a small claims section of its Supreme Court.[29] Under the New Brunswick legislation hearings may be conducted by the clerk of the court or persons appointed by the registrar. The monetary limits are $1000 in New Brunswick and $2000 in Prince Edward Island.[30] In 1984 when Manitoba merged its county court with its superior court, it too located small claims adjudication in the Court of Queen's Bench. In doing so it rejected the advice of the province's Law Reform Commission. The commission, whose report paved the way for the amalgamation of the Court of Queen's Bench and the county court, recommended that small claims adjudication become the responsibility of a special division of the Provincial Court. In the commission's view the Provincial Court system was far "more accessible, especially in rural and northern regions" and "has more experience in dealing with matters speedily despite the high volume of cases which come before it."[31] Instead, Manitoba will continue with a rather lackadaisical approach to small claims under which "officers" of the Court of Queen's Bench (rather like county court clerks) can hear uncontested matters or contested matters with the consent of both parties in claims not exceeding $1000.

Alternative Approaches to Reform

The consumer rights movement and the building of provincial court systems have prompted some institutional "reforms" in the mechanisms and procedures for handling small civil suits. But overall these reforms have been quite modest and tentative. Partly this reflects the low priority of the justice system in the spending priorities of most governments. "The administration of justice" is something politicians like to wax eloquent about in after-dinner speeches, but it is not something on which they are willing to spend a lot of taxpayers' money. Within the justice system, the development of effective and equitable arrangements for dealing with disputes over legal rights and duties involving small amounts of money is apt to be a low reform priority. One reason for this is that small claims work is of little interest to lawyers and the legal profession has a potent influence on the agenda of judicial reform in Canada.

The economic unattractiveness of small claims work to lawyers is of critical importance in shaping the options for the reform of small claims courts. The common law judicial process is fundamentally adversarial in that it relies on representatives of the adversaries—legally trained, professional representatives—not only to advance the strongest arguments which can be marshalled on behalf of each party at trial, but also to advise the parties of their rights before trial, to explore the possibility of settlement without trial, and to ensure the implementation of judgments after trial. But in small claims cases the cost of adequate legal representation may well exceed the amount of money in dispute. Under these circumstances, many adversaries who, whether they know it or not, may well have claims or defences which involve complex legal issues are likely to be unrepresented at any stage of the dispute and the adversary system will not work well.

One response to this problem is to move away from the adversarial mode of adjudication to a more inquisitorial style in which the judge and the court play a more active and interventionist role. This response is evident in Quebec's small claims court and in other jurisdictions that prohibit or restrict the recovery of legal costs. Where legal representation is not formally proscribed, the adjudicative style adopted by the small claims court judge may be fundamentally inquisitorial and discourage lawyers from performing their normal adversarial role. An empirical study of the small claims court in Windsor, Ontario, showed that only 22.6 per cent of plaintiffs were represented by counsel, and those that did use lawyers did not fare significantly better than those who did not.[33] Indeed, when success was measured in terms of the amount collected as compared with the amount originally claimed, unrepresented plaintiffs did better than those who used lawyers. As an explanation, the researchers express the suspicion "that since the small claims court process is designed to operate without lawyers, their presence may prejudice the court against the represented claimant."[34]

Judges who abandon the adversarial style in hearing small claims assume some formidable responsibilities. The chief judge of Quebec's Provincial Court pointed out to this writer that members of his court who presided in Quebec's small claims court were required to play five roles: law professor (to explain the rules of evidence and applicable law to both parties), lawyer for both parties, interpreter, mediator, and finally judge. Professor Axworthy, a strong exponent of the inquisitorial style for small claims courts, puts it this way:

> It is submitted that the best, fastest, and most equitable way for a hearing to take place is with the judge taking the central role, asking the questions, eliciting the required information and helping both parties to state their case. In other words, the judge must be a sort of legal advisor to both parties and an adjudicator at the same time—a complex and demanding combination of tasks.[35]

This profile of the effective small claims court judge would seem to be a long way from the court clerks and part-time lawyers who hear small claims cases in many parts of Canada.

Certainly a good understanding of the relevant law is a prerequisite for the small claims court judge operating in this inquisitorial role. It is interesting that in Australia, where five of the states have developed consumer-oriented small claims tribunals from which legal representatives are normally prohibited, the referee-judges who staff these tribunals are, with but one exception, legally qualified.[36] The referees are authorized to depart from strict legal rules and decide cases on the basis of fairness and equity. But, as G.D.S. Taylor points out, "one major element of fairness and equity is that persons should be entitled to act in reliance on the law. Accordingly . . . there must be substantial reason to depart from the law in pursuance of fairness and equity. The referee must first know the law, secondly appreciate its object and context, and thirdly weigh the law against the facts and their context. Legal qualifications are highly desirable for this."[37] To many of the individuals involved in so-called small claims the amounts of money are not small, nor are their legal rights negligible. However appropriate informality and equity rather than legalism may be in this forum, it is not an arena for legal amateurism. "Small claims judges," writes Terence Ison, "must be men of high intelligence, they must be in some ways more versatile than High Court judges."[38] Ison, who calls for a highly inquisitorial approach to small claims, would require formal legal qualifications or a special twelve-month training program for small claims judges.

It may be that in many jurisdictions in Canada we have the worst of all possible worlds: small claims judges trying to adhere to the adversary system without professional adversaries. That is the key to Ison's negative assessment of small claims courts in Canada and the United States: "The small claims judge tends to imitate his superiors in the adversary system."[39] Even where small claims judges are initially prepared to adopt a more activist approach, the burden of huge and repetitive case loads may after a time blunt their enthusiasm and their skill. Professor Nielson's review of small claims reforms in Canada draws attention to the personal demands on judges who exercise this jurisdiction and the danger of "judicial fatigue or burnout."[40]

An alternative to relying on the activist, inquisitorial judge is to establish adversarial support services in the small claims court. That is the proposal of George Adams. Adams is suspicious of the quality of justice that will be rendered by an inquisitorial system because the judge in that system must form a "premature hypothesis inherent in paternalistic inquiry that promotes biased outcomes."[41] Justice will be more likely done when the parties to the dispute bear the prime responsibility for preparing and putting forward their respective sides of the case. To overcome the absence of adequate legal representation he would institutionalize counselling and advocacy in the small claims court. Each court would maintain a plaintiff's and a defendant's office staffed by personnel qualified to assist each side in understanding its legal situation, in exploring the possibility of settlement, and where necessary, in preparing for trial.[42]

Even if we were to accept that Adams's suspicion of the inquisitorial system has some validity, the trouble with his proposal is the cost of implementing it. As noted earlier, few Canadian provinces have shown much willingness to provide anything remotely close to adequate adjudicative services for small claims courts. The chances of persuading provincial governments to develop an adequate plaintiff's bureau and defendant's bureau in every small claims court are remote. Still, his proposal points to the need for auxiliary court services to assist parties involved in small claims disputes, whether the court to which the services are attached is essentially inquisitorial or adversarial.

The availability of such services is one of the most impressive features of the Montreal small claims court. This court, prominently located on the ground floor of the Palais de Justice, has a large intake office staffed by clerks with a paralegal education. When plaintiffs (bear in mind that corporate plaintiffs are barred from this court) first turn up at the court they are interviewed by one of these clerks. The interviewer explores the possibility of a negotiated settlement; where that is not feasible he counsels the parties on the steps necessary to prepare for trial, including the evidence they will be required to produce. There is nothing approaching this kind of assistance to litigants in most small claims courts elsewhere in the country. By way of contrast with Montreal, the Provincial Court (Civil Division) in Toronto, while providing a very modern court facility staffed by professional judges, offers the barest and most bureaucratic form of assistance to persons who find their way to the court's inquiry counter. In this setting corporate plaintiffs with full-time, veteran court representatives are at a great advantage. This is the kind of situation that gives credence to the charge that small claims courts function too much as a service to the credit industry.

Empirical studies of small claims courts in Canada and the United States continue to report that "small claims courts are clearly dominated by business and professional users of high socio-economic status."[43] The Windsor, Ontario, small claims court study found that 76.9 per cent of the plaintiffs were in the business or professional categories. Among repeat plaintiffs the figures went up to 86.3 per cent.[44] The authors suggest that these data throw into question the idea that the small claims court is a "people's court." Neil Vidmar's research, however, indicates that these studies may have exaggerated the extent to which small claims adjudication is dominated by the business and professional class. His study of the Middlesex County small claims court in London, Ontario, shows that "consumer issues take up a substantial portion of the court's disputed cases."[45] While substantial businesses were the plaintiff in 84 per cent of the *defaulted* cases, in *disputed* cases the picture was considerably different. Over 40 per cent of the plaintiffs in these cases were either individuals or small businesses.

Nevertheless, it is evident that the more simplified and expeditious procedures of small claims courts are not as accessible to all those in the community who might benefit from them. One barrier to accessibility is lack of public knowledge of their very existence. A Winnipeg study has shown that awareness and comprehension of small claims procedures is lowest among low-income groups.[46] A further barrier to accessibility is the failure of small claims courts in many parts of Canada to extend court hours to times when working people can attend. The establishment of evening sittings in a few small claims courts is certainly a step in the right direction.[47]

Better court services are also needed to assist successful small claims plaintiffs collect at least some of what is found to be owing to them. Collection difficulties have been one of the most long-standing grievances of those who use small claims courts. The 1979 study of the Windsor small claims court reported that 31 per cent of successful plaintiffs had not collected after one year.[48] In a few jurisdictions the assistance of referees is available to work out mutually agreeable payment terms.[49] But most provinces have done little to ensure that the "justice" administered in the small claims courts extends to the execution of judgment.

Perhaps the most innovative approach to reforming small claims procedures is to build in a mediation alternative to adjudication. Canada has slowly and cautiously been participating in the alternative dispute resolution (ADR) movement, which is much further advanced in the United States. The ADR movement aims at reversing over-reliance on adjudication as a dispute settlement process by taking advantage of alternatives such as negotiation, mediation, and arbitration which may be more efficient and possibly more conciliatory.[50] In the previous section we referred to the growth of court-sanctioned mediation in the context of family law litigation. As we shall see in the next section, pre-trial conferences have become an important element in the dispute settlement process of some of the higher trial courts. In small claims disputes there is a special need for a court-directed mediation program. Because most of the litigants involved in these disputes are unrepresented, there is little likelihood of lawyers carrying out the informal negotiations that often produce settlements without trial in actions involving larger amounts of money.

Mediation of small claims disputes by court-appointed referees has been used extensively in Ontario. Since 1978 pre-trial "resolution hearings" by non-lawyer referees with work experience in small claims courts have been scheduled for nearly all disputed small claims cases filed with the county (now district) court in Ontario's Middlesex County.[51] Pursuant to rule 22 of the regulation governing procedure in the Toronto-based Provincial Court (Civil Division), most small claims cases (under $1000) and some cases involving larger amounts are sent to referees who are directed to "conduct pre-trial conferences in an effort to settle matters in dispute between the parties."[52] Referees have performed a similar service in the Windsor-Essex Mediation Centre established under the auspices of the Canadian Bar Association.[53] Experimental mediation programs for small claims have also been established in British Columbia and Quebec.[54]

Evaluations of mediation programs demonstrate considerable savings to the court system and to some litigants. For instance in the Windsor-Essex Mediation Centre, 36 per cent of the cases heard by the referee resulted in settlements.[55] Ontario's director of small claims courts estimates that the referee system has saved the province one and a half judges per year.[56] For litigants who settle, there is a saving of time and possibly more satisfactory outcomes. The mediation process may also better prepare some litigants for adjudication in cases that do not settle. Neil Vidmar's analysis of small claims mediations in Middlesex County suggests that mediation is likely to be most successful in cases where the defendant admits partial liability.[57] Where, however, the defendant admits no liability, court-ordered mediation may simply impose an additional step in obtaining an adjudication of the dispute. There is always a danger that coerced mediation will lead to coercion within mediation. Compromise settlements are not always just settlements: sometimes one side is entirely right and the other is entirely wrong. Vidmar's distinction between disputes in which liability is partially admitted and those in which it is not might serve as a guide to those responsible for screening cases for court-directed mediation.

The Future of Small Claims Adjudication

There can be no doubt that there will continue to be a need for special techniques and procedures to adjudicate civil suits involving small amounts of money. The unavailability of professional legal advice and representation for many of those involved in such disputes means that our normal adversary system of justice does not function. Alternatives to professional representatives are needed to inform parties of their legal rights, to bring them together where it is appropriate to attempt settlement without trial, to enable the judge to grasp the basis of the competing claims when adjudication occurs, and to ensure the execution of the court's decisions. There is also a need here (as there is throughout our civil justice system) for adjudicative procedures which are as expeditious as possible and do not burden litigants with unnecessary procedural formalities.

The Canadian justice system has only recently begun, and then most unevenly, to give serious attention to the special requirements of small claims disputes. As with so many aspects of judicial reform, the major improvements have taken place in metropolitan centres. The most extensive reforms have been in central Canada, where small claims courts are now less dominated by creditor interests and where new modes of dispute resolution have been introduced. But in much of Canada today official interest in this dimension of the justice system is still marked by casualness and indifference. In many parts of the country small claims disputes are adjudicated by court officials or part-time judges whose terms of office fail to meet the most minimal conditions required for judicial independence.

We know very little about how this lack of interest in the judicial machinery for small claims actually affects the rights and interests of Canadians. We have no empirical knowledge of what happens to individuals with grievances involving small amounts in those jurisdictions which simply rely on court clerks in their superior courts to adjudicate small claims. Nor do we know much about the impact of the innovative Quebec system on individual and corporate interests. Is adjudication of small claims significantly more accessible to disgruntled consumers in Quebec than in the common law provinces? What happens in the Quebec system to those bad debt cases that corporations cannot take through the small claims procedure?

The empirical study of disputing in Canada—the study of what sorts of civil disputes Canadians have and which ones are taken to court for adjudication—is in its infancy. A pioneering study by Neil Vidmar indicates that only a very small proportion of disputes for which the small claims court is the appropriate legal forum actually are taken to court. Vidmar's data show "that Canadians predominantly handled their own minor problems without the intervention or active help of third parties."[58] This could be good news if adjudication is being avoided for the right reasons. If disputes are being abandoned and people are "lumping it" without serious damage to their interests, or are reaching mutually satisfactory settlements through informal negotiations, then it is clearly best that adjudication be avoided. But it may still be the case that a good many disputes involving small amounts of money fail to be adjudicated for the wrong reasons: because individuals do not know about the small claims procedure, or find it too inconvenient or cumbersome. It cannot be emphasized too much how mistaken it is to assume that simply because the dollar value of a dispute is low the matter is of little importance and devoid of legal complexity. To a person of modest means a dispute over a thousand dollars can be as significant as a million-dollar suit to a large corporation. Indifference to the quality of justice in small claims suits has serious implications for the quality of social justice in Canadian society. As Terence Ison has pointed out it is in this area of litigation that we find the most significant incidence of disputes involving members of different classes.[59]

Making small claims procedures better known and more convenient need not lead to an undue reliance on adjudication as a method of settling disputes. As we have seen, the courts which have been more innovative in their approach to small claims have established mediation opportunities before trial. It is through filing a case with the small claims court that litigants are directed to mediation. American researchers have concluded from a study of mediation in American small claims courts that "informal community justice is unlikely to serve many disputants unless it is intimately connected to some formal legal agency.''[60] Ready access to a judicial tribunal can be a means of promoting use of more informal and conciliatory forms of dispute resolution.

The need to develop economical alternatives to adjudication and innovative modes of adjudication for small claims may suggest that a civil division of the Provincial Court is the best institutional setting for small claims. At present these courts are likely to have more of the flexibility and accessibility needed for small claims than the higher trial courts possess. Most of the provinces and both territories have been developing small claims adjudication as a specialized service of their Provincial Court. Only Manitoba, New Brunswick, and Prince Edward Island rely on their superior courts for the adjudication of small claims.

In the short run, in jurisdictions that maintain a hierarchical system of trial courts, it makes sense to use the more decentralized lower courts with their capacity for handling the high-volume small claims work. But in the long run it would make better sense for the settlement of small civil suits to become a specialized function of the community trial centres we have discussed earlier. Unquestionably, the adjudication of small claims calls for special services and approaches. But, as we have argued with reference to criminal and family courts, specialization should not be equated with stratification. The style of adjudication for small claims should be different but not inferior. It requires first class judges with a strong understanding of the relevant law to know when it is appropriate to deviate from normal procedures. There is no reason to believe that the legal knowledge and skills required for conducting or overseeing small claims adjudication are beneath the ability of county, district, or superior court judges. As we shall see in the next chapter, judges on the higher trial courts are showing an increasing interest in alternative forms of dispute resolution. Some well-qualified judges are trying civil cases in the provincial courts. But there is a real danger of judicial burn-out for judges confined to handling the high-volume, smaller civil suits for the entire duration of their judicial career. Flexibility in the deployment of judges and the development of special adjudicative skills would be greater in a judicial system where trial judges belong to community trial centres which are not hierarchically organized.

The other reason for being wary about building up the civil work of the lower Provincial Courts is the danger of committing Canada to the American dual court system. In chapter 2 we showed that in the modern period the growth areas of the Canadian court system were the purely provincial courts presided over by provincially appointed judges and the purely federal courts. Relatively speaking, the section 96 courts—the linchpin, provincial courts with federally appointed judges—have been declining in importance. This trend threatens to undermine the integrating contribution the section 96 courts make to the Canadian community. A number of the provinces have been building the civil jurisdiction of their purely provincial courts well beyond the small claims level. Quebec has led the way: its Provincial Courts hear cases involving up to $15 000. To reverse this trend, as we have argued throughout this book, provincial governments must participate in the selection of the judges who preside on the higher provincial trial courts.

The other development which must occur if the type of change we have envisaged is to occur, is that the provincial trial courts of general jurisdiction must become less stratified, more decentralized and more innovative in their approach to dispute resolution. As we shall see in the next section, changes in this direction are already occurring in many parts of Canada.

Notes to Chapter 10

1. Hilda Neatby, *The Administration of Justice Under the Quebec Act* (University of Minnesota Press, 1937), pp. 277-79.
2. J.H. Aitchison, "The Courts of Requests in Upper Canada," *Ontario History* (1949), pp. 125-32.
3. For an account of the evolution of division courts, see Ontario Law Reform Commission, *Report on the Administration of Ontario Courts*, (1973), Part III, ch. 12.
4. G.V. LaForest, *Disallowance and Reservation of Provincial Legislation* (Ottawa: Department of Justice, 1955), pp. 92-93.
5. *Magistrates Court of Quebec and A.-G. Quebec* v. *Barreau de la Province de Québec* [1965] SCR 772.
6. Larry H. Moldaver and Jerry Herlihy, *Consumer Litigation in the Small Claims Courts of Metropolitan Toronto: An Empirical Analysis* (Toronto: Osgoode Hall Law School, 1974).
7. Quebec Code of Civil Procedure, Book VIII, ss. 953-98.
8. The exclusion of lawyers was unsuccessfully challenged in *Nissan Automobile Co.* v. *Pelletier* (1978) 97 DLR (3d) 277. This decision, it should be noted, occurred when there was no constitutional Charter of Rights.
9. *Globe and Mail*, 3 Oct. 1984.
10. These cases were discussed in chapter 3.
11. See Jérôme Choquette, *Justice Today* (Québec: Gouvernement du Québec, 1975), pp. 96-110, and *Rapport de Comite directeur sur l'unification de la cour des sessions de la paix, de la cour provinciale et du Tribunal de la jeunesse* (Québec: Ministère de la Justice, 1983).
12. Ontario Law Reform Commission, *Report in the Administration of Ontario Courts* (1973), Part III, p. 347.
13. RSO 1970, c. 439, s. 13.
14. *Report on the Administration of Ontario Courts*, p. 349.
15. RSO 1980, c. 397.
16. Courts of Justice Act, s. 77.
17. *The Law Society of Upper Canada Gazette* (Mar. 1985), p. 27.
18. Ss 1983, c. 43; RSBC 1979, c. 387; ss, c. s-51; SN 1979, c. 34.
19. Small Debt Regulations, RRNWT 1980, Reg. No. 273; Territorial Court Ordinance, ONWT 1978 (2d), c. 16.
20. Judicature Act, RSYT 1975, c. J-1, ss. 50, 1-63; Territorial Court Act, RSYT 1975, c. M-1; Small Claims Act, OYT 1980 (1st), c. 28.
21. SBC 1977, c. 60; Ontario Courts of Justice Act, 1984, s. 86(5).

22. RBC 1960, c. 359; RSS 1965, c. 102, s. 22; OYT 1980, c. 28, s. 2.
23. RSNS 1967, c. 197.
24. Christopher S. Axworthy, "A Small Claims Court for Nova Scotia—Role of the Lawyer and the Judge," *Dalhousie Law Journal* (1978), pp. 311-12.
25. Nova Scotia, *House of Assembly Debates and Proceedings*, 21 May 1980, p. 2455.
26. SNS 1980, c. 16.
27. Ibid., s. 5.
28. RSNB 1973, c. J-2, s. 73(2).
29. RSPEI. 1974, c. J-3, s. 16(2).
30. The Judicature Act of New Brunswick permits the cabinet to make rules for a small claims procedure in the Court of Queen's Bench in cases not exceeding $3000. Rule 75.01(1) has set the limit of the cases which can be heard by this procedure at $1000.
31. Manitoba Law Reform Commission, *The Structure of the Courts; Part II: The Adjudication of Smaller Claims* (Winnipeg, 1983), p. 19.
32. SM 1982-83-84, c. 83.
33. Kai Hildebrandt, Brian McNeely and Peter P. Mercer, "The Windsor Small Claims Court: An Empirical Study of Plaintiffs and their Attitudes," *The Windsor Yearbook of Access to Justice* (1982), p. 86.
34. Ibid., p. 109.
35. Axworthy, "Small Claims Court for Nova Scotia," p. 329.
36. G.D.S. Taylor, "Small Claims in Australia," in M. Cappelletti and J. Weisner, eds., *Access to Justice, Vol. II, Promising Institutions, Bk. 2* (Milan: Sijthoff, 1979).
37. Ibid., p. 631.
38. Terence G. Ison, "Small Claims," *Modern Law Review*, (1972), p. 31.
39. Ibid., 27.
40. William A.W. Neilson, "The Small Claims Court in Canada: Some Reflections on Recent Reforms," *Alberta Law Review* (1982), p. 482.
41. George W. Adams, "Towards a Mobilization of the Adversary Process," in Walter S. Tarnopolsky, ed., *Some Civil Liberties Issues of the Seventies* (Downsview, Ont.: Osgoode Hall Law School, 1975), p. 138.
42. George W. Adams, "The Small Claims Court and the Adversary Process," *Canadian Bar Review* (1973), pp. 614-15.
43. Hildebrandt, McNeely and Mercer, "Windsor Small Claims Court," p. 96.
44. Ibid., table 1.
45. Neil Vidmar, "The Small Claims Court: A Reconceptualization of Disputes and an Empirical Investigation," *Law and Society Review* (1984), p. 545.
46. Cited in Hildebrandt, McNeely and Mercer, "Windsor Small Claims Court," p. 98.
47. In Toronto the small claims court now has evening sessions to hear cases involving $500 or less.
48. Hildebrandt, McNeely and Mercer, "Windsor Small Claims Court," p. 101.
49. For a description of such a service in British Columbia, see Perry S. Millar and Carl Baar, *Judicial Administration in Canada* (Montreal and Toronto: McGill-Queen's University Press, 1981), p. 359.
50. For an examination of this movement in the United States, see the Feb.-Mar. 1986 issue of *Judicature*.

51. For a description and analysis of this program, see Vidmar, "Small Claims Court," p. 515.
52. O. Reg. 158/85.
53. Canadian Bar Foundation, *The Windsor-Essex Mediation Centre: History and Pilot Project Evaluation* (Ottawa, 1984).
54. The British Columbia project is described in Millar and Baar, *Judicial Administration*, pp. 358-59, and the Quebec project in Manitoba Law Reform Commission, *The Structure of the Courts; Part II: The Adjudication of Small Claims*, pp. 29-30.
55. Canadian Bar Foundation, p. 12.
56. Ibid., p. 35.
57. Vidmar, "Small Claims Court."
58. Neil Vidmar, "Seeking and Finding Justice? An Empirical Map of 'Minor' Dispute Behaviour in English Canada," paper presented to annual meeting of the Canadian Law and Society Association, Montreal, 31 May 1985, p. 27.
59. Ison, "Small Claims," p. 23.
60. Craig A. McEwen and Richard J. Maiman, "Mediation in Small Claims Court: Achieving Compliance Through Consent," *Law and Society Review* (1985), p. 46.

CHAPTER 11
GENERAL JURISDICTION TRIAL COURTS

We turn now to the higher trial courts: the superior, county, and district courts. These are the courts specifically provided for in Canada's original Constitution. These were to be the basic courts of an integrated judicial system—the courts themselves established and maintained by the provinces, their judges appointed and paid by Ottawa. These courts, in theory at least, have been responsible for trying the most serious civil and criminal cases in Canada. It is in that sense that their jurisdiction is general. These are the only courts in which jury trials take place. While jury trials have come to constitute only a small fraction of their case load, for many citizens such trials represent the prototype of adjudicative justice.

While there can be no doubt about the importance of these courts at the time of Canada's founding, their centrality in the Canadian justice system today is seriously threatened. Most criminal cases, including most of the cases involving indictable offences, are now heard in the lower Provincial and Territorial Courts. On the civil side, too, these lower courts, as we have seen, have assumed much of the responsibility for settling private suits and disputed family matters. Perhaps of even greater importance is the tendency of contemporary legislative reforms such as no-fault insurance and no-fault divorce to undermine these courts' classic function of determining individual fault in private disputes. In the field of public law, they have been steadily marginalized by the establishment of administrative tribunals to adjudicate disputes under new modes of state regulation. The one important function in this area they have struggled to retain, judicial review of the decisions of administrative tribunals, was significantly reduced by the establishment of the Federal Court of Canada in 1971 with exclusive jurisdiction to review the decisions of federal administrative tribunals.

In seven of the provinces and both northern territories the general trial court function is now performed by one court—a superior court. The term ''superior court'' is used here as a generic term. Only in Quebec does the superior court actually bear this name. Elsewhere in Canada, as can be seen from the first column in table 11.1, this court has such names as Court of Queen's Bench, Supreme Court, and High Court. A two-tier system of general trial courts remains in only three provinces: British Columbia, Nova Scotia, and Ontario. The county and district courts in these provinces continue to function as locally based trial courts of general jurisdiction with a jurisdiction slightly less than that of the province's superior court. All the other common law provinces have recently merged these courts into their superior courts. (Quebec never had county or district courts.) The merger process will be examined later in this chapter.

TABLE 11.1   *PROVINCIAL AND TERRITORIAL GENERAL*
JURISDICTION TRIAL COURTS

PROVINCE OR TERRITORY	COURTS	NO. OF JUDGES*	MERGER SITUATION
Alberta	Court of Queen's Bench	55	Merged, 1979
British Columbia	Supreme Court	30	Merger approved by province
	County Courts	45	in 1969 but not implemented by fed. gov't
Manitoba	Court of Queen's Bench	28	Merged, 1984
New Brunswick	Court of Queen's Bench	22	Merged, 1979
Newfoundland	Trial Division of Supreme Court	18	Merged, 1986
Nova Scotia	Trial Division of Supreme Court	12	No merger
	County Courts	10	
Ontario	High Court of Justice	49	No merger
	District Court	146	
P.E.I.	Trial Division of Supreme Court†	4	Merged, 1975
Quebec	Superior Court	132	Never had county or district courts
Saskatchewan	Court of Queen's Bench	30	Merged, 1980
N.W.T.	Supreme Court	2	
Yukon	Supreme Court	2	

* Based on salaries provided for in *Judges Act*. Does not include supernumerary judges or judges appointed to unified family courts but does include "senior judge" in the territories and chief justices and associate chief justices.

† This anticipates the division of the Supreme Court into separate trial and appeal divisions—a change which is scheduled for 1987.

The Superior Court in British and Canadian History

The provincial superior court is Canada's oldest judicial institution. The superior court of general jurisdiction, like Parliament and constitutional monarchy, is a part of the legacy of British institutions which have survived as basic elements in the Canadian system of government. As was pointed out in chapter 3, for the Fathers of Confederation the provincial superior courts were the key judicial institutions in the new Constitution of Canada. Both the historic lineage of the provincial superior courts and their constitutional centrality were recognized by Mr. Justice Willard Estey of the Supreme Court of Canada when he observed that, "the provincial superior courts have always occupied a position of prime importance in the constitutional pattern of this country. They are the descendants of the Royal Courts of Justice as courts of general jurisdiction."[1]

The Royal Courts of Justice to which Justice Estey referred trace their history back to Norman times. The judicial activities of the King's Court in the years immediately following the conquest were a crucial factor in consolidating the central power of the Norman kings over feudal England. Gradually the judicial functions of the Royal Court came to be exercised by legal experts and "King's Courts" came to signify separate judicial institutions, while "King's Council" referred to the assemblies the king held for other governmental purposes.[2] By the fourteenth century three distinct courts of law had emerged from the King's Court: the Court of Common Pleas (for suits between subjects), the Court of King's Bench (for criminal cases and the supervision of inferior tribunals and royal officials), and the Court of Exchequer (for revenue cases). Over time these courts came to be staffed exclusively by advocates who had practised at their bar. The recorded decisions of the lawyer-judges serving on these courts came to constitute the English common law. This system of common law superior courts was highly centralized. The Royal Courts of Justice were located in London and the judges resided there, although they were also appointed as commissioners of assize and *nisi prius* so that the king's justice could make its presence felt in provincial towns. It was the judges of these superior courts whose independence from the king and the executive was secured by Parliament after the Glorious Revolution through the Act of Settlement in 1701. A major reorganization of the superior courts took place in 1873 when the separate superior courts were consolidated into a single Supreme Court of Judcature with an appeal division and first five, then three, trial divisions: Chancery, Queen's Bench, and Probate, Divorce and Admiralty.[3]

The jurisdiction originally exercised by the judges of the superior court emanated directly from the crown. The judges of these courts administered sanctions and granted relief in the king's name. Parliament, once its supremacy was established, could reorganize the superior courts, reshape their jurisdiction, and even give some of it to "inferior" tribunals; but the superior courts still retained an inherent jurisdiction to try cases and provide remedies. Unlike all other courts in the realm, the superior courts are not entirely dependent on the legislature for their jurisdiction. This inherent jurisdiction is the hallmark of the superior court in the Anglo-Canadian tradition: the scope of the civil and criminal cases it can hear does not depend entirely on statutory definition.

The inherent jurisdiction of the provincial superior courts is more formally secured under the Canadian Constitution than is the jurisdiction of the English superior courts. In chapter 3 we saw how sections 96 to 100 of the Constitution Act, 1867 have been interpreted so as to entrench what the judiciary regards as the essentials of superior court jurisdiction. The Supreme Court of Canada's 1982 decision in *McEvoy*[4] made it clear that the federal Parliament as well as the provincial legislatures are barred from transferring this entrenched jurisdiction to tribunals that lack the constitutional status of superior courts.[4] The Supreme Court's earlier decision in *Crevier* established that an important component of that entrenched jurisdiction was the power of superior courts to review the legality of the activities of administrative tribunals. Although both the provinces and

Ottawa have chipped away at the jurisdiction of the provincial superior courts and assigned some of their adjudicative responsibilities to inferior courts and administrative tribunals, the judiciary itself at the highest levels has through constitutional interpretation set an outside limit to this legislative trend. Today in Canada it would require a constitutional amendment to strip the provincial superior courts completely of their power to hear the most serious civil and criminal cases.

Thus the superior court in Canada as in Britain is the repository of that core of judicial power so essential to the rule of law ideology. When Dicey insisted that the rule of law requires that "disputes as to the legality of actions of government are to be adjudicated by the ordinary courts of the realm,"[5] it was the superior courts he had in mind. And it is the Canadian superior courts which Chief Justice McRuer had in mind when he declared that "the most secure safeguard for the civil right of the individual to have his rights determined according to the Rule of Law lies in the independence of review by the Courts."[6]

The establishment and maintenance of the hierarchical power of the superior courts to review the activities of inferior tribunals and administrative agencies owes much to the influence of lawyers and judges on the structure of government. The legitimacy of this power with the wider public has been fostered by a belief in a politically neutral law administered by apolitical judges. The masking of the political nature of the superior courts' hegemony is perhaps the most salient fact about these courts for the political scientist to understand.[7]

Superior courts came close on the heels of permanent English settlement in British North America. For the English colonialists a superior court of judicature presided over by a legally qualified barrister was clearly an indispensable component of English civilization. The first was the Supreme Court of Nova Scotia founded in 1752 when Jonathan Belcher, an English barrister, arrived in the colony and, apparently without any act or regulation, turned the General Court (consisting of the governor-in-council and established soon after Cornwallis's arrival with the first British settlers) into a Supreme Court of Judicature.[8] A Supreme Court exercising superior court jurisdiction was established in Prince Edward Island in 1769 when the newly founded colony had only 279 settlers,[9] and New Brunswick had a similar Supreme Court from the founding of the colony in 1784.[10] Newfoundland's Supreme Court was established in the 1700s, but the British tried to discourage settlement on the island in the eighteenth and nineteenth centuries, so that it was not until well into the 1800s that the court was functioning effectively as a superior court.[11]

In central Canada a superior court on the English model did not begin to function on a permanent basis until the Constitution Act of 1791 split the colony of Quebec into Lower and Upper Canada. In 1764 the Court of King's Bench, a superior court of judicature exercising civil and criminal jurisdiction, had been established for the newly conquered colony. However, following the Quebec Act of 1774, civil and criminal jurisdiction were assigned to two separate courts: a decentralized Court of Common Pleas for civil cases and a more centralized

Court of King's Bench for the more serious criminal cases. This bifurcation of jurisdiction reflected the legal biculturalism of the Quebec Act: English criminal law and French-Canadian civil law. The Court of Common Pleas was designed basically for Canadiens. The system was much resented by the English merchants, especially the absence of civil jury trials.[12] The Court of King's Bench, on the other hand, administered English criminal law and procedure. It was natural that when the western part of Quebec was reorganized as the separate colony of Upper Canada to serve its burgeoning population of English settlers, an English superior court was soon established. Governor Simcoe was "determined to have the court system in Upper Canada correspond to that in England."[13] Upper Canada's Judicature Act of 1794 established the Court of King's Bench as a centralized superior court of general jurisdiction along the lines of the English Royal Courts. It was to be based in the capital (wherever that was), staffed by legally qualified judges (originally a chief justice and two puisne judges) and its judges were to go on circuit to major towns in the colony. At the same time, district courts (the forerunners of county courts) were established to hear civil disputes up to a monetary limit (originally set at £15) and courts of requests to hear small claims.[14]

In the meantime Lower Canada carried on and extended its more decentralized superior trial court system. In 1793 the Court of Common Pleas was abolished and a new Court of King's Bench established with both civil and criminal jurisdiction. At first it had just two divisions at Montreal and Quebec (a chief justice and two puisne judges each) but in the 1830s Provincial Courts at Three Rivers and Sherbrooke were elevated to the status of the Court of King's Bench. King's Bench judges presided at circuit courts in the various districts to hear cases involving small amounts of money.[15] This distinctive decentralized superior court survived the Act of Union of 1841 and Confederation in 1867. Thus Quebec is the one Canadian province that never developed the English two-tier system of general jurisdiction trial courts (a superior court based in the capital with its judges going on circuit and a lower-level county or district court permanently based in provincial towns), relying instead on a decentralized superior court. As we shall soon see, the Quebec model appears to be the direction in which court reform in the common law provinces is now headed.

In western Canada the first English-style superior courts were established in British Columbia. In 1853 Governor Douglas established a high court of justice initially called the Court of Common Pleas which subsequently became the Supreme Court of Civil Justice of Vancouver Island with jurisdiction in all matters of law and equity over £50.[16] At first this court was presided over by David Cameron, Douglas's brother-in-law, a Hudson's Bay clerk with no legal training. It was not until 1865 that Cameron was succeeded by Joseph Needham, an English barrister. Meanwhile in 1858 Mathew Begbie, the first English barrister to take up residence in British Columbia, had begun to function as a superior court judge. The Colonial Office had intended to appoint a magistrate for British Columbia until "someone realized that a judge with what lawyers call 'original jurisdiction' should be sent out, having power to deal with law suits at all levels.''[17] With the union of the two colonies in 1866, Begbie's and Needham's courts were merged into the Supreme Court of British Columbia.

Manitoba's superior trial court, the Court of Queen's Bench, did not begin to function until 1872, two years after the creation of the province. During the Hudson's Bay Company's regime the principal judicial institution of Assiniboia was not a superior court but the General Quarterly Court presided over by a judge known as the recorder of Rupert's Land, a lawyer employed by the company.[18] However, a full-fledged superior court was established in the Northwest Territories in 1886, nearly two decades before Saskatchewan and Alberta were created and a similar Territorial court was established for the Yukon at the height of the gold rush in 1898.[19] Following the establishment of Alberta and Saskatchewan in 1905, the Territorial Court of the Northwest Territories was disestablished. It was not until half a century later in 1955 that a superior court, the Supreme Court of the Northwest Territories, was established in the modern Northwest Territories north of the sixtieth parallel.

The superior court with its various titles and structural forms was the key judicial institution of the colonial regime in pre-Confederation Canada. The participation of the judges of these courts in colonial government was by no means confined to the judicial branch. When the colonial population included few formally educated or professional people, the English barristers and former American judges who staffed these courts were called upon to participate in the executive and legislative branches of government. As was noted in chapter 4, the process of establishing the formal separation of powers and removing these judges from legislative assemblies and executive and legislative councils was not completed until the middle of the nineteenth century. And it was also not until the end of the 1840s that the guarantee of security of tenure established for the English superior court judges by the Act of Settlement in 1701 was generally available to their counterparts in both parts of the united colony of Canada and the Maritimes. The central importance of the superior courts and their judges in the eyes of the Fathers of Confederation is evident in the fact that it is only the judges of the superior courts whose independence was formally guaranteed by Canada's new Constitution in 1867.

The superior courts were from the beginning very much lawyers' courts. Their key personnel—the judges on their bench and the lawyers who argued at their bar—had come through a lengthy apprentice-like education in which they all imbibed the intricacies of English common law and procedure. Thus the domination of the judicial system by the superior courts had a centralizing and homogenizing effect on legal culture. It also meant that the justice administered by these courts tended to be relatively complex and expensive. However gratifying this may have been to those who were dedicated to ensuring the Britishness of British North America, it must have seemed a mixed blessing to many of the inhabitants. We get a taste of this from the lament of Richard Cartwright, a merchant who as a layman had served on a local court of common pleas, a court of civil jurisdiction eliminated by Governor Simcoe's judicial "reforms" in 1794. Cartwright had this to say about the imposition of the complex English judicial system on the young colony:

> For see it comes with all the glorious uncertainties of the law in its train, holding out wealth and distinction to the man of law but poverty and distress to the unfortunate client . . . it comes with all its hydra of demurrers, rejoinders, surrejoinders, rebutters and surrebutters, and all the monstrous offspring of metaphysical subtlety begotten upon chicaine, to swallow up our simple forms and modes of process which are easy to be understood and followed by any man of plain sense and common education.[20]

Given the paucity of lawyers and the reluctance of the imperial government to spend money on its colonies, it is remarkable how extensive this professional judicial system became. Nova Scotia must surely take the prize. In a speech in the Assembly in 1830, a member indignantly declared that Nova Scotia, with a population of 124 000, had nine judges (the chief justice and four other judges of the Supreme Court, a master of the rolls, and four judges of the Court of Common Pleas), while England with a population of twelve million had only twelve judges![21]

In those colonies most faithful to the British model, namely the Maritimes and Upper Canada, the superior courts developed many of the structural complexities of the contemporary English court system. In the Maritime provinces this meant that there was a separate administration of common law and equity.[22] At first equity was administered directly by the governor as chancellor with some delegation to the chief justice of the Supreme Court.[23] Subsequently, in New Brunswick and Nova Scotia, a master of the rolls was appointed, courts of chancery and finally equity divisions of the Supreme Court were established to hear cases involving claims for equitable relief. Little Prince Edward Island acquired the full paraphernalia of equity judgeships with the appointment of a master of rolls in 1848 and a vice-chancellor in 1869 who also constituted two-thirds of the colony's Supreme Court. Prince Edward Island retained this confusing and cumbersome arrangement of its superior court until 1975.

In Upper Canada the Court of King's Bench was not given equity jurisdiction when it was established in 1794. It was not until 1837 that a Court of Chancery was created presided over by a judge known as the vice chancellor of Upper Canada.[24] In 1849 the superior court structure of Canada West was completely assimilated to the English model with the establishment of three separate courts each with three judges: the Court of Queen's Bench and the Court of Common Pleas—both common law courts with equal, concurrent jurisdiction—and the Court of Chancery as a court of equity. The judicial systems of the two sections of the united colony of Canada were not unified; the superior court system of the predominantly French part of Canada continued to deviate from the English pattern. No equity courts were developed in Canada East and the superior court there maintained its distinctive decentralization: by 1867 it was organized into nineteen districts served by eighteen judges.[25]

The superior courts of pre-Confederation Canada were essentially trial courts. Throughout most of the colonial period the nominal court of appeal was the governor-in-council, with a further appeal to the Privy Council in England in cases involving significant amounts of money. The idea of a right to appeal from a trial court to a separate judicial body higher up in the court hierarchy was not yet a prevailing political norm. Riddell's statement about Upper Canada is probably equally applicable to the other British North American provinces: "Appeals were not unknown; but they were rather infrequent, and almost invariably unsuccessful."[26] Closer to Confederation, the reform movement which had led to responsible government and greater judicial independence began to expand and judicialize the appeal system. The Baldwin-Blake judicial reforms of 1849 established a Court of Error and Appeal for Canada West. Although this change removed judicial functions from the executive, it did not produce a court specializing in appellate work. The nine judges of the three superior trial courts constituted the new Court of Error and Appeal. As Margaret Banks points out, "the result was not entirely satisfactory, because no provision was made to prevent a judge from sitting on an appeal from his own judgment and this, in fact, was quite common."[27] In Quebec a Court of King's Bench was established to hear appeals but its five judges also tried criminal cases. The emergence of courts dedicated exclusively to hearing appeals was a post-Confederation development.

Origin of the County and District Courts

The county and district courts were the other courts explicitly provided for in Canada's Constitution in 1867. Under section 96, the judges of these provincial courts as well as the judges of the superior courts were to be appointed by the federal government, and under section 100 their remuneration was to be provided for by the federal Parliament. But the county and district courts, although clearly key elements in the judicial architecture of the new nation, were not nearly as well developed in pre-Confederation Canada as were the superior courts.

It was in Upper Canada that the county and district courts were first and most fully developed. Thus there may be some historical logic in the fact that contemporary Ontario maintains the largest network of these courts and appears most resistant to merging them into its superior trial courts.

District courts trace their origin to Governor Simcoe's judicial reforms of 1794. The legislation which created the Court of King's Bench also abolished the courts of common pleas and replaced them with a new system of district courts. Like the courts they replaced, the district courts were designed primarily to provide a judicial service for merchants living at considerable distances from the capital. In establishing these courts Simcoe was not following an English model, for it was not until 1846 that a system of county courts was established in England. The district courts had jurisdiction in actions of contract involving sums in excess of the forty-shilling limit of the courts of requests (presided over by justices of the peace) up to £15 and after 1797 to £40. Although this meant that formally their jurisdiction was more limited than the superior courts of common pleas, in fact they could probably handle most of the disputes that would have been taken to those courts. Given the dearth of lawyers in this frontier colony, there was no requirement that the district courts be staffed by professionally qualified judges. Indeed, in the early years they were usually presided over by laymen. Their procedures, however, called for written rather than oral pleadings and thus were more likely to prompt litigants to seek a lawyer's advice.[28]

Under the Union regime the Upper Canadian, locally based intermediate trial courts were professionalized and their role considerably expanded. In 1841 legislation required that district court judges be barristers, that they reside in the district, and that instead of deriving their income from court fees they be paid a salary. These locally based professional district court judges took over some of the major judicial responsibilities of lay justices of the peace. They presided over division courts which replaced courts of requests for small claims cases. Legislation in 1845 required that a district court judge should preside as chairman at the General Quarter Sessions of the Peace. Thus the district court judge began to assume important responsibilities for the administration of criminal as well as civil justice. The civil jurisdiction of these courts also continued to expand with a steady raising of their monetary limit and a widening of the causes of actions they could entertain. In 1849 when counties replaced districts as the basic units of territorial organization in Upper Canada, the district courts became county courts. But to make matters confusing, district courts were re-introduced four years later for those frontier parts of the province organized as districts rather than counties. This combination of county and district courts continued in Ontario right up to 1985.

Well before Confederation, the county or district court of Upper Canada had acquired its distinctive Canadian form: an all-purpose, locally based intermediate trial court. Like the English county courts, they were presided over by legally qualified judges but, unlike their English counterparts, the Canadian county court judges conducted criminal as well as civil trials. While their jurisdiction went well beyond that of lay magistrates, these courts were distinctly "inferior" courts. Their jurisdiction, while extensive, was confined to that set out by statute and excluded what were regarded as the most serious civil and criminal cases. Their inferiority in the judicial hierarchy was marked by the fact that an appeal lay from their decisions on a point of law to the Court of Queen's Bench.[29] The judges on these courts were paid less and had less status than the superior court judges. Their lower status is evident in the failure of the Constitution Act, 1867 to extend the constitutional guarantee of security of tenure to county and district court judges, even though tenure during good behaviour had been conferred on these judges by statute in 1857.

Elsewhere in colonial Canada the county and district courts were much less developed prior to Confederation. Quebec, as we have seen, never established these courts, relying instead on a decentralized superior court and a complex array of locally based lower courts. Nova Scotia's inferior courts of common pleas served much the same function as Upper Canada's district courts. Complaints about the colony's surplus of judges led to the abolition of these courts in 1841. In New Brunswick, on the other hand, the courts of common pleas presided over by lay judges were maintained right up to Confederation when they were replaced by county courts. Similarly, Prince Edward Island, while it did not have Upper Canada's formal county court judicial establishment, had such a system in embryo in the form of courts of the commissioners for the recovery of small debts which were replaced by county courts in 1867. On the Pacific coast the need for a more accessible forum for adjudicating civil disputes involving substantial amounts of money, particularly in the British Columbia gold fields, led in 1866 to the establishment of county courts in the colony of British Columbia and district courts in Vancouver Island. These courts were presided over by stipendiary magistrates most of whom had also served as gold commissioners.[30] In 1867, six of the eleven magistrates (only one of whom had any legal education) were designated county court judges in the United Colony of British Columbia. Elsewhere in the West, county and district courts did not make their appearance until the prairie provinces were formed, although the roots of Manitoba's county courts can be found in the courts of petty sessions which had existed since 1835 under Hudson's Bay Company rule in Assiniboia. The adoption by the other common law provinces of the full Ontario system of locally based, inferior general trial courts, presided over by centrally appointed professional judges, was essentially a post-Confederation project.

Development of the Section 96 Courts since Confederation

From Confederation to the mid-1970s the Upper Canadian–Ontario two-tier system of section 96 trial courts was the basic model for all of the common law provinces. In this system what are deemed to be the most important civil and criminal cases are tried by the superior court whose judges reside in the provincial capital and perhaps one or two other major cities and go on circuit to hear cases around the province. The county and district courts form the second, somewhat lower tier of general trial courts. They are located in cities in all parts of the province and their judges permanently reside in these localities. In principle, the county and district courts were designed as intermediate trial courts: good enough to deal with cases which are too serious to be tried by provincial magistrates, but not quite good enough to handle the really serious cases reserved for the superior courts. Over the years this rationale and the validity of the assumptions on which it is based have come increasingly into question.

Quebec, as has been noted, never established county or district courts. Its superior trial court became the largest and most decentralized in Canada. Its judges are assigned to eight regions of the province. But Quebec's Superior Court is much more centralized than this figure suggests in that a great majority of its judges live in Montreal or Quebec City.[31] Although Quebec has developed the largest superior court bench, still the absence of county or district courts has meant that overall its judicial system has been the least reliant on federally paid and appointed judges. Its purely provincial courts, particularly its Court of Sessions in criminal matters and Provincial Court in civil matters, have done much of the work handled by county and district courts in the other provinces. In this sense Quebec has maintained a more autonomous system of trial courts.

The one other part of Canada in which county or district courts were never established is the northern territories. In the sparsely populated north it has not made sense to post resident judges outside of Whitehorse in the Yukon and Yellowknife in the Northwest Territories.[32] The only section 96 courts in these territories have been superior courts, originally known as territorial courts but today called the Supreme Courts of their respective territories.

Among the common law provinces, while the Ontario model has been dominant, there have been a few structural variations. One kind of variation has to do with the centralization of the superior court. Ontario has adhered closely to the highly centralized English model with all the judges of its High Court (the trial division of its Supreme Court) resident in Toronto. Indeed, the federal Judges Act still requires that the judges in this court reside within forty kilometres of Toronto. In Manitoba, Newfoundland, Nova Scotia, and Prince Edward Island, where the provincial capital is the dominant metropolitan centre, there has been a similar centralization of the superior trial court. But elsewhere the domination of the capital or the largest provincial city was, from the province's beginning, challenged by other metropolitan centres. Hence we find that the rivalries between Vancouver and Victoria, Calgary and Edmonton, and Regina and Saskatoon in the three westernmost provinces, and among Fredericton, Moncton, and Saint John in New Brunswick meant that superior court judges were resident in more than one provincial centre in these provinces.[33]

The continuous presence of superior court judges in the city where they practise is of great importance to lawyers reared in the English tradition. More than convenience is at issue here: it is also a matter of professional status and enrichment. The superior court in the lawyer's mind represents the highest form of justice and professional practice. It is central to the traditional partnership of bar and bench in the English legal world. With changing demographic patterns and population growth many Canadian cities outside the provincial capital have large numbers of professional lawyers. Ontario, for instance, has eleven cities larger than Halifax, but only Toronto has resident superior court judges. Much of the demand for merger of the county and district courts with the superior court comes from lawyers practising in these cities, for merger inevitably means some decentralization of the superior trial court.[34]

Another kind of structural variation concerns divisions of the superior trial court. In the western provinces, the superior courts have always had a simple and unified structure. But in Ontario and the Maritimes these courts were for a time afflicted with some of the complexities of the English system. As might be expected, loyalist Ontario followed the English system most faithfully. It was the only province to replicate the three separate English superior courts: Queen's Bench, Common Pleas, and Chancery. In 1881 legislation mirroring the English reforms of 1873, transformed these three courts into three divisions of a single High Court of Justice, and a fourth division—Exchequer—was created in 1913.[35] In New Brunswick and Nova Scotia the common law and equity courts had been merged before Confederation, but separate equity or chancery justices of the superior courts were retained until after World War Two.[36] The three judges of Prince Edward Island's superior court, as previously noted, bore different titles and held formally different offices right up to the merger of the province's county and superior courts in 1975.

Simplification of the superior court structure does not rule out specialization and functional divisions within the superior courts. Indeed, a number of the contemporary superior courts have specialist divisions. Quebec's Superior Court has gone the furthest in this direction and, under Chief Justice Deschênes, organized its work, particularly in the Montreal area where most of its judges sit, in six divisions as follows: civil, family, criminal, practice (procedural and interlocutory matters), administrative law, and bankruptcy.[37] The Prince Edward Island Supreme Court, since the elmination of the county court in 1975, has had an estates division, family division, and general division.[38] British Columbia, Manitoba, New Brunswick, and Ontario have all developed divisions specializing in family law cases.[39] Since 1972 Ontario has been unique in having a divisional court consisting of three of its High Court judges. The primary function of the divisional court is judicial review of the province's administrative tribunals.[40]

These modern divisions of superior trial courts are much more functional than the earlier more formal divisions. Judges are not permanently attached to divisions but can be assigned to them on the basis of need and aptitude. This kind of flexibility in the deployment of trial judges is one of the distinct advantages of merging the two levels of trial court. As the Manitoba Law Reform Commission pointed out, "To the degree that 'specialization' by the judiciary is required, it can be achieved in a flexible, non-rigid, common sense way within the larger unified court."[41]

Functional specialization in the organization of courts has not been favoured in the common law world as much as in civil law countries. There is a suspicion that a judge who concentrates exclusively on one area of law will become too firmly wedded to a particular orientation within that field and will develop a "tunnel vision" that makes the judge too impervious to the merits of contending points of view and too cut off from the perspectives of other branches of law. On the other hand, the complex and dynamic nature of modern legal systems challenges the reliance on legal generalists in common law systems. Specialist divisions within large superior trial courts may be the best way of striking a balance. Such divisions facilitate the provision of special ancillary services, for instance the mediation services appropriate for a family law division. At the same time, because the judges assigned to these divisions belong to a superior court with a broad jurisdiction, they need not spend an entire career in a single field of trial work.

Between Confederation and the mid-1970s, the most significant and distinctive development in the Canadian system of general trial courts was the expansion of the county and district courts. In 1867, of the four original provinces, only New Brunswick and Ontario possessed these courts. Nova Scotia's county courts were established in 1874. The anti-confederate provincial government had held back this legislation until a Liberal government was installed in Ottawa so that they could be sure their "friends" would be appointed to the county court bench.[42] Each new province to join Confederation followed the Upper Canadian, Ontario model and established a lower tier of locally based general trial courts. In British Columbia, Manitoba, and Prince Edward Island they were based on counties, while in Alberta, Newfoundland, and Saskatchewan they were organized on a district basis. Whereas at Confederation the 42 county court judges constituted less than half of the section 96 judiciary and nearly all were in Ontario, by 1974, 231 judges were serving on these intermediate trial courts, constituting three-quarters of the judges appointed by Ottawa to the trial courts of the common law provinces.

The establishment of county or district courts in all of the provinces outside of Quebec is a clear example of the demonstration effect Ontario institutions have had on other provinces. But it is not generally recognized how much this Ontario model departed from the English system. The Canadian county court acquired much greater responsibilities than its counterpart in England. Unlike the English county court which never exercised criminal jurisdiction,[43] the county and district courts in Canada have, from their earliest days, played a major role in criminal justice. Their civil jurisdiction has also greatly exceeded that of the English county courts. The greater distances in Canada between population centres must surely have been a factor in inducing Anglo-Canadians to make much more of their county and district courts and establish them as major adjudicative agencies in smaller cities throughout the provinces. The expanded use of county and district courts was also a way of retaining and compensating for the highly centralized English superior court. Only Quebec approximated the decentralized superior court model adopted in most of the American states. The common law provinces kept expanding the jurisdiction of their locally based "slightly inferior" general trial courts, gradually weakening the rationale for this hierarchical system and making the Quebec/American system the more appropriate model.

The role of Canada's county and district courts in criminal justice has involved the adoption of a mode of criminal trial unknown in the English upper courts: trial by judge alone without jury. As early as 1869 a federal act provided for trial with the consent of the accused before a judge alone sitting without a jury.[44] At first this legislation applied only in Ontario and Quebec. While in Quebec this jurisdiction came to be exercised by the provincially appointed judge of the Court of Sessions, in Ontario it was exercised by county and district court judges presiding in what came to be known as the "County Court Judge's Criminal Court." Subsequently the so-called speedy trials legislation was applied to all the other provinces and all of them, at least up until merger, followed Ontario, relying primarily on their county or district court judges for delivering this distinctly un-English form of criminal justice. Indeed, in some provinces this option—trial for an indictable offence by judge alone—was reserved exclusively for the county and district court judges.[45]

Trial by judge alone has proved to be a popular mode of trial in Canada for accused persons—or, perhaps more accurately, for their lawyers. Bear in mind that under the Criminal Code, except for those very few offences (for example, murder and treason) reserved exclusively for trial by a superior court judge, and the less serious indictable offences under the exclusive jurisdiction of the Provincial Court judge, an accused has a choice of three modes of trial: trial by magistrate (that is, Provincial Court judge) sitting alone, trial by judge alone, or trial by judge and jury. Very often trial by judge and jury is chosen as a delaying tactic but then abandoned as the trial date approaches. Ejann MacKaay's study of the Montreal courts showed that although 86 per cent of the defendants who pleaded not guilty initially elected trial by judge and jury, 96 per cent of these defendants eventually exercised the right to "re-elect" another form of trial. Ninety per cent of these ultimately chose trial by judge alone.[46]

The county and district court judges' criminal justice responsibilities have not been limited to cases tried without juries. In Ontario from Confederation onward, the county court judge sitting in the Court of General Sessions could try with a jury all indictable offences except those few reserved exclusively for superior courts. Except in Newfoundland, Saskatchewan, and Nova Scotia, the county and district courts in other provinces were given at one time or another jurisdiction to conduct jury trials. This meant that they became the "work horse" courts of the criminal justice system so far as trials for the more serious offences were concerned. In 1953 the minister of justice reported that the county and district courts in Canada tried four times as many cases as the superior courts.[47] Nor have the country and district courts' criminal justice responsibilities been confined to trials. They have also functioned as the courts of appeal from the decisions of magistrates and Provincial Courts in summary conviction matters.

In civil matters the functions assigned to Canada's county and district courts have been extended beyond those of their English counterparts. Like the English county courts, they began with a civil jurisdiction very close to that of a small claims court. At Confederation, the monetary limit on Ontario's county courts was set at $200 for most types of suits and $400 for debt cases, while that on New Brunswick's was just half of Ontario's. These monetary limits were continually raised and considerably beyond the rate of inflation. By the mid-1970s, on the eve of merger, in seven provinces the limit was set at $5000 or above, while the limit on England's county courts by that time had increased to only £750 (about $1950).[48] By 1985 the three provinces which have retained their intermediate trial courts had significantly raised the monetary limit: to $50 000 in British Columbia and Nova Scotia, and $25 000 in Ontario.[49] Much earlier the significance of monetary limits in British Columbia, New Brunswick, and Ontario was greatly reduced by the adoption of a consent jurisdiction which enabled their county courts to hear cases involving any amount of money if both parties agreed to waive the monetary ceiling.[50] Restrictions on the kinds of suit the county and district courts could hear were also eased, although one type of jurisdiction that was generally withheld from them was the review of the decisions of administrative agencies. This important "public law" function was reserved for the superior courts.

Over the years, the county and district court judges were given numerous functions in addition to those flowing directly from their primary appointments. They became in effect "jacks of all trades"—judicial factotums for the communities in which they resided. In most provinces they received appointments as "local judges of the Supreme Court." Under this mantle they could try cases which are constitutionally restricted to the superior court.[51] Through this device Ontario District Court judges, especially outside of Toronto, have borne the brunt of the fastest-growing type of superior court business: litigation on matters ancillary to divorce. Provincial and federal legislation over the years has given a crazy patchwork quilt of jurisdiction to county and district court judges, often as *persona designata*. These assignments cover everything from minor administrative functions such as the approval of cemetery accounts, to important adjudicative matters such as the committal of alcoholics or drug addicts to private sanitaria.[52] In most provinces county and district court judges have served as judges of surrogate or probate courts exercising jurisdiction over the administration of estates and disputes arising in the execution of wills.[53] As we have seen, they also continue in a number of provinces to have a small claims jurisdiction. Their responsibilities have been extended well beyond normal adjudication. In many Ontario cities, for instance, they are appointed local masters of the Supreme Court to handle procedural and interlocutory matters arising in litigation conducted in the superior court.[54]

This unplanned *mélange* of jurisdiction assigned to county and district court judges eroded any rational basis for a division of labour between the two tiers of trial judges. On the one hand, the county and district court judges were called upon to perform all kinds of administrative and routine adjudicative functions which do not require the skills of a superior court judge, while at the same time their jurisdiction to try serious civil and criminal cases approached concurrency with superior court judges. Indeed, on the criminal side it could be argued that they had become a more important criminal trial court than the superior court. The superior courts under the two-tier system increasingly became primarily civil courts devoting most of their time to cases within their exclusive jurisdiction: damage suits and commercial matters where litigants refuse to waive the monetary limit, judicial review of provincial administrative bodies, and a residue of family matters. For some years now the criminal work of Ontario's High Court has constituted less than 10 per cent of its total case load and is confined mostly to homicide cases, the main category of crime reserved under section 427 of the Criminal Code exclusively for trial by a superior court judge.[55] Not only does the criminal trial work of the Ontario District Court quantitatively exceed that of the High Court, but qualitatively it is also probably more important as it includes most of the cases involving armed robbery, fraud, and drug trafficking. To quote the Ontario Law Reform Commission, "It has been said that the Supreme Court (i.e., High Court) judges try only the unique crimes of passion while the county court judges try the professional criminals providing the greatest threat to society."[56]

The Merger Movement

Since 1975 a major change has been taking place in the structure of Canadian trial courts. One by one the provinces have been abandoning the two-tier system of general trial courts and merging their county and district courts into their superior court. The drive toward merger was under way as early as 1934 when the *Canadian Bar Review* reported that representatives of the County Court Judges Association had "waited upon" the attorney general of Ontario with a proposal "that the County Court, the Surrogate Court, the Division Court, the General Sessions Court of the Peace, and the County Judges' Criminal Court be merged in one Court, to be called the Superior Court of Ontario. . . ."[57] At first the merger movement was fostered primarily by county and district court judges themselves and members of the legal profession in centres outside of the home base of the superior court. But by the 1960s merger proposals were becoming attractive to provincial politicians concerned about achieving greater efficiency in the administration of justice. The first province to introduce merger legislation was British Columbia in 1969. Attorney General Leslie Peterson explained the rationale of the legislation in these terms: "The change should provide for a more efficient management of our judicial resources and better service to the public."[58]

Merger was seen to yield two key administrative benefits: the elimination of an awkward circuit system, and the possibility of a more rational use of human and physical resources. Severe scheduling problems have been associated with the two-tier system.[59] The difficulty in anticipating the number of trials the superior court judge will dispose of during a circuit visit to a county or district centre causes delay. Frequently cases scheduled for hearing are postponed, causing considerable inconvenience for the litigants and witnesses. The inconvenience is greatest in civil cases which traditionally have given way to criminal cases on the superior court judge's trial list. From a resource management point of view, assigning judges and court houses to counties or districts regardless of case-load considerations makes little sense. Even where the worst rigidities are eliminated and locally based judges become more mobile through a regional circuit system, jurisdictional gaps between the two tiers of judges impede the most effective use of a province's trial judiciary. While merging the two levels of general trial courts is by no means a panacea for the problems of court administration, the various provincial task forces and commissions that have looked into the merger issue have been in agreement with the basic finding of Manitoba's Law Reform Commission that "The establishment of one trial court would permit, through a single administration and a unified court staff, the flexible and immediate marshalling of resources to meet current and actual requirements. In a single court, it will be possible to assign judges and court personnel and to schedule sittings more efficiently."[60]

The merger movement must also be seen in a larger setting. As Carl Baar has pointed out, this movement is related to "a broader historical evolution of western judicial institutions" which has regarded trial court consolidation as a key to judicial reform.[61] In North America this theme was prominent in the writings of Roscoe Pound and in the advocacy of the American Bar Association. These influences are reflected in the publications of merger supporters in Canada. A memorandum prepared by the chief judge and associate chief judge of Alberta's District Court cites the following "authoritative statement" of the American Bar Association,

> The structure of the (ideal) Court system should be simple, consisting of a trial court and an appellate court each having divisions and departments as needed. The trial courts should have jurisdiction in all cases and proceedings . . . . The judicial function of the trial court should be performed by a single class of judges.[62]

This same ideal, as we have argued, applies to the reform of Canada's so-called lower courts. This model of a non-hierarchical, multi-purpose integrated trial court recognizes differences in the aptitudes and knowledge of judges, but instead of trying to match judges to cases through an unwieldy court hierarchy, proceeds on the assumption that "matching special cases to judicial expertise is a question of administration not structure."[63]

Although British Columbia was the first province to pursue these administrative advantages through amalgamation of its county and superior trial courts, its attempt was abortive. Under the Canadian Constitution a province can pass legislation abolishing its county or district courts and replacing them with an expanded, less centralized superior court. But for such legislation to be effective all of the county or district court judges must be elevated to superior court status and this requires action at the federal level. The federal executive must appoint the lower court judges to the superior court and the federal Judges Act must be amended to provide the additional superior court judgeships and salaries. In 1969 this federal co-operation was not forthcoming. Perhaps the federal government saw the British Columbian measure as a precedent which other provinces were likely to follow and balked at the increased salary cost such a quantity of elevations would entail in the short run. Or perhaps merger was regarded as simply too sharp a departure from the two-tier system provided for in section 96 of the Constitution.

Whatever the reasons—and they were never made public—they did not for long persuade Ottawa to reject provincial pressure for merger. In 1975 the federal government co-operated with Prince Edward Island and took the necessary steps to promote the province's three county court judges to its Supreme Court. Prince Edward Island clearly had the most compelling case for merger as the case loads of its county courts were extremely low.[64] The seven-judge superior court which resulted from merger may seem large for a population of 123 000, but it must be remembered that the Supreme Court judges have also served as the province's court of appeal and that members of its trial division perform virtually all the functions of a family court. This merger has been followed by the consolidation of the two levels of section 96 trial courts in five other provinces: Alberta merged its district courts and the trial division of its Supreme Court to form the Court of Queen's Bench of Alberta in 1978;[65] New Brunswick merged its county courts and the Queen's Bench Division of its Supreme Court to form the Court of Queen's Bench of New Brunswick in 1979;[66] Saskatchewan merged its district courts into its Court of Queen's Bench in 1980;[67] Manitoba did the same with its county courts in 1983;[68] legislation merging Newfoundland's district courts with the trial division of its Supreme Court came into force in 1986.[69]

Court merger in the three Prairie and three Atlantic provinces has not been achieved without a considerable political struggle. The controversy over merger has not been a public debate. The politics involved are professional politics— superior court judges struggling to preserve their status as an elite corps of trial judges, the county and district court judges increasingly resentful of their structural inferiority, sections of the bar objecting to the inconveniences inflicted on lawyers and litigants in cities without resident superior court justices, and other "big city" lawyers enamoured of the traditional English way of linking leaders of the bench and bar together at the centre. Underlying this struggle within professional legal circles are competing theories on how best to provide a high quality of trial adjudication to all the citizens of a province.

Much of the debate over quality has focused on what the Ontario Law Reform Commission referred to as "the delicate question of judicial competence." The commission concluded that an inquiry into competence would show that "there are some County Court judges who are equally competent as some High Court judges, and there are some who are not."[70] The commission did not entertain the third possibility that there might be some High Court judges who were less competent than some county court judges. The only evidence on competence was contained in the dissenting memorandum of Commissioner Richard Bell, which showed that over a five-month period High Court decisions were reversed proportionately more often by the Court of Appeal than county court decisions, thus suggesting a greater propensity to err in the superior court.[71] On the other hand, the Canadian Bar Association's study of judicial appointments found that political favouritism had been a significant factor in county and district court appointments in Ontario but not in High Court or Court of Appeal appointments.[72] This debate over relative competence is bound to be inconclusive and, in any event, is irrelevant to the essential question of whether a difference of quality between locally based and centrally based general jurisdiction trial judges should be maintained as a permanent feature of the administration of justice.

The opponents of merger clearly believe that such a differential makes good sense. They see hierarchy, relative smallness, and collegiality as necessary conditions of excellence. These qualities, they believe, will be best enhanced by maintaining an elite body of trial judges at the centre whose constant interaction will nurture the highest professional standards, and a circuit system through which this elite group of judges will "administer uniform and high quality justice over the most important criminal and civil cases in the province."[73] Judges at the county or district court level, according to this theory, do not have to be quite so good. For as the embodiment of "resident justice" in each county or district of the province they must combine with their adjudicative tasks a host of more ceremonial or administrative functions not entirely suitable for the top flight professional who is skilful enough to try the toughest cases. From this perspective, merger threatens to dilute the quality of the superior court and deprive local communities of the resident justice's services. In the words of Ontario's Law Reform Commission, words publicly endorsed by the judges of Ontario's High Court:[74]

> To merge the two levels would be to sacrifice many of the distinct and desirable features of each level for the sake of increased efficiency. Like the "tail wagging the dog" metaphor, it would be to place considerations of judicial quality in a position secondary to that of administrative convenience and efficiency. This we oppose.[75]

From a more egalitarian perspective, however, this hierarchical approach is unacceptable. It implies, as a permanent feature in the administration of justice, a double standard, with the lower standard for communities outside the provincial capital or one or two major cities. A report on merger submitted to Roy Romanow, the attorney general of Saskatchewan, put the point this way:

> An ideal court system must be one which reduces real inequalities and the appearance of inequality before the law. The location of superior courts, the labels used to identify the "levels" of courts, the allocation of jurisdiction, appeal structures, and even fee schedules reinforce the public conception that "better justice" is available from a superior court.[76]

The force of this point increases when it is recognized that as the two-tier Canadian system evolved, the jurisdiction of the county and district court judges came to encompass the trial of very serious cases, especially in the criminal area. It is difficult to accept that anyone but the most highly qualified trial judge should hear many of the matters dealt with in these courts. If routine administrative and ceremonial tasks have been inappropriately mixed in with serious adjudicative responsibilities, it would seem wiser to assign this part of the job to non-judicial officials than to rely on inferior court judges for the trial of important matters. The trouble with the two-tier system is that it is likely to be the basis of a self-fulfilling prophecy. Precisely because lower status, lower remuneration, and inferior terms of office are associated with positions at the county and district court level, it will be more difficult to recruit outstanding practitioners to judgeships on these courts. (Also, it may very well be that leading lawyers outside of the capital area are reluctant to accept superior court appointments when that means moving their residence and spending as much time on the road as the circuits of a centrally based superior court require.) Further, once appointed, the county or district court judge's relative isolation and lack of collegiality are not conducive to developing professional excellence.

The advantages of having a locally based general jurisdiction trial court can be retained in a merged system by some decentralization of the superior trial court. Legislation in Alberta, New Brunswick, and Saskatchewan requires that one or more judges of the merged superior court reside in certain cities in each province: six in the case of Alberta;[77] eight in the case of the trial division of New Brunswick's Court of Queen's Bench, and six for its family division;[78] ten in Saskatchewan.[79] The Manitoba Act is more flexible, giving the provincial cabinet the responsibility of designating judicial centres in the province with a minimum of three centres outside Winnipeg.[80] The trial division of Newfoundland's merged Supreme Court has eight judicial centres to which judges may be appointed.[81] It will be important to ensure that members of these decentralized superior courts are not isolated from their colleagues and that there is some variety in the trial judges that serve particular communities. Perhaps the best way of combining collegiality and local accessibility is to organize groups of superior court judges around regional centres and to operate mini-circuits in each region. This has been the basic plan for a merged system in Ontario.[82]

Still, it must be conceded that there will be less collegiality within the superior court as a whole under these arrangements. That has been one of the prime reasons for the Ontario High Court judges' opposition to merger. They have expressed concern about "the plight of a court of two hundred judges, divided into eight orbital groups revolving around its own associate chief justice, in maintaining consistency and discipline in following decisions spun off over the whole province."[83] The superior court judges' loss of collective collegiality must, however, be balanced against the gains in collegiality for judges of the former intermediate courts. Also it is not clear, as the High Court judges claim, that merger will produce dangerous jurisprudential inconsistencies. Surely it remains the function of provincial courts of appeal to resolve major discrepancies in the application of laws by a province's trial courts.

The possibility of giving the regions of each province equal acccess to a nucleus of locally based superior court judges would greatly increase once the final step in trial court consolidation is taken and the strict status differential between the lower Provincial Courts and the higher section 96 trial courts is eliminated. In 1979, when the National Task Force on the Administration of Justice took stock of the situation, it reported that the number of communities served by Provincial Courts exceeded the number served by section 96 courts by a ratio of nearly four to one (821 to 221).[84] If, however, the reform of the Provincial Courts discussed earlier were adopted and the hierarchical organization of trial courts were entirely abandoned, elevating all those who are responsible for serious adjudicative work to superior court status, the picture would change dramatically. Under this scheme the sharp differentiation between provincially appointed lower court judges and federally appointed higher court judges would disappear, and communities in every region of each province would have a significant complement of superior court trial judges to provide their adjudicative services.

But at least three provinces—British Columbia, Nova Scotia, and Ontario— are a long way from such a radical dismantling of the trial court hierarchy. These three have not yet taken the first step to trial court consolidation—the merger of their section 96 trial courts. In British Columbia some of the administrative disadvantages of the two-tier system may have been overcome by vesting administrative direction of the county courts in the chief justice of the Supreme Court (British Columbia's superior trial court).[85] Similarly, Ontario, through the recent reorganization of its county courts into a more flexible district court system, may be able to overcome the worst inefficiencies in the deployment of its trial court resources. These provinces may settle for the more moderate approach to trial court reform adopted in England in 1971 following the Beeching Commission Report.[86] The English reforms, at least on the criminal side, merged courts but not the judiciary. Criminal offences (beyond those under the jurisdiction of magistrates) are tried by a new Crown Court staffed by two tiers of judges. The upper tiers are the London-based High Court justices and the lower are former County Court judges and recorders. Aside from the very few offences reserved for High Court judges, there is a considerable degree of flexibility and concurrency in the cases that each tier can hear. On the civil side the county courts remain quite distinct from the High Court with, by Canadian standards, quite a limited jurisdiction. The system is open, however, to greater use of the county courts through practice directions of the Lord Chief Justice concurred in by the Lord Chancellor. One factor which mitigates against going further than this in England is the division in that country's legal profession between solicitors and barristers and the latters' monopoly of the right to argue cases in the superior courts. Total merger of the superior and county courts would threaten the barristers' monopoly.

It will be interesting to see whether, given Canada's more egalitarian North American culture and fused legal profession, the hierarchical English system continues to hold sway in the three provinces which up to now have not merged their higher trial courts. In the long run it seems likely that North American culture and geography will prevail and all the Canadian provinces will abandon the English model for systems more akin to those of Quebec and many of the American states.

Declining Use of the Jury

Years ago trial by jury was the basic form of trial in the superior court. Indeed, trial by jury was considered as essential an ingredient of Canada's British heritage as the superior court or Parliament. The second statute enacted by the legislatures of Upper Canada in 1792 proclaimed that "trial by jury has long been established and approved in our Mother country and is one of the chief benefits to be attained by a free constitution."[87] Although the courts under review in this chapter—the superior, county, and district courts—are the only Canadian courts in which jury trials take place, such trials are now the exception rather than the rule. Today the basic form of trial in these courts is trial by a single judge sitting without a jury.

This decline in the use of jury trials is of major political significance. It means that there has been a great reduction in the participation of the ordinary citizen in the administration of justice in Canada. This change, coupled with the pro-fessionalization of the lower court magistracy, has given state-appointed judges drawn from the legal profession very nearly a monopoly in decision-making in the third branch of government. This is a perplexing development, for it seems to go against the grain of the liberal and egalitarian currents of thought that have been influencing the reform of Canadian institutions. It also appears to conflict with contemporary public opinion. When the Law Reform Commission con-ducted a survey of the public in the late 1970s, it found that 37 per cent felt a jury was more likely to arrive at a just and fair verdict while only 9 per cent thought that a judge was more likely to be just and fair (5.4 per cent rated them both equally).[88]

The main factor in reducing the relative frequency of jury trials in criminal cases has been the steady increase in the number of criminal offences for which the jury trial is either not permitted at all or is only an option. It should be recalled from chapter 8 that the vast majority of criminal offences—all summary offences and indictable offences with the lowest range of penalties—can be tried only in the lower criminal court before a Provincial or Territorial Court judge sitting alone. In the middle are most of the more serious indictable offences for which the accused has three options: trial by a federally appointed judge and jury, trial by judge alone or trial in a lower court before a Provincial or Territorial Court judge. Before the Charter of Rights Canadian legislators were not con-stitutionally restricted in regulating the use of jury trials. The Canadian Consti-tution contained nothing like the sixth amendment of the American Constitution which guarantees the right to trial by jury in all criminal prosecutions, or the seventh amendment right to jury trials in civil suits where the value in controversy exceeds $20. The guarantee of the right to trial by jury in section 11(f) of the new Charter of Rights and Freedoms will not significantly change the situation. The guarantee applies only to offences for which the maximum penalty is five years or some punishment more severe—a requirement which the existing pro-visions of the the Criminal Code appear not to violate.[89]

To some extent Canada has been following British practice in making the right to jury trials inaccessible in the great bulk of minor offences that litter the modern statute book. But there is one significant difference. In England, when offences are put under the exclusive jurisdiction of the lower court, this means throughout most of the country that the cases will be heard by banks of lay justices. In Canada, on the other hand, at least since the middle of the last century, the lower criminal court has not had this kind of citizen participation but instead has been presided over by stipendiary or police magistrates and later by professional judges. We should also note that in criminal justice England did not develop the other Canadian alternative to jury trials—trial by a higher court judge sitting alone. Thus, British criminal justice has remained open to more popular participation than has the Canadian system.

It is not just the legislature alone that has reduced trial by jury in criminal cases. For that large group of indictable offences for which trial by judge and jury remains as an option, the jury trial is clearly the least popular option. As far back as 1906, jury trials occurred in only 7.4 per cent of cases involving indictable offences. By 1966 the figure was down to 2.1 per cent.[90] A number of disincentives are attached to the jury option: a longer period to wait for a jury trial and the prospect of a lesser sentence in the lower court may be the most important. Election of the forum in most cases will be heavily influenced by the accused's lawyer. Legal counsel may initially opt for trial by judge and jury as a delaying device, but in the end "advise" the accused to elect one of the other forums. An experienced crown attorney, S.G. Leggett, has observed that jury trials "are avoided by many lawyers because under the legal aid system they can make more money out of a larger volume of shorter trials."[91] A more respectable reason for avoiding jury trials arises from the fact that juries do not give reasons for their decisions. As Brian Bailey, a Nova Scotia defence lawyer, points out, "If the nature of the charge or the circumstances of the offence are such that complex questions of law arise then the advocate may be better advised to consider trial in a lower court."[92] A judge deciding a case alone will often give reasons which can be challenged on appeal. Thus a variety of factors have rendered the theoretically most popular form of criminal trial the least popular option in practice.

Provincial legislatures have drastically curtailed the right to trial by jury in civil cases. Until 1856 in Upper Canada trial by jury in civil cases was the only form of trial in the courts of common law. By 1868 the situation had been reversed and all civil actions in Ontario were to be tried by a judge alone unless a jury was requested by one of the parties.[93] The other provinces have generally followed Ontario. Except for actions involving personal reputation or liberty such as libel, false imprisonment, and malicious prosecution, the general rule in civil cases is trial by judge alone unless a party requests that a jury decide issues of fact or assess damages. Even then a jury trial may be denied if the judge deems it inappropriate. As a result, jury trials in civil cases are relatively infrequent in Canada: not more than 5 or 6 per cent of civil actions tried in the superior courts of most jurisdictions and even less than that in others.[96] But the use of juries in civil cases has not declined quite as much as in England where, since Lord Denning's decision in *Ward* v. *James*, jury trials are available in personal injury cases only in the most exceptional circumstances.[95]

Canadian judges have followed Lord Denning in questioning the competence of juries to decide complex factual issues.[96] An Ontario judge justified precluding jury trials in medical malpractice suits by this attack on jury competence:

> If during a trial a judge has difficulty understanding technical evidence he is in a position to ask questions to obtain the necessary explanation . . . . It is frequently difficult enough for an expert to explain a technical matter so that one person can understand it. It is substantially more difficult to explain it in a way that a number of different persons, each with different educational and occupational backgrounds, can do so. There are practical constraints upon the amount of time that can be taken in the education of the tribunal so that it can comprehend the complexities of someone else's field of expertise. . . . It is, we think, more probable that within some reasonable time constraints one person—the judge—can be educated than can a group of people—the jury.[97]

Along with alleged incompetence, the other judicial charge against the jury is its lack of consistency and uniformity in the application of legal rules. A Manitoba judge put it this way:

> The results of a trial before a Judge sitting alone can be predicted with much greater confidence, and prospective litigants can be advised with much greater certainty than is the case where the determination of liability and the assessment of damage is left to a jury untrained in evaluating either.[98]

Another Manitoba judge cited both of these contentions in holding that the denial of a jury trial in civil cases does not violate the guarantee of "fundamental justice" under section 7 of the Charter of Rights.[99]

The reduction of jury trials has occurred in a very closed policy system dominated by lawyers and judges. Judicial critiques of jury competence have been based on impressionistic evidence rather than solid empirical research. Nor have they objectively compared the competence and fairness of the alternative to juries as triers of fact—namely, judges sitting alone. Indeed, there is a certain immodesty in judges' assertions of their own superiority. Awareness of possible flaws in the jury as a fact-finder has not been sufficiently balanced by sensitivity to the positive values of the jury system. Those values are fundamentally political and concern the democratic quality of our justice system. They were never more succinctly put than in these words from Alexis de Tocqueville's *Democracy in America*:

> The jury is pre-eminently a political institution; it must be regarded as one form of the sovereignty of the people; when that sovereignty is repudiated, it must be rejected, or it must be adapted to the laws by which that sovereignty is established. The jury is that portion of the nation to which the execution of the laws is intrusted, as the houses of parliament constitute that part of the nation which makes the laws.[100]

The democratic value of the jury system is multi-faceted. To begin with, jury service provides one of the few opportunities for the citizen in a representative democracy to participate directly in government decision-making. Even if, as the federal Law Reform Commission's survey indicates, only 5 per cent of the Canadian population have had this opportunity, the experience may be widely shared: the commission found that 29 per cent of those surveyed knew someone who had served on a jury.[101] The 5 per cent figure can be an argument for expanding rather than contracting jury opportunities. The jury has the potential not only for contributing to citizen participation in Canadian democracy but also for keeping the law in touch with community standards and modifying the strict application of legal rules with considerations of equity.[102] This dimension of jury decision-making is a possible answer to allegations of jury lawlessness. The refusal of four Canadian juries (three in Quebec and one in Ontario) to convict Dr. Henry Morgentaler of violating Canada's abortion laws is a case in point. These juries were signalling a general dissatisfaction with the application of criminal sanctions to an issue on which there is no moral consensus. In doing so they gave reality to Patrick Devlin's famous dictum that "Each jury is a little parliament."[103]

The democratic attributes of jury trials should not be purchased at any price. If juries have difficulty assessing complex, technical information or tend to be arbitrary or unduly biased, then there may well be grounds for severely restricting, if not eliminating, them from the justice system. But in fact we have very little hard knowledge of how juries perform and what we have scarcely supports the case against the jury. The only empirical study of Canadian juries, conducted by Professor Allen Linden and Richard Sommers and focusing on decisions of Ontario juries in motor vehicle cases, showed that, contrary to rumour, juries were not overly generous in assessing damages. The one significant difference between jury awards and those of judges in similar cases was a much greater tendency of juries to apportion liability to both parties—an outcome which the authors suggest "may well accord better with the true position with regard to blameworthiness."[104] Incidentally, they also found that there was somewhat less delay in reaching jury trials than trials by judge alone and that the average length of jury trials compared with trials by judge alone was only marginally longer: 2.4 versus 1.9 days.[105] These findings were one of the factors which prompted Manitoba's Law Reform Commission to recommend that the law governing civil juries in that province be reversed so that trial by jury would be the rule rather than the exception.[106]

There has been much more research on the jury in the United States and Britain. The best-known American study, directed by Harry Kalven and Hans Zeisel, found that in both civil and and criminal cases judges disagreed with only 22 per cent of the jury verdicts and that these disagreements could not be accounted for by the complexity of the evidence.[107] Although a recent study of criminal jury trials in England found a greater frequency of questionable jury verdicts, it did not consider that this constituted support for reducing or elimi-nating jury trials.[108] Before being any further disenfranchised from the admin-istration of justice, the Canadian public might well require that the jury's critics provide more convincing evidence of jury incompetence or unfairness. We are inclined to agree with a contemporary social science assessment of the jury that "those who would wish to curtail its powers or abolish it should bear the burden of proof."[109]

There is also the possibility of reforming the jury system so as to reduce its deficiencies and reinforce its strengths. Law Reform Commission reports and scholarly publications contain a plethora of recommendations, few of which have been acted upon. Among those which stand out are permitting the jurors to take notes and submit questions to witnesses, and the preparation of accurate and understandable guidelines for judges' instructions to juries on the relevant points of law.[110] Consideration should also be given to widening the grounds of appeal in jury cases.[111] If juries are to be truly representative of the community, then jury service must be made attractive to all walks of life and biases in jury selection eliminated. Some local systems of selecting jurors are highly questionable: one town reported to Manitoba's Law Reform Commission that it only chose jurors "personally known to the selectors," and another that "no ladies with large families (i.e., with two children) would generally be considered."[112] The democratic functions of jury trials should also make us question the reduction in the size of juries from twelve to six in some jurisdictions. Six-person criminal juries in the northern territories have been found to violate the Charter of Rights.[113] Finally, the migration to Canada of "scientific" jury selection techniques developed in the United States should be carefully monitored.[114] Such techniques, with their potential for packing juries with persons sympathetic to the accused, could put in jeopardy the jury's capacity to represent the breadth of community values.

Promoting Settlement

The adversary system, along with jury trials, were central features of the English common law legal culture that originally was the dominant influence on the Canadian judicial system. Procedure and practice in the higher trial courts traditionally adhered closely to the adversarial model in which the judge's primary role is to adjudicate a dispute on the basis of submissions made by the adversaries in open court. But just as the jury trial has become a declining feature of justice in the higher trial courts, similarly there has been some movement in these courts away from strict adherence to the adversarial system. This modification of the judge's traditional adjudicative role has not been as marked as the decline of the jury. It may also be a more progressive kind of change.

The principal innovation in Canada's higher trial courts has been the introduction of judicially conducted pre-trial conferences. These conferences may serve to clarify issues and identify those which need adjudication. Approached in this way, pre-trial conferences are a way of preparing for adjudication. But they may also be a vehicle for avoiding adjudication by promoting settlement before trial. Much will depend on the orientation of the judge who conducts the conference. An "activist" judge who considers that a great many trials are unnecessary and takes pride in bringing the parties to a negotiated settlement will approach the pre-trial conference as an occasion for conciliation.[115] It must be emphasized that what is new here is not simply an interest in pre-trial settlement. The judicial branch has always counted on the vast majority of disputes, in both criminal and civil justice, being settled without a trial. The novel and problematic dimension of the pre-trial conference is the active intervention of judges in promoting or "managing" negotiated settlements.[116]

Pre-trial conferences in civil cases were used in state courts in the United States as early as the 1920s and provision for them was written into the rules of the federal courts in 1938. Since then the pre-trial conference has come to be widely used in both state and federal courts, with increasing emphasis on settlement promotion rather than its trial preparation dimension. It is now a key component of the ADR (alternative dispute resolution) movement in the United States.[117] Typically, and inevitably, this movement has begun to influence Canada. We have already seen its influence at work on family courts and small claims courts. Its primary manifestation up to now in the higher trial courts is the pre-trial conference. These conferences have been used sparingly in British Columbia since 1961 and Alberta since 1969, more extensively in Nova Scotia, and perhaps most systematically in more recent years in Ontario.[118] Since a national inventory of innovations in Canada's civil trial courts has not been made, it is difficult to say how widespread their use is in Canada today. In 1985 an amendment to the Criminal Code (which, as of June 1986 had not been proclaimed in force) made pre-trial conferences mandatory in any case to be tried with a jury. But the purpose of these conferences in criminal cases, at least in theory, is not to serve as a formal opportunity for reaching a negotiated settlement but to "promote a fair and expeditious trial."[119]

The best-documented use of pre-trial conference is in Ontario's High Court. Between 1976 and 1978 a controlled experiment was conducted in this court.[120] All the cases on its civil non-jury list (this does not include divorce cases) were randomly assigned to two groups: one group (the test group) had pre-trial conferences, the other group (the control group) did not. The results of this experiment are interesting. They showed that, contrary to research results in the United States,[121] the pre-trial conference in Ontario contributed substantially to the rate at which cases settled before trial: pre-trial settlements occurred in 25 per cent more of the test group cases than in the control group. The researchers also found that the contribution the pre-trial conference made to promoting settlements was unaffected by either the type of litigation or the amount of money in dispute. One factor which does appear to affect the results is the attitude of the judge conducting the conference. The pre-trial settlement rate was much higher in the early stages of the experiment when settlement-oriented judges conducted a larger proportion of conferences.[122]

The Ontario experiment suggests that the pre-trial conference in civil cases can contribute to what Marc Galanter has identified as the cool rationale for greater judicial involvement in the settlement process.[123] The emphasis in the cool theme is on more efficient management of judicial institutions: reduction of court case loads, less delay and expense for the litigants. From the perspective of the cool theme, the achievement of the pre-trial conference, although not negligible, should not be overrated. While the conferences may cut down on the time judges spend as adjudicators, they do take up some judge time in conciliation. In the Ontario experiment it is estimated that the pre-trial conference resulted in a 13 per cent net reduction in the amount of judge time required to dispose of cases. Also, in assessing the savings in delay and cost to the litigants, it is important to bear in mind that the pre-trial conference takes place shortly before trial after many months, if not years, of litigation and that "it is generally accepted that a range of ninety to ninety-five per cent or more of actions commenced in the High Court settle at some stage, without a pre-trial conference."[124] Still, there will be a substantial saving in time and money for litigants in that residue of cases where the pre-trial conference enables the parties to avoid a trial. If the court-induced pre-trial settlement yields a more satisfactory resolution of the dispute, the conference will surely make a positive contribution to society.

But this brings us to the central normative issue in the movement toward the judge as conciliator and to the "warm" theme underlying it. The warm theme, to quote Galanter, "refers to the impulse to replace adversary conflict by a process of conciliation to bring the parties into a mutual accord that expresses and produces community among them."[125] From this perspective, the pre-trial conference aims at supplementing and reinforcing informal settlement processes in society and producing dispute resolutions which are more satisfactory in the sense that they are mutually agreeable to both parties. The pre-trial conference's capacity to enhance the quality of dispute resolution cannot be inferred solely from the increase in pre-trial settlements. It would be instructive to ascertain the views of the actual parties to these disputes with regard to the negotiated outcomes. In Ontario the conference usually takes the form of "a business-like meeting between counsel and the presiding judge, in the absence of parties."[126] Thus there is a danger that one or both of the parties will be pressured into accepting a court-sanctioned settlement negotiated behind closed doors. Ontario and other Canadian jurisdictions have tried to avoid the danger that the pre-trial conference will undermine the prospect of a fair trial by insisting (unlike many American jurisdictions) that the judge who conducts the conference not try the case should it go to trial.

The American scholar Owen Fiss has questioned the notion that the judicial process should give priority to reaching agreeable settlements. The function of judges as public adjudicators, he has written, "is not to maximize the ends of private parties, nor simply to secure the peace, but to explicate and give force to the values embodied in authoritative texts such as the Constitution and statutes: to interpret those values and to bring reality into accord with them."[127] This attack on the pro-settlement movement reminds us that the purpose of adjudication is not simply to settle disputes, but to render authoritative decisions on disputes about legal rights and duties. This fundamental adjudicative function, however, need not be performed on all the disputes filed with trial courts. For private disputes where there is no significant legal issue at stake, and both parties admit to some liability, negotiated settlements would seem beneficial both for the parties and for society. The trial court's role in clarifying and vindicating rights will be more appropriate in the field of public law, especially in Canada where the new Charter of Rights has stimulated a host of constitutional claims.

Pre-trial conferences are by no means the only approach to reforming the operations of the general jurisdiction trial courts. Various forms of summary procedure for civil suits have been introduced in several jurisdictions.[128] These simplified forms of procedure are designed to accommodate more intermediate-sized claims that are considered too large for informal small claims procedures but not large enough to risk the cost and delay of going through all the traditional stages of litigation. The aim here is to ensure that meritorious claims are not abandoned or compromised because of the cost and inconvenience of submitting them to a full-blown trial. As Allan Hutchison has put it, "the civil justice system must not allow an inequitable settlement to become less burdensome than the cost of justice."[129] There are a number of other alternatives to traditional adjudication—for instance, court-administered arbitration and summary jury trials —which have been introduced in the United States that might be considered by Canadian trial courts.[130] It may, however, be some time before Canadian courts acquire the internal administrative strength and managerial skills required for the research and development of these alternative forms of dispute resolution.

One of the advantages of the community trial centres we have envisaged as the logical culmination of the merger movement is the greater flexibility such centres would have in matching disputes to appropriate resolution procedures. Accessibility to different forms of justice should not depend on the jurisdictional rules of a trial court hierarchy. Procedures developed in the lower civil and family courts of the provinces may be well suited for disputes that are still reserved for the higher trial courts. Accessibility to the appropriate form of case-processing is likely to be considerably greater in the "multi-door" community court house.[131] If trial courts of general jurisdiction have a long-term future in Canada, it is in this direction that they must continue to evolve.

Notes to Chapter 11

1. *A.G. Canada* v. *Law Society of B.C.* [1982] 2 SCR, at 326-27.
2. For a brief description of the process, see R.M. Jackson, *The Machinery of Justice in England*, 7th ed. (Cambridge: Cambridge University Press, 1977), ch. 1. For a more in depth account, see John P. Dawson, *The Oracles of the Law* (Ann Arbor: University of Michigan Law School, 1968), ch. 1.
3. See Brian Abel Smith and Robert Stevens, *Lawyers and the Courts* (London: Heinemann, 1967), ch. 2.
4. There is some doubt as to whether federally created courts have the constitutional status of superior courts. While there would be general agreement that the Supreme Court of Canada is a superior court, constitutional writers differ as to courts established under s. 101 for "the better Administration of the Laws of Canada."

5. A.V. Dicey, *Introduction to the Study of the Law of the Constitution*, 10th ed. (London: Macmillan, 1961), p. 193.
6. *Royal Commission of Inquiry into Civil Rights*, vol. 1 (Toronto: Ontario Ministry of Government Services, 1968), p. 279.
7. For an analysis of this phenomenon in England, see H.W. Arthurs, *"Without the Law": Administrative Justice and Legal Pluralism in Nineteenth-Century England* (Toronto: University of Toronto Press, 1985).
8. Charles J. Townshend, "Historical Account of the Courts of Judicature in Nova Scotia," *Canadian Law Times* (1899), pp. 25, 58, 87, 142.
9. Frank MacKinnon, *The Government of Prince Edward Island*, (Toronto: University of Toronto Press, 1951), p. 12.
10. Hon. Justice McKeown, "The First Supreme Court of New Brunswick," *Canadian Law Times* (1917), p. 830.
11. S.J.R. Noel, *Politics in Newfoundland* (Toronto: University of Toronto Press, 1971), p. 6.
12. See Hilda Neatby, *The Administration of Justice Under the Quebec Act* (Minneapolis: University of Minnesota Press, 1937).
13. W.R. Riddell, *The Bar and the Courts of the Province of Upper Canada or Ontario* (Toronto: Macmillan, 1928), p. 86.
14. See Margaret A. Banks, "The Evolution of the Ontario Courts, 1788-1981," in David H. Flaherty, ed. *Essays in the History of Canadian Law*, II (Toronto: Osgoode Society, 1983).
15. See Leo Pelland, "Aperçu historique de notre organisation judiciaire depuis 1760,"
    La Revue du Droit (1933), p. 14.
16. See David M.L. Farr, "The Organization of the Judicial System in the Colonies of Vancouver Island and British Columbia, 1849-71," *University of British Columbia Law Review* (1967), p. 1.
17. David R. Williams, *The Man for a New Country, Sir Mathew Baillie Begbie* (Sidney, B.C.: Gray's Publishing, 1977), p. 33.
18. See Dale and Lee Gibson, *Substantial Justice* (Winnipeg: Peguis, 1972), pp. 23-58.
19. See Horace Harvey, "The Early Administration of Justice in the Northwest," *Alberta Law Quarterly* (1934), pp. 1, 171.
20. Quoted in Bora Laskin, *The British Tradition in Canadian Law* (London: Stevens, 1969), p. 18. For an analysis of the practical inconveniences of Upper Canada's new judicial system, see William N.T. Wylie, "Instruments of Commerce and Authority: The Civil Courts in Upper Canada 1789-92," in Flaherty, ed., *Essays in the History of Canadian Law*, II.
21. J. Murray Beck, *The Government of Nova Scotia* (Toronto: University of Toronto Press, 1957), ch. 8.
22. *Black's Law Dictionary* defines equity as "Justice administered according to fairness as contrasted with the strictly formulated rules of common law. It is based on a system of rules and principles which originated in England as an alternative to the harsh rules of common law and which were based on what was fair in a particular situation."
23 Laskin, *British Tradition in Canadian Law*, pp. 10-13.
24. Banks, "Evolution of Ontario Courts," pp. 504-506.

25. Pelland, "Aperçu historique . . . ," p. 27.
26. Riddell, *The Bar and The Courts*, p. 191.
27. Banks, "Evolution of Ontario Courts," p. 513.
28. Wylie, "Instruments of Commerce and Authority," p. 18.
29. This was introduced in 1845, see Banks, "Evolution of Ontario Courts," p. 510.
30. Farr, "Organization of the Judicial System," p. 21.
31. See Monique Giard and Marcel Proulx, *Pour comprendre l'appareil judiciaire québécoise* (Sillery: Presses de l'Université du Québec, 1985).
32. For a vivid account of the peripatetic life of a superior court judge in the north, see Jack Sissons, *Judge of the Far North* (Toronto: McClelland and Stewart, 1973).
33. British Columbia appears to have had the most decentralized superior court: in 1897 residential Supreme Court judges were required for New Westminister, Clinton, Vancouver, and Kamloops as well as the capital, Victoria.
34. See, for example, the brief of the Carleton Law Association, "Proposing the Merger of the High Court of Justice with the County and District Courts," prepared by lawyers in the Ottawa area in 1982.
35. See Banks, "Evolution of the Ontario Courts."
36. In Nova Scotia until 1948, the "Judge in Equity" constituted the court of divorce and matrimonial causes because of doubts as to the province's constitutional powers to change arrangements that existed at the time of Confederation. See Beck, *Government of Nova Scotia*, p. 290.
37. Justice James Huggesson, "Issues of Merger and Specialization: a Quebec View," paper presented at annual conference of the Canadian Institute for the Administration of Justice, Osgoode Hall Law School, Toronto 1976. (At the time Justice Huggesson was the associate chief justice of the Superior Court of Quebec.)
38. Supreme Court Reorganization Act, SPEI 1975, c. 27.
39. Only New Brunswick's was established by statute; see amendment to the Judicature Act, RSNB 1979, c. 36.
40. The Divisional Court also hears appeals from lower courts; see R.F. Reid, "The Ontario Divisional Court," *Law Society of Upper Canada Gazette* (1983), p. 71.
41. Manitoba Law Reform Commission, *The Structure of Courts; Part I: Amalgamation of the Court of Queen's Bench and the County Courts of Manitoba* (Winnipeg, 1982), p. 11.
42. George Patterson, "The Establishment of the County Court in Nova Scotia," *Canadian Bar Review* (1943), p. 394.
43. County court judges in England were often selected to serve as chairmen of the county quarter sessions, and since 1972 they have served as circuit judges on England's new criminal court, the Crown Court. See I.R. Scott, *The Crown Court* (London: Butterworths, 1972).
44. See Banks, "Evolution of Ontario Courts," pp. 521-22. According to the Ontario Law Reform Commission, Ontario did not make use of this jurisdiction until 1873; see *Report on Administration of Ontario Courts*, Part 1, p. 47.
45. In Ontario, until 1984, a High Court judge had no jurisdiction to try criminal cases without a jury except under the Combines Investigation Act.
46. Ejann MacKaay, *The Paths of Justice: A Study of the Operation of the Criminal Courts in Montreal* (Montréal: Faculté de droit Université de Montréal, 1976), pp. 94-96.

47. Helen Kinnear, "The County Court Judge in Ontario," *Canadian Bar Review* (1954), p. 35.
48. Fred L. Morrison, *Courts and the Political Process in England* (Beverly Hills: Sage, 1973), p. 50.
49. SBC 1984, c. 25, s. 2; SNS 1978, c. 41, s. 7; SO 1984, c. 11, s. 32.
50. See, for example, SO 1896, c. 19, s. 3.
51. The assignment of divorce jurisdiction to county court judges sitting as local judges of a superior court was found to be constitutional by the Supreme Court of Canada in *A.G.B.C.* v. *McKenzie* [1965] SCR 490.
52. For a discussion of this type of jurisdiction, see Ontario Law Reform Commission, *Report on Administration*, pp. 171-81.
53. In some provinces these functions related to testamentary matters were shared with the superior court. For information on the assignment of surrogate and probate jurisdiction in the provinces and territories today, see Canadian Centre of Justice Statistics, *Civil Courts in Canada* (Ottawa, 1985).
54. See Ontario Law Reform Commission, *Report on Administration*, p. 160.
55. For instance, Chief Justice Evans reported that the High Court in 1983 disposed of 295 criminal cases as compared with 343 contested divorces and 4962 other civil cases. *Law Society of Upper Canada Gazette* (1984), p. 19.
56. Ontario Law Reform Commission, *Report on Administration*, p. 52.
57. *Canadian Bar Review* (1934), p. 600.
58. Leslie R. Peterson, "Proposed Reorganization of the Courts of the Province," *Advocate* (1969), p. 26.
59. For an account of these difficulties, see J.C. Anderson, "Some Thoughts on Court Reorganization," *Canadian Bar Journal* (1969), p. 72.
60. Manitoba Law Reform Commission, *The Structure of the Courts: Part 1, p. 10.*
61. Carl Baar, "Courts and Constitutions: The Institutional Setting of Judicial Administration," paper presented at Conference on Judicial Administration, State University of New York at Albany, 17 June 1986.
62. Quoted in J.N. Decore and P.P. Kerans, *Criteria and considerations which should apply to the study of the question of amalgamation of the District and Supreme Courts of Alberta* (Edmonton, 9 Nov. 1976).
63. Ibid., p. 9.
64. A strong recommendation for merger was contained in the 1973 study of the Prince Edward Island justice system conducted by a Calgary lawyer, R.A. MacKimmie, for the provincial attorney general; see *MacKimmie Report* (Charlottetown, 1973), pp. 15-20.
65. SA 1978, c. 51. The legislation was not implemented until 1979.
66. SNB 1979, c. 41.
67. SS 1979-80, c. 78, c. 91.
68. SM 1982-83-84, c. 81, c. 82.
69. Bill 38, An Act to Revise the Judicature Act, 1986.
70. Ontario Law Reform Commission, *Report on Administration*, p. 91.
71. Ibid., p. 98.
72. *Report of the Canadian Bar Association Committee on the Appointment of Judges in Canada*, p. 57.
73. Ontario Law Reform Commission, *Report on Administration*, p. 88.
74. See "Observations of the High Court of Justice to a Proposal that it be Merged

with the County and District Courts," *Law Society of Upper Canada Gazette* (1983), p. 166.

75. Ontario Law Reform Commission, *Report on Administration*, p. 91.

76. *A Study Relating to the Proposed Merger of the District Court for Saskatchewan with the Court of Queen's Bench for Saskatchewan* (Regina, 1979).

77. RSA 1980, c. 29, s. 6.

78. Judicature Act, s. 4 as amended by SNB 1981, c. 36, s. 3 and SNB 1982, c. 34, s. 2.

79. SS 1979-80, c. 91, s. 5.

80. SM 1982-83-84, c. 82, s. 10.

81. SN 1986, c. 38, s. 22.

82. An eight-region plan was originally put forward by Richard Bell in his Memorandum of Dissent in the Ontario Law Reform Commission Report and has more recently been put forward in a brief adopted by the County of Carleton Law Association; see Colin D. McKinnon, "A Brief Proposing the Merger of the High Court of Justice with the County and District Courts," *Law Society of Upper Canada Gazette* (1983), p. 108.

83. *Law Society of Upper Canada Gazette* (1983) , p. 168.

84. National Task Force on the Administration of Justice, *Justice Services in Canada, 1977-78* (Vancouver, 1979), p. 87.

85. SBC 1973, c. 196, s. 2.

86. Courts Act 1971, 20 Elizabeth, c. 2, c. 23. For an account of these reforms, see Scott, *The Crown Court.*

87. Quoted in Laskin, *The British Tradition,* p. 42.

88. Law Reform Commission of Canada, *The Jury in Criminal Trials* (Ottawa: Supply and Services, 1980), pp. 15-16.

89. Thus far Canadian judges have not been liberal in their approach to this right. The B.C. Court of Appeal rejected a challenge to the Combines Investigation Act's denial of the right to trial by jury on the grounds that s. 11(f) of the Charter does not apply to corporations; *Re PPG Industries and A.-G. Canada* (1983) 146 DLR (3d) 261. Two courts have rejected arguments that a person charged with contempt of court should have a right to a jury trial; *Re Layne and the Queen* (1984) 14 CCR (3d) 149; *R. v. Cohn* (1984) 15 CCC (3d) 150.

90. Laskin, *The British Tradition,* p. 48.

91. *Globe and Mail,* 7 Feb. 1977.

92. Brian F. Bailey, "Use of the Non-Jury Forum," in Sandra Oxner, ed., *Criminal Justice* (Toronto: Carswell, 1982), p. 144.

93. For a survey of statutory developments concerning civil juries in all jurisdictions, see Ontario Law Reform Commission, *Report on Administration*, pp. 329-35.

94. Ibid., pp. 331-34.

95. [1965] 1 All ER 563.

96. For an extreme judicial critique of jury competence, see Jerome Frank, *Courts on Trial* (New York: Atheneum, 1967), ch. 8.

97. *Soldwisch v. Toronto Western Hospital* (1983) 43 OR (2d) 449.

98. *Kisiw v. Dietz* (1969) 5 DLR (3d) 764, at 766.

99. *Martin v. Idiffe and Health Science Centre* [1984] 4 WWR 61.

100. Quoted in Valerie Hans and Neil Vidmar, *Judging the Jury* (New York: Plenum, 1986), p. 248.

101. *The Jury in Criminal Trials*, p. 14.
102. For a good discussion of this aspect of jury trials, see W. Neil Brooks and Anthony N. Doob, "Justice and the Jury," *Journal of Social Issues* (1975), p. 171.
103. Patrick Devlin, *Trial By Jury* (London: Methuen, 1956), p. 164.
104. Allen M. Linden and Richard J. Sommers, "The Civil Jury in the Courts of Ontario: A Postscript to the Osgoode Hall Study," *Osgoode Hall Law Journal* (1968), p. 255.
105. Ibid., pp. 256-57.
106. Manitoba Law Reform Commission, *The Administration of Justice in Manitoba, Part II—A Review of the Jury System* (Winnipeg, 1975).
107. Harry Kalven and Hans Zeisel, *The American Jury* (Boston: Little Brown, 1966).
108. John Baldwin and Michael McConville, *Jury Trials* (Oxford: Clarendon Press, 1979).
109. Hans and Vidmar, *Judging the Jury*, p. 251.
110. See Law Reform Commission of Canada, *The Jury in Criminal Trials*, chs. 6-7.
111. This point is emphasized as a check on criminal juries by Baldwin and McConville, *Jury Trials*, and for civil jury awards by the British Columbia Law Reform Commission, *Review of Civil Jury Awards* (Vancouver, 1984).
112. Manitoba Law Reform Commission, *Administration of Justice*, p. 10.
113. *R. v. Punch* (1985) 22 CCC (3d) 289.
114. For an analysis of these techniques, see Hans and Vidmar, *Judging the Jury*, ch. 6.
115. For profiles of some activist judges in Canada, see Jack Batten, "A New Kind of Justice," *Saturday Night*, Dec. 1982, p. 30. For a critical analysis of this approach to judging in the United States, see Judith Resnik, "Managerial Judges," *Harvard Law Review* (1982) p. 376.
116. See D. Marie Provine, "Managing Negotiated Justice: Settlement Procedures in the Courts," paper presented at Conference on Judicial Administration Research, Rockefeller College, State University of New York at Albany, 18 June 1986.
117. For an overview of these developments, see Marc Galanter, "The Emergence of the Judge as a Mediator in Civil Cases," *Judicature*, (Feb.-Mar., 1986), p. 257.
118. R.M.J. Werbicki, "The Pretrial Conference in the Supreme Court of Ontario," *Canadian Bar Review* (1981), p. 489. Pre-trial conferences are now mandatory in Ontario in all civil cases, and strongly encouraged in criminal cases in the Supreme and district courts.
119. Criminal Code of Canada, s. 553.1(2).
120. Garry D. Watson, "Judicial Mediation: The Results of a Controlled Experiment in the Use of Settlement-Oriented Pretrial Conferences," paper presented at annual meeting of the Law and Society Association, Boston, 7-10 June 1984.
121. The leading American study is M. Rosenberg, *The Pretrial Conference and Effective Justice* (New York: Columbia University Press, 1964).
122. For a presentation of the early results, see M. Stevenson, G. Watson and E. Weissman, "The Impact of Pretrial Conferences: An Interim Report on the Ontario Pretrial Conference Experiment," *Osgoode Hall Law Journal* (1977), p. 591.
123. Galanter, "The Judge as Mediator."
124. Werbicki, "The Pretrial Conference," p. 508.

125. Galanter, "The Judge as Mediator," p. 257.
126. Werbicki, "The Pretrial Conference," p. 495.
127. Owen M. Fiss, "Against Settlement," *Yale Law Journal* (1984), p. 115.
128. See W.A. Bogart, "Summary Judgment: A Comparative and Critical Analysis," *Osgoode Hall Law Journal* (1981), p. 552.
129. Allan C. Hutchinson, "The Formal and Informal Schemes of the Civil Justice System: A Legal Symbiosis Explored," *Osgoode Hall Law Journal* (1981), p. 492.
130. These alternatives are the subject of the entire Feb.-Mar. 1986 issue of *Judicature*.
131. For a description of such a centre, see Lind J. Finkelstein, "The D.C. Multi-Door Courthouse," *Judicature* (Feb.-Mar. 1986), p. 305.

CHAPTER 12
PROVINCIAL COURTS OF APPEAL

In the four previous chapters we examined courts whose primary adjudicative function is to serve as courts of first instance, deciding cases through trial before a judge or a judge and jury. In this chapter our attention will be on courts that perform the appellate function, reviewing the decisions of the trial courts. Although the provincial courts of appeal are by no means the only courts of appeal in Canada and not always the final courts of appeal, they do perform the great bulk of the appellate work in Canada's third branch of government.

On a national basis we can think of these courts as the country's primary intermediate courts of appeal—intermediate in the sense that they are between the provincial and territorial trial courts and Canada's highest court of appeal, the Supreme Court of Canada. In civil cases, except for small claims cases and some family cases where the first appeal goes from a Provincial Court to a section 96 trial court and that small but growing special body of federal law matters which are handled by the Federal Court of Appeal, the basic right of appeal from the court of first instance is to a provincial court of appeal. In criminal matters, except for summary offences where the initial appeal is again from the Provincial Court to a section 96 trial court, the accused and the prosecution can appeal both the verdict and the sentencing decision of the trial court directly to the provincial court of appeal.[1]

In the vast majority of appeals, the decision of the provincial court of appeal is final. With very few exceptions, there is no automatic right to a second appeal from the provincial courts of appeal to the Supreme Court of Canada.[2] To go on to the Supreme Court, the losing party in the provincial court of appeal must seek "leave to appeal" either from the provincial appeal court itself (an option few lawyers choose) or from the Supreme Court of Canada.

In deciding the cases that come before them the provincial appeal courts must serve two rather different purposes in the justice system. Their first function is to correct injustices or errors that may have occurred in the lower court. This is the function that will be readily understood by most citizens. Our modern liberal society has come to accept as a fundamental justice need the opportunity for the party who has lost in the court of first instance to have the trial court's decision reviewed by a higher court. This ideal of a basic right of appeal to at least one higher court is now, as the Ontario attorney general's study of the provincial appeal court observes, "so firmly entrenched in the traditions of our courts that any effective restriction on the ability of the dissatisfied litigant to call for a review by a superior court might well be looked upon by the public as a denial of a time-honoured right."[3] In Canada today it is only in the smallest of small claims cases (for instance cases under $500 in Ontario) that the decisions of the court that first tried a case must be accepted as final. For most civil and criminal cases the provincial court of appeal performs this essential error-correcting function.

The second function of the provincial court of appeal is less recognized by the public. That is its jurisprudential, law-making function. In reviewing trial court decisions the appeal court is concerned primarily (although not exclusively) with legal issues rather than factual issues or questions of evidence. As was argued in chapter 1 and is today widely acknowledged by judges and lawyers, judicial decisions on contested points of law inescapably have a creative legislative dimension. While the decisions of trial courts, especially superior trial courts, partake of this legislative dimension, they are not nearly as important in this regard as decisions of the provincial courts of appeal. The principle of *stare decisis* in our common law system means that the decisions of the provincial court of appeal are binding on all courts below it in the same province and are "strongly persuasive" authorities for trial courts in other provinces.[4] This law-making function of the provincial courts of appeal affects the development of all three streams of Canadian law: common law, statute law—both provincial and (except for matters reserved exclusively for the Federal Court of Canada) federal—and constitutional law. As the Supreme Court of Canada focuses more and more on cases involving the interpretation of federal statutes and the Constitution, the provincial appeal courts' work in developing common law and interpreting provincial statutes has become increasingly important. In these areas the provincial courts of appeal tend to function as final courts of appeal. In one crucial area of criminal law, sentencing, they have long served as our final courts of appeal, since the Supreme Court of Canada does not review the decisions of provincial courts of appeal on the fitness of sentences unless a sentencing decision involves an important question of law.[5]

Today provincial courts of appeal in Canada are hard pressed to perform both appellate functions well. A continuing growth in the propensity of Canadians (and their lawyers) to exercise their basic right of appeal makes it difficult for courts of appeal in the larger provinces to dispose expeditiously of the high volume of routine appeals and still find time to produce well-crafted decisions on those new and important legal questions which are coming before them in ever-increasing numbers. Tension between these two functions and the problem of trying to do justice to both through a single institution are generating proposals for the restructuring of provincial appellate systems.

Emergence of Separate Courts of Appeal

In the previous chapter we noted that at the time of Confederation the provincial courts of appeal were staffed by judges who also served on the superior trial courts. Ontario was the first province to move toward a full-fledged court of appeal with judges who did nothing but appellate work. In 1874 it made provision for a chief justice and three other judges of appeal to serve full-time on the Court

TABLE 12.1 PROVINCIAL AND TERRITORIAL COURTS OF APPEAL

PROVINCE OR TERRITORY	COURT	NO. OF JUDGES*	DATE SPECIALIZED COURT OF APPEAL ESTABLISHED‡
Alberta	Alberta Court of Appeal	10	1919
British Columbia	British Columbia Court of Appeal	11	1907
Manitoba	Manitoba Court of Appeal	6	1906
New Brunswick	New Brunswick Court of Appeal	6	1966
Newfoundland	Newfoundland Court of Appeal	4	1974
Nova Scotia	Appeal Division of Supreme Court	7	1966
Ontario	Ontario Court of Appeal	16	1874
P.E.I.	Appeal Division of Supreme Court	3	1987†
Quebec	Quebec Court of Appeal	16	1974
Saskatchewan	Saskatchewan Court of Appeal	7	1915
N.W.T.	N.W.T. Court of Appeal	Alta. Ct. of Appeal & N.W.T. Sup. Ct.	–
Yukon	Yukon Court of Appeal	B.C. Ct. of Appeal & Yukon Sup. Ct.	–

* Based on salaries provided for in the Judges Act. Judges serving on a supernumary basis are not included.

† The establishment of a separate appeal division of P.E.I.'s Supreme Court is scheduled for 1987.

‡ Specialized means a court of appeal with judges who do only appellate work.

of Error and Appeal, although when necessary judges from the superior trial courts could serve on the appeal court. Over the next five decades Ontario's superior court was frequently restructured, with judges from the appeal division and the High Court (Trial Division) sharing the appellate function. It was not until 1931 that the structure we know today was in place. The Court of Appeal for Ontario was established then as a branch of Ontario's Supreme Court with its own full-time judges. The other branch of the Ontario Supreme Court is the High Court, which is basically a trial court.

As table 12.1 shows, the development of separate provincial courts of appeal did not occur in the other provinces until the twentieth century. The situation was complicated in Quebec by the fact that following Confederation the Court of Queen's Bench in that province functioned both as the provincial court of appeal and a trial court for the most serious criminal offences. When exercising original criminal jurisdiction it was called the Court of Queen's Bench, Crown Side. Over the years this trial function became more and more nominal as most of the criminal trial work was done by judges of the Superior Court. Still, the nominal duality of the Court of Queen's Bench continued until 1974, when the Court of Queen's Bench was abolished and the Quebec Court of Appeal established.[7] Prince Edward Island, not surprisingly, is the last province to establish a separate court of appeal. In 1986 the federal Judges Act was amended in anticipation of provincial legislation reorganizing the Supreme Court of Prince Edward Island into a three-judge appeal division and a four-judge trial division.[8] The two northern territories are still deemed to be too small to warrant having their own courts of appeal. Their courts of appeal consist of the judges serving on the superior courts of the territories plus members of the British Columbia Court of Appeal in the case of Yukon and members of the Alberta Court of Appeal in the case of the Northwest Territories.

The provincial courts of appeal have not totally severed their links with the superior trial courts from which they emerged. They are considered to be one of the province's superior courts. In most provinces, the court of appeal is legislatively defined as a branch of the province's Supreme Court, the other branch being the superior trial court. Thus references to the "Supreme Court" of a province are likely to be confusing in Canada. In a province such as Ontario or Nova Scotia, "Supreme Court" may refer to the province's court of appeal, its superior trial court, or both. In British Columbia, on the other hand, the Supreme Court is the province's second highest court, the superior trial court. Nowhere is the title used, as the uninitiated might expect, to refer solely to a province's highest court, its court of appeal. A similar confusion attaches to the title of chief justice. Both the superior trial court and the provincial court of appeal have "chief justices" (the heads of all other provincial courts are "chief judges"). But the chief justice of the court of appeal is referred to as the chief justice of the province. In some provinces the judges of one branch of the Supreme Court can, under certain conditions, serve in the other branch.[9] The equality of professional status between the judges of the two provincial superior courts is underlined by the fact that under the Judges Act they are paid the same salaries.

The emergence of the provincial courts of appeal, reflects profound changes in Canada's legal and political culture. The right of appeal, which is now apparently a "time honoured" right, was scarcely recognized a century or so ago. Canadians in the late nineteenth century were not particularly troubled by the fact that when an appeal occurred the panel of judges hearing it might include the trial judge whose decision was being reviewed. Today Canadians would find this situation intolerable. This change in attitude concerning the requirements of justice represents a strengthening of liberal ideals in Canada. A more liberal society is less inclined to acquiesce in the unbridled authority of the trial judge and more likely to insist on the right of appeal as an essential ingredient of justice. A growing egalitarian sentiment in the latter decades of this century has through legal aid programs made the right of appeal more accessible to all classes. This development still has some way to go: the opportunity to appeal is often denied in cases involving small amounts of money which may be of great concern to persons with low incomes; even in serious civil and criminal cases its availability normally depends on the discretion of legal aid officials; those with limited resources much more often than governments, corporations, or the wealthy would be deterred by the prevailing system of court costs in Canada under which the losing side is required to indemnify the successful party for a significant portion of its lawyers' fees and expenses.[10]

In one respect Canada has been more liberal than the United States in extending the right to appeal. The Criminal Code of Canada provides an opportunity to appeal with leave against the sentence imposed by the trial court in cases involving indictable offences. In the United States, appellate review of sentences is not available in the federal courts or in most of the state court systems. On this issue the American judicial system would appear to place a higher value on institutional convenience than the rights of the individual.[11] But the "tory" side of Canada's political tradition can also be seen in its treatment of appeals. The state has appeal opportunities in criminal cases that are very nearly reciprocal with those of the accused.[12] Americans are often shocked to learn that the crown (that is, the prosecutor) in Canada can with leave of the court appeal against an acquittal on an issue of law and against a sentence.[13] The provincial court of appeal in reviewing the fitness of a sentence may increase the punishment as well as lessen it. This tory touch in the Canadian appeal system cannot be attributed to Canada's English heritage. There is only a very limited right of the crown to appeal in England.[14]

In the emergence of courts of appeal as distinct institutions at the top of the provincial court hierarchy we can also see a growing understanding of the legislative role of appellate courts. Once the policy-making elite in the justice field come to recognize that the court of appeal is not simply correcting error but is also developing the law of the province, there is a greater emphasis on the need for continuity and collegiality in its structure and operation. An ad hoc rotating membership of trial judges is unacceptable for a body of jurists writing the jurisprudence of a province. Some perception of the policy-making role of the provincial court of appeal has probably also been a factor in the insistence of even tiny Prince Edward Island, with a population of only 125 000, on having its own court of appeal. The idea of a Maritime Court of Appeal was put forward by the Rowell-Sirois Royal Commission in 1940 and again in the 1973 MacKimmie Report on the Prince Edward Island judicial system.[15] Indeed, both MacKimmie and Rowell-Sirois suggested a regional court of appeal for the Prairie provinces also but these proposals did not gain a following in either region. The provincial court of appeal has come to be seen as an essential element in the governing structure of a province.

Case-Load Pressures

Case loads can raise very different problems for provincial appellate structures. The provincial population may be too small to generate enough appeals to justify appointing three judges (the minimum number for a court of appeal) on a full-time basis to a provincial court of appeal. That is certainly why Canada's two smallest provinces, Newfoundland and Prince Edward Island, have been the last to establish courts specializing in the appellate function. But nowadays it is the reverse problem that is becoming more severe. Mushrooming case loads are threatening the capacity of courts of appeal in the larger provinces to function effectively.

A remarkable growth in the volume of appeals appears to be a general North American phenomenon over the last twenty-five years. Marc Galanter's review of research on patterns of litigation in the United States shows that increases in the case loads of American appeal courts have outpaced those of trial courts. He reports, for instance, that the number of appeals filed in the federal courts of appeal nearly quintupled from 1960 to 1980.[16] Unfortunately, we do not have good case-load data for all Canadian courts of appeal (or, for that matter, for any type of provincial court). However, what fragmentary evidence we do have points to substantial increases in appeals in Canada. In 1978 the Kelly Report on Ontario's Court of Appeal disclosed that criminal appeals heard by that court had increased twice as fast as the province's population.[17] Piecing together data from this report with statistical information included in the annual opening of courts address by Ontario's chief justice,[18] we can see that the number of appeals heard by Ontario's Court of Appeal in civil and criminal matters doubled from 1967 to 1983. Data contained in a report of the Canadian Centre for Judicial Statistics on workload pressures indicate that other provincial courts of appeal may be experiencing similar pressures to Ontario's. For the three provinces participating in that study, British Columbia, Quebec, and Saskatchewan, civil appeal rates considerably in excess of Ontario's are reported.[19]

Factors already referred to in this book have certainly contributed to the expansion of appeal court business: an increase in litigation and trial court business, the growth of the legal profession, publicly funded legal aid, new legislation, and constitutional provisions. The development of legal aid plans across Canada from the late 1960s through the 1970s may account for a sizeable portion of the increase in appeals (particularly criminal appeals) during this period. Now that these programs have reached maturity we might expect some levelling off in the rate of increase. The shift in litigation patterns from traditional areas of private and commercial law to family law (in 1982 one-third of the appeals heard by the Ontario Court of Appeal dealt with family law[20]) new kinds of private suits (wrongful dismissal, for instance) and many new areas of public law, ranging from environmental regulation to the new Charter of Rights, tend to increase not only the quantity of cases coming before the provincial courts of appeal, but also the complexity and novelty of the issues they must decide.

The public interest groups which, partly through the stimulus of the Charter of Rights, are making more use of the courts as an arena of political combat, have the resources and incentive to push cases to the appeal court level. At the appeal level they have an opportunity to obtain rulings on disputed points of law that have more legislative force than the decisions of trial courts.[21] Provincial governments have used the reference question device to bring major constitutional questions before their courts of appeal. Manitoba, Newfoundland, and Quebec all initiated challenges in their courts of appeal to the Trudeau government's attempt to patriate the Constitution unilaterally.[22] Ontario has recently sought opinions from its court of appeal on the adequacy of francophone education in its school system and the constitutional validity of full public funding of the Roman Catholic separate schools.[23]

Up to a point, heavier case-load burdens can be dealt with simply by expanding the membership of provincial appeal courts. Certainly this has been done in Canada. Since 1970 the number of judgeships on provincial courts of appeal has increased by 65 per cent. But as the size of these courts creeps up through the teens, we begin to approach the limit of this particular response to the expansion of appellate business. With a sixteen-judge court of appeal, such as Canada's two largest provinces now have, let alone the twenty-plus benches which, if the present approach is continued, they will have in the near future, it becomes virtually impossible to retain the minimal amount of collegiality and consistency required of these courts. Here we must remember that with regard to a great many issues the provincial courts of appeal function as final courts of appeal. The Supreme Court of Canada hears about one hundred cases a year while the provincial courts of appeal are deciding somewhere between four and five thousand. This means that, at most, only 2 to 3 per cent of the provincial appeal court decisions are reviewed by the Supreme Court. To an ever-increasing extent the provincial court of appeal acts, in effect, as the supreme court of the province. It is interesting to observe that not one of the American states has permitted its supreme court to grow beyond nine judges.[24] In Canada four provincial courts of appeal are already beyond that size.

Provincial courts of appeal normally sit in three-judge panels. Occasionally, for extremely important cases, five-judge panels will be used. Five-judge panels of both the Manitoba and Quebec courts of appeal, for example, answered the reference questions concerning unilateral patriation. Justice John Morden of Ontario's Court of Appeal calculates that with sixteen judges it is possible to have 560 different three-judge panels and 4368 different five-judge panels. As he points out, "the experience of any appellate court that sits in divisions is that the danger of conflicting decisions is a real and constant one."[25] This problem is clearly exacerbated the larger the courts of appeal become. The problem is not simply increasing likelihood of inconsistencies in the rulings of different panels on similar points of law but diminishing interaction and coherence in developing the province's jurisprudence. There should be plenty of scope for a diversity of outlooks and dissenting opinions on a lively court of appeal;[26] but this pluralism works best when it is experienced through the interaction of judges hearing cases together and articulating their differences in majority and dissenting opinions.

In continental civil law systems, where the creative, personal dimension of adjudication is not acknowledged, there is little concern about the collegiality of courts of appeal. France's highest court, Le Cour de Cassation, has a membership of close to one hundred.[27] But the prime function of that court, as its name connotes, is to break or overcome mistakes made by the lower courts. In the legal culture of the English-speaking common law world, where courts of appeal are expected to write coherent jurisprudence to guide the courts below as well as correct their errors, collegial interaction in the production of that jurisprudence is essential. The governing law of the province should not depend on the luck of the draw in the composition of the panel that happens to decide the appeal.

Responses to Case-Load Pressures

Increasing case loads bring pressure on courts of appeal to deal more expeditiously with cases. To keep abreast of the case load and avoid delay, appeal court judges find that reserving judgment after the hearing in order to write well-researched and well-reasoned opinions increasingly becomes a luxury. In Alberta and Ontario over 90 per cent of the provincial appeal courts' judgments are delivered at the conclusion of the hearing.[28] If the appeals which are dealt with in this assembly-line fashion really do not raise any important legal issues requiring clarification by the court of appeal, then nothing is lost. However, it is doubtful that this is the case. As R.A. Macdonald has argued, "Since, in theory, appellate argument is generally restricted to questions of law, even a *pro forma* appellate judgment will almost never be a strictly logical piece of deductive reasoning from precise black-letter rules."[29] In some of the appeals which are dealt with summarily, the court of appeal may without any express justification be dismissing an alternative approach to the law. This approach can camouflage a quiet, unaccountable conservative approach to an appeal court's law development function. Also, by failing to provide written judgments that clarify and resolve contested legal issues, the assembly-line approach to the appellate function may actually foster appeals and perpetuate the congestion problem in the appeal courts.

Other steps have been taken to improve the operational efficiency of provincial courts of appeal which are more in keeping with their jurisprudential responsibilities. Some use is being made of pre-appeal conferences. In Ontario, beginning in 1984, in appeals expected to last longer than a day such conferences were conducted by the associate chief justice "in order to narrow the issues and shorten the length of the hearings."[30] But no research comparable to that done on pre-trial conferences in the high courts has been carried out to test the effectiveness of these conferences in conserving judge time or in giving the appeal a sharper focus. Indeed, empirical research on the operations of Canada's intermediate courts of appeal is even more underdeveloped than research on the higher trial courts.[31] One innovation in these courts that follows an earlier development in the Supreme Court of Canada is the hiring of law clerks to assist the judges in their law-making function. The law clerks are recent graduates from the university law schools who spend their "articling" year in the court of appeal researching material on new legal issues. In the provinces where they are used (for instance, British Columbia and Ontario) they will likely be of particular importance in cases involving the Charter of Rights where many constitutional concepts are being interpreted for the first time. The law clerk is yet another essentially American innovation in the administration of justice in Canada and one that tends to modify the adversary system of decision-making by bringing to the judge's attention arguments and material not submitted or examined by the parties.

Another American approach to appellate decision-making, however, which is not likely to gain acceptance in Canada is the application of strict time limits on oral arguments. Canadian appellate procedure is distinctively Anglo-American. In the English courts of appeal there are no written submissions and oral arguments are all-important. In the United States, appeal courts place much more emphasis on written briefs and usually place strict time limits on oral arguments—frequently no more than a quarter or a half hour for each side.[32] Canadian lawyers like to have the best of both worlds. Briefs, or "factums," as they are called, are submitted in advance summarizing the facts and law relevant to the issues on appeal and hearings take place without any formal time limits. Just how time-consuming the oral argument stage can be is indicated by a passage in the 1986 report of Chief Justice Howland of Ontario's Court of Appeal in which he reports that one lawyer recently suggested he would need thirty days to argue an appeal. The chief justice remarked that "the court is reluctant to place fixed time limits on oral argument but expects all counsel to be succinct and only to take such time as is absolutely necessary to present their clients' position."[33] The chief justice's polite admonition is not likely to have much effect. Lawyers nurtured in the traditional adversarial system will resist any significant restriction on their freedom to control the conduct of a case.

Aside from professional resistance, another consideration that should make Canadians cautious about any drastic curtailment of the oral part of appellate proceedings is the closed nature of the appellate process. It is a process dominated by legal professionals—lawyers and judges. Ordinary citizens do not participate as witnesses or jurors. The actual parties are generally only observers at the hearing.[34] One practice which opens the appellate process somewhat in Canada is the granting of intervenor status to public interest groups to argue issues not fully developed by the principal parties. This practice may be particularly important in complex public law cases. In the reference case examining the adequacy of Ontario's French-language school facilities in terms of the guarantee of minority language education in the Charter of Rights, in addition to the federal and Ontario governments, twenty organizations and groups (including the two opposition political parties) were represented in the proceedings. Case-load pressures may lead to some modification of this liberal approach to granting intervenor status.

Instead of cutting down severely that part of the appellate process which contributes to public accessibility, it might be wiser to consider structural changes designed to enable the highest courts of the provinces to focus their energy more effectively on the legislative function of appeal courts. The most fully elaborated structural reform of this kind is that recommended in 1977 to Ontario's attorney general by a committee chaired by Arthur Kelly, a retired member of the Ontario Court of Appeal.[35] The Kelly Report proposed that the Court of Appeal be divided into a juristic section and a general section. The juristic section would be a comparatively small and integrated body of eight judges whose members could "work in close and continuing community in the development of the law."[36] The general section would deal with "the prepondering number of appeals which do not require that consideration be given to questions of general importance." While the juristic section would remain fixed in size, the general section would have all the remaining judges on the court of appeal and would continue to expand as case levels require. Litigants could proceed directly to the juristic section if they could persuade judges in that section that their case involved an issue worthy of engaging the law-development section's attention. Otherwise they would take their appeal to the general section, with the further possibility of later applying to the juristic section to review the decision of the general section.

The Kelly proposal was not adopted. It suffers from an overly simplistic distinction between appeal cases that have a "policy" or "law-development potential" and those that are "ordinary" or "precedent-bound." Most legal scholars today would agree with R.A. Macdonald's blunt assertion that "this dichotomy simply does not exist."[37] A case that reaches the appeal stage must raise an issue on which there are two possible views as to what the relevant law is or how it should be applied. The theory of adjudication put forward earlier in this book would certainly prompt us to question the Kelly Committee's assumption that most appeals can be decided mechanically without any creative input by the judiciary. This is not to say that as we move up the appellate ladder there is no need to ration access to the highest court in a jurisdiction. But it is one thing to ration access on the basis of the public importance of the legal issues at stake as is now done with the Supreme Court of Canada; it is quite another to assume that judges lower in the hierarchy should decide appeals without a view to their law-development potential. The Kelly proposal also posed a serious personnel problem. Telling members of a provincial court of appeal that they are about to be relegated to a division which deals only with intellectually unchallenging routine matters would be rather like telling the majority of professors in a university department that they will teach only the large elementary courses. Being assigned to the realm of the ordinary does not go down well with any group of reasonably ambitious, self-respecting professionals.

There are two alternatives to the Kelly approach to restructuring the appellate system which have been used in other countries. One is to have the provincial court of appeal function through panels specializing in different areas of law. The large European courts of appeal endeavour to maintain continuity and collegiality in this fashion. The French Cour de Cassation has five specialist sections (*chambres*).[38] Similarly the German appellate structure assigns judges to divisions which cluster together related areas of law.[39] As we noted earlier in discussing superior trial courts, the common law legal mind is attracted to the generalist judge and tends to resist organizing the higher levels of the judiciary around this kind of subject matter specialization. But perhaps the time has come to reconsider the traditional objections to this approach. Paul Carrington has shown how the work of the circuit courts of appeal in the American federal court system might be grouped around a broad enough range of subjects to minimize the danger of fostering the tunnel vision which may arise from too narrow a specialization.[40] Assignments to particular sections need not be permanent. The procedure of having the court sit *en banc* to resolve differences between its sections might be adapted from the circuit courts of appeal in the United States.[41]

A more modest version of the specialized chamber approach would be to establish a criminal law division of the provincial court of appeal. A few American states, notably Alabama and Texas, have organized their appellate systems this way.[42] There is also English precedent for such an arrangement. A Court of Criminal Appeal for England and Wales was established in 1907. It was recently replaced by the criminal division of the Court of Appeal (the intermediate high-volume court of appeal in the English judicial system).[43] Any proposal that comes wrapped in the Union Jack is still more likely to find favour with Canada's legal establishment. In the Canadian context, given our liberal treatment of the right to appeal in criminal cases, a criminal division would likely absorb more than half the court of appeal. In England the volume of appeals is kept down through a very tight screening process administered by individual members of the Queen's Bench Division of the High Court (the superior trial court).[44] It is doubtful that this method of controlling appeal opportunities in criminal cases would be acceptable in Canada. Eventually there may be a stronger case for establishing a special criminal court of appeal on a national basis just below the Supreme Court than for creating criminal divisions of provincial courts of appeal.

The other major structural alternative to the Kelly proposal is the establishment of an intermediate court of appeal between the trial courts and the highest court of appeal in the province. This is the change in appellate structure that is most likely to be adopted in Canada. As far back as 1968 Ontario's Chief Justice James McRuer observed that "All states in the United States with a population comparable to that of Ontario have intermediate Courts of Appeal as part of the appellate structure."[45] This is the change the appellate judges themselves seem to be pressing for. It was recently proposed to the Ontario government by the Ontario Court of Appeal and the chief justice of the British Columbia Court of

Appeal has made a strong case for it.[46] It is a change which is already partially in place in Ontario.

Toward an Intermediate Provincial Court of Appeal

This partial step toward an intermediate court of appeal was taken in 1972 when the Ontario Divisional Court was established.[47] The Divisional Court is a division of the High Court (Ontario's superior trial court). It functions through three-judge panels established on an annual basis. The primary function of the Divisional Court is to hear appeals from administrative tribunals and applications for judicial review of administrative agencies in the province.

Technically, judicial review of administrative activities is not considered to be an appellate function. It is a jurisdiction developed by judges of superior courts as a means of giving relief to those who claim that an administrative agency has exceeded its lawful authority, deviated from required procedure or misinterpreted the law. Traditionally this jurisdiction has been exercised by individual members of superior trial courts and, indeed, was the essential basis for maintaining the power of the judiciary to intervene as a check on the ever-expanding activities of the modern administrative state. Setting up a special branch of the High Court to carry out the judicial review function represents an effort to strengthen this form of judicial power by making it more collegial, more coherent, and more accessible.[48] A similar objective, as we shall see in the next chapter, inspired the establishment of the Federal Court of Canada in 1971. These efforts at shoring up judicial review of administrative activity, however debatable they may be as public policy,[49] like the Charter of Rights, have the effect of strengthening the judicial branch of government in Canada. They show a high-level deference on the part of legislators for the judiciary in the contemporary Canadian state.

The Divisional Court was also given some appellate jurisdiction over the decisions of trial judges. Decisions of High Court judges under the Business Corporation Act, the Assessment Act, or on interlocutory matters (that is, procedural or technical issues arising in the course of the trial), decisions of district court judges acting as local superior court judges and judgments or orders of masters of the supreme court are among the hodge-podge of matters that can be appealed to the Divisional Court.[50] A considerably bigger step toward making the Divisional Court an intermediate court of appeal was taken in 1984 when it was given jurisdiction to hear civil appeals from the High Court or the district court in cases involving not more than $25 000.[51] This change still falls far short of establishing a full intermediate appeal court and does virtually nothing to improve the court of appeal's capacity to develop the law of the province in a coherent and collegial way.

A full intermediate court of appeal would presumably absorb the Divisional Court's jurisdiction and become the court to which a right of appeal would lie from all trial courts and tribunals. Not only would it hear appeals which now go as of right from the higher trial courts to the court of appeal, but it would also hear appeals from the "lower" Provincial Courts which are now heard by single judges of the district court or High Court. Although there might be a further right of appeal to the province's highest court where there is a dissent in the court of appeal or in cases involving constitutional interpretation, generally appeals to the highest court would require (as they do now from the Divisional Court) leave of that court. Thus the province's highest court would become truly a supreme court selecting most of the cases on its docket on the basis of the importance of the policy issues in them for the province and the country.

Such an appellate hierarchy is much more appropriate for provincial judicial systems than the existing hierarchy of trial courts. With the up-grading of the qualifications and quality of appointments to the Provincial Courts, it makes little sense to have their decisions reviewed, as in many instances they are now, by single judges of the section 96 trial courts. Indeed, when this occurs in appeals from the family divisions of Provincial Courts it may frequently mean that the appeal is heard by a judge who is less knowledgeable about family law than the judge being appealed from. An intermediate appeal court would thus fit in well with merger of the trial courts and the development of regional trial centres envisaged in earlier chapters. In the larger provinces the court would be large enough to organize on a regional basis. This would make the right of appeal considerably more accessible than it is now. Quebec's Court of Appeal has always had a Montreal and a Quebec City division and the three western provinces have made provision for the hearing of appeals in the two major provincial cities. But elsewhere the appellate function has been concentrated in the provincial capital.[52]

The creation of an intermediate appeal court would undoubtedly add to the cost of Canada's judicial system. But just how much the net additional cost would be and whether this cost would be offset by benefits to be obtained through a smaller, more effective final court of appeal in the province are questions which have not been carefully considered. These are precisely the kind of questions which, under the joint federal-provincial "management" of section 96 courts, tend to be neglected. In British Columbia and Ontario merger of the county and district courts with the superior trial courts might create a surplus of trial judges who could be used to staff a new intermediate appeal court. Promotion to a court of appeal might soothe the egos of those superior court judges who are unhappy about the implications of merger for their elite status. On the other hand, there is the problem of fashioning smaller provincial supreme courts out of the over-sized courts of appeals. Justice John Morden has suggested this might be done gradually through attrition.[53] Given the human problems involved and the strong possibility that some members of the provincial courts of appeal not elevated to a new provincial supreme court would launch an attack in the courts on the constitutional validity of what they would see as a demotion from the apex of the province's judicial system, the attrition approach, expensive as it may be, is perhaps the most viable transition strategy.

The cost to the litigant rather than the taxpayer has been the strongest argument against the intermediate court of appeal. Both McRuer in 1968 and Kelly in 1977 dismissed the two-tiered appellate system because of the inconvenience, added delay, and expense they felt it would inflict on litigants. A two-tier system does confront cases flowing through the provincial judicial system with the possibility of being processed at four levels before final resolution: trial, two levels of provincial appeal, and the Supreme Court of Canada. The threat of further appeal can be used as a bargaining device to force the winning side in a lawsuit to accept less than it is entitled to. However, we must remember that Ontario with its Divisional Court and appeals from Provincial Courts to single judges of section 96 trial courts already has developed a partial, ramshackle, two-tier system without producing any of the offsetting advantages of a smaller, more cohesive provincial court of appeal. Also, it is possible to mitigate some of the problems associated with the introduction of another layer of appeal. R.A. Macdonald has suggested a form of interim payment following trial that could discourage "tactical appeals" by economically stronger parties.[54] Where there is a need for a fairly quick resolution of a major issue of public law, provincial governments can continue to use the reference case procedure to bring these questions directly to the highest court in the province.

The time has certainly come to consider a fundamental restructuring of provincial appellate systems. Our contemporary political and legal culture, whether we like it or not, will produce an appeal rate that is going to generate at least five hundred appeals per million of population.[55] Appeal systems in provinces with populations at or over the two million level are likely to experience case loads in excess of one thousand a year. Thus far, the larger provinces have been coping with these case loads simply by adding more judges to their courts of appeal and dealing with an increasing proportion of appeals in a summary fashion. The intermediate court of appeal, with all of its warts, would seem to have more to offer in terms of both quality and accessibility as a long-run solution for provincial appeal systems in at least the larger provinces.

The Provincial Courts of Appeal in National Perspective

Up to now in this chapter we have been considering provincial courts of appeal mainly in terms of their role in provincial judicial systems. But these courts must also be viewed from a national perspective. It is from the provincial courts of appeal that the Supreme Court receives most of its cases. Their only rival in this regard is the Federal Court of Appeal. But the Federal Court, as we shall see in the next chapter, focuses on a narrow range of federal legal issues arising out of the review of federal administrative agencies. Although appeals from the Federal Court have grown over the last decade and half, they still constitute only about 10 per cent of the Supreme Court's docket.[56] The provincial courts of appeal are still, nation-wide, the principal intermediate courts of appeal for federal law and constitutional law as well as provincial law.

Earlier in the chapter we pointed out that in the vast majority of appeals the provincial court of appeal makes the final decision. Unless there is some radical change in the structure or functioning of the Supreme Court of Canada, this tendency of provincial courts of appeal to become, in effect, final courts of appeal is bound to increase. While the number of cases the provincial appellate courts handle keeps going up, the number decided by the Supreme Court is at best stable, and in fact in recent years has been declining.[57] The legislation recently introduced in Parliament to eliminate the automatic right of appeal in criminal cases will increase the finality of provincial appeal court decisions in this important field of federal law.[58] The only kind of case in which there will be a right of appeal to the Supreme Court is in reference cases initiated in the provincial courts of appeal.[59] In all other cases, access to the Supreme Court will require leave of that Court (or of the court being appealed from) based on an assessment of the public importance of the issues in the case.

The importance of provincial courts of appeal as national law makers is by no means confined to those of their decisions which are final. In those that are appealed to the Supreme Court, the reasoning contained in the opinions written by members of the provincial appeal courts will usually provide the primary material for the Supreme Court's deliberations. The quality of these opinions can have a very great influence on the work of the Supreme Court. A provincial court of appeal bold enough to deviate from what it considers to be an out-dated precedent established by the Judicial Committee of the Privy Council (Canada's final court of appeal until 1949) or from an earlier decision of its own predecessors, can put law reform possibilities on the Supreme Court agenda.[60] Provincial court of appeal judges will often be influential pioneers in working out interpretations of new statutory or constitutional provisions. That has certainly been the case with the new Charter of Rights. Sometimes a provincial appeal judge's opinion will be adopted in whole or in part by the Supreme Court of Canada. This can happen even with a dissenting opinion. A case in point is Justice Samuel Freedman's dissenting opinion in the *Dominion News* case on the meaning of obscenity in the Criminal Code. Although it was a dissenting opinion in the Manitoba Court of Appeal, it was adopted by a unanimous Supreme Court and became in effect the law of Canada.[61]

The provincial courts of appeal have exhibited a considerable pluralism in their decision-making. Professor F.L. Morton's statistical study of the decisions of Canadian courts on the Charter of Rights indicates that the courts of appeal have been less liberal in their treatment of the Charter than trial courts.[62] The success rate of Charter cases in provincial courts of appeal from 1982 to 1985 was 24 per cent as compared with 28 per cent in the section 96 trial courts and 40 per cent in the trial courts presided over by provincially appointed judges.[63] But among the provincial courts of appeal there were some significant differences: the Nova Scotia Appeal Court stood out "as the most pro-Crown in its approach to Charter cases," with a success rate of 14 per cent while Ontario's was "the most libertarian," upholding Charter claims in 29 per cent of the cases it decided.[64]

In an earlier, more fragmentary study of provincial appeal court decisions in criminal cases, Philip Lister saw evidence of "two definite and distinct tendencies or approaches."[65] Among one group of courts—Alberta, Manitoba, Nova Scotia, Saskatchewan, and the Supreme Court of Canada—he found the success rate in criminal appeals ranged from 12 to 20 per cent, whereas among a more "liberal" group—British Columbia, New Brunswick, Ontario, and Quebec—they ranged from 41 to 47 per cent. Evidence of diverse approaches among provincial appeal courts is all the more interesting when we bear in mind that their judges are all appointed by the federal government. They are selected, however, from the legal profession in their respective provinces. It may be that the prevailing legal culture in a province has an ideological flavour that accounts for the distinctive approaches of its federally appointed judges.

One questionable kind of pluralism in the provincial courts of appeal occurs in reviewing sentences. The Criminal Code gives provincial courts of appeal a very wide power to "consider the fitness of the sentence" and, within the limits prescribed by law (which are very wide) to vary the sentence downward or upward.[66] Some years ago J.V. Decore pointed to the "extraordinary discrepancies in almost all aspects of sentencing, not only as between territorial jurisdictions, but sometimes within the jurisdictions themselves."[67] The Quebec Court of Appeal, for instance, in one case approved a twenty-five-year prison term for a youth convicted, on a first offence, of armed robbery, whereas in another armed robbery case it reduced a sentence of ten years and ten lashes to three years and five lashes.[68] The concern here is not the lack of uniformity in sentencing but the absence of a coherent set of principles as to the weight that should be given to the various factors that affect the fitness of a sentence. In chapter 8 we drew attention to the fact that judges in the lower criminal courts in carrying out their important sentencing function have not had the benefit of a clear and consistent set of guidelines evolved by the provincial courts of appeal.

Some may conclude that the remedy lies in giving the Supreme Court of Canada the power to review the sentencing decisions of provincial appeal courts. But such a reform would be of dubious merit. The Supreme Court, as we shall see in chapter 14, is already bogged down coping with its existing responsibilities, especially interpreting the new Charter of Rights and Freedoms. It is not in a position to take on another major policy responsibility. But a more fundamental point must be raised: an appellate court—be it the Supreme Court of Canada or some new national court of appeal on criminal matters—may not be the best kind of institution for developing the country's sentencing policy. At issue in working out a sentencing policy are the questions of why we punish—to deter, to reform, to right wrongs—and how to achieve the agreed-upon purposes of punishment. The range of experience and knowledge from the humanities and social sciences required to generate intelligent answers to these questions might be better assembled on a non-judicial commission. Such a body could also work more accountably and flexibly with elected legislatures in making sentencing policy. Must we always turn to the judicial branch to resolve complex ethical issues of public policy? It is to be hoped that the Canadian Sentencing Commission which will issue its report in the spring of 1987 will not rely on appellate court jurisprudence as the only mechanism for reforming sentencing policy in Canada.[69]

Up to a point, pluralism among Canada's provincial courts of appeal does not pose a serious problem for the Canadian federation. In matters of law subject to provincial jurisdiction, different approaches by courts of appeal to common law issues or statutes in similar fields should, in principle, be no more objectionable than different approaches by provincial legislatures. Those who object to this kind of diversity would prefer that Canada be a unitary rather than a federal state. Even in fields of federal law and constitutional interpretation there is room for some diversity of approach among Canada's second-highest courts of appeal. Different approaches at this level can articulate options for the Supreme Court before it attempts final resolution of major controversies. But demands on the Supreme Court's resources may become so heavy that differences among the provincial courts of appeal on key issues are left unresolved so that the Criminal Code and other federal statutes come to mean very different things in different parts of the country.

Concerns of this kind have made the creation of a national intermediate court of appeal an imminent possibility in the United States.[70] In 1984 Justice Willard Estey of the Supreme Court of Canada put forward the idea of a national intermediate court of appeal for Canada made up of members of provincial courts of appeal sitting a few times a year.[71] In the United States, with nearly ten times the Canadian population and nearly ten times as many applications per year for appeal to the Supreme Court, there may well be a strong case for such an intermediate national court of appeal. In Canada we still have a considerable way to go in improving the efficiency of our Supreme Court before Canadians should be asked to give serious consideration to establishing another layer of appeal between the provincial courts of appeal and the highest court in the land. For the time being the argument for an intermediate court of appeal is much more compelling in a provincial than in a national context.

Notes to Chapter 12

1. On questions of law there is a right to appeal. Otherwise the appeal requires leave of the appeal court. See Criminal Code, ss. 603-5.
2. The right to appeal to the Supreme Court in civil cases involving $10 000 or more was abolished in 1974. In criminal cases there has been a right to appeal to the Supreme Court in indictable cases on an issue of law where the provincial court of appeal was not unanimous or reversed the verdict of the trial court. Legislation to repeal this automatic right of appeal was introduced in the federal Parliament in 1986 (Bill C-105).
3. *Report on the Attorney General's Committee on the Appellate Jurisdiction of the Supreme Court of Ontario* (Toronto, 1977), p. 14. The committee that produced

this report was chaired by Arthur Kelly, a retired member of the Ontario Court of Appeal. It will be referred to hereafter as the Kelly Report.

4. See Gerald L. Gall, *The Canadian Legal System*, 2nd ed. (Toronto: Carswell, 1983), ch. 10, for a more detailed exposition of the operation of *stare decisis* in the Canadian judicial system.

5. The Supreme Court has ruled that as a matter of law it could grant leave to review a sentence, but as a matter of policy it will not unless there is an important question of law arising out of sentencing. *R. v. Gardiner* [1982] 2 SCR 368.

6. For a summary of these developments, see Margaret A. Banks, ''The Evolution of the Ontario Courts, 1788-1981,'' in David H. Flaherty, *Essays in the History of Canadian Law*, II (Toronto: Osgoode Society, 1983).

7. Jérôme Choquette, *Justice Today* (Québec: Gouvernement du Québec, 1976), pp. 77-78.

8. SC 1986, c. 35, s. 1.

9. In Ontario, for instance, the patents of all Supreme Court judges appoint them to one branch and ex officio to the other branch. The chief justice of the Court of Appeal can assign members of his court to sit in the High Court in Toronto or, with the concurrence of the chief justice of the High Court, members of the High Court to sit in the Court of Appeal; Courts of Justice Act, ss. 9-10.

10. This indemnity in Ontario amounts to one-half to two-thirds of the successful party's legal bill. See John W. Morden, ''Appellate Judging—Some Canadian Features,'' *Law Society of Upper Canada Gazette* (1985), p. 72.

11. See Paul D. Carrington, ''Crowded Dockets and the Courts of Appeal: The Threat to the Function of Review and the National Law,'' *Harvard Law Review* (1969), p. 578.

12. A major exception is that only the accused can with leave of the court of appeal, appeal a question of fact or mixed law and fact.

13. The Ontario Court of Appeal has ruled that the crown's right of appeal does not violate the protection against double jeopardy guaranteed in section 11(h) of the Charter of Rights. *R. v. Morgentaler, Smoling and Scott* (1985) 22 DLR (4th) 641. The Supreme Court of Canada will deal with this issue on appeal.

14. See Martin L. Friedland, *Double Jeopardy* (Oxford: Clarendon Press, 1969), ch.10.

15. MacKimmie Report (Charlottetown: Minister of the Attorney General, 1973), pp. 49-52. *Report of the Royal Commission on Dominion-Provincial Relations* (Ottawa, 1940), Book 2, pp. 170-71.

16. Marc Galanter, ''Reading the Landscape of Disputes: What We Know and Don't Know about the Allegedly Contentious and Litigious Society,'' *UCLA Law Review* (1983), p. 38.

17. Kelly Report, p. 7.

18. ''Reports on the Administration of Justice in Ontario on the Opening of the Courts for 1984,'' *Law Society of Upper Canada Gazette* (1984), p. 14.

19. Canadian Centre for Judicial Statistics, *Court Management Studies: Workload Measures Project* (Ottawa, 1985). Table 9 in this report shows a rate of civil appeals per one million population varying from 119 in Quebec to 212 in British Columbia. Ontario's in 1983 was 66. The rates of criminal appeals for British Columbia and Saskatchewan are also higher than Ontario's.

20. *Law Society of Upper Canada Gazette* (1982), p. 16.

21. See, for example, Canadian Advisory Council on the Status of Women, *Women and Legal Action: Precedents, Resources and Strategies for the Future* (Ottawa, 1984).

22. For a summary of these cases, see Peter H. Russell, *Leading Constitutional Decisions*, 3rd ed., (Ottawa: Carleton University Press, 1982) p. 502.

23. *Reference Re Education Act* (1984) 10 DLR (4th) 491; *Reference re Bill 50, An Act to amend to Education Act* (1986) 53 OR (2d) 513.

24. H. Ted Rubin, *The Courts: Fulcrum of the Justice System* (Pacific Palisades: Goodyear Publishing, 1976), table 4, pp. 128-29. While the state supreme courts have been kept small, the thirty-eight states with intermediate courts of appeal have expanded these courts indefinitely.

25. John W. Morden, "Appellate Judging," p. 55.

26. For an empirical account of policy differences within the Ontario Court of Appeal, see J.T. Holmes and E. Rovet, "The Ontario Court of Appeal: Some Observations on Judicial Behavior," *Osgoode Hall Law Journal* (1969), p. 81.

27. See Henry J. Abraham, *The Judicial Process*, 4th ed. (New York: Oxford University Press, 1982), p. 275.

28. John W. Morden, "The Partnership Between Bench and Bar," *Law Society of Upper Canada Gazette* (1981), p. 77.

29. R.A. Macdonald, "Speedy Justice for the Litigants: Sound Jurisprudence for the Province?" *Osgoode Hall Law Journal* (1978), p. 608.

30. "Reports on the Administration of Justice in Ontario on the Opening of the Courts in 1985," *Law Society of Upper Canada Gazette* (1985), p. 9.

31. For an assessment of the state of research on appellate courts in the United States, see Stephen L. Wasby, "The Study of Appellate Court Administration: The State of the Enterprise." paper presented at Conference on Judicial Administration Research, Rockefeller College, State University of New York at Albany, 16-18 June 1986.

32. For a comparison of British and American practice, see Delmar Karlen, *Appellate Courts in the United States and England* (New York: New York University Press, 1963).

33. "Reports on the Administration of Justice in Ontario or the Opening of the Courts in 1986," *Law Society of Upper Canada Gazette* (1986), p. 11.

34. Under s. 615 of the Criminal Code an accused person who is represented by counsel is not entitled to be present at the appeal.

35. *Kelly Report*.

36. Ibid., p. 18.

37. Macdonald, "Speedy Justice for the Litigants," p. 607.

38. Abraham, *The Judicial Process*.

39. Daniel J. Meador, "Appellate Subject Matter Organization: The German Design," *Comparative Law Review* (1969), p. 532.

40. Carrington, "Crowded Dockets," pp. 587-96.

41. For a discussion of their procedure, see ibid., p. 581.

42. Rubin, *The Courts*, p. 127.

43. Abraham, *The Judicial Process*, p. 264.

44. Kelly Report, p. 81.

45. *Report of Commission of Inquiry Into Civil Rights* (McRuer Commission), 2 (Toronto, 1968), p. 663.

46. John W. Morden, ''Appellate Judging—Some Canadian Features,'' pp. 55-56, and N.T. Nemetz, address delivered to the Canadian Institute for Advanced Legal Studies, Stanford University, July 1986.

47. For an account of this court by one of its members, see R.F. Reid, ''The Ontario Divisional Court,'' *Law Society of Upper Canada Gazette* (1983), p. 71.

48. This indeed was the basic theme of the McRuer Commission Report which recommended the Divisional Court.

49. For a recent debate on the subject, see Canadian Institute for the Administration of Justice, *Judicial Review of Administrative Rulings* (Montreal: Yvon Blais, 1983).

50. For a more detailed account of the jurisdiction originally assigned to the Divisional Court, see Ontario Law Reform Commission, *Report on the Administration of Ontario Courts* (1973), Part I, ch. 8.

51. Courts of Justice Act, so 1984, c. 11, ss. 15, 36.

52. In Ontario panels of the Divisional Court sit on circuit in different parts of the province. Also in Ontario the Court of Appeal hears some appeals in Kingston Penitentiary.

53. John W. Morden, ''Appellate Judging—Some Canadian Features,'' p. 55.

54. Macdonald, ''Speedy Justice for the Litigants,'' p. 610.

55. The Canadian Centre of Judicial Statistics, *Workload Measures Project*, reports appeal rates for civil and criminal cases combined for Saskatchewan in excess of 500 per million and a slightly lower rate for British Columbia. The rate shown for Quebec is well below this level but the report says that this is likely due to under-reported case-load data for criminal appeals in Quebec.

56. Statistics released by the registrar of the Supreme Court show that 29 of the 266 cases heard by the Supreme Court from 1983 to 1985 come from the Federal Court of Appeal.

57. The Supreme Court's case load is discussed below in chapter 14.

58. See note 2, *supra*.

59. Supreme Court Act, s. 37.

60. For a discussion of provincial appeal courts' treatment of *stare decisis*, see Mark MacGuigan, ''Precedent and Policy in the Supreme Court,'' *Canadian Bar Review* (1967), p. 71.

61. *Dominion News and Gifts Ltd.* v. *The Queen* [1964] scr 253.

62. F.L. Morton and Michael J. Withey, ''Charting the Charter, 1982-1985: A Statistical Analysis,'' paper presented at annual meeting of the Canadian Political Science Association, Winnipeg, 6-8 June 1986.

63. Morton and Withey note that there may be a bias in reporting decision of Provincial Courts toward including decisions in which the Charter claim is successful. So the actual success rate in Provincial Courts may be substantially lower than 40%.

64. Ibid., p. 11.

65. Philip G. Lister, ''Criminal Trends in Appellate Courts of Canada,'' *Chitty's Law Journal* (1975), p. 84. Lister's study is based on cases reported in the *Canadian Criminal Cases* reporting service between late 1970 and early 1974.

66. Criminal Code, s. 614.

67. J.V. Decore, ''Criminal Sentencing: The Role of the Canadian Courts of Appeal and the Concept of Uniformity,'' *Criminal Law Quarterly* (1964), p. 373.

68. The cases are described in ibid. pp. 344-48.

69. The Canadian Sentencing Commission's Report was released in March 1987.
70. For a discussion of various alternatives for dealing with the workload problems of the u.s. Supreme Court, see "Of High Designs: A Compendium of Proposals to Reduce the Workload of the Supreme Court," *Harvard Law Review* (1983), p. 307.
71. For a discussion of Justice Estey's proposal and other restructuring alternatives, see the editorial "Entre Nous" in *The Advocate* (1986), pp. 11-13.

CHAPTER 13
THE FEDERAL COURT

The Federal Court of Canada first opened its doors on 1 June 1971. The establishment of the Federal Court represented the first major expansion in nearly a century of what we have called "the purely federal courts": that is, courts whose judges are appointed by the federal government and which are organized and maintained by the federal Parliament and government. The addition of this court to the Canadian judicial system had important implications for the judicial branch of government. It was designed to strengthen judicial involvement in federal administration and, as we have already noted in chapter 3, it moved Canada a step closer to the American dual court system.

Despite the significance of these implications, the founding of the Federal Court received little political attention. There were a couple of days of discussion in the House of Commons, a handful of lawyers and law professors made submissions to a House of Commons committee, and a few back-page newspaper articles noted the Court's opening day.[1] Again the political scientist should be struck by how closed the policy-making process is in the field of judicial structure. Political scientists, indeed, have virtually ignored the Federal Court. Little empirical research has been done on it and textbooks on Canadian government at most devote only a few lines to it.[2] And yet, when we consider the Federal Court's role, the work assigned to it, and the cases that flow through it, it is evident that the court has a considerable potential for altering the way Canada is governed and for shaping the rights and freedoms actually enjoyed by Canadian citizens and those who would like to become Canadian citizens.

Reasons for Establishing the Court

The establishment of the Federal Court did not result from any widespread public clamour for reform of the federal court system. Nor is it evident that there was any pressure for it within the legal profession. On the contrary, much of the professional comment at the time of its founding and since has been negative. It would appear that the creation of the court was primarily an "inside job"; its principal architects were officials in the federal Justice Department, the minister of justice at the time, John Turner, and possibly members of the Exchequer Court (which the Federal Court absorbed), especially its president, W.R. Jackett. The court was designed to achieve two improvements in the administration of justice in Canada: first, to relieve the Supreme Court of Canada of the burden of hearing routine appeals from the Exchequer Court and certain federal administrative tribunals, and secondly, to strengthen judicial review of federal administration.

The Exchequer Court, it will be recalled from chapter 3, was the purely federal trial court created by Parliament, along with the Supreme Court of Canada, in 1875. As the court's name implies, its main function, initially, was to hear cases involving claims against the federal treasury.[3] Besides its jurisdiction over disputes arising from the enforcement of federal revenue laws, the Exchequer Court was the only court in which an action could be brought against the federal crown and it had concurrent jurisdiction with the provincial superior courts to hear civil suits in which the federal crown was the plaintiff. The Exchequer Court also tried cases in several very technical fields of federal law: namely, admiralty law, and the law relating to patents, copyright, trademarks (what lawyers call "intellectual property"). Because the Exchequer Court was a court of first instance, there naturally had to be a right of appeal from it and, in the absence of any intermediate federal court of appeal, that appeal was to the Supreme Court of Canada. Since 1887 the losing party in any case involving more than $500 had the right to appeal a final judgment of the Exchequer Court to the Supreme Court of Canada.[4] Although the volume of these appeals had not been great in the past, in recent times, according to the minister of justice, they were taking up "a very high percentage" of the Supreme Court's time.[5]

Now most of this appellate burden would be assumed by the Appeal Division of the new Federal Court. The trial division of the Federal Court would replace the Exchequer Court and the appeal division (also to be known as the Federal Court of Appeal) would hear appeals as of right from the trial division. The Federal Court of Appeal would also replace the Supreme Court as the first court of appeal from federal administrative tribunals such as the Immigration Appeal Board and the Tariff Board. An appeal from the Federal Court of Appeal to the Supreme Court would be available as of right from judgments in cases involving more than $10 000 and otherwise with the leave of the Supreme Court.[6]

This part of the Federal Court package should be seen as the first step toward reshaping the role of the Supreme Court. By 1970 there was a growing recognition that if the Supreme Court was to discharge its function effectively as Canada's highest court of appeal in all areas of law, it could not afford to fritter away its time on routine appeals which did not involve the resolution of major controversies about the proper meaning and application of the law. The crucial step was not taken until 1974, when appeals as of right from both provincial courts of appeal and the Federal Court of Appeal to the Supreme Court of Canada in civil cases, regardless of the amount of money in dispute, were abolished.[7] The Supreme Court of Canada from that point on became, in effect, its own gatekeeper, granting leave to appeal on the basis of the public importance of the issues raised in the case. The Federal Court Act, by removing from the Supreme Court's docket routine appeals in such areas as contested income tax cases, patent controversies, and maritime suits, enabled the Supreme Court to move closer to fulfilling its essential mandate.

The second objective of the Federal Court project—the reform of judicial review of federal administrative agencies—was given more emphasis by its sponsors and was the source of considerable controversy. Here it is important to bear in mind the difference between rights of appeal and what the lawyers call "judicial review." There was and continues to be a right of appeal from some of the independent administrative agencies Parliament has created. This right of appeal on some policy issues might be to a higher executive body—for instance, to the cabinet in the case of the National Energy Board—or on matters of law to a court. Under the Federal Court Act, as we have noted, the Federal Court of Appeal would replace the Supreme Court of Canada as the primary forum for hearing appeals from federal boards and tribunals. But, quite aside from statutory appeal provisions, judicial review of administrative decisions can often be obtained through the common law remedies which have been fashioned by the superior courts over many years. These remedies include the so-called prerogative writs such as *certiorari* (quashing the decision of a tribunal) or *mandamus* (ordering an agency to perform a duty required of it by law) or court orders such as injunctions (ordering government to halt an action jeopardizing someone's legal rights).[8] In Canada this kind of judicial review of federal or provincial adminstrative activity was generally obtainable only in the provincial superior courts.[9] Under section 18 of the Federal Court Act this jurisdiction (except for the writ of *habeas corpus*) so far as it applies to agencies of the federal government was taken away from the provincial superior courts and assigned exclusively to the trial division of the Federal Court.

The main rationale for this transfer of jurisdiction was to provide a basis for developing federal administrative law in a more unified and cohesive fashion. Judicial review of administative activity usually calls for an interpretation of the legislation that establishes an agency and defines its powers and procedures. There was an apprehension, in the words of one commentator, "that, with the provincial superior courts all having jurisdiction at times over a particular federal tribunal, there was a serious chance of a multiplicity of interpretations across Canada of that tribunal's empowering statute."[10] With federal agencies regulating activities across Canada (for instance, the Canada Labour Relations Board) it was sometimes difficult to ascertain which provincial superior court was the appropriate forum in which to challenge an administrative decision. A federal court would have a clear Canada-wide jurisdiction and could develop expertise in administrative law issues.

A strong case can be made for the advantages of specialization in this area. There is a need on the part of judges exercising judicial review powers in the modern administrative state to be sensitive to both the collective interests served by regulatory agencies and the rights of individuals. An overly activist court in this field can paralyse effective administration and substitute the biases of amateur judges for policies developed by expert and representative boards. On the other hand, judicial restraint should not be taken to the point where highly autonomous agencies of the state can become a law unto themselves, effectively accountable to no one for the balance they strike between administrative efficiency and fair procedure. In France this entire area of adjudication is handled by a special branch of the judiciary, the Conseil d'État. In modern times all the English-speaking common law countries have evinced some dissatisfaction with the way administrative law has been developed by the ordinary courts. Reform efforts have generally involved some movement toward codifying administrative law and establishing more specialized and collegial forms of judicial supervision. This movement is evident in the establishment of Ontario's Divisional Court and again here in the establishment of the Federal Court.

Besides the transfer of traditional judicial review jurisdiction to the trial division of the Federal Court, the Federal Court Act contained another component which its authors advertised as a major innovation in the reform of administrative law. This was section 28 of the act which established a new remedy available only in the appeal division of the new court and only against decisions or orders of administrative bodies required to be made "on a judicial or quasi-judicial basis." Section 28 set out a mini-code of the grounds upon which such decisions could be overturned. These grounds included a failure to observe "a principle of natural justice" or basing a decision on "an erroneous finding of fact . . . made in a perverse or capricious manner." How this new approach to judicial review of federal administrative activities administered by the appeal division would co-exist with the traditional remedies to be administered under section 18 by the trial division, and with the statutory rights of appeal from some federal tribunals, would become a major source of confusion in the Federal Court's early years.

The motivation for establishing the Federal Court went beyond these rather technical, law reform interests. The Federal Court was also part of the Trudeau government's political agenda. The late 1960s and early 1970s were the years when the federal government was beginning to mount a counter-offensive against province-building. Many of the new public services which had developed since World War Two, though deriving much of their financial support from the federal government, were delivered to citizens by provincial governments. There was concern in Ottawa with the centrifugal implications of this trend and a desire to augment the ways in which the federal government could make its presence felt in the daily lives of citizens other than as a tax collector. The Federal Court was part of this strategy. By opening offices and hearing cases in major cities across the country, a federal justice flag would be visible to the people. Some of the critics of the Federal Court Act argued that reform in federal administrative law did not require the establishment of a new court and that the real motive behind the legislation was this political objective of establishing a larger "federal presence."[11]

In the House of Commons, John Turner emphasized the new court's accessibility. Litigants, he said, "will be able to obtain not only a trial on their doorstep . . . but they will be able to obtain as well an appeal at their doorstep."[12] Under Justice Jackett's presidency, the Exchequer Court had been making itself more available to hear cases outside of Ottawa. The Federal Court would continue this trend: both of its divisions would be "itinerant" or "circuit" courts. Of course, while the Federal Court might be more accessible than the Exchequer Court, it was questionable whether it would be more accessible than provincial superior courts. The Conservative opposition criticized the Federal Court bill on this ground, especially the clause requiring all members of the court to reside within twenty-five miles of Ottawa.[13] Turner defended this provision as a means of ensuring some measure of collegiality within the court. The accessibility of the Federal Court to litigants outside Ottawa would depend on its judges becoming "frequent flyers."

One other facet of the nation-building dimension of the Federal Court project was the additional jurisdiction given to the court under section 23 of the act to try private suits in three areas of federal legislative competence: bills of exchange and promissory notes, aeronautics, and interprovincial works and undertakings. The Federal Court's jurisdiction in these areas, as in cases involving maritime law, would be exercised concurrently with provincial courts. The constitutional validity of this part of the Federal Court's jurisdiction was to be thoroughly undermined by subsequent rulings of the Supreme Court of Canada.

Although the creation of the Federal Court was at least in part politically motivated, it did not provoke much political reaction. Most of the criticism at the time of its founding came from experts in administrative law concerned about the confusion they predicted (rightly as it turned out) would arise from the bill's provisions dealing with administrative law. Later on provincial leaders questioned both the constitutional validity of certain sections of the Federal Court Act and the practical disadvantages of this move toward a dual court system. The provinces "unanimously expressed these concerns" about the Federal Court at a federal-provincial conference of attorneys general in 1975.[14] The federal attorney general indicated that he was reviewing the role and jurisdiction of the court but no proposals were forthcoming at the time. Since then the court has not been on the country's political agenda.

The Court's Basic Structure and Functions

The new Federal Court of Canada when it was first established was a twelve-judge court—not much larger than the eight-judge Exchequer Court whose judges and jurisdiction it absorbed. The judges were appointed to the court's two divisions: the chief justice and three judges to the Court of Appeal, and the associate chief justice and seven judges to the Trial Division. Although in law judges appointed to one division are *ex officio* members of the other division,[15] in practice the judges stick to their own division.

In Table 13.1 we can see how the Federal Court has more than doubled in size in a decade and a half. The table also shows how the appeal division has grown from one-third to nearly 45 per-cent of the court. This reflects the fact that in some respects the appeal division is a court of first instance. Under section 28, applications for judicial review come to it directly from administrative bodies as do appeals under a number of federal statutes. Also, the appeal division is

TABLE 13.1   GROWTH OF THE FEDERAL COURT, 1971-1985

YEAR	TRIAL DIVISION	APPEAL DIVISION	TOTAL
1971	A.C.J. * + 7	C.J. † + 3	12
1973	A.C.J. 9	C.J. + 5	16
1983	A.C.J. + 11	C.J. + 9	22
1985	A.C.J. + 13	C.J. + 10	25

*A.C.J. = Associate chief justice
†C.J. = Chief justice
Source: Revised Statutes of Canada, 1970, c. 6 (2nd Supp.); Statutes of Canada: 1974-1975-
1976, c. 48, s. 2; 1980-81-82-83, c. 157, s. 1; 1985, c. 38, s. 11. Reproduced with
permission of the Minister of Supply and Services Canada.

more extravagant in its use of judges as its cases must be heard by panels of at least three judges, whereas in the trial division judges hear cases sitting alone. The court's judicial staff can be supplemented by the appointment of members of the provincial superior, county, or district courts as deputy judges.[16] Such appointments require the approval of the associate chief justice and provincial attorney general. Deputy judges have come to be used less and less, but the provision for them in the Federal Court Act bears witness to the integrated nature of the Canadian judicial system.

As was discussed in Part Three, the method of appointment, remuneration, qualifications, and terms of office (except for mandatory retirement at seventy rather than seventy-five)[17] of Federal Court judges are essentially the same as for the judges of the provincial superior courts. One distinctive feature of the Federal Court's composition is its bicultural character. When it was enacted, the Federal Court Act stipulated that at least four of the judges had to be appointed from the bar or section 96 bench of Quebec.[18] As the court expanded, this requirement was not adjusted to ensure that one-third of the justices were from Quebec. In 1985 it was changed to a requirement that eight of the court's twenty-five members come from Quebec.[19] The point of this requirement is not simply to provide francophone judges but to ensure there are judges with a background in Quebec's distinctive civil law system. This may seem like an odd rationale for a court established for the better administration of federal laws. However, we must bear in mind that the court has exclusive jurisdiction to hear suits against the federal crown and when these suits arise in Quebec, civil liability, contractual obligations, and other such matters will be determined according to Quebec's civil law.

As can be seen from table 13.2, the work of the trial division of the Federal Court basically consists of the jurisdiction formerly exercised by the Exchequer Court plus the responsibility, transferred from the provincial superior courts, of exercising the traditional forms of judicial review over the federal administration. The items are listed in table 13.2 according to the frequency with which they

TABLE 13.2   WORK OF THE TRIAL DIVISION OF THE FEDERAL COURT, 1971-1985

TYPE OF PROCEEDING	AVERAGE NO. OF CASES INSTITUTED PER YEAR
Admiralty	944
Matters instituted against the crown	630
Tax appeals	357
Patent, copyright, and trademark	313
Matters instituted by the crown	256
Prairie Grain Advance Payment Act	177
Section 18, judicial review of administration	173
Other	107

Source: *Federal Court of Canada Statistics*, Federal Court of Canada (Ottawa, 29 Jan. 1986), pp. 60-78.

are instituted in the court. The top five represent the principal Exchequer Court areas of jurisdiction. The fifth of these, "matters instituted by the crown," has declined sharply since the 1970s as the result of constitutional restrictions imposed on the Federal Court's jurisdiction by the Supreme Court of Canada, which we shall discuss later in the chapter. The item just below this, the Prairie Grain Advance Payment Act, takes up very little of the court's time: initiating proceedings in the Federal Court is simply a step the government must take in order to recover advances made to farmers under the act.[20] Here the court is serving primarily as a debt collection agency. It is also noteworthy that very little use has been made of the court's "nation-building" jurisdiction in the area of federal legislative competence covered by section 23 of the Federal Court Act.

The magnitude of the numbers shown in table 13.2 is apt to be misleading. The figures refer to actions filed with the court, not to cases actually tried. As with all trial courts, most cases registered with the court are settled before trial. In the Federal Court's case, pre-trial settlements owe little to the intervention of the court. Pre-trial conferences are relatively rare and are used primarily to prepare for a long trial rather than to promote settlement. Since 1974 the average number of trials per year has been just under 250, and has not risen significantly in recent years. But trials constitute only 16 per cent of the matters heard by the court.[21] Much of the court's time is taken up handling (not always with a hearing) procedural requests or "motions," which are a prominent aspect of litigation in the areas of law (especially patent law) dealt with by the court.

Turning now to the appeal division, table 13.3 shows how its work has been distributed over the three sources of its jurisdiction. What stands out is the predominance of applications for the novel form of judicial review under section 28 of the act. However confusing its scope and application may have been, clearly a great many people have tried to use section 28 as a way of attacking

TABLE 13.3   *WORK OF THE FEDERAL COURT OF APPEAL, 1971-1985*

TYPE OF PROCEEDING	NUMBER INSTITUTED	AVERAGE PER YEAR	%
Section 28, judicial review of administrative bodies	8376	572	69
Appeals from trial division	3172	211	25
Appeals from administrative bodies	760	51	6
Applications for extension of time	1576	105	50
Applications for leave of appeal	962	64	56

Source: *Federal Court of Canada Statistics*, Federal Court of Canada (Ottawa 29 Jan. 1986), pp. 36, 37, 39.

decisions of federal administrative boards and tribunals. These figures do not show how successful these efforts were. The jurisdictional muddle we will discuss in the next section may have meant that a fair number of applications resulted in a ruling that the party was seeking relief in the wrong division of the court.

Clearly the Federal Court of Appeal's time is largely taken up with administrative law. Although the appeal division deals with traditional Exchequer Court matters in hearing appeals from the trial division, even within this branch of its work cases involving administrative law under section 18 are the fourth-largest category of appeals from the Trial Division. The right to appeal questions of law directly to the Federal Court of Appeal from certain administrative tribunals is provided for under a number of statutes. Although these appeals account for only 6 per cent of the business instituted in the Federal Court of Appeal, it can exercise greater power in deciding these appeals than it can in handling cases under section 28. With the latter, if it finds fault with an administrative tribunal's decision it can only set the decision aside, whereas in dealing with appeals it can substitute its own decision for that of the tribunal.[22]

The Federal Court of Canada has acquired a number of other functions in addition to its core jurisdiction. The federal government has tended to treat the court as *its* superior court and assign a variety of judicial and semi-judicial tasks to "its" judges rather as the provinces are prone to do with judges of "their" superior courts. For instance, the trial division of the Federal Court serves as the citizenship court hearing appeals from citizenship "judges."[23] One of the most onerous burdens on the court is imposed by the Unemployment Insurance Act under which the cabinet appoints members of the Federal Court to serve as "umpires" to hear appeals from boards of "referees."[24] Since 1977 these appeals have averaged over one thousand a year.[25] The Law Reform Commission of Canada has suggested that this work might more appropriately be done by a specialized administrative tribunal.[26] Other legislation has given the Federal Court responsibilities that have an important bearing on the quality of democratic government and civil liberties. Under the Access to Information Act and the

Privacy Act, it is to the Federal Court's trial division that disgruntled citizens or a frustrated information commissioner can appeal.[27] When the new Canadian Security Intelligence Service was set up in 1984, the Federal Court was given an important role in controlling its use of intrusive investigatory powers. Permission to plant bugs, open mail, conduct surreptitious entries, or access confidential private information would depend on the issuance of a warrant granted by a judge of the Federal Court.[28] The 1986 reforms of competition policy designate Federal Court judges to sit with lay persons on the new Competition Tribunal.[29] The federal government has certainly found it convenient to have its own judicial reservoir. But it does not appear to give much thought to the appropriateness of the mix of functions assigned to the Federal Court.

The Jurisdictional Muddle

From its inception the Federal Court has been plagued with a number of jurisdictional complexities. The worst of these has concerned whether a case challenging administrative activity should be brought before the court's trial or its appeal division. The new remedies against federal administrative bodies created by the Federal Court Act were to be available only in the Federal Court of Appeal. Indeed, when these section 28 remedies are available they take precedence over any of the traditional remedies available in the trial division. But these new remedies cannot be applied to "a decision or order of an administrative nature not required by law to be made on a judicial or quasi-judicial basis." This distinction between purely administrative activities and activities which are to be carried out in a judicial manner may sound simple enough on the surface, but in practice it is extremely difficult to apply. Over a great many years courts in the English-speaking world have not been able to establish guidelines for applying this distinction with any certainty. Thus the division of labour between the court's two divisions was based on language which had the effect, in the words of David Mullan, of "cementing the follies of the past."[30] This uncertainty has meant that often lawyers have appeared before one division only to be told that their case must be taken to the other division.

An additional source of uncertainty has been the concept of a "decision or order." An early decision of the Federal Court of Appeal held that section 28 cannot be used against an order or decision which an agency makes in the course of proceedings but which is not its final decision.[31] As a result, judicial review of a case before a federal administrative tribunal may often be fragmented: interlocutory rulings (given in the course of proceedings) are challengeable in the trial division, while the final decision is challengeable only in the Appeal Division.

Uncertainty concerning the division of labour between the court's two levels was not the only source of confusion. Numerous questions arose about the proper limits of both divisions' jurisdiction to review federal administration activities. The judicial review of both divisions applies to any "federal board, commission or agency.'' But section 2(g) of the Federal Court Act defines "federal board, commission or tribunal" very broadly to include anybody or person "exercising . . . powers conferred by or under an Act of the Parliament of Canada" except persons appointed under provincial authority and section 96 judges.[32] Some crown corporations such as the CBC have been held to be inappropriate targets for judicial review by the Federal Court, but it is far from clear how to draw the line between included and excluded agencies.[33] Even the exclusion of section 96 judges has been problematic. A 1975 decision of the Supreme Court of Canada found that when a section 96 judge decides an extradition case, he or she does so as a specially designated person (*persona designata*) and a decision made in this capacity was a decision of a "federal board, commission or tribunal."[34] This had the unfortunate consequence of dealing the Federal Court into the review of provincial superior court decisions in criminal law, an area in which the Federal Court had little competence.[35]

These and other jurisdictional issues were the dominant theme in most of the early writing on the new Federal Court. Clearly the drafting of the Federal Court Act had been less than brilliant. It reminded one of Canada's leading practitioners in the field of administrative law of the ditty:

I am the Parliamentary draftsman;
I compose the country's laws,
And of half the litigation
I am undoubtedly the cause.[36]

The reform proposals generated by this critical writing went beyond merely clarifying the terms describing the court's jurisdiction. The principal focus was on the possibility of consolidating all of the judicial review jurisdiction in one of the court's divisions. When the Federal Court Act was before the House of Commons, both opposition parties had urged that the trial division's responsibility for administering the traditional forms of judicial review be given to the appeal division so that there would be no confusion as to which division of the court a case challenging federal administrative activity should be brought.[37] Later this proposal gave way to the idea of consolidating judicial review in the trial division. This was the approach favoured by the Law Reform Commission of Canada,[38] by the Canadian Bar Association,[39] by leading academics,[40] and eventually by the federal government itself.[41] This approach would have the practical advantage of cutting down on the frequency with which three-judge panels have to be flown to different parts of the country to review decisions of federal administrative agencies. On the other hand, it would subject the collective decisions of expert tribunals to review by single judges of the trial division and eliminate the experiment of three-judge review at first instance.[42]

Despite the agitation for restructuring the Federal Court, no legislative proposals have been forthcoming. It may be that many of the professionals working in the field of administrative law have come to agree with Norman Fera that "there appears to be nothing in the present federal supervisory system of review that is so intolerable as to warrant immediate major or radical change.''[43] Lawyers are an adaptive lot. They will rail at departures from established ways and will use their ingenuity to exploit any ambiguities in the laws governing new institutions. But their instinct for professional survival and precedent leads them eventually to find some new form of order. Perhaps the Federal Court of Canada, with the initially confusing and still illogical division of judicial review responsibilities between its two levels, has reached this stage of acceptance.

Constitutional Problems

Jurisdictional complexities built into its governing statute were not the only problem to beset the Federal Court in its early years. At the outset there was a cloud of constitutional doubt hanging over this new federal judicial agency. The most fundamental question was whether the federal Parliament could take away from the provincial superior courts their power to apply the traditional common law remedies against federal administrative bodies and give that power to a new "superior court." Here the Federal Court project encroached on the whole superior court mythology which is so deeply embedded in common law legal culture. G.V.V. Nichols, a leading scholar in administrative law, on the eve of the court's founding, gave strong expression to this concern:

> Superior-court judges in the provinces, whose status goes back to pre-Confederation times, sit as personal representatives of the Crown when exercising a prerogative power. For Parliament to say that statutory judges appointed under a federal act have exclusive power to review what Crown servants do under federal statutes is an interference with the royal prerogative that existed before Confederation, and still exists.[44]

Norman Fera also speculated that because of the inherent nature of the provincial superior courts' jurisdiction to administer the common law writs, there was a good possibility that the attempt to give the Federal Court exclusive jurisdiction in this field would not stand up.[45] This fundamental constitutional doubt animated the provincial attack on the Federal Court at the 1975 meeting of attorneys general.

This question concerning the constitutional power of the federal Parliament to give the Federal Court exclusive jurisdiction to apply the traditional remedies to federal tribunals has turned out not to be a serious problem. Except for the writ of *habeas corpus*, which is not included under section 18 of the Federal Court Act, the provincial superior courts have not claimed any residue of inherent power to administer the prerogative writs against the federal government. Two Quebec scholars, Nicole Vallières and Denis Lemieux, have demonstrated in convincing terms the fallacy of the theory that the power of the provincial superior courts to administer the common law writs is beyond the reach of the legislature.[46] To be sure, the Federal Court does not have the inherent jurisdiction of a true superior court which we discussed at the beginning of chapter 11. Unlike the provincial superior courts, the Federal Court can exercise only those powers explicitly bestowed upon it by Parliament. But it has been able to exercise its exclusive jursdiction in the area of federal administrative law without serious challenge. However, the Supreme Court of Canada has established an outside limit to this monopoly. In 1982, in the *Jabour* case, the Supreme Court firmly rejected the contention that the Federal Court Act had removed from the provincial superior courts their power to determine the constitutional validity of federal laws. To do that, Justice Estey thundered, "would strip the basic constitutional concepts of judicature of this country, namely the superior courts of the provinces, of a judicial power fundamental to a federal system as described in the *Constitution Act*."[47] Judicial review of the constitutional validity of federal legislation remains a power which the Federal Court shares with the provincial superior courts.

A quite different constitutional issue which was not anticipated at the time of the Federal Court's founding has created a much more serious problem. This has been created by the Supreme Court through a series of decisions which have given the narrowest possible interpretation of the federal Parliament's power under section 101 of the Constitution to create "additional courts for the better Administration of the Laws of Canada." These decisions were reviewed in chapter 3. It will be recalled that the Supreme Court's rulings have the effect of preventing the Federal Court from taking jurisdiction in any proceedings which are not governed by "applicable and existing federal law."[48] It is not enough that the subject matter of the suit be one that is within the federal Parliament's legislative powers. There must also be existing federal legislation, not common law, governing the relationships at issue. Thus the Federal Court's jurisdiction, which it shares with the provincial superior courts, to hear cases in which the federal government is a plaintiff asserting common law rights has been rendered virtually null and void, as has its jurisdiction to hear suits in such areas of federal competence as aeronautics and inter-provincial transportation if they involve provincial civil rights. Even where existing federal law is at the centre of a case, the Supreme Court has been unwilling to stretch the Federal Court's jurisdiction so that it could deal with peripheral matters or ancillary proceedings which, although not strictly governed by operative federal law, are "functionally incidental"[49] to a matter that is properly before the court.

The tight constitutional restrictions the Supreme Court has imposed on the Federal Court have been severely criticized. Stephen Scott has shown that a much more plausible reading of the Constitution would support the proposition that "Parliament's power to create courts, and to confer judicial jurisdiction, is (*regardless* of the ambit of s. 101) *coextensive with its power of law-making—* not merely coextensive with *substantive federal law*."[50] The rigidity with which the Supreme Court has treated the ambit of Federal Court jurisdiction stands in marked constrast to the much more functional and accommodating approach to federal court jurisdiction taken by the highest courts in two sister federations, Australia and the United States. The explanation of the Supreme Court's rigidity lies, it would appear, not in the text of the Constitution but in the Court's strong commitment to "the idea of a single system of Canadian Courts which comprise the Provincial Courts."[51] The Court's posture on this issue should surely discourage federal legislators from any major moves in the direction of a dual court system.

Whatever ideological merit the Supreme Court stand may have, it has inflicted practical inconveniences on Canadian litigants. Given that the federal crown can be sued only in the Federal Court but that in disputes involving the federal crown as a defendant counter-claims made by the federal crown as plaintiff and third-party claims may now be excluded from the Federal Court's jurisdiction, the resolution of a single dispute may require the initiation of lawsuits in several courts. There is also the indeterminant nature of the test as to whether the Federal Court has jurisdiction—the requirement of "applicable and existing federal law." Peter Hogg has pointed out that this concept is "exceedingly difficult to apply," and as a result litigation is often required "to determine the appropriate forum for cases in which the applicable laws come from a variety of sources."[52]

The Court's Performance

Despite all that the Federal Court has had going against it—the jurisdictional muddle, constitutional challenge, provincial suspicions, professional criticisms, not to mention the appointment of persons closely associated with federal politics and administration (the Court has been facetiously referred to as Senate II)—it has been used a great deal, especially for the judicial review of federal administrative activities. The court's administrative law case load has steadily built up over the years. In the 1980s, the number of applications launched under section 28—(the section establishing a new remedy and providing for review in the first instance by the Federal Court of Appeal) has been averaging over 900 a year.[53] During the same period just under 250 cases a year involving traditional common law remedies have been initiated in the Trial Division.[54]

These figures make it clear that the federal administration is subjected much more frequently to judicial review in the Federal Court than it ever was in the provincial superior courts. In 1973 David Mullan reported that "a survey of the Dominion Law Reports reveals very few cases of provincial courts having been called upon to review the decisions of federal administrative bodies."[55] Yet now the Federal Court's case load in this area is around a thousand a year. This increase must be attributed in part to a general growth in public law litigation. More and more Canadians have been turning to the judicial arena to challenge the other branches of government. The adoption of a Charter of Rights in 1982 is only the culmination of this trend. In 1977 Mullan pointed out that "the last five years or so seem to have witnessed an incredible upsurge in judicial review applications across Canada."[56] Ontario's Divisional Court, which as we noted in chapter 11 is primarily a provincial administrative law court, by 1983 had a case load of 450 a year.[57] Still, while no doubt there are broad trends at work in generating the Federal Court's judicial review case load, one cannot help speculating that at least some of the increase stems from the very existence of a new, specialized judicial forum.

Certainly the court has struggled manfully to make itself accessible. It has established registry offices in sixteen locations across Canada. It hears cases in major cities in every province and in the northern territories. Despite the requirement that all of the court's judges reside in Ottawa, only 14 per cent of the matters heard by the court since 1978 have been heard in the national capital. This is just 2 per cent higher than the proportion of cases heard in Vancouver. Two-thirds of the cases since 1978 have been heard in Montreal and Toronto.[58] The Federal Court judges have indeed become frequent flyers! The court has also been innovative in streamlining the processing of cases.[59] Unnecessary formal steps which cause delay and expense have been eliminated; many matters are dealt with by correspondance so that as much as possible non-contentious matters do not require court appearances. The Canadian Bar Association has given the Federal Court high marks for the expeditious way in which it conducts its business. The association's study of the court states that "overall, it is clear that from the time the Court was established it has been noted for the efficiency and dispatch with which it has performed its functions."[60] It is doubtful that the association would make that comment of any other court in Canada. The court's geographic accessibility and its efficiency, unquestionably, have promoted its use by Canadians and have helped overcome its somewhat negative original image.

The areas of federal administration on which the Federal Court has had the greatest impact are set out in table 13.4 The table lists the top eight sources of cases instituted in each of the three streams through which challenges to administrative decisions may come before the Federal Court. On the left are applications to the trial division for the prerogative writs and other traditional remedies available under section 18. In the middle are applications directly to the Court of Appeal for the new remedy established in section 28. The appeals listed on the right are not appeals from the trial division but appeals available under various statutes directly to the Court of Appeal. Two general points about the Federal Court's review of federal administrative activities emerge from this table. First, it is the new remedy with the codified grounds for review in section 28 that has attracted the most business. But it must be noted that the figures given refer to matters instituted, not cases actually decided. No data are available on how many of these section 28 applications have been found to fall outside the section. Secondly, it is clear that the court's work in reviewing decisions of federal agencies is heavily concentrated in a few areas of activity. Immigration clearly stands out, heading all three jurisdictional sources. Many of these immigration cases are "routine and taken simply for delay."[61] The Canadian Bar Commission has suggested that to avoid swamping the Federal Court with immigration cases consideration should be given to establishing a special tribunal for immigration matters with a limited appeal on questions of law to the Federal Court of Appeal.

TABLE 13.4   SOURCES OF ADMINISTRATION LAW MATTERS INSTITUTED IN THE FEDERAL COURT OF CANADA, 1971-1985

SECTION 18		SECTION 28		APPEALS TO COURT OF APPEAL	
Immigration Act	722	Immigration Act	5851	Immigration Appeal Board	223
Penitentiaries	198	Unemployment Insurance	633	Commissioner of Patents	156
Parole Board	119	Public Service Commission	490	Tariff Board	124
Public Service Commission	67	Public Service Staff Relations	287	Canadian Transport Commission	74
Indian Act	63	Ministry of National Revenue	111	Min. of National Revenue	60
Canadian Labour Code	53	CRTC	63	CRTC	44
Unemployment Insurance	41	Canadian Transport Commission	58	Customs and Excise Act	27
RCMP	34	Canadian Human Rights Commission	46	National Energy Board	20

Source: *Federal Court of Canada Statistics*, Federal Court of Canada (Ottawa, 29 Jan. 1986), pp. 41-42, 79-88.

Recent developments in administrative and constitutional law may expand
the judicial review activity of the Federal Court. In 1980 the Supreme Court of
Canada in the *Martineau* case ruled that an alleged breach of procedural fairness
by a prison disciplinary board could be the subject of *certiorari* proceedings in
the trial division of the Federal Court, even though the board was not exercising
a judicial function.[62] The writ of *certiorari* to quash an administrative decision
is "the most common administrative law remedy sought in Canada."[63] But prior
to *Martineau* it was available only where a judicial function was being exercised.
The Court of Appeal's power under section 28 to quash administrative decisions
applies only to decisions required to be made on a judicial or quasi-judicial basis.
Martineau reduces the problem of applying the judicial/administration distinction
and opens the trial division to reviewing the fairness of procedures employed
by branches of the federal administration such as prison disciplinary boards that
are not classified as judicial.[64] The Charter of Rights and Freedoms will have a
similar effect in expanding the grounds for judicial review. The trial division of
the Federal Court, for instance, has applied the guarantee of fundamental justice
in section 7 of the Charter as a requirement of procedural fairness in decisions
affecting a person's liberty made by the National Parole Board.[65] Before the
Charter, the Supreme Court had ruled that because the Parole Board was not
performing a judicial function it was not required to observe the rules of natural
justice.[66]

While there can be no doubt that from a purely quantitative perspective the
new Federal Court's review of the federal administration has been significant,
what about its qualitative significance? What difference has it really made? How
much has it fulfilled the high hopes of its founders who, to use the rhetoric of
John Turner, believed that the Federal Court was a "further step toward balancing
the rights between the citizen and the state, providing some sort of recourse
against bigness, remoteness, alienation, distance from the decision-making
power?"[67] Or has it been too activist and fulfilled the expectations of those who
fear that judicial review may be used by private interests to hamstring the administration of valuable government programs? These conflicting hopes and fears
indicate how ideological any assessment of the court's judicial review work is
likely to be.

No overall study of the Federal Court's supervision of federal administration
has been attempted, but a few scholars have surveyed decisions in key areas of
administrative law. Norman Fera found that the trial division in its early years
was relatively conservative in administering the traditional remedies under section
28.[68] Fera suggested that this cautious attitude reflected the fact that most of the
court's original members were former Exchequer Court judges with little experience
in administrative law. David Mullan, in the background study prepared for the
federal Law Reform Commission, concluded that the appeal division appeared
sensitive to the need to maintain a reasonably balanced approach when applying
the rules of natural justice to administrative activities. When citizens challenged
the refusal of officials to provide them with copies of pertinent documents, the

court frequently overruled government decision makers. On the other hand, it was reluctant to impose elaborate court-like procedures on the administration of personnel policies by the Public Service Commission. There is no evidence that section 28(1)(c) of the Federal Court Act inviting the Court of Appeal to review the factual determinations of administrative bodies has led to a lot of judicial second-guessing of the policy decisions of expert boards and commissions. On the contrary, the Federal Court of Appeal appears to have drawn a "tight net" around 28(1)(c) as a ground of review, so that in effect it amounts to no more than the traditional requirement that there be some evidence to support the decision under review.[70] As far as the Charter of Rights is concerned, the Federal Court's record, from a statistical perspective, is not far off that of the section 96 provincial courts: 27 per cent of Charter claims initiated in the trial division have been successful, which is just slightly above the average for section 96 trial courts; only 19 per cent have been successful in the appeal division, which is a little below the average for provincial courts of appeal.[71]

Much more empirical research is needed before we can ascertain how the Federal Court is influencing the quality of public administration at the federal level of government. Besides looking at the extent to which the court has checked abusive exercises of authority or, alternatively, imposed unreasonable procedural requirements on regulatory schemes, such research should consider the characteristics of the individuals and groups who make use of the Federal Court. An examination of table 13.4 suggests that there are vast areas of the federal bureaucracy untouched by the judicial review functions of the Federal Court. If the court is to be assessed in terms of John Turner's goal of making the federal bureaucracy less remote and insensitive to the needs of citizens, consideration should be given to alternatives to judicial review.[72] It may be that a federal ombudsman (which has never been established at the federal level in Canada) or substantially increasing the size of the House of Commons and reducing the size of the constituencies served by federal members of Parliament, could do considerably more than the Federal Court to achieve Turner's ideal. However, one has a sense that the contemporary enthralment with judicial protection of rights will make it difficult for more informal political remedies to get a hearing.

Curtailing the Drift Toward a Dual Court System

One of the contributions the Federal Court has made to the Canadian judicial system is to make Canadians more conscious of the dangers of federalizing our judicial system and drifting toward an American system of dual courts. The Supreme Court's rigid approach to the division of jurisdiction between federal and provincial courts has accentuated the drawbacks of a dual system in Canada. Perhaps that was the Court's underlying intent. However much the decisions of the Supreme Court might be faulted for inconveniencing litigants, they have served as a deterrent to any judicial empire-building schemes federal politicians may harbour.

It is not only the jurisdictional complexities and confusion of overlapping forums that should make Canadians wary of gravitating toward a fully developed dual court system. There is also the unfortunate tendency we have noted for politicians and officials at the federal level to think of federal courts as "their courts." An episode which occurred shortly after the Federal Court was established illustrates the danger. In 1973 leaders of the Dene people in the Mackenzie Valley applied to the Supreme Court of the Northwest Territories to file a caveat on 450 000 square miles of territory based on the allegation that Treaty 11 was fraudulent. The hearing was about to take place before Justice William Morrow in the Northwest Territories Supreme Court when the federal government took steps to have the case removed to the Federal Court. To native people in the territory it appeared that the government was trying to take the case away from a judge who had been administering justice in the territories for some years and might be sensitive to the significance of aboriginal rights and put it in the hands of its own Ottawa-based court. Fortunately, Justice Frank Collier of the Federal Court rejected this crude jurisdictional ploy.[73]

The assignment of special national functions to Federal Court judges, such as hearing requests from the Canadian Security Intelligence Service for warrants to investigate threats to national security, may make sense in terms of the convenience of having these judges in Ottawa. But it is unfortunate if there is any intimation in this assignment that Federal Court judges are in some sense more "national" or committed to Canada than the judges of provincial superior courts. It cannot be emphasized too strongly that the section 96 courts are neither purely provincial nor purely federal, but are the nucleus of an integrated national judiciary. A central argument of this book is that if Canada is to have a truly national judiciary it must be built around these courts.

It may seem that in establishing the Tax Court of Canada in 1983, the federal government was once again moving towards the dual court system. However, this would be a questionable reading of that event. As was pointed out in chapter 3, the new Tax Court is not a new tribunal but the judicialization of an existing administrative tribunal.[74] Its work is limited to a very specialized field of adjudication which in no sense encroaches on the jurisdiction traditionally exercised by the section 96 courts.

In the same year that the Tax Court was created, the federal minister of justice, Mark MacGuigan, in a discussion paper on proposals to amend the Federal Court Act stated that "there is no desire or intention to establish a dual-court system in Canada."[75] In that paper the minister said that consideration was being given to repealing section 23 which gives the Federal Court jurisdiction to adjudicate actions between citizens concerning such subjects as bills of exchange, aeronautics, and interprovincial works. The minister pointed out that the court had no special expertise in these areas and that in any case, this part of the court's jurisdiction had "largely been ignored by the legal profession."[76] He also proposed that the provincial superior courts be given concurrent jurisdiction over claims against the federal government. This change would reduce the hardships inflicted on litigants by the Supreme Court's narrow interpretation of the constitutional limits of Federal Court jurisdiction. As long as the federal crown can be sued only in the Federal Court and the Federal Court is denied jurisdiction to deal with third-party claims and counter-claims by the federal crown, there will be suits that cannot be litigated in a single forum.

We would go further and ask why the Federal Court should retain any jurisdiction to hear civil suits involving the federal crown? If the legal rights and obligations at issue in these suits are essentially based on the common law and Quebec's Civil Code, it is difficult to see that the Federal Court can claim any special expertise in this field. A system of concurrent jurisdiction would seem to be a source of unnecessary jurisdictional tangles and an invitation to forum-shopping. The very notion of a "crown court"—a court with a special empathy for the interests of the executive—is an anachronism today. It may have been the original rationale for the Exchequer Court, the Federal Court's predecessor, but it is out of keeping with contemporary ideals of the separation of powers and the independence of the judiciary.

The future of the Federal Court must surely lie in those areas where it has the advantage of specialized knowledge and experience. Those areas are essentially admiralty, industrial property (copyright, patents, and trademarks) and federal administrative law. It is in this last area that the court is likely to experience the greatest growth in its case load in future years. Rather than simply adding judges to the court to cope with this expansion in administrative law cases, the government should pursue the proposals set out in the 1983 MacGuigan paper and reduce the court's role in fields where it has no special expertise and which overlap with the jurisdiction of the provincial superior courts. In this way the benefits of developing a court with a special competence in some complex areas of federal law can be realized while curtailing the drift toward a dual court system.

Notes to Chapter 13

1. See, for instance, Farrell Crook, "Federal Court Born," *Globe and Mail*, 1 June 1971.
2. See, for instance, R.J. Van Loon and Michael S. Whittington, *The Canadian Political System*, 3rd ed. (Toronto: McGraw-Hill Ryerson, 1981), p. 213-14. Van Loon and Whittington conclude their brief discussion of the court with these words; "The overall verdict on the Federal Court has to be that it has proven successful."
3. For an account of the Exchequer Court's early work, see Louis Arthur Audette, *The Practice of the Exchequer Court of Canada* (Ottawa: Thoburn, 1895); for a more contemporary account, see W.R. Jackett, "Practice and Procedure in the Exchequer Court," *Canadian Bar Journal* (1968), p. 45.
4. 50-51 Victoria, c. 16, ss. 51-52.
5. House of Commons, *Debates*, 25 Mar. 1970, p. 5470.
6. Federal Court Act, RSC 1970, c. 10, s. 31.

7. SC 1974-75-76, c. 18, s. 5.
8. There are many texts on administrative law discussing these remedies. An account which is particularly useful for political scientists is David P. Jones and Anne S. de Villars, *Principles of Administrative Law* (Toronto: Carswell, 1985).
9. For the few, essentially nominal, exceptions, see D.J. Mullan, "The Federal Court: A Misguided Attempt at Administrative Law Reform?" *University of Toronto Law Journal* (1973), p. 14.
10. Ibid., p. 22.
11. See, for example, the submission of Professor Garry Watson in *Proceedings of the House of Commons Standing Committee on Justice and Legal Affairs*, 14 May 1970, pp. 10-11.
12. House of Commons, *Debates*, 25 Mar. 1970, p. 5470.
13. Ibid., 28 Oct. 1970, pp. 662-65. This clause is s. 7(1) of the Federal Court Act. Twenty-five miles has been changed to forty kilometres.
14. *Report of the Western Premiers' Task Force on Constitutional Trends*, May 1977, p. 46.
15. Federal Court Act, s. 5.
16. Ibid., s. 10.
17. As was pointed out in chapter 7, this provision of the Federal Court Act has been found by the trial division of the Federal Court to violate the equality guarantee in the Charter of Rights.
18. Federal Court Act, s. 5(4).
19. SC 1985, c. 38, s. 11.
20. RSC 1970, c. 24 (2nd Supp.), s. 4.
21. *Federal Court of Canada Statistics* (1986), p. 22. This table shows an average of forty-nine pre-trial conferences per year since 1980.
21. Ibid., pp. 19-20, and 36-39.
22. See Gordon F. Henderson, "Federal Administrative Tribunals in Relation to the New Federal Court of Canada," *Law Society of Upper Canada Lectures* (Toronto: De Boo, 1971), p. 57.
23. S. 21 of the Federal Court Act gave the trial division exclusive jurisdiction to hear appeals that could be taken to the Citizenship Appeal Court. In 1978 s. 21 was amended to transfer jurisdiction of the Citizenship Court to the trial division; SC 1974-75-76, c. 108, s. 38.
24. SC 1980-81-82-83, c. 158, s. 55.
25. *Federal Court of Canada Statistics*, p. 102.
26. Law Reform Commission of Canada, *Report on Judicial Review and the Federal Court* (Ottawa, 1980), p. 19 and recommendation 3.7.
27. SC 1980-81-82-83, c. 111, ss. 41-42.
28. SC 1983-84, c. 21, ss. 2, 21. Members of the court who are eligible for this work are designated by the chief justice of the Federal Court.
29. Competition Tribunal Act, SC 1986, c. 26.
30. D.J. Mullan, "The Federal Court," p. 16.
31. *National Indian Brotherhood* v. *Juneau (No.2)* [1971] FC 73.
32. Decisions of the governor-in-council, the Treasury Board, a superior court or the Pension Appeals Board are explicitly excluded from review under s. 28(6).
33. *Canada Metal Co . Ltd.* v. *C.B.C. (No.2)* (1975) 11 OR (2d) 166.
34. *Commonwealth of Puerto Rico* v. *Hernandez* [1975] 1 SCR 228.

35. See D.M. Goldie, "Notes on the Federal Court," *The Advocate* (1977), p. 17.
36. The ditty is from Robert Megarry's *Miscellany-At-Law* and was cited by Gordon Henderson, in his "Comments on the Federal Court" at the conference of the Canadian Institute for the Administration of Justice, on the Canadian Court System, Osgoode Hall, Toronto, 1976.
37. House of Commons, *Debates*, 28 Oct. 1971, pp. 670-71.
38. The Law Reform Commission of Canada, *Judicial Review and the Federal Court*, recommendation 3.1.
39. A. Lorne Campbell, D.M.M Goldie and B.A. Crane, *Report of the Canadian Bar Commission on the Federal Court* (Ottawa, 1977).
40. See, for example, David J. Mullan, *The Federal Court Act: Administrative Law Jurisdiction* (Ottawa: Law Reform Commission of Canada, 1977).
41. Mark MacGuigan, minister of justice, "Proposals to Amend the Federal Court Act" (Ottawa: Department of Justice, 29 Aug. 1983).
42. The MacGuigan proposals would retain some of the statutory appeals from administrative tribunals directly to the Federal Court of Appeal.
43. Norman M. Fera, "LRC's Proposals for Reform of the Federal Judicial Review System—A Critical Examination and Counterpoise," *Manitoba Law Journal* (1977), p. 547.
44. G.V.V. Nicholls, "Federal Proposals for Review of Tribunal Decisions," *Chitty's Law Review* (1970), p. 257.
45. Norman M. Fera, "The Federal Court of Canada: A Critical Look at Its Jurisdiction," *University of Ottawa Law Journal* (1973), pp. 106-107.
46. Nicole Vallières and Denis Lemieux, "Le Fondement constitutionnel du pouvoir de controle judiciaire exercé par la cour fédérale du Canada," *Dalhousie Law Review* (1975), p. 268.
47. *Jabour* v. *Law Society of British Columbia et al.* [1982] 2 SCR 307, at 328.
48. *Quebec North Shore Paper Co.* v. *Canadian Pacific* [1977] 2 SCR 1054, at 1065-66.
49. The phrase comes from Steven B.A. Bardy, "The Federal Courts: the necessity, the desirability and the problems of the creation, development, and continued existence of the Federal Courts of Australia and Canada" (Master of Laws thesis, Queen's University, Kingston, 1982), p. 300.
50. Stephen A. Scott, "Canadian Federal Courts and the Constitutional Limits of Their Jurisdiction," *McGill Law Journal* (1982), p. 189.
51. Bardy, "The Federal Courts," p. 300.
52. Peter W. Hogg, *Constitutional Law of Canada*, 2nd ed. (Toronto: Carswell, 1985), p. 145.
53. *Federal Court of Canada Statistics*, 29 Jan. 1986, p. 43.
54. Ibid., p. 78.
55. Mullan, "The Federal Court," p. 24.
56. Mullan, *The Federal Court Act*, p. 62.
57. R.F. Reid, "The Ontario Divisional Court," *Law Society of Upper Canada Gazette* (1983), p. 72.
58. *Federal Court of Canada Statistics*, p. 27.
59. For a summary of its efforts in this area, see *Federal Court of Canada, 1986-87 Estimates, Part III Expenditure Plan*, p. 113.
60. *Report of the Canadian Bar Commission on the Federal Court*, p. 15.

61. Ibid., p. 47.
62. *Martineau* v. *Matsqui Disciplinary Board* [1980] 1 SCR 602.
63. Mullan, "The Federal Court," p. 31.
64. For a discussion of the duty of fairness in administrative law, see R.A. Macdonald, "A Theory of Procedural Fairness," *Windsor Yearbook of Access to Justice* (1981), p. 3.
65. *Re Cadieux and Director of Stony Mountain Institution et al.* (1984) 13 CCC (3d) 330; *Latham* v. *Solicitor General of Canada et al.* (1984) 12 CCC (3d) 9.
66. *Howarth* v. *National Parole Board* (1975) 50 DLR (3d) 349.
67. House of Commons, *Debates*, 25 Mar. 1970, p. 5474.
68. Norman M. Fera, "Conservatism in the Supervision of Federal Tribunals: The Trial Division of the Federal Court Considered," *McGill Law Journal* (1976), p. 234.
69. Mullan, *The Federal Court Act*, pp. 56-59.
70. Norman M. Fera, "Review Under 28(1)(c) of the Federal Court Act: Error of Law Not an Appeal on the Merits," *Queen's Law Journal* (1978), p. 148.
71. F.L. Morton and M.J. Withey, "Charting the Charter, 1982-85: A Statistical Analysis," Research Study 2.1, Occasional Paper Series. (Research Unit for Socio-Legal Studies, University of Calgary, 1986).
72. For a discussion of the limits of judicial review and the need to consider alternatives, see W.H. Angus, "The Individual and the Bureaucracy: Judicial Review— Do We Need It?" *McGill Law Journal* (1974), p. 177.
73. *A.G. Canada* v. *Hon. William George Morrow* [1973] FC 889.
74. For a discussion of the Tax Court's role, see Ronald Appleby and A. Lorne Greenspoon, "The Tax Court of Canada and the Tax Appeal Process," *The Advocates' Journal* (1984-85), p. 331.
75. Proposals to Amend the Federal Court Act," p. 18.
76. Ibid., p. 5.

CHAPTER 14
THE SUPREME COURT OF CANADA

We come now to the highest court in the land, the Supreme Court of Canada. As the court that sits at the apex of the Canadian judicial system it would appear to be the most powerful court and therefore the court of most interest to the student of politics. Although the Supreme Court decides far fewer cases than any other Canadian court, its decisions are binding on all the courts below. So far as the judicial branch of government is concerned, it has the last word in all areas of law: provincial, federal, and constitutional.

The Supreme Court is primarily a court of appeal. Occasionally, under the reference case procedure, the federal governement refers a question directly to the Court.[1] But these reference cases are few and far between (only ten since 1950).[2] The great bulk of the Court's cases are appeals from lower courts, and nearly all have already been appealed at least once.[3] The Supreme Court deals with disputed questions of law (not facts) which have already been decided, typically, by a trial court and a provincial court of appeal or the Federal Court of Appeal. The point of a second appeal to the Supreme Court of Canada is not primarily to correct errors but to obtain ''an authoritative settlement of a question of law of importance to the whole nation.''[4]

To understand the Supreme Court's role it is instructive to think of the country's legal system as a pyramid with a very wide base narrowing to a sharp point with the Supreme Court at the apex. Forming the base of this pyramid are the myriad situations involving the legal rights and duties of Canadians. Some of these situations—perhaps several million in the course of a year—will give rise to disputes most of which will be either abandoned or settled informally. But a few hundred thousand of these disputes will be taken to the next level of the pyramid to one of the provincial or territorial trial courts or the Federal Court of Canada. A few of these—somewhere around five to six thousand—will be appealed a step higher to a provincial court of appeal or the Federal Court of Appeal. And finally, a very small fraction of the cases decided at this second-highest level—somewhere between 1 and 2 per cent—will be appealed to the Supreme Court of Canada at the peak of the pyramid. The Court which presides at the apex cannot be expected to review all that has gone on below it. Henry Hart, the American jurist, has explained what we should expect from the highest court of appeal. His words are as applicable to the Canadian Supreme Court as to its American counterpart:

> The hard fact must be faced that the Justices of the Supreme Court . . . can at best put their full minds to no more than a tiny handful of the trouble cases which year by year are tossed up to them out of the great sea of millions and even billions

of situations to which their opinions relate. When this fact is fully apprehended, it will be seen that . . . what matters about Supreme Court opinions is not their quantity but their quality. And it will be seen that the test of quality of an opinion is the light it casts, outside the four corners of the particular lawsuit, in guiding the judgment of the hundreds of thousands of lawyers and government officials who have to deal at first hand with the problems of everyday life and of the thousands of judges who have to handle the great mass of litigation which ultimately develops.[5]

Seen in this light the Supreme Court's function is essentially legislative. Here we must refer back to our discussion of the paradox of adjudication in chapter 1. At the heart of that paradox, it will be recalled, is the fact that courts, in the very process of deciding disputes about legal rights and duties, often shape the law. They do that by applying general rules to particular circumstances, thus giving flesh and substance to the law, and by sorting out conflicts and priorities of principles and values within the legal system. While all courts perform this "creative" function, appeal courts perform it more often then trial courts and the Supreme Court most of all. In virtually all the cases the Supreme Court hears it reserves judgment so that the justices can write opinions which can serve as additions to the law on the subjects under consideration. These opinions are the Court's principal product. Their significance lies not so much in the way they serve as resolutions of the particular disputes giving rise to the cases coming before the Court, as in the prospective light they throw on relationships in our society affected by the principles and rules they enunciate.

The significance of the highest court's work will very much depend on whether it applies its legislative energies to legal questions of fundamental importance to society. Until quite recently the Supreme Court of Canada was poorly placed to play a major role in the development of the country's legal system. The criterion which determined most of the cases it heard was the amount of money in dispute, not the importance of the legal questions at issue. The 1974 amendment to the Supreme Court Act eliminating the automatic right of appeal in civil cases has largely cured this situation. With few exceptions, the Court is now its own gate-keeper, with a mandate to select the cases it hears on the basis of their public importance. As we shall see later in this chapter when we examine the Court's contemporary jurisdiction and case load more closely, the Supreme Court of Canada has become primarily a "public law" court, its docket dominated by criminal law, the interpretation of regulatory statutes, and constitutional issues. In this respect it has come to resemble the Supreme Court of the United States much more than Britain's highest court, the House of Lords.[6] Some would argue that there is a danger in moving too far in this direction, for it would surely be a mistake to regard the law governing private commercial transactions or the duties of citizens to one another as no longer of public importance.

Today the relative importance of the Supreme Court's role in the Canadian polity has the potential of surpassing that of the United States Supreme Court in the American polity. Unlike the United States, where state supreme courts are the final courts of appeal on matters of purely state law, in Canada the national Supreme Court is a general court of appeal. The Supreme Court of Canada has the final say in all areas of law, including all areas of provincial law. In the constitutional field the Supreme Court continues to function as the umpire of Canada's federal system defining the powers of the two levels of government, whereas the contemporary United States Supreme Court, although occasionally imposing limits on the states, has abdicated to the Senate the responsibility of applying federal restrictions on Congress.[7] Now, with the Charter of Rights, the Supreme Court of Canada becomes the arbiter not only of the division of power between governments but also of the line between the powers of both levels of government and the rights and freedoms of citizens. Thus, added to its already weighty responsibilities, is the civil liberties adjudication which has been the most prominent function of the United States Supreme Court since World War Two.

The Supreme Court's Long Adolescence

The powerful role the Supreme Court is now assuming in Canadian government is one for which neither the Court nor the public have had much preparation. For most of its history the Supreme Court of Canada was a subordinate, secondary institution. It took the better part of a century for the Court to assume a position in our affairs where it could be truly regarded as the head of the third branch of government in Canada. The Court's long period of underdevelopment tells us something both about the slowness of Canada to mature as a nation and the slowness of the judiciary to acquire the status of a separate branch of government in Canada.

The Fathers of Confederation did not regard the Supreme Court as an immediately necessary element in the government of the new Dominion. They did not establish the Court in the Constitution but left it to the federal Parliament to decide whether to create a "General Court of Appeal for Canada."[8] One reason for the lack of urgency in establishing such a court was the fact that Canadians would continue to have access to the supreme court of the British Empire, the Judicial Committee of the Privy Council. As good colonialists, most of the founding fathers were content to see that tribunal, at least for a time, remain Canada's highest court of appeal. In 1867 an appreciation of the creative legislative function of the national supreme court simply was not part of the legal or political culture. There was a dim recognition of the possibility that such a court might play a role in interpreting the constitution (mainly by enforcing limits on the provinces) but no conception of a supreme court enforcing a broad set of constitutional guarantees against the political branches of government.[9] Parliamentary sovereignty, not a liberal system of checks and balance, was the central principle in prevailing notions of good government.

The legislation which established the Supreme Court, introduced by Alexander Mackenzie's government in 1875, was the source of a good deal of controversy.

The legislation's supporters were certainly moved by some nation-building enthusiasm. Establishing a national court of appeal could be viewed as a necessary step in completing the Confederation project—as putting "the keystone to the arch of Confederation."[10] But the legislation also had its critics. This criticism had two main streams. First there was the concern of Quebeckers that the new court with just two of its six members from Quebec was ill suited to decide appeals concerning Quebec's civil law. Some of these Quebec critics had more confidence in the erudite law lords who sat on the Judicial Committee than in the backwoods lawyers who would serve on the new court in Ottawa.[11] The other line of attack came from imperialist Canadians who wished to retain the appeal to the Judicial Committee of the Privy Council or, to use their romantic rhetoric, "the appeal to the foot of the throne." Sir John A. Macdonald's Conservative party, which dominated federal politics for the first three decades after Confederation, championed this cause. Macdonald favoured the establishment of the Supreme Court but not as a court of last resort. His own administration's plans to establish the Court left the Privy Council appeal intact. So did the Liberals' original Supreme Court bill. But they subsequently accepted a backbench member's amendment, clause 47, making the judgment of the Supreme Court "final and conclusive," except for "any right which her Majesty may be graciously pleased to exercise by virtue of Her Royal Prerogative." Clause 47 looked as if it were designed to eliminate the statutory basis for appeals to the Privy Council, leaving only the occasional appeal that might be granted by the royal prerogative. It was bitterly but unsuccessfully opposed by the Conservatives. However, through what virtually amounted to a "smoke and mirrors" operation, the imperial authorities in London prevailed upon the Canadian government to acquiesce in their view that clause 47 left the appeal to the Privy Council unchanged.[12]

Not until 1949 was the Privy Council appeal abolished. This meant that for its first seventy-five years the Supreme Court of Canada was supreme in name only. In fact, it functioned as an intermediate court of appeal within the Canadian judicial system, and not a very powerful intermediate appeal court at that. Not only could its own decisions be appealed to the Judicial Committee, but the Supreme Court could be bypassed altogether. Although the percentage of Privy Council appeals in which the Supreme Court was bypassed declined somewhat over the years,[13] it is significant that nearly half the Privy Council's decisions on the Canadian Constitution (77 out of 159) were rendered in cases that were appealed directly from provincial courts of appeal.[14] Occupying this secondary position in the judicial hierarchy, the Supreme Court had little incentive to develop its own jurisprudence. After an initial spurt of independence, it followed the Judicial Committee's decisions conscientiously.

This subordination of the Supreme Court to the Judicial Committee aroused little opposition in Canada until well into the twentieth century. If, as Bora Laskin put it, the Supreme Court until 1949 was a "captive court,"[15] it was a reasonably contented captive. The Canadian legal establishment was in awe of the English bench and bar. In 1895 the English moved to strengthen the Judicial Committee as an imperial supreme court by providing that senior judges from Canada and several other "self-governing colonies" could be eligible to sit on the Judicial Committee.[16] From this time on Supreme Court justices participated in the judicial work of the Privy Council. Only two—typically the chief justice and one puisne judge—were eligible at one time. The Supreme Court justices revelled in this opportunity, even if it was often a strain on their pocket books (for the British did not pay for this colonial participation). It meant a summer in Europe and the privilege of sitting on a panel with the most renowned English judges. Far from bridling at being in the shadow of the Privy Council, the Supreme Court, for the most part,[17] happily followed its lead. Sir Lyman Duff, whom many would regard as the strongest jurist to serve on the Supreme Court before 1949, in discussing the Judicial Committee's role in interpreting the Canadian Constitution, referred to it as "a tribunal supremely equipped for that task."[18]

During this long period of subordination, the Supreme Court was a thoroughly second-rate institution and was treated as such by the federal government. James Snell and Frederick Vaughan in their history of the Court have documented its poor performance and shabby treatment by government. It was at times grossly inefficient in rendering judgment in the cases it heard. A footnote to an 1884 case reports that "the learned judge [Strong], having mislaid his judgement, directed the reporter to report the case without it."[19] The judges often did not get along with one another and, on occasion, were extremely discourteous to lawyers and court staff. The process of selecting judges was not exactly a talent hunt. As the list of Supreme Court justices in chapter 5 (table 5.1) indicates, prime ministers and justice ministers in making appointments were highly susceptible to pressures from their federal and provincial political friends. Indeed, three justice ministers engineered their own appointment to the Supreme Court bench and one, Charles Fitzpatrick, to the chief justiceship. Even when it tried, the government did not have an easy time attracting juristic talent to the Supreme Court. The salary level was far below the income of successful lawyers. Members of the Court were required to reside within five miles of Ottawa,[20] a city which for most Canadian judges and lawyers was distant and drab. Working conditions went from grim to appalling. The Court did not obtain its own premises until 1882—a refurbished portion of Parliament's West Block formerly used as stables and workshops. By the 1930s the condition of this building had deteriorated to the point that it was condemned by building and health inspectors "as being injurious to the health of the occupants and totally inadequate for the purpose for which it is used."[21]

Far from viewing the Supreme Court as the head of a separate branch of government, politicians and officials were more inclined to see the Court and its justices as instruments of the federal government. This view of the Court is reflected in the reference procedure, whereby the federal cabinet was empowered to elicit advisory opinions from the Court "on any matters whatsoever."[22] Archival material examined by Snell and Vaughan shows the close links that existed between the Court and the cabinet. "Government leaders saw the courts as one of a variety of institutions through which political plans for the nation might be achieved."[23] They were not above trying to manoeuvre the Court into positions advantageous to the government,[24] or attempting to influence the outcome of individual cases.[25] Indeed, when the abolition of Privy Council appeals was being discussed in the 1920s, Sir Lyman Duff suggested to his Privy Coucil colleague, Lord Haldane, that Mackenzie King would support this change because a court in Ottawa would be more amenable to influence. "You can have very little idea," he wrote, "of the liberties some Canadian Ministers will allow themselves in influencing judges where they think it is safe to bring pressure to bear."[26] Supreme Court justices were called upon to perform all kinds of assignments off the bench, ranging from drafting legislation to handling appeals under the Military Service Act to service on numerous royal commissions. Perhaps the most questionable of the latter was the inquiry provoked by the Gouzenko revelations in 1946. It was conducted by Justices Kellock and Taschereau of the Supreme Court and ran roughshod over such traditional liberties as the right to counsel and *habeas corpus*.[27]

The Abolition of Privy Council Appeals

The final move to abolish appeals to the Privy Council and make the Supreme Court truly supreme owed nothing to admiration for the Supreme Court. It was part and parcel of the general movement toward national autonomy and was spurred on by some controversial decisions of the Privy Council. One of these was the Judicial Committee's decision in *Nadan* v. *The King*, a criminal appeal, in 1926.[28] In 1888, three years after the Privy Council heard Louis Riel's appeal, Parliament passed legislation prohibiting appeals in criminal cases.[29] This law was not challenged until 1926 in the *Nadan* case. The Privy Council then ruled that this Canadian law was inoperative because it conflicted with British legislation governing the Judicial Committee's jurisdiction which under the Colonial Laws Validity Act took precedence over Canadian legislation. This decision led to a debate in the House of Commons and calls for the abolition of appeals.[30] The Statute of Westminster in 1931, by repealing the Colonial Laws Validity Act with respect to Canada and the other autonomous dominions, removed any imperial obstacle to ending Privy Council appeals. This was confirmed by the Privy Council in 1935 in the *British Coal Corporation* case when it upheld the section of the Canadian Criminal Code banning appeals in criminal cases from any Canadian courts to any courts in the United Kingdom.[31]

But the real catalyst for terminating Canadian appeals to the Privy Council was a series of constitutional decisions rendered by the Judicial Committee in 1937. In these decisions the Judicial Committee found unconstitutional legislation which formed part of the Canadian "New Deal" introduced in 1934 and 1935 by R.B. Bennett's Conservative government.[32] There was nothing new about the basic approach the Privy Council took to the Canadian Constitution in these cases. Its concern for provincial autonomy and restrictive interpretation of the major federal powers had been established in earlier cases. But the application of this approach in the circumstances of the Great Depression convinced many Canadians that the Constitution as interpreted by the Judicial Committee robbed the federal government of the capacity to deal effectively with both the causes and consequences of the major social and economic problems confronting a modern industrial society. Some turned to constitutional amendment to overcome the consequences of the Privy Council's decisions. But there was also increased support, even within the Conservative party, for getting rid of the Privy Council as Canada's highest court. Indeed, a former member of Bennett's cabinet, M.C. Cahan, in 1938 launched the parliamentary assault on the Privy Council.[33] The socialist CCF were keen to see the Privy Council's decentralizing tendencies reversed. Mackenzie King's Liberals, now in power in Ottawa and traditionally more nationalist than the Conservatives, could now proceed with the abolition of Privy Council appeals knowing they would not meet with serious opposition from either the left or the right.

This consensus at the federal level, however, did not reflect opinion throughout the country. In provincial capitals there was considerable fear that an Ottawa-based Supreme Court unshackled from the Privy Council would push the Constitution in a highly centralized direction. This feeling was particularly strong in Quebec where the Privy Council was widely respected as a guardian of provinical rights. Legal scholars in English Canada could attack the constitutional jurisprudence of the Privy Council and express the belief that when Canadian judges had the final word in interpreting the Constitution they would see the light and give much more power to the federal government.[34] But so strong was the strength of provincial rights sentiment in the country that federal politicians dared not proclaim this rationale for making the Supreme Court supreme. They preferred to present the idea simply as a logical step in Canada's attaining full national sovereignty.

In April 1939, Cahan's bill terminating Privy Council appeals in all matters from all Canadian courts had its second reading in the House of Commons.[35] The bill took the form of an amendment to the Supreme Court Act. The Liberal government gave the measure its full support but, because there were lingering doubts about Parliament's power to accomplish such a change, decided that an opinion on the constitutional validity of the legislation should be obtained from the Supreme Court. Early in 1940 the Supreme Court brought down its decision upholding the legislation four judges to two.[36] A common theme in the dissenting opinions of Justices Crocket and Davis was their view that Parliament's power under section 101 did not extend to regulating appeals in provincial law matters from provincial courts to the Judicial Committee. Four provinces wished to appeal the Supreme Court's decision to the Privy Council but the hearing of the appeal was postponed until after the war. In a judgment, already discussed in chapter 3, the Judicial Committee of the Privy Council in effect signed its own death warrant upholding the proposed legislation in its entirety.[37] Although by January 1947 the way was clear to pass the legislation, the Liberal government proceeded cautiously—a good indication, as Snell and Vaughan suggest, that "public opinion was still ambivalent."[38] It was not until the Liberal party had adopted a convention resolution favouring complete abolition of the Privy Council appeal and a Liberal government, now led by Louis St. Laurent, had been re-elected in June 1949 that the amendment to the Supreme Court Act giving the Court "exclusive ultimate appellate civil and criminal jurisdiction within and for Canada"[39] was reintroduced and passed.

During the debate on the abolition bill, George Drew, the leader of the opposition Conservative party, urged that a clause be inserted requiring that the rule of *stare decisis* be applied to all past decisions of the Supreme Court and the Judicial Committee.[40] This proposal had the backing of the Canadian Bar Association. The government did not accept the amendment but had to tip-toe around the suggestion that the Supreme Court might deviate from the path laid out by the Judicial Committee. Prime Minister St. Laurent accepted the spirit of the Conservative motion but said it was unnecessary. He loftily asserted that he was "unable to see that it [the legislation abolishing appeals] could have any effect upon provincial or minority rights."[41] All of this indicates that while the Supreme Court was now indeed supreme, the political and legal elites in Canada were not yet prepared to acknowledge that it might play a creative role in the governance of the country.

The Court Slowly Comes of Age

Nineteen forty-nine marks the date of the Supreme Court's formal ascendence to the head of the Canadian judicial system. The Court now had the final word on all matters of Canadian law[42] and, the Conservatives' motion to legislate *stare decisis* having failed, it was not formally bound by either the Privy Council's or its own previous decisions. The 1949 Supreme Court Amendment Act added two members to the Court so that it now had its modern complement of nine judges. It also had an impressive new home. In 1946 it moved into the imposing edifice designed by Ernest Cormier in the general style of the existing buildings on Parliament Hill, but suitably distanced from them. Although the essential legal, personnel, and physical components of supremacy and independence were now in place, making full use of this capacity has been a more gradual process.

After 1949 the Supreme Court continued to show great deference for English jurisprudence. This respect for English authorities was especially marked in cases dealing with the common law. It extended to decisions of the House of Lords as well as to Judicial Committee precedents and to criminal law as well as the law governing private suits. In 1955 we find, for instance, Justice Rand, one of the Court's more innovative members, dismissing a lawyer's attempt to persuade the Court not to follow an English precedent with the words "the authorities in England have pronounced."[43] Legal scholars who attacked the Court for its lack of intellectual independence had little immediate impact.[44] The Supreme Court gradually inched away from a strict and mechanical rule of precedent with regard to both its own and English decisions. It did not issue a clear, corporate policy statement like that of the House of Lords announcing its willingness "to depart from a previous decision when it appears right to do so."[45] But it would on occasion "distinguish" English decisions as not applicable to contemporary Canadian circumstances[46] and in more recent years became, to use Chief Justice Laskin's phrase, "more receptive to re-examination" of previous decisions.[47] In the late 1970s it explicity overruled three of its own decisions and a Privy Council decision.[48]

The Supreme Court's tendency to cling for so long to English precedents was based more on the judges' general approach to judicial decision-making than on legal anglophilia. The attraction of writing opinions that appeared to be logical deductions from rules established in earlier cases is that it relieves the justices of any obligation to direct their inquiry and reasoning toward "the values and social policies which ought to influence the direction in which the courts take our law."[49] By treating the common law as a closed book the judges could deny themselves a creative role in adapting the law to contemporary Canadian circumstances. It is only when this timidity about the judicial function begins to wane that the Supreme Court will loosen "the mooring ropes of binding precedent."[50] The Court's decision in *Cherensky*[51] indicates that as late as 1979 there was still some way to go in overcoming this timidity. In this case the majority denied to newspaper owners the defence of fair comment for defamatory statements contained in letters to the editor. While the dissenting opinion of Justice Dickson carefully weighed the competing values at issue, the majority stuck narrowly to the words of selected English precedents.

In constitutional law the Judicial Committee left a legacy of conflicting precedents for the Supreme Court. A 1946 decision of the Privy Council took a very broad view of the scope of the federal Parliament's power to make laws for "the peace, order and good government of Canada."[52] According to this decision, a legislative subject could be brought under this power if it went "beyond local or provincial concern or interests and must from its inherent nature be the concern of the Dominion as a whole." This seemed to be a much more generous interpretation of this power than the approach in earlier cases, which confined its use to national emergencies such as wars or famines. In one of the Court's earliest constitutional decisions after becoming supreme, *Johannesson* v. *West St. Paul*,[53] decided in 1952, the Court moved boldly in a centralist direction. Six of the seven judges taking part in the case held that under the peace, order and good government power federal jurisdiction must pre-empt any local control over the location of airports because of the "inherent national importance" of aeronautics. The reasoning of several of the judges explored in some depth why the development of Canada required such extensive federal control over commercial aviation.[54] Later in the 1950s a number of decisions manifested a more nationalist understanding of the reach of the federal trade and commerce power, and a concern that provincial power over property and civil right not be used to impede the flow of trade across provincial borders.[55]

The centralist tone of these early decisions of the emancipated Supreme Court did not have a major impact on the distribution of power in the Canadian federation. Nor did it establish a permanent trend. Throughout the two decades following 1949 and at least part of the third the most significant adjustments in federal-provincial relations were effected through executive agreements between the two levels of government. In the middle of the 1960s the Supreme Court again took the ''inherent national importance'' approach to Parliament's general power as a basis for federal jurisdiction, first over the national capital region[56] and second for federal control of offshore mineral resources.[57] But now this treatment of the division of powers evoked a loud and hostile reaction from provincial leaders and Quebec legal scholars.[58] This criticism in an era of aggressive province-building helped create a climate of opinion that was to put a brake on the Supreme Court's centralist tendencies.

With regard to civil liberties, the Supreme Court played a very activist role in the 1950s in reversing policies and practices of the Duplessis regime in Quebec. In a sequence of seven decisions, the Court granted appeals from the Quebec Court of Appeal brought by members of religious and political minorities (principally Jehovah's Witnesses and communists) challenging restrictions on political and religious freedom.[59] Although the Quebec judges tended to form a dissenting bloc in most of these decisions, the Court's decisions did not arouse popular resentment in Quebec. As I have argued elsewhere, the Supreme Court's majority in these cases ''acted as a judicial vanguard for significant forces which were beginning to agitate Quebec society and which, during the 1950s, were in the process of becoming the predominant element in the province's political life.''[60]

While the results of these 1950s Quebec civil liberties cases were liberal, the Supreme Court's constitutional jurisprudence was conservative. Only three of the seven cases involved constitutional interpretation, and in these a majority of the judges refused to endorse the thesis expounded by Chief Justice Duff in the 1938 *Alberta Press* case[61] that the provisions of the BNA Act establishing parliamentary government contained an implicit guarantee of the freedoms necessary for the functioning of a parliamentary democracy. The position the Court had arrived at by the end of the 1950s was to treat civil liberties essentially as questions of federalism. There was a consensus that provinces could not use criminal sanctions to restrict freedom of speech or religion because that would encroach on the federal Parliament's exclusive jurisdiction over criminal law. But only Justice Abbott supported the idea that fundamental political freedoms were beyond the reach of both levels of government.[62] By backing away from Duff's implied constitutional bill of rights, the Supreme Court did much to encourage the advocates of an explicit bill of rights.

The agitation for an American style bill of rights scored its first breakthrough with Parliament's enactment of the Canadian Bill of Rights in 1960. This was a very weak instrument. It was not part of the formal Constitution but simply an ordinary act of Parliament. It did not apply to the provinces. The Supreme Court judges did not sense that the Bill of Rights gave them a clear mandate from the Canadian body politic to enforce its terms against the political branches of government. Their treatment of the bill was anything but robust. At first the Court appeared to take the position that the bill could not be used as a basis for overturning federal legislation that pre-dated it.[63] There was a surprise flip-flop in 1970 when the majority in the *Drybones* case ruled long-standing provisions of the Indian Act inoperative because of their conflict with the Bill of Rights.[64] But then the Court retreated to a very narrow interpretation of the bill's substantive provisions, especially the right to equality before the law. The Supreme Court's halting and unenthusiastic approach to the bill discouraged lawyers from using it.[65] Between 1960 and 1982 only thirty-four cases involving claims based on the Bill of Rights reached the Supreme Court, and in only five of these did the Court uphold claims based on the bill.[66]

By 1949 there was a much stronger inclination in Ottawa to treat the Supreme Court as the head of a seperate branch of government. Snell and Vaughan record that direct contacts between the justices and members of the legislative and executive branch which had been so frequent in the Court's early years "became much less common" in the era after World War Two.[67] In 1954 Douglas Abbott, the minister of finance, was appointed directly to the Court to fill a Quebec vacancy. The adverse public reaction to this appointment indicated that "the government was out of touch with public expectations of how one should be chosen for such an important judicial office."[68] Since then governments have refrained from using the Court as a dumping ground for old politicians, although it is a matter of record that some of John Diefenbaker's colleagues tried to ease him out of the prime ministership by "offering" him the position of chief justice. Diefenbaker, we are told, "resolutely refused."[69]

During the two decades following 1949 the Supreme Court's work, without any change in the rules governing its jurisdiction, began to shift toward public law. Whereas questions of private law were at issue in 53 per cent of the cases decided by the Court between 1875 and 1949, they were involved in just over one-third of the cases decided between 1950 and 1969.[70] Criminal cases, which had constituted only 5 per cent of the Court's pre-1949 work, now replaced tort cases at the top of the docket: between 1950 and 1969, just under 15 per cent of the cases involved criminal law. Taxation disputes flowing up through the Exchequer Court were now second in frequency: 13 per cent as compared with 12 per cent for tort cases. Constitutional cases, however, showed no increase, remaining a paltry 4 per cent of the Court's docket.

The Supreme Court after 1949 was still not in charge of its own agenda. Nearly all the cases that came before it were appeals as of right. This meant that the Court heard the cases not because they raised an important and unsettled legal issue, but because the losing party in a provincial court of appeal or the Exchequer Court (and after 1970 the Federal Court of Appeal) had a statutory right to a second appeal to the Supreme Court of Canada.[71] In civil cases this

TABLE 14.1   *CHANGES IN JURISDICTIONAL SOURCES OF*
             SUPREME COURT CASES, 1970-71 TO 1980-81

TERM	NO. OF CASES HEARD	LEAVE OF THE SUPREME COURT	APPEALS AS OF RIGHT	LEAVE OF COURT OF APPEAL	OTHER
1970-71	151	15%	83%	1%	1%
1980-81	117	74%	16%	4%	6%

Source: S.I. Bushnell, "Leave to Appeal Applications to the Supreme Court of Canada: A Matter of Public Importance," *Supreme Court Review* (1981), table 2, p. 497, University of Chicago Press.

right depended on whether more than $10 000 was at issue in the case. In criminal cases involving indictable offences it depended (and at the time of writing still does) on whether there was a division on a point of law in the courts below— either within the court of appeal or between the trial court and the court of appeal.[72] Because so many of the Supreme Court's cases were not screened by the Court, it often dismissed the appeal after hearing the appellant's arguments without any need to hear the other side. This author's study of the minute book for the Court's 1964-65 session revealed that about one out of every eight appeals were treated in this way.[73]

The Court Becomes Its Own Gate-Keeper

Nineteen seventy-five is almost as significant a date in the history of the Supreme Court as 1949. It was in late 1974 that an amendment to the Supreme Court Act eliminated the appeal as of right in civil cases involving more than $10 000 and replaced it with an appeal requiring leave of the Court. Leave to appeal would be granted if

> The Supreme Court is of the opinion that any question involved therein is, by reason of its public importance or the importance of any issue of law or any issue of mixed law and fact . . . one that ought to be decided by the Supreme Court or is, for any other reason, of such a nature or significance as to warrant decision by it. . . .[74]

This legislation implemented the principal proposal of a Canadian Bar Association study of the Supreme Court's case load commissioned in 1972 by John Turner, the minister of justice.[75] Like the 1970 legislation creating the Federal Court of Appeal, it was designed to relieve the Supreme Court of the burden of hearing routine appeals. The Court now had much more control over its own work. The then chief justice of Canada, Bora Laskin, hailed the change as confirming "the Court's status as Canada's ultimate appellate Court."[76]

Since 1975, through the leave process the Court has selected most of the cases it has heard. The figures on table 14.1, based on Professor S.I. Bushnell's research, demonstrate the change which took place over a decade in the Court's control over its docket. At the beginning of the 1970s only 15 per cent of the Court's cases reached the Court through the Court's granting of leave; by the end of the decade roughly three-quarters of the Court's cases came by this route. The Court grants leave in both civil and criminal cases. But in some criminal cases, as we have noted, there is a right of appeal to the Supreme Court. These cases constitute most of the residue of appeals of right which by the 1980s accounted for 16 per cent of the cases on the Court's docket. The sections of the Criminal Code creating this right of appeal to the Supreme Court were not touched by the 1974 amendment to the Supreme Court Act. But they are likely to be repealed in the near future. The Supreme Court of Canada has been reeling under workload pressures generated by the Charter of Rights. It cannot afford the gap in its control over its case load that results from these Criminal Code provisions. In April 1986 the federal Parliament gave first reading to legislation (Bill C–105) removing the automatic right of appeal to the Supreme Court provided for in the Criminal Code and several other statutes.[77] There is still a right of appeal from decisions of provincial courts of appeal in reference cases initiated by provincial governments. This right of appeal will likely remain as these cases usually raise important constitutional questions that should be brought before the Supreme Court for final resolution.

The two columns at the right-hand side of table 14.1 mark further breaches in the Court's control over its docket. The column at the far right includes a miscellany of provisions which in all likelihood will continue. These include section 55 of the Supreme Court Act empowering the federal government to refer questions directly to the Court. The practice of having the courts render advisory opinions at the beck and call of the executive seems out of keeping with the separation of powers appropriate in the age of the Charter. Reference cases have certainly been declining. Barry Strayer reports that whereas roughly 25 per cent of the constitutional cases that reached the highest court in Canada's first century were references, from 1967 to 1981 only 10 per cent were references.[79] But the reference case procedure is probably too ingrained in the Canadian tradition and too handy to politicians to be abandoned. Indeed, since Strayer did his survey, references have experienced something of a revival, with 17 per cent of the Supreme Court's constitutional decisions reported from 1982 to 1985 (nine out of fifty-two) occurring in reference cases.[80]

The column second from the right in table 14.1 shows that in a small number of cases it is the provincial court of appeal or the Federal Court of Appeal not the Supreme Court that grants leave. Apparently very few lawyers avail themselves of the opportunity of seeking leave to appeal from the court in which they have lost, and when they do these intermediate courts are quite restrained in granting leave.[81] There would seem to be little point in retaining this double-track system of leave-granting. Only the Supreme Court is in a position to see the whole picture and to judge which issues are most in need of resolution by the ultimate court of appeal.

With the changes in the rules governing its jurisdiction which have been made

TABLE 14.2   THE SUPREME COURT'S WORKLOAD, 1983-1985

	1983	1984	1985
Applications for leave	501	479	415
Applications granted	117(23%)	123(26%)	64(15%)
Cases heard	89	89	88
Judgments rendered	89	63	84

Source: *Bulletin of the Supreme Court*, 3 Feb. 1984, and statistical reports issued by the Office of
Registrar, Supreme Court of Canada. Reproduced with permission of the Minister of
Supply and Services Canada.

and are in the offing, the Canadian Supreme Court becomes, as did the United
States Supreme Court sixty years ago, a discretionary court; the work it does
depends essentially on the exercise of its own discretion. Selecting the cases it
will hear is an important policy-making function of the Court. Up to now the
Court has performed this function in a time-consuming and fragmented fashion.
Each application for leave is heard by a panel of three judges and decisions are
by majority vote.[82] This means that two judges can grant or block access to the
Court. Applications to be heard in the United States Supreme Court are handled
in a more corporate and expeditious manner.[83] There they take the form of
petitions for the writ of *certiorari*. Between four and five thousand of these are
filed with the United States Supreme Court annually. Any of these petitions
which are deemed worthy of consideration by any one justice are put on a list
for discussion at the Court's weekly conference. The full Court meeting in
conference makes decisions on petitions soley on the basis of written materials.
Decisions are made by "the rule of four": acceptance of a request to be heard
requires the agreement of four of the nine justices.

Case-load pressures may soon force the Supreme Court of Canada to adopt
a more American-style procedure for handling leave applications. Applications
for leave to appeal have increased in volume from less than 150 a year in the
middle of the 1970s to between 400 and 500 a year in the 1980s.[84] The highest
number appears to be the 501 applications filed in 1983, the first year applications
raising Charter of Rights issues reached the Court. That same year the Court
made it possible for lawyers to apply for leave via two-way satellite television
communications.[85] While this saved lawyers and their clients a trip to Ottawa,
it did not save the judges' time. But more than the conservation of judicial time
is at issue. There is also growing evidence of the need for more coherent institutional control over the flow of cases into the Court. In the 1980s the Court
has been biting off considerably more than it can chew. Table 14.2 shows that
in 1983 and 1984, the year in which the Charter avalanche was reaching the
Court, the justices' generosity in granting leave far exceeded their capacity for
hearing cases and rendering judgment. The data for 1985 suggest that there was

TABLE 14.3   CASES HEARD BY THE SUPREME COURT, 1983-1985

	1983	1984	1985
Private Law	21(24%)	10(11%)	14(16%)
Public Law			
Charter of Rights	2(2%)	14(16%)	14(16%)
Other constitutional	12(13%)	8(9%)	2(2%)
Criminal	24(27%)	23(26%)	26(30%)
Other public	30(34%)	34(38%)	32(36%)
Totals	89(100%)	89(100%)	88(100%)

Source: *Bulletin of the Supreme Court*, 3 Feb. 1984, and statistical reports issued by Office of the Registrar, Supreme Court of Canada. Reproduced with permission of the Minister of Supply and Services Canada.

some orchestration of the leave-granting process, as the percentage of successful leave applications plummetted to 15 per cent—lower than it has been since 1975.[86]

The bill which would eliminate appeals as of right in criminal cases would also eliminate the oral hearing as a regular part of leave application proceedings. This would become the exception rather than the rule and would be ordered only when the court finds it cannot make a decision on the basis of the written submissions.[87] The legislation does not push the Court into a more corporate mode of decision-making on leave applications: a quorum of three is to be retained for determining leave applications. However, once the Court's gate-keeping decisions are made in a less formal and less public setting, it should be easier to ensure that they respond more deliberately to institutional capacity and priorities.

The Supreme Court does not give reasons for its leave-granting decisions. Hence, to obtain some sense of the judges' priorities we can only look at the results of their decisions. These results point clearly in the public law direction. Bushnell's research showed that for the four sessions from 1977 to 1981, applications involving public law out-numbered private law application 61 per cent to 39 per cent and the rate of acceptance for public law applications was 30 per cent as compared with 23 per cent for private law applications.[88] More recent figures released by the Court indicate that in the early years of the Charter era this public law trend has intensified. For the years 1983 to 1985, only 14 per cent of private law applications were granted as compared with 25 per cent in public law.[89] Table 14.3 shows how this approach to leave-granting is affecting the Supreme Court's work in the 1980s. Criminal law continues to be the largest single category on the Court's docket. But constitutional law, especially the Charter, is far more prominent than ever before, while private law has fallen even further below the one-third level it had reached at the end of the 1960s.

There have been objections that the Court may be moving too far in the public law direction. Professors MacKay and Bauman, in a study of the Supreme Court prepared for the Royal Commission on the Economic Union, make the important observation that "the criterion of 'national importance' is not coextensive with, or a subsidiary of, 'public law'."[90] These and other commentators point to the way in which judicial decisions on so-called private law issues can have important consequences for the functioning of economic and social institutions.[91] Cases dealing with the rights of corporate directors or the division of property in marriage break-ups, for example, though technically classified as private law, concern relationships and interests which are of great public import. Conflicting decisions among provincial courts of appeal on questions of commercial law can be a source of confusion, increasing the cost of transactions for firms doing business on a national basis. Only the Supreme Court is in a position to establish a uniform method for resolving the kinds of conflict of law situations which arise in disputes between parties from different provinces.[92] Michael Goldie suggests that at the very least the Supreme Court should grant leave to appeal "from the common-law provinces in civil matters . . . when there is a conflict between or among provincial appellate courts."[93] The provincial appeal courts might be inclined to be more innovative in developing the common law if there was some assurance that interprovincial conflicts would be resolved by the Supreme Court of Canada.

In chapter 3 we pointed out that the classical federalist objection to the Supreme Court's jurisdiction in civil law and provincial law matters no longer has any significant political following in the country. Quebec's historic fear that a Supreme Court dominated by common law judges might adulterate its distinctive system of civil law has also evaporated. The federalist politicians who are dominant in contemporary Quebec do not want to see their province's legal culture left out of the Supreme Court's work. The Supreme Court in modern times has hewed closely to the practice of having civil appeals from Quebec decided by five-judge panels that include the three Quebec judges. Common law participation in Quebec civil law today "is essentially a non-issue."[94] This political and intellectual consensus on the positive integrative value of the Supreme Court's exercise of ultimate authority in the field of private law means that the Supreme Court will likely remain as it is described in the Constitution, a general court of appeal. But we may well see shifts away from the mix of legal categories set out in table 14.3. After its initial enthusiastic embrace of the Charter the Supreme Court might become pickier about the Charter cases it decides to hear. It might also begin to respond to those who advocate that it be more active in the field of commercial law and in developing the common law. The Court will also be under pressure to take more cases from the Federal Court of Appeal. The creation of that court, as we saw in the last chapter, has relieved the Supreme Court of the burden of hearing routine appeals in federal public law matters. But the Federal Court of Appeal is a very active court and often a court of first instance in cases involving federal administrative law. In the future, then, the Supreme Court is likely to be called upon frequently as a final arbiter in disputes involving federal administrative agencies, while its criminal law case load should decline when the automatic right of appeal in criminal cases is repealed.

Although constitutional cases have become and will remain a much bigger component of the Supreme Court's work than they were throughout its first century, the Court is not on its way to becoming a "constitutional court." Remaining a general court of appeal need not, however, detract from its power. Quite the contrary: it is only the worst kind of formalism that views ultimate courts of appeal as powerful only when they are interpreting a constitution. By exercising its gate-keeping responsibilities shrewdly, the Supreme Court of Canada is now in a position to fashion a docket that will include cases penetrating into every significant area of the legal system. This gives the Court the potential for exercising more power to shape the law of Canada than the United States Supreme Court has over American law.

The Court's Decision-Making System

The evolution of the Court's decision-making system has not kept pace with the changes in its role. Like so many Canadian institutions, the Supreme Court has been moving from an English toward an American model. In the traditional English approach to appellate decision-making, the judges after listening to the arguments retire to their individual chambers to write their judgments.[95] The court's decision is simply the sum of these individual opinions. In the American model, decision-making is more collegial and less dependent on oral argument. The American-style appellate court functions more as a research institution and its decisions are the products of a more sustained and systematic internal process of collaboration and bargaining. The Supreme Court of Canada is closer to the American model than are Canada's intermediate courts of appeal. The very large role it has taken on in the governance of Canada will force it to move even further in that direction.

The Supreme Court of Canada rarely sits as a full court. In this respect it is in marked contrast with its American counterpart, where all nine judges participate in all of the court's decisions. The Canadian Supreme Court sits most often in panels of seven or a bare quorum, which is five. There is an effort to avoid even-numbered panels so as to prevent tie votes (in the case of a tie the decision being appealed stands). Bora Laskin, both as an academic and as chief justice, believed strongly that all nine members of the Court should sit at least for important cases.[96] Of course, after 1974 when "public importance" became the criterion for most of the cases the Court heard, this meant that the full Court should hear most cases. Under Laskin's leadership the Court made rapid progress toward meeting that objective. The proportion of cases heard by nine judges rose rapidly after he became chief justice in 1973, reaching a high of 64 per cent in the 1976-77 term, as compared with less than 10 per cent at the beginning of the 1970s. But after that it slid back.[97] In 1979-80 only 5 per cent of the

Court's cases were heard by a full bench. A combination of workload pressures and illnesses was taking its toll. In the 1980s panels of seven or five judges became the norm. For the 1983-85 period 50 per cent of the Court's judgments were rendered by seven-judge panels, 29 per cent by five-judge panels, and only 7 per cent by the full Court.[98] Even in cases raising Charter issues, full Court participation has been rare. In only three of the eighteen Charter cases reported in the *Supreme Court Reports* up to late 1986 did all nine judges take part.

For Quebec civil law appeals a five-judge panel may be appropriate as a means of ensuring that the majority of judges hearing such cases have an extensive background in Quebec's legal system. But for other cases it is a questionable means of coping with workload problems. The decisions of a national court of appeal which are essentially legislative in nature should emerge from an exchange of ideas among all of the Court's members representing all points of view and all parts of Canada. "Failure to make progress in this regard means that the Court is increasingly exposed to the criticism that the outcome of cases, especially those with a high political profile, is influenced by the selection of judges to hear particular cases."[99] If the Court is to achieve the degree of collegiality appropriate for its new role in Canadian government, it will have to find some alternative to the panel system as a means of dealing with its workload problem.

Since 1949 the Court has developed greater coherence in the production of opinions. For many years now the judges, after hearing the oral argument, have been meeting in conference to discuss the case. At these conferences each judge gives his or her views on the case, beginning with the most recently appointed judge and proceeding in reverse order of seniority. This is the same order as is used in the English House of Lords but exactly opposite to the American Supreme Court where the chief justice speaks first. Justice Bertha Wilson has explained that the Canadian order is designed to reduce the risk of junior members feeling pressure to side with their elders, a risk she assures us no longer exists.[100] From what one can gather, the Canadian Supreme Court judges do not go at one another in these conferences with quite the same degree of vigour as is characteristic of debate in the America Court's conference chamber. Nor do they conclude, as the American court does, with a formal vote (in reverse order of seniority). In recent years a much more concerted effort has been made before and after the conference to produce a majority opinion. Justice Wilson describes the contemporary practice:

> The first tentative expression of views at our conference will usually disclose whether there is any prospect of unanimity or whether there is clearly going to be more than one judgement. We decide at the conference who is going to prepare the first draft. This will be a member of the group which appears likely to form the majority. One of that group will normally volunteer or, if there is no volunteer, the Chief Justice will ask one of the group to take it on. The other judges then set aside their record in the case until a draft is circulated.[101]

It is in the circulation of draft opinions and comments on drafts that much of the internal politics of the Court are played out. Although these politics may not be as strenuous as they tend to be in the United States Supreme Court, in important and controversial cases there is likely to be a concerted effort to consolidate a majority position.

Increased collegiality in the formation of opinions has enabled the Court, as F.L. Morton has observed, to speak "more authoritatively."[102] The Court has moved away from the traditional English practice of seriatim opinion writing, in which the puzzled consumer of the Court's product must piece together a number of separate opinions to ascertain the court's position on the disputed point of law. Again, Bora Laskin's leadership was a turning point. Since his chief justiceship, in most cases the opinion of one judge is endorsed by a majority, with perhaps one or two shorter concurring opinions agreeing with the majority's basic conclusion but differing with some of their reasons. On occasion the Court has gone further and fashioned a single "opinion of the Court" which is not attributed to the authorship of any particular judge. Most of these cases have involved highly charged political controversies, such as control over British Columbia's offshore resources, or the federal Parliament's unilateral power to reform the Senate, or whether Quebec had a veto over fundamental constitutional change.[103] By putting an institutional imprint on its opinions in these cases the Court attempts to depersonalize its decisions and give them greater authority.

But this can only occur when the judges are unanimous. There has been no inclination in the Supreme Court of Canada to push the institutional approach to decision-making as far as the Privy Council did. During the time the Privy Council was Canada's highest court it never permitted dissents. In theory, the Judicial Committee was regarded as giving advice to the sovereign and it was thought that the sovereign should not be confused by conflicting opinions. Dissenting opinions are and will continue to be an important part of the Supreme Court's output, as is the case with most final courts in the common law world.[104] The value of dissenting opinions is that they point to alternative directions in which the law may develop in the future. To use the more elegant language of a former United States chief justice, "a dissent in a court of last resort is an appeal to the brooding spirit of the law."[105] Dissenting opinions also help us to identify the problematic issues in a case and to understand what has persuaded judges to follow different paths in their reasoning. The amount of dissent which occurs in a final appellate court depends on many factors, including the contentiousness of the issues coming before the court and the leadership of the chief justice. It seemed reasonable to expect the frequency of dissents in the Supreme Court to increase after 1974 because a much higher proportion of cases would raise difficult, problematic issues. However, Bushnell's research shows that this did not happen in the period up to 1981. He suggests that workload pressures gave the justices little time for authoring dissenting opinions.[106] Perhaps it is workload pressures that have continued to keep the percentage of unanimous decisions high. Indeed, for the 1983-85 period 87 per cent of judgments rendered by the Court were unanimous.[107] This is about 10 per cent higher than the 1970s and much, much higher than in the United States Supreme Court, where in recent years the unanimity rate has been barely 20 per cent.[108]

The Charter of Rights might over time reduce the degree of consensus within the Canadian Supreme Court. The Court's first few decisions on the Charter were unanimous: the first dissents occurred in its eighth Charter case, *Therens*, on the issue of excluding illegally obtained evidence.[109] But the Court's more recent decisions have manifested more divisions.[110] As differences within the Court on Charter issues become a matter of public controversy, external politics may well stir up the Court's internal politics. American experience has shown that if the majority within the court is perceived to be out of line with majority opinion in the nation, elected governments will try to use their appointing power to reverse the balance of power within the court. When this occurs a supreme court can become an arena of spirited ideological combat!

The use of law clerks, first instituted in the late 1960s, has significantly increased the Supreme Court's research capacity. Most Supreme Court judges have two clerks, and they are now used more extensively in the Supreme Court than in any other court in Canada. The law clerks are young law school graduates who are appointed for one- or two-year terms. The assistance they may give a judge ranges from researching legal issues and serving as a sounding board to summarizing material submitted to the Court and even drafting sections of an opinion. As Mackay and Bauman point out, they can "keep the isolated judiciary in touch with current social and legal trends."[111] But the American book *The Brethren* demonstrates that law clerks can have a down side: immoral arrogance on the part of young lawyers and dereliction of duty by old judges.[112] Let us hope that in Canada both the judges and law clerks are on guard to these dangers. In any event, law clerks are here to stay. Their extensive use in the Supreme Court is another measure of how far the Court has moved from the pure adversary model of the judicial process in which the judicial decision is fashioned entirely out of the adversaries' submissions.

One feature of the traditional adversary system to which the Supreme Court has clung is the large amount of time the judges spend listening to lawyers' arguments. Well in advance of every hearing the judges have an opportunity to study a record of the proceedings and reasons for judgment in the courts below and the factums of the parties setting out their arguments in written form. So they should be reasonably well acquainted with the issues in the case when the oral proceedings begin. Yet there are no time limits imposed on counsel in making their oral arguments. The presiding judge can indicate that a lawyer is taxing the court's patience but some counsel ignore these signals and drone on for hours after tediously reading aloud material that the judges can quite easily read. All this is in marked contrast to proceedings in the American Supreme Court where normally each side is given half an hour to address the court.

The time problem is compounded by the Canadian practice of granting intervenor status to governments and interest groups. In reference cases where the constitutional validity of legislation is at issue the Supreme Court Act gives all the provincial governments the right to participate in the proceedings and empowers the Court to appoint counsel to represent "any interest that is affected and as to which counsel does not appear."[113] Under the rules of the Court any person "interested in an appeal" may seek the Court's leave to intervene.[114] It is this rule that has facilitated the intervention of public interest groups in private litigation. Intervenors make both written and oral submissions to the Court. In major constitutional cases half a dozen or more provincial governments, the federal government, and several major interest groups will often take part in the proceedings. Oral argument in these cases is likely to go on for several days— sometimes for a week or more.

In response to the severe workload problems it has been experiencing in the early years of the Charter, the Supreme Court has cut down severely on inter- ventions by public interest groups. In December 1983 it revoked a rule which it had introduced in January 1983, giving automatic intervenor status in th Supreme Court to those who had been intervenors in the courts below. The Court became considerably tougher in granting leave to intervene: in 1983 it rejected six out of twenty-three applications and ten out of sixteen in 1984.[115] In principle, the beginning of the Charter era would seem exactly the wrong time for the Supreme Court to be suddenly swerving away from a participatory approach to constitutional adjudication. Charter cases raise many new legal issues which affect major public policies and fundamental social values. In making decisions on these issues the Court should not be narrowing the range of opinion and expertise to which it is exposed. In the United States the rules governing the filing of *amicus curiae* (friend of the court, the American common law equivalent of intervenor) briefs have been applied in an increasingly liberal fashion, es- pecially in constitutional cases. *Amicus curiae* participation in non-commercial suits is "now the norm rather than the exception" in the US Supreme Court.[116] But *amicus curiae* briefs take the form of written briefs without any oral argu- ment. A similar practice in Canada would enable the Supreme Court to revert to the fairly generous tradition of granting intervenor status without putting an undue burden on the judges' time. The Canadian Civil Liberties Association has proposed that the Court "might selectively invite counsel for intervenors to appear for oral argument for the purpose of speaking to whatever limited issues, in the discretion of the court, would assist in the disposition of the case at bar."[117] This may well be an appropriate Canadian compromise.

Somehow the Supreme Court will have to become more efficient. Its annual output of judgments is now in the sixty to ninety range—about 50 per cent below what it was in the 1970s. Temporarily it is coping with its backlog by granting leave to appeal in fewer and fewer cases. But this is not a satisfactory long-term solution. It means that more and more of the decisions of the provincial courts of appeal and the Federal Court of Appeal become final decisions. As we saw in the last chapter, these courts are extremely busy courts, hard pressed to find the time needed to fulfill their law development functions. Besides, the decisions of the provincial courts of appeal do not have national authority. The changes in Bill C-105, especially eliminating oral hearings as a standard feature of leave applications, will afford the Court some relief. But further reforms of the Supreme Court's *modus operandi* may be necessary. The most logical candidate for reform is the open-ended nature of the oral hearing. The quality of the United States Supreme Court's decisions would not appear to have suffered from reducing the oral argument stage to a well-focused hour in which the judges draw counsel out on the soft spots in their positions. Canadian lawyers may rail at this departure from traditional procedure. But they must come to recognize that the Supreme Court of Canada is no longer performing a traditional function.

Moving to Centre Stage

From the mid-1970s on the Supreme Court of Canada has been moving closer to centre stage in Canadian government. Well before it began to grapple with the Charter of Rights the Court's work as a constitutional arbiter was becoming of much greater importance in the life of the nation. The Court was beginning to respond to those of its critics whose expectations of a supreme court in a constitutional democracy were shaped by the dazzling performance of the Warren Court in the United States. Looking back now, it is evident that in the 1970s and early 1980s the Court was being conditioned for the Charter challenge.

The Court's position at the head of a separate branch of government was now being more firmly recognized. In 1977 the Supreme Court Act was amended so that the registrar, the chief administrative officer of the Court, would no longer report to the minister of justice but to the chief justice.[118] The Supreme Court would henceforth have more administrative autonomy than any other Canadian court. The chief justice's position as the chief justice of Canada was also made more meaningful during the 1970s by the establishment of the Canadian Judicial Council with the chief justice as its chairman. It will be recalled from chapter 7 that this council has the primary responsibility for the professional development and discipline of the federally appointed judiciary. At a more informal level, Chief Justice Laskin and his successor, Brian Dickson, have functioned much more than any of their predecessors did as the chief representative of the judiciary in Canada. Both these chief justices made themselves and their court more accessible to the media than they had ever been in the past.[119]

The Court's work made it increasingly worthy of media attention. In the constitutional area, where public interest is greatest, the volume of cases dealt with by the Court increased considerably. Between 1975 and 1983, the last non-Charter year, the Court decided ninety constitutional cases as compared with seventy-eight for the entire quarter-century from 1949 to the end of 1974.[120] Not only was the volume of constitutional litigation up, but so was its political salience. These cases frequently involved judicial review of major public policy initiatives: challenges to the federal government program of wage and price controls, provincial and federal resource policies, and the regulation of television broadcasting are just a few leading examples.[121] In a series of cases dealing with the constitutional amendment process—the reference concerning reform of the Senate, the *Patriation Reference* and the *Quebec Veto* case—the Court was drawn directly into the turbulent politics of constitutional renewal.[122]

The frequency with which the Supreme Court was called upon to adjudicate controversies between the two levels of government reflects the more combative style of federal-provincial politics that prevailed during the latter years of the Trudeau era and a breakdown in the mechanisms of informal accommodation. But such an explanation cannot account for all of the escalation in constitutional litigation. Most of the constitutional cases coming before the Court were initiated by private corporations and individuals, not governments. The Court's jurisprudence may have encouraged this litigation. From the late 1960s on, the Supreme Court drew away from the marked centralism that characterized its interpretation of the Constitution in the years immediately following 1949. The treatment of the federal peace, order and good government power that was adopted by a majority on the Laskin court was not the expansive "inherent national concern" test favoured by the chief justice, but the much narrower emergency doctrine.[123] The federal trade and commerce power was given a fairly wide interpretation as a basis for overruling provincial regulation encroaching on the flow of interprovincial or international trade, but the Court refused to give any significant weight to that power as a basis for the "general regulation of trade affecting the whole Dominion."[124] In the latter half of the 1970s the Supreme Court for the first time since 1949 began to veto federal legislation that in its view encroached on provincial rights.[125] The federal government to be sure still won some important cases, but the Supreme Court's approach to the federal division of powers throughout the Trudeau years, and beyond, has been remarkably balanced.[126] As I have suggested elsewhere, the very balance the Court has exhibited in its treatment of federal issues by making it reasonable for those on either side of a division of powers issue to think they might win is an incentive to lawyers to raise these issues.[127]

This balanced approach to federal issues has done much to consolidate the Court's legitimacy as a constitutional arbiter. In a very broad sense the Court has responded to its political environment. In contemporary Canada there is no consensus to push the balance of power in the federal system decisively one way or the other. The Supreme Court has kept in the political mainstream. In the words of Guy Tremblay, "The understanding of the Canadian political system articulated by the Court corresponds generally to the expectations of the governments and the people."[128] The most important decision the Court has ever made, the 1981 *Patriation Reference*, is a case in point. By giving both sides exactly half a loaf, the Court—or, more accurately, a majority of its members— forced Ottawa and the provinces to negotiate a compromise settlement of their constitutional differences.[129] This is probably about as close as the Court could come to producing a result acceptable to the Canadian people.

But the consensus behind the constitutional accord, like the Court's legitimacy, was by no means complete. The accord was bitterly attacked by the Quebec government and a portion of the Quebec people. A few months after patriation and the proclamation of the "new constitution" the Court was dangerously exposed as part of what Robert Dahl refers to as "the dominant national alliance"[130] when it was called upon to pronounce upon the legitimacy of excluding Quebec from the constitutional accord. In a short and very unconvincing decision the Court ruled that there had not been in Canadian history an informal political convention giving Quebec a veto over constitutional changes affecting its powers.[131] The Court spent some of its own legitimacy in upholding a constitutional bargain that lacked Quebec's support. As the Supreme Court assumed a significant role in national governance, it was finding that Canada is not an easy country to govern.

In the period immediately preceding the Charter of Rights, accessibility to constitutional litigation was considerably broadened by the Court's decisions on "standing." Standing refers to the right of members of the public to challenge the validity of legislation in the courts. Earlier in its history the Court had denied standing to challenge legislation to those who were not directly affected in some distinct and personal way by the legislation. But in 1975 in *Thorson*[132] the Court granted standing to a retired judge to challenge the validity of the Official Languages Act, and in *McNeil*[133] to a journalist to challenge Nova Scotia's censorship laws, and in 1981 in *Borowski*[134] to a male leader of the right-to-life movement to challenge the law permitting women to have abortions. These cases, said Justice Martland, establish that to be given standing in the courts to request a declaration that legislation is invalid, "a person need only show that he is affected by it directly or that he has a genuine interest as a citizen in the validity of the legislation and that there is no other reasonable and effective manner in which the issue may be brought before the court."[135] This, as it turned out, provides a more liberal basis for turning on the tap of judicial review than the remedy section of the Charter itself (section 24), which extends only to someone "whose rights or freedoms, as guaranteed by this Charter, have been infringed."[136]

In these pre-Charter years there were signs that the Court was moving toward a bolder, more innovative style of jurisprudence. We have already mentioned that the Court's first overrulings of previous decisions of its own and the Privy Council occurred in the latter half of the 1970s. While the Court's majority delivered a knock-out blow to the doctrine of an implied constitutional bill of rights[137] and showed little inclination to breathe new life into the Canadian Bill of Rights, the Court as a whole evinced a very "activist" approach to the bilingual rights guaranteed in Canada's original Constitution. In 1979 in *Blaikie*[138] the Court vetoed portions of the Parti Québécois' recently enacted Bill 101 making French the official language of government, and in *Forest*[139] it overturned legislation which had been in force in Manitoba for ninety years making English the sole language of government in that province. The Court justified its very liberal approach to the bilingual guarantees by talking vaguely about treating the Constitution as a "living tree" and the desirability of avoiding overly technical constructions when dealing with a constitutional guarantee.[140] It was almost as if the Court were sending out a signal that it was to not to be judged on the basis of its previous performance and that if a constitutional bill of rights were adopted, the Supreme Court was prepared to treat constitutional guarantees in a broad and liberal fashion.

The constitutional issues the Court was being called upon to adjudicate during these years made it difficult to adhere to a narrow, legalistic mode of reasoning. In the *Anti-Inflation Reference* the Supreme Court accepted submissions which included economists' arguments that Canada's economic circumstances at the time did not constitute an emergency. Although the Court was not persuaded by these arguments, their acceptance has widened the range of material submitted to the Court in constitutional cases.[141] In the *Senate Reference* the Court's decision that the federal Parliament could not unilaterally abolish or make major changes in the Senate was based on a broad understanding of the historic purpose of the Senate as a guardian of regional interests. In answering the questions about constitutional conventions in the *Patriation* and *Quebec Veto* references, the Court was dealing with questions which on the basis of its own analysis were political, not legal in nature.

Manitoba's difficulty in complying with the Court's decision in *Forest* generated litigation that again stretched the Court's capacity for statecraft. Following the *Forest* decision, Manitoba had ninety years of legislation to translate into French. This obviously could not be done overnight. The question then arose: were untranslated laws unconstitutional? The politicians' failure to push through a constitutional amendment which would have given Manitoba a breathing spell forced this question before the Supreme Court.[142] The Court was not prepared to plunge Manitoba into a state of anarchy by declaring most of its laws unconstitutional. On the other hand, it was unwilling to condone non-compliance with its constitutional rulings. So, drawing heavily on the doctrine of state necessity developed in other jurisdictions (in the United States following the Civil War, in Rhodesia during the illegal Smith regime, in Cyprus during conditions of emergency), the Court justified temporarily upholding laws which were enacted in an unconstitutional manner. At a subsequent hearing the Court approved a maximum of five years for the translation exercise.[143] As we noted in the first chapter, the justices of the Supreme Court of Canada were cutting their teeth on the problems of compliance associated with the judicial enforcement of constitutional guarantees—problems so familiar to their colleagues south of the border!

At the very least this experience in dealing rather explicitly with practical political and policy questions made it more difficult for members of the Court to view the adjudicative task in a court of last resort as simply a formal exercise in deductive reasoning from fixed legal categories. It would be going too far to suggest that the Court's view of the adjudicative function was entirely transformed. It is one thing to come to recognize more realistically the kind of choices that are inescapable in adjudication; it is quite another to establish a clearly worked-out methodology for reasoning through and justifying those choices. As we have seen in chapter 1, this latter problem has been the central theoretical issue in modern jurisprudence. In the years leading up to the Charter members of the Supreme Court were listening to the debate going on in academic circles about the nature of the judicial role.[144] Some of the judges serving on the Supreme Court of Canada had had leading roles in Canadian law schools earlier in their careers. They would be sensitive to the academics' critique of the sterility that had traditionally characterized the Court's work. While it would be impossible to predict exactly how judges might respond to this criticism, at least one could be fairly certain that the Court that was to have the definitive role in interpreting the Charter of Rights was much better prepared than it had been a generation earlier to deal more openly and confidently with the questions of principle and policy which that task entails.

Interpreting the Charter

The Canadian Charter of Rights and Freedoms came into force on 17 April 1982. Since then cases raising Charter issues have been initiated in the lower courts at the rate of about five hundred a year. In 1983 the Supreme Court began to receive requests for leave to appeal from litigants on the losing side of Charter decisions in the provincial courts of appeal and the Federal Court of Appeal. The Court was understandably generous in granting leave in these initial applications. It agreed to hear thirty-nine of the sixty-eight Charter cases in which leave was sought in 1983 and 1984. These cases represented an extraordinary challenge to the Court's decision-making capacity. They raised novel questions of constitutional law involving the interpretation of such broad and general concepts as "the principles of fundamental justice," limits to rights that are "reasonable" and "demonstrably justified in a free and democratic society," "freedom of conscience," and protection against "unreasonable search or seizure." For Canada, as for any country with a written constitution and judicial review, there is more than a little truth in the adage that "the constitution is what the judges say it is." In writing their opinions on the meaning of the general language of the Charter, the Supreme Court justices are literally writing the constitutional law of Canada. No wonder they laboured over these early decisions. And labour they did. They were soon far behind in rendering decisions in the Charter cases they had heard. Although by the end of 1985 they had granted leave to appeal in forty-eight Charter cases, near the end of 1986 they had rendered judgment in only eighteen of these cases.[145]

From its very first Charter decision, *Law Society of Upper Canada v. Skapinker*, rendered on 3 May 1984,[146] it was evident that the Supreme Court had a strong sense of the weighty responsibility it was assuming as the final interpreter of a written constitution which now purported to guarantee the fundamental rights and freedoms of the people. In this first decision, Justice Willard Estey who wrote the Court's opinion, stated:

> We are here engaged in a new task, the interpretation and application of the *Canadian Charter of Rights and Freedoms* . . . . It is part of the constitution of a nation adopted by constitutional process which, in the case of Canada in 1982, took the form of a statute of the Parliament of the United Kingdom. The adoptive mechanisms may vary from nation to nation. They lose their relevancy or shrink to mere historical curiosity value on the ultimate adoption of the instrument as the Constitution.[147]

While the Court had long experience with interpretation of the Constitution Act, 1867 and its division of power between governments, Estey acknowledged that the Charter of Rights introduces

> a new dimension, a new yardstick of reconciliation between the individual and the community and their respective rights, a dimension which like the balance of the Constitution remains to be interpreted and applied by the Court.[148]

Estey referred to the famous case of *Marbury* v. *Madison*[149] in which the United States Supreme Court first asserted its power to overrule laws which conflict with the constitution as authority for the kind of responsibility the Court was now assuming. For guidance in exercising this power he cited the dictum of Chief Justice Marshall from a subsequent case that ''we must never forget, that it is a *constitution* we are expounding.''[150] In interpreting a constitution which is to shape and serve the Canadian community for a long time, ''Narrow and technical interpretation, if not modulated by a sense of the unknown of the future can stunt the growth of the law and the community it serves.''[151] Ironically, in *Skapinker*, as in *Marbury* v. *Marshall*, the specific constitutional challenge to legislation was dismissed. The case involved the claim that Ontario legislation making Canadian citizenship a condition for practising law violated section 6, the mobility rights section, of the Charter. In the Court's view the Ontario law was not designed to impede movement across provincial borders and therefore did not offend the mobility guarantee. But again, as in *Marbury* v. *Madison*, although the Court did not exercise its power of veto, it used the case to herald its entry into a new age of judicial power.

In the four cases immediately following *Skapinker* the Court upheld the Charter claims. In the *Protestant School Boards*[152] case it struck down the section of Quebec's Bill 101 which closed Quebec's English school system to children of citizens who had received their English education in the English-speaking provinces. The Court found this in direct violation of the ''Canada clause'' in section 23(1)(b) of the Charter guaranteeing Canadian citizens the right to educate their children in English or French wherever they move in Canada. In *Southam*[153] the Court overturned the search powers of officials acting under the federal Combines Act on the grounds that they violated the right in section 8 of the Charter to be secure against unreasonable search and seizure. The issue in *Singh*[154] concerned provisions of the Immigration Act under which resident aliens could be denied refugee status and deported without a hearing. While three justices found this violated the right to a fair hearing in the Canadian Bill of rights, three others in an opinion written by Justice Wilson found that there was a violation of the right to ''security of the person'' in section 7 of the Charter and ''the right not be be deprived thereof except in accordance with the principles of fundamental justice.'' Justice Wilson rejected the government's argument that providing hearings for thousands of refugees was so costly it was reasonable to limit their right to due process. ''A balance of administrative convenience,'' she wrote, ''does not override the need to adhere to those principles [of fundamental justice].'' In

Big M Drug Mart[155] the Court found the long-standing federal Lord's Day Act in conflict with the right to freedom of religion in section 2 of the Charter. In doing so it repudiated the Court's 1963 holding in *Robertson* and *Rosetanni*[156] that the Lord's Day Act did not conflict with the right to freedom of religion under the Canadian Bill of Rights.

Not only were the results of these early Charter cases in marked contrast to the Court's treatment of the Bill of Rights, but the methods the judges used to interpret the Charter also went well beyond the traditional legalistic approach. Chief Justice Dickson took the lead in expounding a purposive approach to the task of defining the nature and scope of the rights and freedoms entrenched in the Charter. This method of interpretion calls upon judges to consider the broad historical and philosophical reasons which have made the right or freedom a cherished value in our society. In *Southam* Dickson traced the right to security from unreasonable searches back to the common law concept of trespass and its application by English judges in the 1700s to make an Englishman's home his castle. He then followed the evolution of this private property interest into a wider concern with personal privacy as a fundamental value of a liberal society. Similarly, in *Big M Drug Mart* the chief justice identified the essential core of religious freedom by reflecting on how western civilization through the religious wars of post-Reformation Europe learned how both political freedom and genuine religious experience are endangered when the state attempts to enforce the tenets of a particular faith.

The Court's treatment of the Charter was not all, however, in the "activist" direction. In some of their early decisions on the Charter members of the Court began to exhibit some sensitivity to the judiciary's limitations in reviewing public policy. A key example is the Court's response, in *Operation Dismantle*[157] to the attempt by a coalition of peace groups to use the Charter to overturn the agreement of the Canadian government to test the American cruise missile in Canada. The peace groups wished to argue that this agreement increased the likelihood that Canada would be involved in a nuclear war and thus threatened to deprive Canadians of their right to security of the person under section 7 of the Charter. The Supreme Court decided that this was not a proper question to bring before the courts. It did not base this decision on the "political questions" doctrine developed by the United States Supreme Court, according to which questions of foreign and defence policy may be too political to be reviewed by the courts. Indeed, Chief Justice Dickson writing for the majority said he had "no doubt that disputes of a political or foreign policy nature may be properly cognizable by the courts."[158] Operation Dismantle's claim was inappropriate for adjudication not because it was too political but because, even with the best available evidence, judges could do no more than speculate about the consequences of cruise missile testing. Here the Court was indicating that Charter claims should be rejected by the judiciary when they turn on causal connections between challenged government policies and Charter rights involving complex determinations about future behaviour which cannot be satisfactorily assessed through the judicial process.

Even in what many regard as the Court's most activist decision, the *B.C. Motor Vehicle Act Reference*,[159] the Court registered a note of self-restraint. In this case the Court found that British Columbia legislation making it an offence punishable by imprisonment to drive with a suspended licence regardless of whether the driver knew that the licence was suspended violated the right in the Charter's section 7 not to be deprived of one's liberty "except in accordance with principles of fundamental justice." The Court, in an opinion written by Justice Lamer, took a very liberal view of the meaning of fundamental justice. It was not impressed by evidence from the parliamentary debates showing that the Charter's drafters intended fundamental justice to refer only to essential procedural, due process, requirements. The Court took the position that laws depriving citizens of their life, liberty, or personal security must not only be procedurally just but must be just in their very substance. But to guard against the danger of the judiciary becoming a "super-legislature," the Court indicated that it was not prepared to apply the guarantee of substantive justice to every area of public policy. Principles of fundamental justice, wrote Justice Lamer, "do not lie in the realm of general public policy but in the inherent domain of the judiciary as guardian of the justice system."[160] The issue in this case—the absence of *mens rea* (a guilty mind) in the definition of a criminal offence attracting penal consequences—was squarely in the field of criminal justice, a policy area over which the judiciary has traditionally had a great deal of influence. The Court may well have been signalling that it would not look kindly on a section 7 claim alleging fundamental injustice in economic and social policy fields where the judiciary has little experience or competence.

The first dissenting opinions on the Charter did not appear until the Court's eighth charter decision, the *Therens* case.[161] *Therens* tested the justices' position on one of the most important new powers assigned to the judiciary by the Charter—the responsibility, under section 24(2) of the Charter, to exclude evidence obtained by the police in a manner that violates the accused's constitutional rights if in the judge's view admitting the evidence would bring the administration of justice into disrepute. In *Therens* the judges all agreed that the police had violated Therens's right under section 10(b) to be informed, upon arrest or detention, of the right to retain and instruct counsel when they administered a breathalyzer test without informing him of his right to contact a lawyer. But they split seven to two on the question of whether the breathalyzer evidence showing Therens was impaired was admissible. The majority regarded the police violation of the charter as "flagrant" and therefore as fully justifying exclusion of the evidence. Justices Le Dain and McIntyre disagreed. Indeed, Justice McIntyre contended that the exclusion of the evidence in a case like *Therens* would go far to bring the administration of justice into disrepute.

Divisions of the Court in Charter cases since *Therens* indicate that the justices are not all equally enthusiastic about the Charter. At the beginning of his majority judgment in *Mills*, decided in June 1986, Justice McIntyre stated that "the Charter was not intended to turn the Canadian legal system upside down."[162] In this case proceedings involving a charge of armed robbery were stopped at the preliminary hearing stage while the accused's claim that his right under section 11(b) of the Charter to be tried within a reasonable time was appealed all the way up to the Supreme Court. The majority refrained from deciding the 11(b) issue, sending it back to be dealt with by the trial judge in the normal course of proceedings. Chief Justice Dickson and Justices Lamer and Wilson in dissent would have ordered a stay of proceedings on the grounds that Mills's right under section 11(b) had been violated. Justice Lamer in his dissenting opinion argued for the need to back up the Charter with strong enforcement mechanisms to ensure that it "will be a vibrant and vigorous instrument."[163] Although it is too early to discern any clear and firm groupings of judges on the Charter, the evidence to date suggests that the following alignment may be emerging: Justice Wilson on the far left taking the most liberal or activist approach;[164] the chief justice and Justice Lamer more likely than any others to side with Justice Wilson; Justices Beetz, Chouinard, LaForest, Le Dain, and McIntyre somewhat inclined now to put the brakes on the Charter express at least a little bit; with Justice Estey being the least predictable.

But, however these alignments work out, until 1991 when the next *scheduled* vacancy occurs, the Court will likely remain relatively liberal overall in its treatment of the Charter. The justices clearly sense that they have a much stronger mandate from the Canadian body politic to give force and substance to the Charter of Rights than was ever the case with the Canadian Bill of Rights. They would surely all agree with Justice Wilson's statement in *Singh* that

> the recent adoption of the *Charter* by Parliament and nine of the ten provinces as part of the Canadian constitutional framework has sent a clear message to the courts that the restrictive attitude which at times characterized their approach to the Canadian Bill of Rights ought to be re-examined.[165]

The Supreme Court has been sending that message down to the courts below. In explaining this degree of support for the Charter in the Supreme Court, it is of some relevance to point to the fact that seven members of the Dickson Court were appointed by the Trudeau government, the same government that pushed so hard for the Charter. There is not as yet in the Canadian judicial selection process anything like the clear ideological bias that influences the American process. Still, it would seem fairly safe to predict that through the 1980s Canada will have a Supreme Court considerably more liberal than that of the United States, dominated as it is by judges selected by Republican presidents.

Not Quite Supreme

The Supreme Court's long process of maturation is nearly complete. No longer should it be "viewed in our political and legal culture as a body subsidiary to the legislature and the political executive." In the words of the Court's biographers, James Snell and Frederick Vaughan, today it is "in a position . . . to make itself a truly significant participant in the Canadian polity."[166] But there are still some limitations on the Court's supremacy.

The most formal of these limitations is the fact that the Court is not yet a creature of the Constitution. The Supreme Court was created by an act of Parliament and its jurisdiction, composition, the terms of office of its judges, and their method of appointment are provided for in that statute, not in the formal Constitution. Failure to establish the Court in the Constitution is essentially a symbolic concern. As was pointed out in Part Two of this book, there may be a number of ways in which the Court's structure as well as its power to review the constitutional validity of legislations are entrenched. And in any case, there are great political disincentives facing any federal government that might contemplate unilaterally restructuring or dismantling the Supreme Court of Canada. Still, it does seem anomalous in terms of the logic of constitutionalism "that the court which is the final authority in determining the meaning of the constitution is not itself established by the constitution."[167]

For quite some time there has been a consensus among Canadian politicians in support of the general idea of giving the Supreme Court formal constitutional status. Proposals to put the Supreme Court in the Constitution were on the constitutional reform agenda from the late 1960s to 1980. The contentious issue throughout was how to involve the provincial governments in the appointment of Supreme Court judges. An acceptable solution to this problem was negotiated at Victoria in 1971 and again, it would appear,[168] at the September 1980 Ottawa conference, the last broad-based effort at constitutional renewal. When Prime Minister Trudeau proceeded unilaterally to force through some changes in the Constitution, the Supreme Court was not on his agenda. Nor should it have been: the Court's legitimacy as a constitutional arbiter would be imperilled if new constitutional provisions concerning the Court were not agreed to by the provinces. It was probably also fortunate that the federal and provincial politicians who hammered out the constitutional accord of Novemeber 1981 kept their hands off the Supreme Court. A last-minute bargaining session in a conference centre kitchen is not the best place to work out the constitutional terms defining the role and structure of the Supreme Court.

So the Supreme Court remains one of the country's more important items of unfinished constitutional business. The effort to complete the constitutional accord and gain Quebec's official support for the Constitution Act, 1982 may put the Supreme Court back on the constitutional bargaining table. The Bourassa government in Quebec has made Quebec's participation in the appointment of the Quebec members of the Supreme Court one of the points it wishes to secure as a condition of Quebec's acceptance of the "new constitution."[169] If Quebec's proposal is to be dealt with, it must be negotiated as part of a larger constitutional amendment dealing with those features of the Supreme Court which should be entrenched in the Constitution. It would be a pity to see one piece of the Court's constitutionalization broken off and treated in isolation by politicians at the constitutional bargaining table.

Even when the Supreme Court's place at the head of the Canadian judicial system is enshrined in the Constitution, its status and power will be limited by the political system. If Canada's political leaders and people are beginning to see the Supreme Court as heading up the third branch of government, it is still a somewhat junior branch of government. There is no better illustration of this than the Mulroney government's appointment of Mr. Justice Estey as a one-person royal commission into some bank failures, an appointment that went directly against the expressed views of Chief Justice Brian Dickson and came at a time when the Court was facing a tremendous workload crisis. Clearly, Mr. Mulroney and his colleagues put the interests of their own administration ahead of the Court's.

A more enduring and benign constraint on the Court is the ambivalence of Canadians about judicial power. As a people, our expectations about the power it is appropriate for courts to exercise have been enlarged. But our trust in the courts or law makers is not unqualified. Notions of parliamentary supremacy still dance in our heads. This ambivalence is well expressed in section 33 of the Charter—the so-called override section—which permits legislatures to immunize legislation for five years at a time from claims based upon the fundamental freedoms, legal rights, or equality sections of the Charter. The inclusion of this section in the Charter at the insistence of eight provincial premiers shows that Canadians are not as inclined as Americans to abdicate so completely to their Supreme Court final responsibility for making decisions about fundamental rights and freedoms.[170] This clause, by relieving judges of the burden of finality, may encourage some to be bolder than they might otherwise have been. But in the long term, for citizens as for judges, it should serve as a reminder of the limited nature of the judicial mandate.

Summary and Conclusion to Part Four

In Part Four we have examined the structure and function of the seven basic types of court that make up the Canadian judicial system. Most of the courts are components of provincial or territorital judicial systems with converging lines of appeal through provincial courts of appeal to a common general court of appeal, the Supreme Court of Canada.

These provincial and territorial systems are the primary elements of Canada's third branch of government. Their entry points are the provincial and territorial trial courts. These trial courts have evolved in two tiers. In the higher tier are the section 96 courts, the linchpin courts of the original constitution, exercising a general jurisdiction in civil and criminal matters, established and maintained by the provinces but staffed by federally appointed judges. For the first century after Confederation this higher level of trial courts in the common law provinces had two layers: metropolitan based, circuit-riding superior courts, and locally based county or district courts slightly inferior in jurisdiction and status to the superior court. Only British Columbia, Nova Scotia, and Ontario have retained their county and district courts. It is in the lower tier of trial courts that most Canadians will have their only first-hand experience with the justice system. These courts, presided over by locally appointed judges, have expanded the most since Confederation and in modern times have been the focus of the reforming efforts of provincial and territorial governments. Today virtually all criminal cases begin in the criminal branch of these Provincial and Territorial Courts and the vast majority of criminal cases end there. On the civil side, in varying degrees across the country, the Provincial and Territorial Courts are involved in disputes involving small amounts of money and family disputes. Above the trial courts are the increasingly besieged provincial courts of appeal, trying to cope with the ever-growing body of litigants exercising their basic right of appeal, from the courts of first instance. And beyond these courts in 1 or 2 per cent of the cases they handle there is a second appeal to the Supreme Court of Canada.

Off to the side of these provincial and territorial judicial systems is a very small federal court system. Up until 1971 this system consisted of a single eight-judge Exchequer Court. Since then it has expanded considerably with the establishment of the Federal Court and, more recently, the Tax Court of Canada. This federal court system still handles only a tiny fraction of the country's judicial business and it is highly specialized. The primary function of the Federal Court and its enduring raison d'être in the Canadian judicial system is the judicial supervision of the host of near courts—administrative tribunals, boards and commissions—created by the federal government in the modern era.

This last point should remind the reader of our discussion in Part One of the fact that the adjudicative function of government—settling disputes about legal rights and duties—is by no means carried out exclusively by institutions formally labelled "courts." Canada, like most modern administrative states, has assigned adjudicative functions in a wide range of specialized areas to non-curial agencies.

In terms of sheer volume, probably more adjudication takes place in these administrative bodies than in the formal judicial system. But there has been a continuous struggle on the part of lawyers and judges to maintain a supervisory role for the formal judiciary over adjudication by non-courts. The development of Ontario's Divisional Court and the Federal Court is evidence of the continuing strength of this movement. Behind this tendency is the single fountain of justice ideology: the notion that justice in the resolution of disputes about legal rights and duties can only be had when the judicial branch of government retains a monopoly of final control over adjudication. The merits of this ideology have been much disputed by legal scholars but have scarcely been examined by political scientists.

All the courts we examined perform an adjudicative function. But the courts vary a good deal in the extent to which their work concentrates on adjudication. The purest adjudicative bodies are the courts of appeal. Their energies are dedicated almost exclusively to rendering authoritative decisions on legal issues appealed from courts of first instance. In rendering these decisions, as we have argued throughout this book, courts of appeal perform, inescapably, a legislative function. However, the provincial courts of appeal, particularly in the larger provinces, because of case-load pressures, find it increasingly difficult to perform this legislative function properly. The proportion of cases in which they can take time to craft written reasons in a reasonably collegial fashion is rapidly diminishing. We are coming to rely too much on an overburdened Supreme Court of Canada to develop Canadian jurisprudence in all areas of law. The solution supported here is the establishment of intermediate courts of appeal to handle the mass of appeals as of right within provinces. This would permit smaller, more collegial provincial supreme courts to deal with appeals raising issues of the greatest complexity and public importance.

It is in the trial courts that we find the greatest mixture of functions. Little of what goes on in the lower criminal court could be termed adjudication. The determination of guilt or innocence is not their central activity. These courts spend much of their time processing cases through the initial stages of the criminal justice system. Their judiciary's deliberative task which is of the greatest social consequence is the sentencing function. In courts exercising civil jurisdiction increasing use is being made of alternative forms of dispute resolution. This trend is furthest advanced in courts dealing with disputes involving family relationships. Court-sanctioned mediation is becoming a standard feature of both higher and lower trial courts in this field. Similarly, civil courts, whether at the small claims provincial court level, or the section 96 superior court level, are endeavouring to steer cases toward modes of pre-trial settlement which are more economical and conciliatory.

A major challenge to the administration of justice in Canada today is to improve the capacity of our courts to direct disputants to the most appropriate form of dispute resolution. Due process should not always mean having one's day in court. The process which is due and appropriate in terms both of the cost to society and the parties in time and money, as well as in doing justice to the disputants' claims, may well be one of those alternatives to adjudication we identified in chapter one: negotiation, mediation, or arbitration. The alternatives to adjudication can certainly be established outside of court settings. But in a litigious society, where so many disputes are initially put on court registers, courts are well placed to foster the use of alternatives to adjudication.

While it is enlightening to recognize the dangers of excessive reliance on adjudication, there is also a danger in excessive optimism about its alternatives. Blanket programs designed to push whole categories of cases such as family or commercial disputes into some pre-trial form of settlement are a mistake. In every area of law disputes arise which require adjudication. When legally advised citizens seriously contest those obligations to one another which can be backed by the coercive powers of state, or deny the legitimacy of the coercive powers which the state proposes to exercise over them, forcing disputes into non-adjudicative channels will at best simply add a costly stage to the settlement process and at worst coerce people into abandoning their rights. Where legal rights are claimed but disputed, negotiation and the more economic forms of third party dispute resolution may go on in the shadow of the court. But the adjudicative services of the courts should not be pushed so far into the background that they are accessible only to the most persistent and the most affluent. It is important to bear in mind that the amount of adjudication we have is conditioned by the expansion of our legal system. The more we decide to regulate our social and political relationships by formal legal rules—the more legal rights and duties we establish—the more adjudication we will have. We cannot be turning the adjudication tap off while we are turning the rights tap on.

Historically the Canadian trial courts have evolved in an hierarchiacal manner: superior courts at the top, county and district courts in the middle, magistrates' and then provincial courts at the bottom. This heirarchical organization of the trial function has become increasingly questionable. It produces irrational jurisdictional rigidities, the worst example of which is the fragmented jurisdiction over family disputes. The fragmentation of courts into separate, hierarchically arranged structures frustrates attempts at systematic reform of court administration. Most objectionable is the tendency of the hierarchical system to relegate adjudication that is of most concern to the rights of lower-income persons—small claims, child welfare, criminal justice—to "inferior" courts. This class bias in the organization of our trial courts is unacceptable in today's society.

In the reform model put forward in this and other parts of the book, the traditional hierarchy of trial courts would give way to multi-faceted, regional dispute resolution centres staffed by superior court judges. These regionally based superior courts would be courts of general jurisdiction. Their judicial staff would contain specialists in different areas of law and different adjudicative technologies. But specialization would not be confused with hierarchy. Nor would judges be frozen into one specialist line of work for their entire career. In both the civil and criminal areas routine matters not involving serious disputes about legal rights could be handled through summary procedures administered by properly trained justices of the peace. It would be the responsibility of the judicial management of the centres to supervise this para-judicial activity. By assembling a broad mix of judicial resources in regional justice centres the metropolitan bias of our traditional court system would be overcome. The full range of judicial services would be more accessible to people living outside the one or two largest cities in the province. In the larger provinces the introduction of intermediate courts of appeal could lead to some decentralization of the appeal process, so that the basic right of appeal could be exercised at some of the regional centres.

A crucial step in the direction of this model has been taken by the six provinces which in recent years have merged their county or district courts into their superior trial courts. This is a step which Quebec and the two northern territories never had to take, as they never had the lower level, section 96 trial courts. It is a step which may well be recommended by the Ontario Courts Inquiry currently being carried out by Justice Thomas Zuber. If Ontario takes the plunge, can British Columbia and Nova Scotia be far behind?

Merger of the section 96 trial courts is the first and earliest step toward the model of court reform advocated in this book. The second step, elevation of the Provincial and Territorial Court judges and their major adjudicative functions to superior court status, will be much more difficult to accomplish. Such a change in judicial structure will not likely be on the reform agenda of politicians or of the most influential lawyers and judges of the present generation. But the next generation may come to see that it is not such a revolutionary idea. For it would really bring our judicial system back to where it began in 1867 with the superior court as the central institution of the Canadian judicial system.

But to recover the superior court as the core institution of our judicial system one basic change or adaptation will have to be made in the Confederation arrangements: the provinces must be able to participate in the selection of section 96 judges. Unless some satisfactory method of involving provincial governments in appointing the judges of the provincial superior courts is worked out, the provinces—especially the larger provinces with extensive provincial lower court systems staffed by provincially appointed judges—will not and should not agree to the upward unification of their lower courts with the superior courts. The reform of court structure proposed in Part Four requires the reform of the judicial appointment system proposed in Part Three.

The consequence of not making these changes is to abandon the integrated judicial system provided for by the Fathers of Confederation in 1867. The key to that integrated system, it will be recalled, was the section 96 provincial courts with their federally appointed judges. The basic section 96 court, the building block of the system envisioned by the Constitution, was the provincial superior trial court of general jurisdiction. Since 1867 the Canadian judicial system has drifted steadily away from that original conception. As the volume of litigation and adjudication has expanded, the provincial superior court has become marginalized with the bulk of the country's new judicial business being taken on by the lower courts of the provinces and territories and, more recently, by the purely federal courts. If we continue on this path, the third branch of government in Canada, like the other two branches, will be federalized and on a two-class basis, with provincial lower courts and a fragmented set of federal higher courts dominating the judicial scene. It is doubtful whether many Canadians want their judicial system to develop in that way. It is equally doubtful whether many Canadians have the slightest idea that the system is drifting in that direction.

The other instrument of integration in our third branch of government is the Supreme Court of Canada. Only in the last decade has the Supreme Court acquired the legal and political authority as well as the freedom to manage its own work, which it must have if it is to be the effective head of the judicial branch. Today the Supreme Court is an institution under considerable stress as it copes with the burden of decision thrust upon it by the Charter of Rights and Freedoms. That burden may distract it, temporarily, from its superintendence over the development of other areas of law, especially the common law, which is also an essential part of the Court's integrative role in Canada's legal system. But we can hardly fault the Supreme Court justices for the time and attention they are devoting to the initial Charter cases. For in deciding these cases, not only are they drawing the boundary between the legitimate authority of governments and the rights and freedoms of citizens, but in the course of making these decisions they will also be drawing new boundaries for the judicial branch of government. The judgments which result from this decision-making should be read with interest and respect but not uncritically. In a democracy the last word on the metes and bounds of judicial power must rest with the citizenry, not the judges.

Notes to Chapter 14

1. This procedure is provided for in s. 55 of the Supreme Court Act, RSC, C. S-19, c. 44 (1st Supp.). For a discussion of the procedure see chapter 4.
2. Reference cases initiated by the provincial governments in the provincial courts of appeal and then appealed to the Supreme Court have been more numerous. There have been twenty-two of these since 1950. These figures are based on cases reported in the *Supreme Court Reports*.
3. It is possible to jump over the provincial court of appeal and in a civil case appeal a matter of law directly to the Supreme Court from a section 96 trial court. But such *per saltum* appeals require the leave of the Supreme Court and the consent of the parties, Supreme Court Act, s. 39. They are very rare. In 1982 S.I. Bushnell reported that he could find only three such cases since 1970; "Leave to Appeal Applications to the Supreme Court: A Matter of Public Importance," *Supreme Court Review* (1982), p. 495.
4. Peter H. Russell, "The Jurisdiction of the Supreme Court of Canada: Present Policies and a Programme for Reform," *Osgoode Hall Law Journal* (1969), p. 29.
5. Henry Hart, "The Time Chart of the Justices," *Harvard Law Review* (1959), p. 96.
6. For an account of the United States Supreme Court's docket, *see Henry J. Abra-*

ham, *The Judicial Process*, 4th ed. (New York: Oxford University Press, 1980), ch.5; for the House of Lords, see Louis Blom-Cooper and Gavin Drewry, *Final Appeal: A Study of the House of Lords in its Judicial Capacity* (Oxford: Clarendon Press, 1972), ch. 12.

7. *Garcia* v. *San Antonio Metropolitan Transit Authority* (1985) 471 U.S. 1049.
8. Constitution Act, 1867, s. 101
9. See Jennifer Smith, "The Origins of Judicial Review in Canada," *Canadian Journal of Political Science* (1983), p. 115.
10. Quoted in James G. Snell and Frederick Vaughan, *The Supreme Court of Canada: History of the Institution* (Toronto: The Osgoode Society, 1985), p. 5.
11. See Peter H. Russell, *The Supreme Court of Canada as a Bilingual and Bicultural Institution* (Ottawa: Queen's Printer, 1969), pp. 11-17.
12. For an account of this episode, see Frank H. Underhill, "Edward Blake, the Supreme Court Act and the Appeal to the Privy Council, 1875-6," *Canadian Historical Review* (1938), p. 245.
13. See Snell and Vaughan, *The Supreme Court*, table 4, p. 180.
14. Peter H. Russell, *Leading Constitutional Decisions*, 3rd ed. (Ottawa: Carleton University Press, 1982), p. 6.
15. Bora Laskin, "The Supreme Court of Canada: A Final Court of Appeal of and for Canadians," *Canadian Bar Review* (1951), pp. 106-109.
16. 58-59 Victoria, c. 70. For a general discussion of the Judicial Committee see Loren Beth, "The Judicial Committee: Its Development, Organization and Procedures," *Public Law* (1975), p. 22.
17. In the Court's earliest days some discontent was registered. In 1885 Justice Strong, in explaining why the Court would not give reasons in the *McCarthy Act Reference* case, said that "The matter will be sure to go to the Privy Council. Our judgements will not make any difference there; as a matter of fact they never do." Quoted in Alexander Smith, *The Commerce Power in Canada and the United States* (Toronto: Butterworths, 1963), p. 50.
18. Sir Lyman Duff, "The Privy Council," *Canadian Bar Review* (1925), p. 279. For a detailed account of Duff's work as a member of the Judicial Committee, see David R. Williams, *Duff: A Life in the Law* (Vancouver: University of British Columbia Press, 1984).
19. Quoted in Snell and Vaughan, *The Supreme Court*, p. 37.
20. Supreme Court Act, s. 8. They are now required to live within twenty-five miles of the National Capital Region.
21. Snell and Vaughan, *The Supreme Court*, p. 174.
22. 38 Victoria, c. 11, s. 52.
23. Snell and Vaughan, *The Supreme Court*, pp. 47-48.
24. A case in point is an attempt to exclude David Mills from a panel hearing a reference case; ibid., p. 93.
25. See, for example, the account of Mackenzie King's attempt to influence the outcome of a suit involving the publication of a biography of his rebel grandfather in Williams, *Duff: A Life in the Law*, p. 73.
26. Ibid., pp. 129-30.
27. See M.H. Fyfe, "Some Legal Aspects of the Report of the Royal Commission on Espionage," *Canadian Bar Review* (1946), p. 777.
28. [1926] AC 482.

29. RSC 1906, c. 146, s. 1025.
30. For a summary, see Coen G. Pierson, *Canada and the Privy Council* (London: Stevens, 1960), p. 45.
31. *British Coal Corporation* v. *The King* [1935] AC 500.
32. For the major cases, see Russell, *Leading Constitutional Decisions*, pp. 113-30. For a more detailed account of the whole episode see W.H. McConnell, "The Judicial Review of Prime Minister Bennett's 'New Deal'," *Osgoode Hall Law Review* (1968), p. 39.
33. House of Commons, *Debates*, 10 Feb. 1938, p. 313.
34. For an analysis of the Judicial Committee's academic critics, see Alan C. Cairns, "The Judicial Committee and Its Critics," *Canadian Journal of Political Science* (1971), p. 301.
35. House of Commons, *Debates*, 14 Apr. 1939, pp. 2811-16.
36. [1940] SCR 49.
37. *A.G. Ontario* v. *A.G. Canada* [1947] AC 128.
38. Snell and Vaughan, *The Supreme Court*, p. 189.
39. This is now in s. 54 of the Supreme Court Act.
40. House of Commons, *Debates*, 23 Sept. 1949, p. 194.
41. Ibid., p. 198.
42. The legislation abolishing appeals came into force on 23 Dec. 1949. Cases commenced before that date could be appealed to the Privy Council. It was not until 1959 that the Privy Council decided its last Canadian appeal.
43. *Beaver* v. *McCauley* (1955) 1, DLR (2d) 415. For a discussion, see Gilbert D. Kennedy, "Supreme Court of Canada — *Stare Decisis* — Role of Canada's Final Court," *Canadian Bar Review* (1955), pp. 340 and 632.
44. See, for example, H.E. Read, "The Judicial Process in Common Law Canada," *Canadian Bar Review* (1959), p. 267; and Mark MacGuigan, "Precedent and Policy in the Supreme Court," *Canadian Bar Review* (1967), p. 627.
45. For a discussion of this statement see W.B. Leach, "Revisionism in the House of Lords: The Bastion of Stare Decisis Falls," *Harvard Law Review* (1967), p. 797.
46. A leading example is *Fleming* v. *Atkinson* [1959] SCR 513. For a discussion, see Paul Weiler, *In the Last Resort: A Critical Study of the Supreme Court of Canada* (Toronto: Carswell/Methuen, 1974), ch. 3.
47. Quoted in Gerald L. Gall, *The Canadian Legal System*, 2nd ed. (Toronto: Carswell, 1983), p. 230.
48. The four decisions are: *Hill* v. *The Queen (No. 2)*, [1977] SCR 827; *R*. v. *Paquette* [1977] 2 SCR 189; *McNamara Construction Ltd.* v. *R.* [1977] 2 SCR 654; and *Reference re the Agricultural Products Marketing Act* [1978] 2 SCR 1198.
49. Weiler, *In the Last Resort*, p. 50.
50. The expression is from Gordon Bale, "Casting off the Mooring Ropes of Binding Precedent," *Canadian Bar Review* (1980), p. 255. Bale's article contains a critical analysis of the Court's decision in *Cherensky*.
51. *Cherensky* v. *Armadale Publishers Ltd.* [1979] 1 SCR 1067.
52. *A.G. Ontario* v. *Canada Temperance Federation* [1946] AC 193.
53. [1952] 1 SCR 292.
54. See especially the opinion of Justice Locke.
55. The principal cases were: *Reference re the Farm Products Marketing Act (Ontario)* [1957] SCR 198; and *Murphy* v. *C.P.R.* [1958] SCR 626.

56. *Munro* v. *National Capital Commission* [1966] SCR 663.
57. *Reference re the Offshore Mineral Rights of British Columbia* [1967] SCR 792.
58. For political reactions, see Russell, *Leading Constitutional Decisions*, p. 179. For an example of Quebec legal scholars' concerns, see Jean Beetz, "Les Attitudes changeantes de Québec a l'endroit de la constitution de 1867," in P.-A. Crépeau and C.B. Macpherson, eds., *The Future of Canadian Federalism* (Toronto: University of Toronto Press, 1965).
59. The seven cases were *Boucher* v. *The Queen* [1951] SCR 265 (interpretation of the seditious libel section of the Criminal Code); *Saumur* v. *Quebec* [1953] SCR 299 (Quebec City by-law requiring police chief's permission to distribute pamphlets in the street), *Chaput* v. *Romain* [1955] SCR 834 (police powers to break up religious meetings); *Birks and Sons* v. *Montreal* [1955] SCR 799 (compulsory closing of businesses on Catholic holy days); *Switzman* v. *Elbling* [1957] SCR 285 (Padlock Law outlawing propagation of communism); *Roncarelli* v. *Duplessis* [1959] SCR 121 (Quebec premier's removal of a Jehovah Witness supporter's restaurant liquor licence); and *Lamb* v. *Benoit* [1959] SCR 321 (police power to detain persons for distributing pamphlets considered by the police to be seditious).
60. Russell, *The Supreme Court as a Bilingual and Bicultural Institution*, pp. 204-205.
61. *Reference Re Alberta Statutes* [1938], SCR 100.
62. See his opinion in *Oil, Chemical and Atomic Workers International Union* v. *Imperial Oil Ltd.* [1963] SCR 584.
63. See Justice Ritchie's majority opinion in *Robertson and Rosetanni* v. *The Queen* [1963] SCR 651.
64. *The Queen* v. *Drybones* [1970] SCR 282.
65. See Peter W. Hogg, *Constitutional Law of Canada*, 2nd ed. (Toronto: Carswell, 1985), pp. 787-91.
66. F.L. Morton, "The Political Impact of the Charter of Rights," *Occasional Papers Series, Research Study 2.2* (Research Unit for Socio-Legal Studies, University of Calgary, 1986), p. 5. Only the *Drybones* decision rendered federal legislation inoperative. The other four cases upholding Bill of Rights claims were: *Brownridge* v. *The Queen* [1972] SCR 917; *Lowry and Lepper* v. *The Queen* [1974] SCR 195; *A.G. Canada* v. *Cosimo Reale* [1975] 2 SCR 624; and *R.* v. *Shelley* [1981] 2 SCR 196. In these cases Bill of Rights requirements were read into federal criminal legislation.
67. Snell and Vaughan, *The Supreme Court*, p. 134.
68. Ibid., p. 199.
69. Ibid., p. 703. Snell and Vaughan's account of this episode is based on Gordon Churchill's diary and differs from the account in Peter Newman, *Renegade in Power* (Toronto: McClelland and Stewart, 1963), pp. 370-71.
70. All the figures in this paragraph are based on a survey of the Court's reported decisions carried out by the author and Professor Sidney Peck of the Osgoode Hall Law School and reported in Peter H. Russell, "The Political Role of the Supreme Court of Canada in Its First Century," *Canadian Bar Review* (1975), p. 576.
71. For an analysis of the Supreme Court's jurisdiction at this time, see Peter H. Russell, "The Jurisdiction of the Supreme Court of Canada; Present Policies and a Programme of Reform," *Osgoode Hall Law Journal* (1969), p. 1.
72. The right of appeal for indictable offences is governed by ss. 618, 620, 621 and

719 of the Criminal Code. The right of appeal is slightly wider for the accused than it is for the attorney general. Both have a right to appeal a question of law on which a judge or the court of appeal dissents. But the accused also has a right of appeal when the appeal court overturns an acquittal (except where there was a verdict of not guilty on account of insanity) and where an application for *habeas corpus* has been refused.

73. Russell, *The Supreme Court as a Bilingual and Bicultural Institution*, p. 83.
74. SC 1974-75-76, c. 18, s. 5. These words are now found in s. 41 of the Supreme Court Act.
75. For a discussion of the background to this legislation, see S.I. Bushnell, "Leave to Appeal Applications to the Supreme Court of Canada," pp. 480-84.
76. Bora Laskin, "The Role and Function of Final Appellate Courts: The Supreme Court of Canada," *Canadian Bar Review* (1975), p. 474.
77. House of Commons, *Debates*, 25 Apr. 1986, p. 12649. The other federal statutes giving a right of appeal to the Supreme Court are the Combines Investigation Act, the Dominion Controverted Elections Act, and the National Defence Act. The right of appeal from refusals of *habeas corpus* does not appear to be eliminated by the draft legislation. Also, it retains a right of appeal from the Court Martial Appeal Court in cases confirming a death sentence. The minister of justice has indicated his intention to reintroduce this legislation. *Globe and Mail*, 1 Nov. 1986.
78. This column also includes rehearings and motions to quash.
79. Barry L. Strayer, *The Canadian Constitution and the Courts*, 2nd ed. (Toronto: Butterworths, 1983), p. 295.
80. This is based on the *Supreme Court Reports* for these years. Two of the nine references were initiated by the federal government. The other seven were initiated by the provincial governments and appealed from the provincial courts of appeal.
81. See Bushnell, "Leave to Appeal Applications to the Supreme Court," pp. 499-502. Bushnell reports that applications to the Quebec Court of Appeal for leave to appeal to the Supreme Court are non-existent.
82. RSC 1970, c. 44 (1st Supp.), s. 3.
83. For a description of the United States Supreme Court's procedure, see Abraham, *The Judicial Process*, pp. 182-99.
84. For data on the volume of leave applications up to 1980-81, see S.I. Bushnell, "Leave to Appeal Applications to the Supreme Court," pp. 504-505. Data for years after that were contained in *Bulletin of the Supreme Court of Canada* for 3 Feb. 1984 and in statistical reports obtainable from the Office of Registrar of the Supreme Court.
85. *Globe and Mail*, 6 Dec. 1983.
86. See Bushnell, "Leave to Appeal Applications to the Supreme Court," table 8, p. 507. From 1975 to 1981 the percentage of leave applications granted ranged from 30% to 27%. It was 28% in 1982.
87. Bill C-105, s. 4.
88. Bushnell, "Leave to Appeal Applications to the Supreme Court," p. 521.
89. These figures are derived from statistics presented in the *Bulletin of the Supreme Court*, 3 Feb. 1984 and statistical reports released by the Office of Registrar of the Supreme Court of Canada.
90. A. Wayne MacKay and Richard W. Bauman, "The Supreme Court of Canada: Reform Implications for an Emerging Institution," in Claire Beckton and

A. Wayne MacKay, eds., *The Courts and the Charter* (Toronto: University of Toronto Press, 1985), p. 65.

91. See, for example, Donovan Waters *et al.*, "The Future of the Supreme Court of Canada as the Final Appellate Tribunal in Private Law Litigation," *Canadian Business Law Journal* (1982-83), p. 389.

92. See W.R. Lederman, "Current Proposals for Reform of the Supreme Court," *Canadian Bar Review* (1979), pp. 215-17.

93. D. Michael Goldie, "The Supreme Court of Canada and the Common Law—A Future Consideration," in Gerald A. Beaudoin, ed., *The Supreme Court of Canada: Proceedings of the October 1985 Conference* (Cowansville: Yvon Blais, 1986), p. 122.

94. David J. Wheat, "Disposition of Civil Law Appeals by the Supreme Court of Canada," *Supreme Court Law Review* (1980), p. 454.

95. This model refers to the traditional English approach. In the contemporary House of Lords, conferences do take place after the hearing, although the production of opinions continues to be characterized by a laissez-faire approach. See Alan Paterson, *The Law Lords* (Toronto: University of Toronto Press, 1982), ch. 5.

96. As an academic, Laskin thought the full court should sit for constitutional cases; see Bora Laskin, "The Supreme Court of Canada: A Final Court of and for Canadians," *Canadian Bar Review* (1951), p. 1038. But when he became chief justice he thought that panels should not be used at all in a final court; see Bushnell, "Leave to Appeal Applications to the Supreme Court," p. 491.

97. Figures for 1970 to 1981 are from ibid., table 1, p.491. Bushnell's figures for a full bench include eight-judge panels.

98. The remainder were heard by even-numbered panels. *Bulletin of the Supreme Court*, 3 Feb. 1984, and reports released by the Office of Registrar of the Supreme Court of Canada.

99. Peter H. Russell, "Constitutional Reform of the Judicial Branch Symbolic vs. Operational Considerations," *Canadian Journal of Political Science* (1984), p. 238.

100. Bertha Wilson, "Decision-Making in the Supreme Court," *University of Toronto Law Journal* (1986), p. 236.

101. Ibid.

102. F.L. Morton, "The Changing Role of the Supreme Court: From Adjudicator Toward Policy-Maker," paper presented at annual meeting of the International Political Science Association, Paris, July 1985, p. 59.

103. Ibid. Morton identifies four other judgments rendered as decisions of the court, all since 1978.

104. See Edward McWhinney, "Judicial Concurrences and Dissents: A Comparative View of Opinion-Writing in Final Appellate Tribunals," *Canadian Bar Review* (1953), p. 595.

105. C. Evan Hughes, *The Supreme Court of the United States* (New York: Columbia University Press, 1928), p. 68.

106. Bushnell, "Leave to Appeal Applications to the Supreme Court," pp. 547-49.

107. See note 89, supra.

108. Abraham, *The Judicial Process*, p. 214.

109. *R. v. Therens* [1985] 1 SCR 613.

110. See esp. *Mills* v. *R*. [1986] 1 SCR 863. This case is discussed further below.
111. MacKay and Bauman, "The Supreme Court," pp. 87-88.
112. B. Woodward and S. Armstrong, *The Brethren* (New York: Simon and Schuster, 1979).
113. Supreme Court Act, s. 55(5).
114. For an account of public interest interventions, see Jullian Welch, "No Room at the Top: Interest Group Intervenors and Charter Litigation in the Supreme Court of Canada," *University of Toronto Faculty of Law Review* (1985), 204.
115. See *ibid.*, and Kenneth P. Swan, "Intervention and Amicus Curiae Status in Charter Litigation," in Robert Sharpe, ed., *Charter Litigation* (Toronto: Butterworths, 1987).
116. Karen O'Connor and Lee Epstein, "Amicus Curiae Participation in U.S. Supreme Court Litigation: An Appraisal of Hallman's 'Folklore'," *Law and Society Review* (1981-82), p. 318.
117. See Swan, "Intervention and Amicus Curiae Status."
118. SC 1976-77 c. 25, s. 20. For a discussion, see Jules Deschênes, *Maîtres Chez Eux* (Ottawa: Canadian Judicial Council, 1981).
119. On 28 Sept. 1981 for the first time national television broadcast live the rendering of a Supreme Court decision. The occasion was the Court's decision in the *Patriation Reference*.
120. These figures are based on cases reported in the *Supreme Court Reports*. Cases dealing with the Canadian Bill of Rights were not considered to be constitutional cases.
121. *Reference Re Anti-Inflation Act* [1976] 2 SCR 373; *Caloil Inc.* v *A.G. Canada* [1971] SCR 543; *Canadian Industrial Gas & Oil Ltd.* v. *Gov't of Saskatchewan* [1978] 2 SCR 545; *Central Canada Potash Co. and A.-G. Canada* v. *Gov't of Saskatchewan* [1979] 1 SCR 42; *Re Exported Natural Gas Tax* [1982] 1 SCR 1004; *Capital Cities Communications* v. *C.R.T.C.* [1978] 2 SCR 141; *Public Service Board* v. *Dionne [1978]* 2 SCR 191; *A.-G. Quebec* v. *Kellogg's Co.* [1978] 2 SCR 211.
122. *Reference Re Legislative Authority of Parliament to Alter or Replace the Senate* [1980] 1 SCR 54; *Reference re Patriation of the Constitution* [1981] 1 SCR 914; *Reference Re Objection to a Resolution to Amend the Constitution* [1982] 2 SCR 793.
123. *Reference Re Anti-Inflation Act* is the leading decision.
124. See esp., *Dominion Stores Ltd.* v. *The Queen* [1980] 1 SCR 139; *Labatt* v. *A.-G. Canada* [1980] 1 SCR 914.
125. *MacDonald* v. *Vapor Canada Ltd.* [1977] 2 SCR 914; *McNamara Construction* v. *The Queen* [1977] 2 SCR; *Quebec North Shore Paper Co.* v. *C.P.R.* [1977] 2 SCR 1054.
126. For other assessments that reach this general conclusion, see P.W. Hogg, "Is the Supreme Court of Canada Biased in Constitutional Cases?" *Canadian Bar Review* (1979), p. 721, Gilbert L'Ecuyer, *La cour suprême du Canada et la partage des compétences 1949-1978* (Québec: Gouvernement du Québec, 1978).
127. Peter H. Russell, "The Supreme Court and Federal Provincial Relations: The Political Use of Legal Resources," *Canadian Public Policy* (1985), p. 101.
128. Guy Tremblay, "The Supreme Court of Canada: Final Arbiter of Political Dis-

putes,'' in Ivan Bernier and Andree Lajoie, eds, *The Supreme Court of Canada as an Instrument of Political Change* (Toronto: University of Toronto Press, 1985), p. 200.

129. See Peter Russell, Robert Decary, *et al.*, *The Court and the Constitution* (Kingston: Institute of Intergovernmental Relations, Queen's University, 1982).

130. Robert Dahl, ''Decision-Making in a Democracy: The Supreme Court as a National Policy-Maker,'' *Journal of Public Law* (1958), p. 294.

131. *Reference Re Objection to a Resolution to Amend the Constitution.* For a critical analysis of this decision, see Marc Gold, ''The Mask of Objectivity: Politics and Rhetoric in the Supreme Court of Canada,'' *Supreme Court Review* (1984), p. 455.

132. *Thorson* v. *A.-G. Canada* [1975] 1 SCR 138.

133. *McNeil* v. *Nova Scotia Board of Censors* [1976] 2 SCR 265.

134. *Borowski* v. *Minister of Justice of Canada* [1981] 2 SCR 575.

135. Ibid., at p. 598.

136. For a discussion, see Dale Gibson, ''Enforcement of the Canadian Charter of Rights and Freedoms (Section 24),'' in Walter Tarnopolsky and G.-A. Beaudoin, *Canadian Charter of Rights and Freedoms* (Toronto: Carswell, 1982).

137. The key decision was *A.-G. Canada and Dupond* v. *Montreal* [1978] 2 SCR 770. The Court upheld a Montreal by-law restricting freedom of assembly during emergencies. Writing for the majority, Justice Beetz stated that ''None of the freedoms (of speech, of assembly and association, of the press and of religion) . . . is so enshrined in the constitution as to be above the reach of competent legislation.''

138. *A.-G. Quebec* v. *Blaikie* [1979] 2 SCR 1016.

139. *A.G. Manitoba* v. *Forest* [1979] 2 SCR 1032.

140. The ''living tree'' metaphor was taken from Lord Sankey's judgment in *Henrietta Muir Edwards* v. *A.G. Canada* [1930] AC 124.

141. Hogg, *Constitutional Law of Canada*, p. 183.

142. *Reference Re Manitoba Language Rights* [1985] 1 SCR 721.

143. *Order: Manitoba Language Rights* [1985] 2 SCR 347.

144. For the reflections on these questions of the two justices who became chief justice in this period, see Bora Laskin, ''The Institutional Role of the Judge,'' *Israeli Law Review* (1972), p. 329, and Brian Dickson, ''The Judge as Lawmaker: Comment,'' in A.M. Linden, ed., *The Canadian Judiciary* (Toronto: Osgoode Hall Law School, 1976).

145. Leave-granting figures are based on the sources referred to in note 89. In counting judgments in Charter cases, I have included only cases in which the Charter was the central issue and have considered *Therens*, *Trask*, and *Rahn* to be a single judgment.

146. [1984] 1 SCR 357.

147. Ibid., at p. 365.

148. Ibid., at pp. 366-67.

149. (1803) 5 US (1 Cranch) 173.

150. *M'Culloch* v. *State of Maryland* (1819) 17 US (4 Wheaton's).

151. *The Law Society of Upper Canada* v. *Skapinker*, p. 366.

152. *A.-G. Quebec* v. *Quebec Association of Protestant School Boards* [1984] 2 SCR 66.

153. *Hunter et al.* v. *Southam Inc.* [1984] 2 SCR 145.
154. *Singh et al.* v. *Minister of Employment and Immigration* [1985] SCR 177.
155. *R.* v. *Big M Drug Mart* [1985] 1 SCR 295.
156. *Robertson and Rosetanni* v. *The Queen* [1963] S.C.R. 651.
157. *Operation Dismantle* v. *The Queen* [1985] 1 SCR 441.
158. Ibid., at p. 459.
159. *Re British Columbia Motor Vehicle Act* [1985] 2 SCR 486.
160. Ibid., at p. 503.
161. *R.* v. *Therens.*
162. *Mills* v. *The Queen* [1986] 1 SCR 863, at p. 953.
163. *Ibid.*, at p. 881.
164. See esp. her dissent in *Jones* v. *The Queen* (not yet reported), where she is the only judge willing to uphold a claim based on s. 7 of the Charter against legislation restricting the ways in which an exemption from compulsory school attendance can be obtained.
165. *Singh et al.* v. *Minister of Employment and Immigration*, at p. 209.
166. Snell and Vaughan, *The Supreme Court*, p. 258.
167. Peter H. Russell, "Constitutional Reform of the Judicial Branch," *Canadian Journal of Political Science* (1984), p. 230.
168. See ibid., pp. 240-41.
169. *Globe and Mail*, 25 Sept. 1986.
170. For a discussion of the political theory of the override clause, see Paul C. Weiler, "Rights and Judges in a Democracy: A New Canadian Version," *University of Michigan Journal of Law Reform* (1984), p. 51.

INDEX

Abbott, Douglas, 343
Aboriginals in the judiciary, 165, 166
Abraham, Henry, 139
Access to Information Act, 35
Act to Promote Access to Justice (Que.),
   238-39
Act of Settlement, 1701 (Br.), 81-82,
   255
Adams, George, 244
Addy, G.A., 85, 86
Adjudication
   alternative structures for, 17-20
   compliance, need for, 8
   constitutional interpretation, powers of,
      9-10
   dispute settlement, as form of, 5-6
   influence on law and policy, 13-17
   and judicial law-making, 9-10
   legal disputes, limited to, 6
   nature of, 40
   non-voluntary nature of, 5-6
   normative dimensions of, 20-27
   policy-making roles, 14-15
      court decisions, 15
   procedural features, judiciary, 25-27
   reasons for decision, 26
   scope and application of, 7
   social control function of, 18
   structural features, judiciary, 20-25
   through administrative tribunals, 19-20
   vs. arbitration, 5-6
   vs. mediation, 5-6
Adjudicative functions, judiciary, 5-10
Adjudicative tribunals, need for, 31-32
Administration, judicial, 11-12
Administrative tribunals, adjudicative role
   of, 19-20
   provincial creation of, 57
Adoption Reference, 1938, 57, 227
Adversary system, 25, 26, 278
Advisory Committee on Confederation
   (Ont.), 55

Alberta
   merger movement, 270
   small claims court, 240
Alberta Press case, 342
Anti-Inflation Reference, 357
Anti-monopoly legislation and judicial
   law-making, 9
Appeal(s)
   in Quebec, British domination of, 36
   right of, 289, 292-93
   s. 101, national court of, 50
Appointment of judges
   British system, 107-108
   candidates selection, 112
   career judiciary, 110
   comparative perspective, 107-12
   election of, 108-109
   federal process, 112-17
      consultation with provinces, 121-30
      reform of, 118-21, 130
   four historical stages in, 115-16
   government service as factor in,
      163-64
   involvement in professional activities,
      163-64
   judicial councils, 111
   legislative election, 109-10
   nominating commissions, 127, 130
      for federal appointments, 130-35
   patronage, extent of, 113-16
   political links with government, 110
   provincial systems, 124-30
      centralized control, 125
      lay judges, elimination of, 127
      lower status of, 126
      patronage, 125-26
      policy implications, 126
      selection of candidates, 27-30
   s. 96 judges, 121-22
   as source of political influence, 116-17
   strengthening justice minister's support
      staff, 133

379

Institute of Law Research and Reform
(Alta.), 228
Integration of judicial system, 49-54
constitutional provisions, 49-50
court procedure, 50-51
national court of appeal, 50
provincial criminal courts, 50
Intervenor status, 352-53
Ison, Terence, 243, 247

Jackett, W.R., 311, 314
Jackson, R.M., 165
Jerome, James, 141
Jewett, Pauline, 165, 166
Johanneson v. West St. Paul, 341
John East Iron Works, 57-58
Joint Parliamentary Committee on the
Constitution Report 1972, 66
Judges
administrative role of, 11-12
ages of, 162-63
appointment of—See Appointment of
judges
deputy, Ontario, 240
discipline, 182-85
distribution of in courts, 51-52, 107
during good behaviour, 176
education and professional development, 185-91
federally appointed, number of, 51, 52
federal monopoly of appointment of,
56
impartiality, need for, 20-21
importance of, 36-37
independence—See Judicial
independence
lawmakers, as, 37
limits to political activities of, 87-88
linguistic representation, 166-67
mandatory retirement, 173-75
mentor schemes, 187
numbers of, 33
part-time, 188
performance review, 189-90
personnel management of, 12
power structures, connections to, 21-21
professional qualifications, 160-62
promotion, 135-41

provincially appointed, number of, 51,
52
recruitment patterns, 162-64
regional representation, 167-69
removal of—See Removal of judges
remuneration—See Remuneration of
judges
royal commissions, appointment to,
12-13
salary, termination of, 184
s. 96, provisions for, 56
status of, 37
tenure, constitutional guarantees, 81-85
salary suspension, 84-85
s. 99 protection of, 83-84
ten-year rule, 161
unrepresentative character of, 164-66
variety of backgrounds, 163
Judges Act, 184
amendments, 1971, 174
Judges affair, 1976, 78-81
Judicial Committee of the Privy Council,
36, 50, 54-55, 64, 335-37
Judicial councils, 12
Alberta, 129
British Columbia, 127-28
discipline of judges, 182-85
judges appointments, 111, 127-30
Newfoundland, 129
Northwest Territories, 129
Ontario, 128-29
provincial and territorial, composition
of, 185
Quebec, 129-30
Saskatchewan, 128
Yukon, 129
Judicial independence
constitutional entrenchment of power,
75, 81-85, 95-98
court administration, 77
differences in extent of, 23-24
entrenchment of judicial review, 93-95
freedom from political attack, 87-88
historical antecedents, Britain, 81-82
interference with, 22-23
judges promotion, effect on, 140
judges tenure, 81-85
minimum standards of, 22